W9-BVE-054

Northern Beltrami County

Clearwater County Area

Your complete guide to over 160 lakes in the Grand Rapids & Bemidji Areas

SPORTSMAN'S connection®

Leading Publisher of Fishing Map Guides

The lakes selected for this guide are confined to those that are accessible to the public. Test surveys were performed by Minnesota Department of Natural Resources personnel to assist in their evaluation of fisheries. Note that some lakes test with more reliability than others and weather and other factors can skew results. Secchi disk readings indicated are typically averaged over a period of time, and actual water clarity may vary according to season. Information regarding public access is based upon sources available at time of publication, and is subject to change. Maps are not intended for navigation. Publisher is not responsible for errors or omissions.

Length to weight conversion scale																		
Northern Pike																		
Inches	24	25	26	27	28	29	30	31	32	33	34	35	36	37	38	39	40	41	42
Pounds	3.9	4.4	5.0	5.6	6.2	7.0	7.7	8.5	9.3	10.2	11.2	12.2	13.3	14.5	15.7	16.9	18.3	19.6	21.2
Walleye																		
Inches	14	15	16	17	18	19	20	21	22	23	24	25	26	27	28	29
Pounds	1.0	1.2	1.5	1.8	2.2	2.5	3.0	3.4	3.9	4.5	5.1	5.7	6.5	7.2	8.1	9.0
Largemouth Bass																		
Inches	12	13	14	15	16	17	18	19	20	21	22	23
Pounds	1.0	1.3	1.7	2.1	2.5	3.0	3.6	4.2	5.0	5.7	6.6	7.6
Crappie																		
Inches	8	9	10	11	12	13	14	15	16	17
Pounds	0.4	0.6	0.8	1.1	1.4	1.8	2.2	2.8	3.4	4.1

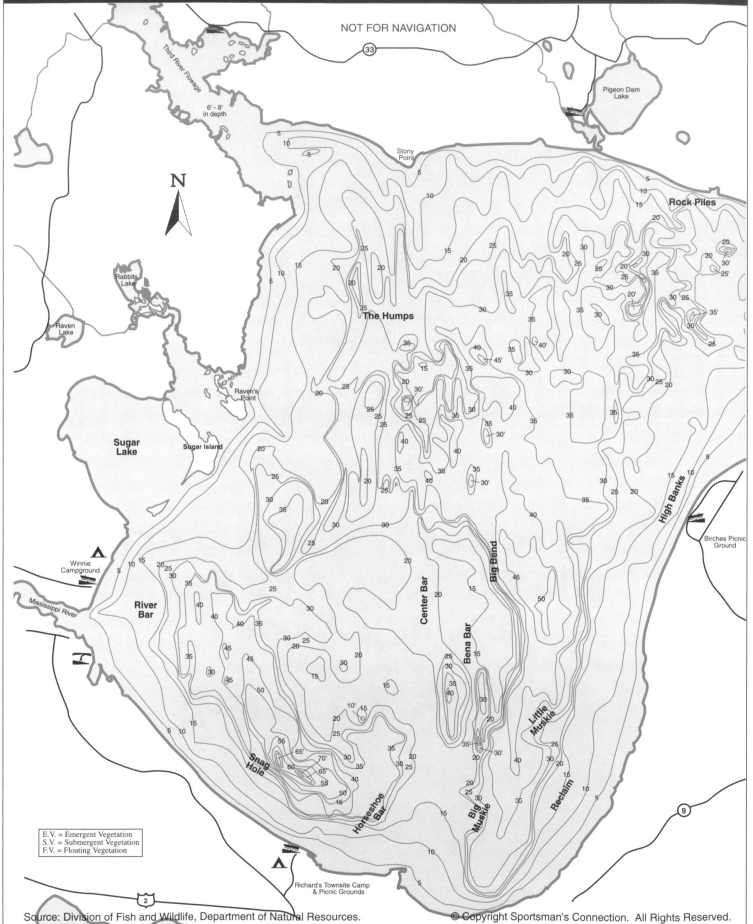

NOT FOR NAVIGATION

33

Third River Flowage

6' - 8' in depth

Pigeon Dam Lake

Stony Point

Rock Piles

N

Rabbits Lake

Raven Lake

The Humps

Raven's Point

Sugar Lake

Sugar Island

High Banks

Birches Picnic Ground

Winnie Campground

Mississippi River

River Bar

Center Bar

Big Bend

Bena Bar

Little Muskie

Reclaim

9

Snag Hole

Horseshoe Bar

Big Muskie

E.V. = Emergent Vegetation
S.V. = Submergent Vegetation
F.V. = Floating Vegetation

2

Richard's Townsite Camp & Picnic Grounds

Lake Winnibigoshish

NOT FOR NAVIGATION

Map labels:
Day Creek Lake
Seelye Point
Battle Point
Deer Lake
Cut Foot Sioux Lake
The Gap
Sugar Bush Point
William's Narrows
Cut Foot Flowadge
Mosomo Point
McAvity Bay
Bowen's Flats
Satellite Dishes
Cabbage Patch
Wild Rice
Tamarack Point Campground
Plug Hat Point Camp and Picnic Grounds
Winnibigoshish Dam
Tamarack Lake
Mississsippi River

N

Interview text:

Mike Auger, Blue Horizon Guide Service out of Pokegama Sports in Grand Rapids, has logged many hours on this famous Walleye factory. Following is an excerpt from our interview with Mike:

Sportsman's Connection: Where do you fish around opening weekend on the big lake?

Auger: On opening weekend from Bowen's Flats through The Gap is real good. The whole north shore is also real good the first couple weeks of the season in seven to 12 feet of water. The Pigeon River Flowage area is good on up to Stony Point. At this time of year 12 to 15 feet is the deepest water you'll want to fish on a calm, sunny day. Most of the fish are caught along here early in the season. Do you know about the migration of Winnie?

Sportsman's Connection: No, not really.

Auger: About 90 percent of the Walleyes migrate from the area around Cut Foot Sioux called "The Gap" and along the north shore, down around the east side and on up onto Bena Bar, which is a huge area that includes the Center Bar, Big Muskie, Big Bend and the Little Muskie areas. The top of Bena Bar averages around 13 feet. Fish right at the breakline in about 17 feet.

Sportsman's Connection: So this whole area is the Bena Bar?

Auger: Yeah. A good spot in early June is Big Bend, almost straight out from the access to the middle of the lake (actually about a third of the way across). Follow the schools along the High Banks area a couple of weeks after opener into the first week of June. Then follow the migration right down the shore, moving 300 to 400 yards each day.

Sportsman's Connection: Just follow them as spring progresses?

Auger: Right. Then move out onto the Bena Bar, usually around the second or third week of June and also up into the area called "The Humps," which drops down and comes back up. The top of the break actually tops out about 15 feet of water (the two 20-foot circles just above the name "The Humps" on the map are what he is referring to).

(Continued on page 6)

Source: Division of Fish and Wildlife, Department of Natural Resources.

(Continued from page 5)

Fish the breaklines right at the top of the break in about 17 to 18 feet of water.

Sportsman's Connection: What's the best fishing method: jigging, drifting?

Auger: Drift, jig, troll, cast, everybody seems to be doing a little bit of each. Jig-and-minnow and lindy rigs with leeches are the most common. We hit 'em real good over at Raven's Point the third week of June. We worked the south side of the point where it's real rocky and we nailed them. It's probably also good earlier, because you can catch the fish that spawn up in Raven Lake and Sugar. Horseshoe Bar is real good in a northwest wind all along the breakline. It's a good area from early June all the way through summer. Late summer can be real good.

Sportsman's Connection: What about Big Muskie?

Auger: Bena Bar is the whole flat area down there. Fish the east side of the breakline all the way down. A sunken island not shown on the map off of Big Muskie is good when you get a hard northwest wind. Everything including bait fish gets pushed off the bar up onto the east side of the sunken island. You can line up straight north with the Bena radio tower and follow the Bena bar.

Sportsman's Connection: What's in Sugar Lake?

Auger: Sugar Lake has some good Northern and Bass.

Sportsman's Connection: What about the area around Cut Foot?

Auger: Cut Foot Sioux has three or four sunken islands straight out from The Gap toward Battle Point which come up to 13 feet. Early in the season, they're all good. Just fish the edges again, 13 to 17 feet. A breakline runs right behind Sugarbush Point, and that's real good at 17 feet. The weedline runs right around there, from about 13 to 17 feet.

Sportsman's Connection: What's the average Walleye caught out of Winnie?

(Continued on page 30)

Location: Township 145 - 147 Range 26 - 29
Watershed: Mississippi Headwaters
Size of lake: 69,821 acres
Shorelength: 35.0 miles
Secchi disk (water clarity): 6.9 ft.
Water color: NA
Cause of water color: NA

Maximum depth: 65.0 ft.
Median depth: 15.0 ft.
Accessibility: Plug Hat Point, Tamarack Point, Birches, W. Winnie Campgrd, Third River, Winnie Dam
Boat Ramps: All concrete
Parking: Ample
Accommodations: Campground, Resorts, Picnic Areas

Shoreland zoning classification: General Development
Dominant forest/soil type: No Tree/Wet
Management class: Walleye
Ecological type: Hard-water Walleye

FISH STOCKING DATA

year	species	size	# released
83	Walleye	Fry	6,000,000
85	Walleye	Fry	3,000,000
86	Walleye	Fry	8,000,000
89	Walleye	Fry	8,500,000
91	Walleye	Fry	3,000,000
92	Walleye	Fry	3,400,000
93	Walleye	Fry	5,236,400

NET CATCH DATA

survey date: 6/30/97

species	Gill Nets # per net	Gill Nets avg fish wt. (lbs.)	Trap Nets # per set	Trap Nets avg fish wt. (lbs.)
Yellow Perch	96.0	0.23	-	-
White Sucker	1.0	1.98	-	-
Walleye	7.3	0.96	-	-
Tullibee (Cisco)	35.5	0.41	-	-
Shorthead Redhorse	trace	4.30	-	-
Rock Bass	trace	1.20	-	-
Northern Pike	6.9	2.90	-	-
Muskellunge	trace	8.70	-	-
Black Bullhead	trace	0.30	-	-

LENGTH OF SELECTED SPECIES SAMPLED FROM ALL GEAR

Number of fish caught for the following length categories (inches):

species	0-5	6-8	9-11	12-14	15-19	20-24	25-29	>30	Total
Yellow Perch	360	1,559	384	-	-	-	-	-	2,303
Walleye	-	9	35	103	19	7	2	-	175
Tullibee (Cisco)	2	320	509	20	-	-	-	-	851
Rock Bass	-	-	2	-	-	-	-	-	2
Northern Pike	-	-	1	7	54	59	30	14	165
Muskellunge	-	-	-	-	-	-	-	1	1
Black Bullhead	-	1	-	-	-	-	-	-	1

FISHING GUIDE TO OVER 90 LAKES IN THE GRAND RAPIDS & WINNIBIGOSHISH AREAS

Grand Rapids & Bemidji Area
Fishing Map Guide
Table of Contents

See back cover for alphabetical index of lakes

MAPS IN THIS GUIDE ARE NOT FOR NAVIGATION

(Continued on next page)

Grand Rapids & Bemidji Area Fishing Map Guide
by Sportsman's Connection

Editor: James F. Billig
Editorial/Research: Jack Tyllia, Steve Meyer, Jon Wisniewski, Chuck Hartley
Cartography: Hart Graphics, Janet Billig
Typesetting/Layout: Shelly Wisniewski

**Sportsman's Connection
Superior, Wisconsin**

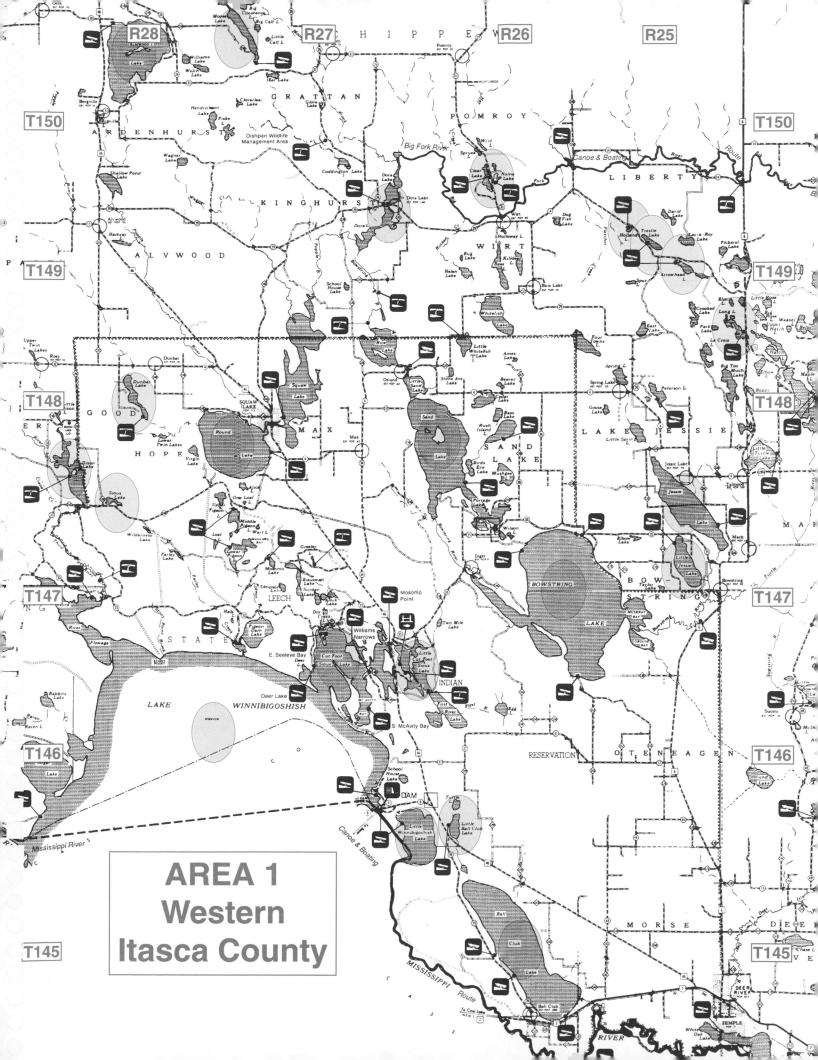

AREA 1
Western
Itasca County

CUT FOOT SIOUX LAKE   LITTLE CUT FOOT SIOUX LAKE

Itasca County

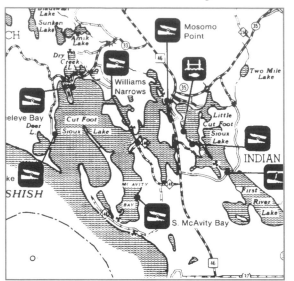

Location: Township 146,147 Range 26, 27
Watershed: Mississippi Headwaters
Size of lake: 2,851 acres
Shorelength: 18.2 miles
Secchi disk (water clarity): 7.3 ft.
Water color: NA
Cause of water color: NA
Maximum depth: 78.0 ft.
Median depth: 23.6 ft.
Accessibility: North shore (1), west shore (1), east shore (2), at channel (1); see map
Boat Ramp: Concrete; Earth
Parking: Ample
Accommodations: Campground, resorts
Shoreland zoning classif.: Rec. Dev.
Dominant forest/soil type: NA
Management class: Walleye
Ecological type: Hard-water Walleye

Location: Township 146,147 Range 26, 27
Watershed: Mississippi Headwaters
Size of lake: 660 acres
Shorelength: 2.9 miles
Secchi disk (water clarity): 6.0 ft.
Water color: Brown
Cause of water color: Algae
Maximum depth: 20.0 ft.
Median depth: 9.4 ft.
Accessibility: USFS earth ramp at Onegume campground; USFS carry-in access at First River Campground
Boat Ramp: Earth
Parking: Ample
Accommodations: Campground, resorts, fishing pier
Shoreland zoning classif.: Rec. Dev.
Dominant forest/soil type: Decid/Sand
Management class: Walleye
Ecological type: Hard-water Walleye

DNR COMMENTS:
Walleye and Northern Pike populations above local median levels. Evidence suggests that Walleye fry stocking in Little Cut Foot Sioux may be benefitting the population in Big Cut Foot Sioux; direct fry stocking in Big Cut Foot Sioux, however, is having little apparent effect on the population. Yellow Perch and Cisco numbers high. Other fish populations within normal limits for lake class.

FISH STOCKING DATA

year	species	size	# released
89	Walleye	Fry	NA
89	Walleye	Fry	14,555,000
92	Walleye	Fry	10,000,000
93	Walleye	Fry	11,824,800
94	Walleye	Fry	9,955,000
95	Walleye	Fry	6,400,000
96	Walleye	Fry	4,660,000
97	Walleye	Fry	5,880,000

NET CATCH DATA
survey date: 7/26/93

	Gill Nets		Trap Nets	
species	# per net	avg fish wt. (lbs)	# per set	avg fish wt. (lbs)
Black Crappie	1.3	0.47	-	-
Bluegill	0.1	0.30	-	-
Burbot	0.1	2.78	-	-
Northern Pike	3.6	2.09	-	-
Pumpkin. Sunfish	0.4	0.20	-	-
Rock Bass	1.1	0.64	-	-
Shorthead Redhorse	0.3	2.80	-	-
Tullibee (Cisco)	15.0	0.47	-	-
Walleye	5.6	1.43	-	-
White Sucker	2.6	2.85	-	-
Yellow Perch	58.3	0.02	-	-

LENGTH OF SELECTED SPECIES SAMPLED FROM ALL GEAR
Number of fish caught for the following length categories (inches):

species	0-5	6-8	9-11	12-14	15-19	20-24	25-29	>30	Total
Black Crappie	1	4	5	-	-	-	-	-	10
Bluegill	-	1	-	-	-	-	-	-	1
Northern Pike	-	-	-	4	12	9	3	1	29
Pumpkin. Sunfish	2	1	-	-	-	-	-	-	3
Rock Bass	1	1	6	1	-	-	-	-	9
Tullibee (Cisco)	-	54	41	23	2	-	-	-	120
Walleye	-	2	14	5	18	6	-	-	45
Yellow Perch	129	324	13	-	-	-	-	-	466

FISH STOCKING DATA

year	species	size	# released
89	Walleye	Fry	13,000,000
90	Walleye	Fry	11,190,000
91	Walleye	Fry	14,100,000
92	Walleye	Fry	12,015,364
93	Walleye	Fry	13,197,600
94	Walleye	Fry	14,936,000
95	Walleye	Fry	7,700,000
96	Walleye	Fry	4,970,000
97	Walleye	Fry	6,935,000

NET CATCH DATA
survey date: 6/19/95

	Gill Nets		Trap Nets	
species	# per net	avg fish wt. (lbs)	# per set	avg fish wt. (lbs)
Black Crappie	trace	0.52	3.6	0.54
Bluegill	trace	0.51	5.9	0.57
Bowfin (Dogfish)	-	-	trace	3.86
Hybrid Sunfish	-	-	trace	0.35
Northern Pike	14.6	1.92	2.3	0.63
Pumpkin. Sunfish	0.5	0.44	12.0	0.38
Rock Bass	-	-	0.3	0.51
Tullibee (Cisco)	32.8	0.78	-	-
Walleye	1.1	1.47	0.2	0.86
Yellow Perch	65.2	0.34	11.8	0.34

LENGTH OF SELECTED SPECIES SAMPLED FROM ALL GEAR
Number of fish caught for the following length categories (inches):

species	0-5	6-8	9-11	12-14	15-19	20-24	25-29	>30	Total
Black Crappie	1	4	38	1	-	-	-	-	44
Bluegill	-	58	14	-	-	-	-	-	72
Hybrid Sunfish	-	1	-	-	-	-	-	-	1
Northern Pike	-	1	24	35	60	55	26	2	203
Pumpkin. Sunfish	2	133	-	-	-	-	-	-	135
Rock Bass	-	3	1	-	-	-	-	-	4
Tullibee (Cisco)	-	1	82	68	24	-	-	-	175
Walleye	-	-	2	3	8	2	-	-	15
Yellow Perch	9	268	136	1	-	-	-	-	414

DNR COMMENTS:

NOT AVAILABLE

FISHING INFORMATION: Cut Foot is probably the most popular fishing spot in the entire region on opening weekend as well as at other times. A classic spawning area for Big Winnie's Walleyes, the heavy concentrations are fished relentlessly boat to boat at times, especially around William's Narrows. One- to 1-1/2 pound males are usually the most active early in the year with some 8- to 10-pound females' becoming more responsive after the post-spawn period. Many of the spawners are residents of the Cut Foot Lakes and simply move out to deeper water as the season progresses. The Gap, Battleship Point and the island to the east of Battleship give up some good fish around autumn. As in most Walleye lakes, plan on some Northern line bite-offs. Slab Crappies are found throughout the Cut Foot Lakes with 3/4-pound-plus fish being the norm. (See Lake Winnibigoshish pages for more information on Cut Foot).

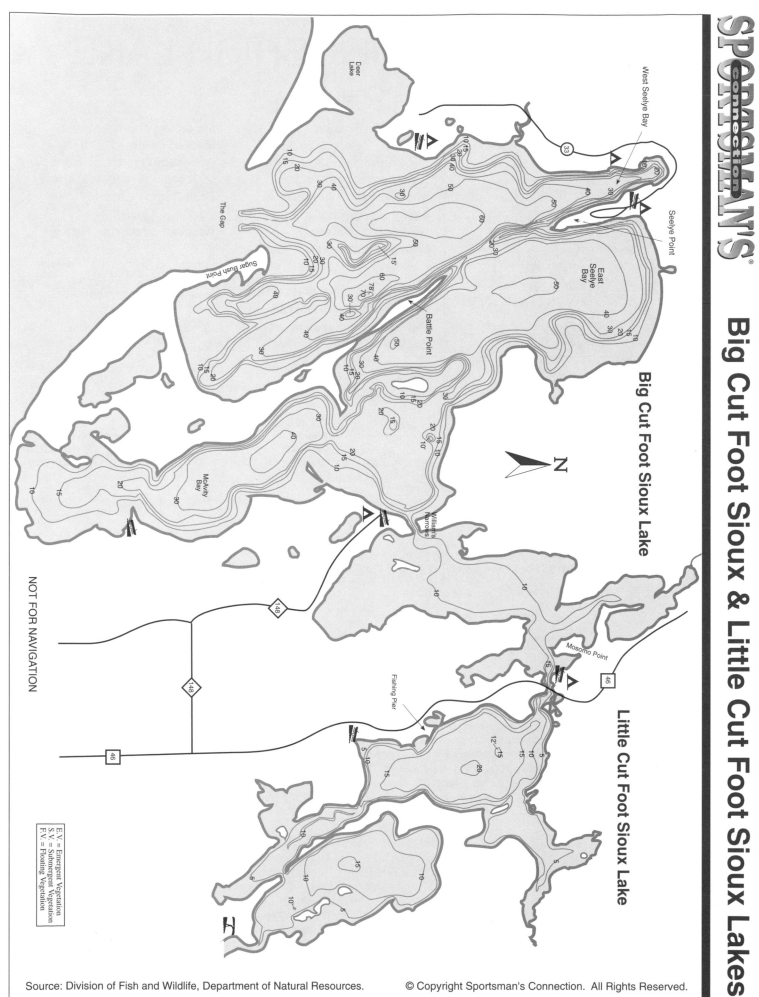

SPORTSMAN'S Connection®

Big Cut Foot Sioux & Little Cut Foot Sioux Lakes

Big Cut Foot Sioux Lake

Little Cut Foot Sioux Lake

Deer Lake

West Seelye Bay

Seelye Point

East Seelye Bay

The Gap

Sugar Bush Point

Battle Point

McAvity Bay

William's Narrows

Mosomo Point

Fishing Pier

N

NOT FOR NAVIGATION

E.V. = Emergent Vegetation
S.V. = Submergent Vegetation
F.V. = Floating Vegetation

LITTLE WINNIBIGOSHISH LAKE
Cass County

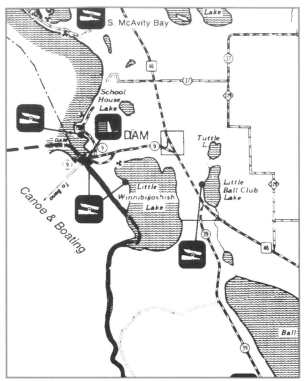

Location: Township 145, 146
Range 26, 27
Watershed: Mississippi Headwaters
Size of lake: 1,287 acres
Shorelength: 5.0 miles
Secchi disk (water clarity): 4.9 ft.
Water color: Green
Cause of water color: Algae

Maximum depth: 26.0 ft.
Median depth: 17.5 ft.
Accessibility: USFS-owned public access on northwest shore
Boat Ramp: Earth
Parking: Limited
Accommodations: Resort

Shoreland zoning classification: Recreational Development
Dominant forest/soil type: No tree/Wet
Management class: Walleye
Ecological type: Hard-water Walleye

FISH STOCKING DATA

year	species	size	# released
90	Walleye	Fry	1,300,000
92	Walleye	Fry	1,300,000
94	Walleye	Fry	1,300,000

NET CATCH DATA

survey date: 7/25/94

species	Gill Nets # per net	Gill Nets avg fish wt. (lbs.)	Trap Nets # per set	Trap Nets avg fish wt. (lbs.)
Black Bullhead	0.3	0.88	-	-
Black Crappie	5.9	0.75	2.5	0.71
Northern Pike	4.4	2.18	0.3	2.09
Pumpkin. Sunfish	trace	0.34	0.4	0.38
Rock Bass	trace	0.97	-	-
Shorthead Redhorse	trace	2.23	-	-
Tullibee (Cisco)	12.6	0.40	-	-
Walleye	6.3	1.25	0.2	2.65
White Sucker	4.6	1.46	1.1	2.69
Yellow Perch	24.3	0.21	4.5	0.16

LENGTH OF SELECTED SPECIES SAMPLED FROM ALL GEAR

Number of fish caught for the following length categories (inches):

species	0-5	6-8	9-11	12-14	15-19	20-24	25-29	>30	Total
Black Bullhead	-	-	3	1	-	-	-	-	4
Brown Bullhead	-	-	97	2	-	-	-	-	99
Northern Pike	-	-	-	1	22	28	4	1	56
Pumpkin. Sunfish	-	5	-	-	-	-	-	-	5
Rock Bass	-	-	1	-	-	-	-	-	1
Tullibee (Cisco)	-	75	35	15	-	-	-	-	125
Walleye	-	11	1	23	38	5	-	-	78
Yellow Perch	61	197	41	-	-	-	-	-	299

DNR COMMENTS: Walleye population near median level for lake class and stable; mean size 14.9 inches and 1.2 lb.; natural reproduction may be sufficient to support population. Northern Pike numbers about average for lake class; mean size of 21.2 inches and 2.2 lb. is the largest observed since 1974. Muskellunge, Largemouth Bass, Black Crappies and Bluegills present in low numbers. Yellow Perch population near lake class median values; mean length 7.3 inches. Cisco numbers high; mean length 9.1 inches; 90 percent of this species is free of parasites. Rock Bass, Whitefish, Pumpkinseed and Bullheads also present.

FISHING INFORMATION: Little Winnibigoshish – or "Little Winnie" – is less famous and receives considerably less fishing pressure than its larger namesake. The Mississippi River flows in and out of the lake, providing excellent spawning grounds for Northern and Walleye – both of which reach trophy size. According to Joe, at the River Rat Trading Post on Highway 2 near Cohasset, a good population of 20-pound-class Northerns roam the lake, and the Walleye fishing can be very good. Trolling the weedline produces good Northern action, especially early in the season after ice out. Little Winnie also holds some big Muskies. George, at The Bait Shop in Deer River, told us of a 50-inch Muskie caught from shore by a Walleye angler a few years back. If you locate a school of Crappie, count on some nice sizes, typically 3/4-pound-plus, with an occasional 2-pounder. Little Winnie is a fairly dark, relatively shallow lake, which warms up earlier than many of the clear, deep lakes in the area. Try the north end and river inlet and outlet for early Crappie. Sam, of Fred's Live Bait and Tackle in Deer River, said anglers get good Walleye catches up river toward the Big Winnie dam early in the year. Move out to the deep side of the weedline of the lake later in the season.

SPORTSMAN'S
connection

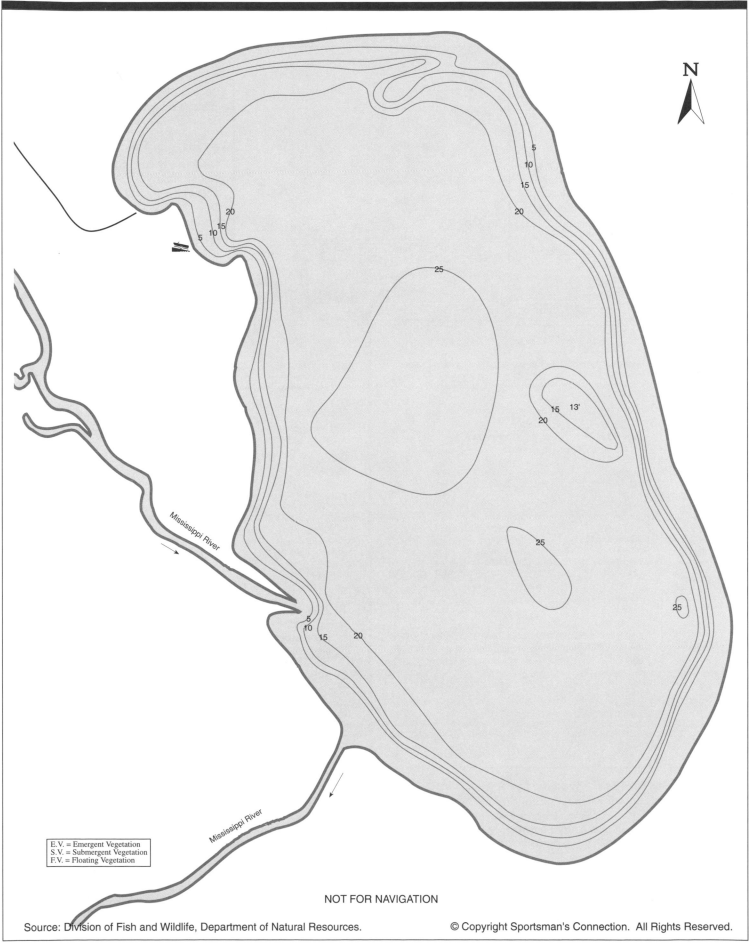

N

Mississippi River

Mississippi River

E.V. = Emergent Vegetation
S.V. = Submergent Vegetation
F.V. = Floating Vegetation

NOT FOR NAVIGATION

Source: Division of Fish and Wildlife, Department of Natural Resources.

BALL CLUB LAKE   LITTLE BALL CLUB LAKE

Itasca County

Location: Township 145 Range 25, 26
Watershed: Mississippi Headwaters-
Size of lake: 4,951 acres
Shorelength: 15.0 miles
Secchi disk (water clarity): 11.3 ft.
Water color: Light green
Cause of water color: Algae bloom
Maximum depth: 85.0 ft.
Median depth: 45.0 ft.
Accessibility: County-owned public access on south shore off Hwy. 2; state-owned public access on west shore
Boat Ramp: Earth (S); Concrete (W)
Parking: Ample
Accommodations: Resorts
Shoreland zoning classif.: Rec. Dev.
Dominant forest/soil type: NA
Cause of water color: Algae bloom
Management class: Walleye
Ecological type: Hard-water Walleye

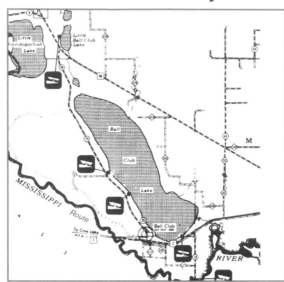

Location: Township 145 Range 25, 26
Watershed: Mississippi Headwaters
Size of lake: 132 acres
Shorelength: 3.3 miles
Secchi disk (water clarity): 6.5 ft.
Water color: Brown
Cause of water color: Bog stain and suspended silt
Maximum depth: 29.0 ft.
Median depth: 20.0 ft.
Accessibility: USFS-owned public access on west shore
Boat Ramp: Gravel
Parking: Ample
Accommodations: Resorts
Shoreland zoning classif.: Rec. Dev.
Dominant forest/soil type: Decid./Wet
Management class: Walleye-Centrarchid
Ecological type: Centrarchid-Walleye

DNR COMMENTS:
Walleye Population about average for lake class; average weight 1.5 lb.; natural reproduction apparently successful for this species. Northern Pike in good condition; average size 20.8 inches and 2.4 lb., but fish to 31 inches captured. Black Crappie sampled in low numbers; average length 10 inches. Bluegills scarce. Yellow Perch, Cisco, and Whitefish populations good.

FISH STOCKING DATA: NO RECORD OF STOCKING

NET CATCH DATA

survey date: 8/9/93

species	Gill Nets # per net	Gill Nets avg fish wt. (lbs)	Trap Nets # per set	Trap Nets avg fish wt. (lbs)
Black Crappie	trace	0.67	0.5	0.65
Bluegill	-	-	trace	0.66
Bowfin (Dogfish)	-	-	0.1	5.35
Northern Pike	5.6	2.37	0.5	0.58
Rock Bass	0.1	0.82	0.3	0.77
Tullibee (Cisco)	2.5	0.61	-	-
Walleye	3.3	1.48	trace	0.42
White Sucker	0.9	1.82	trace	2.87
Yellow Perch	25.0	0.21	4.6	0.09

LENGTH OF SELECTED SPECIES SAMPLED FROM ALL GEAR
Number of fish caught for the following length categories (inches):

species	0-5	6-8	9-11	12-14	15-19	20-24	25-29	>30	Total
Black Crappie	-	-	9	-	-	-	-	-	9
Bluegill	-	1	-	-	-	-	-	-	1
Northern Pike	1	4	3	5	36	27	15	1	92
Rock Bass	-	3	4	-	-	-	-	-	7
Tullibee (Cisco)	-	5	21	11	-	-	-	-	37
Walleye	-	-	5	16	23	6	-	-	50
Yellow Perch	148	161	51	1	-	-	-	-	361

FISH STOCKING DATA

year	species	size	# released
89	Walleye	Fingerling	30
89	Walleye	Yearling	333
91	Walleye	Yearling	81
96	Walleye	Fingerling	1,170

NET CATCH DATA

survey date: 6/3/93

species	Gill Nets # per net	Gill Nets avg fish wt. (lbs)	Trap Nets # per set	Trap Nets avg fish wt. (lbs)
Black Crappie	4.0	0.45	3.6	0.38
Bluegill	0.2	0.22	4.3	0.37
Bowfin (Dogfish)	0.3	5.97	0.5	5.70
Northern Pike	6.8	2.55	0.9	0.95
Pumpkin. Sunfish	0.2	0.24	1.8	0.26
Walleye	0.5	2.30	0.1	2.40
Yellow Bullhead	0.2	0.40	-	-
Yellow Perch	42.7	0.15	7.8	0.08

LENGTH OF SELECTED SPECIES SAMPLED FROM ALL GEAR
Number of fish caught for the following length categories (inches):

species	0-5	6-8	9-11	12-14	15-19	20-24	25-29	>30	Total
Black Crappie	-	35	17	1	-	-	-	-	53
Bluegill	8	25	2	-	-	-	-	-	35
Northern Pike	-	1	5	5	11	13	9	3	47
Pumpkin. Sunfish	8	7	-	-	-	-	-	-	15
Walleye	-	-	-	-	3	1	-	-	4
Yellow Bullhead	-	1	-	-	-	-	-	-	1
Yellow Perch	75	163	5	-	-	-	-	-	243

DNR COMMENTS:
Walleye population low for lake class and in decline since 1973; good average weight of 2.3 lb. Yellow Perch numbers up, with a few fish reaching 8 inches. Bluegill numbers up slightly but still below average for lake class. Black Crappie lengths range from 7 to 12 inches.

FISHING INFORMATION: Renowned as a panfish lake, **Big Ball Club** also provides some nice Northern Pike, hefty Walleye, and big Largemouth Bass. Jeff Kremers of the Be-Mah-Quat Resort confirms the lake's reputation as a top panfish producer, one yielding with Crappies in the 1 1/2- to 2-pound range and 1- to 1 1/2-pound Bluegills. Trophy Walleye are available, with the average fish going 2 1/2 to 3 1/2 pounds. They are caught by working the various points and other Walleye structure, including the sandbars on the south end of the lake. Try working off of the large point (Cook's Point); the Ball Club River outlet; and the creek on the southeast shoreline. Action heats up in June, with minnows being the preferred bait earlier and leeches later in the summer. Northern fishing can yield some 3 1/2- to 20-pound-plus fish. There's even an occasional Muskie taken. Shoreline dropoffs along the lake's cattails are productive for Pike, as are the weedbeds near the sandbars on the south end. Ball Club's sandy bottom and deep, cold water provide excellent-tasting fish year round. **Little Ball Club** is small (lakes on map page are not in scale) and has little in common with Big Ball Club. The little lake does have a history of producing some nice Crappies and Bluegills, however. And it gives up some decent Walleyes and Northern Pike to anglers casting or trolling the shorelines. Try working the bulrushes and weedbeds, too, for Largemouth Bass and panfish.

NOT FOR NAVIGATION

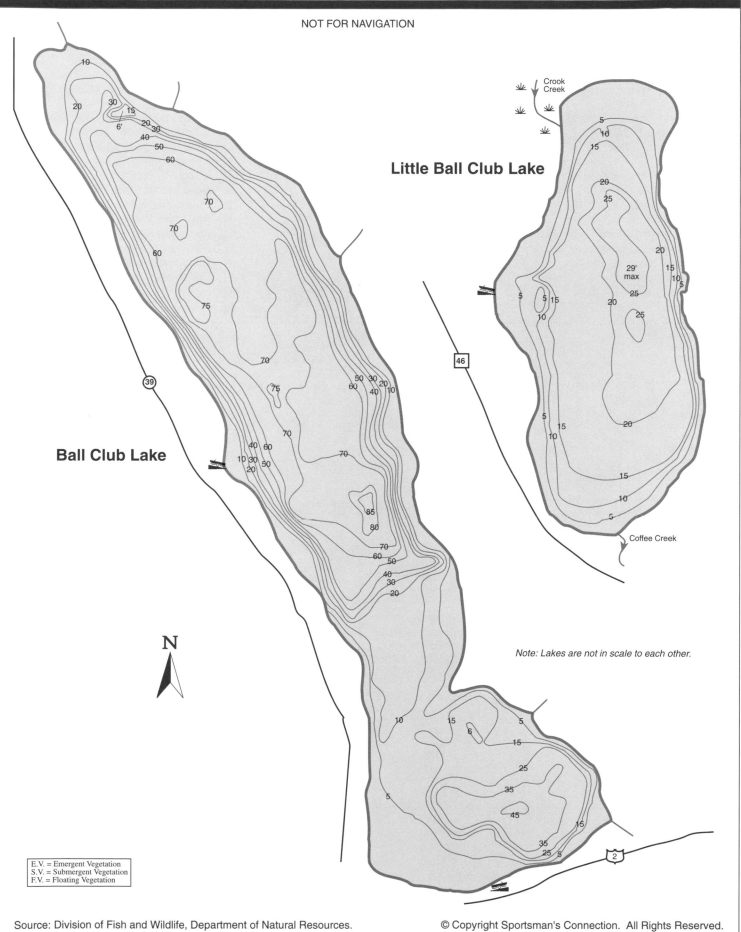

Little Ball Club Lake

Ball Club Lake

Crook Creek

29' max

Coffee Creek

Note: Lakes are not in scale to each other.

N

E.V. = Emergent Vegetation
S.V. = Submergent Vegetation
F.V. = Floating Vegetation

Source: Division of Fish and Wildlife, Department of Natural Resources.

DIXON LAKE

Itasca County

Location: Township 148 Range 28, 29
Watershed: Mississippi Headwaters-
Size of lake: 666 acres
Shorelength: 9.3 miles
Secchi disk (water clarity): 4.5 ft.
Water color: Green
Cause of water color: Algae bloom
Maximum depth: 29.0 ft.
Median depth: 12.0 ft.
Accessibility: Township-owned carry-in access on NW shore of south basin
Boat Ramp: Carry-down
Parking: Limited
Accommodations: Resorts
Shoreland zoning classif.: Rec. Dev.
Dominant forest/soil type: Decid/Loam
Management class: Walleye
Ecological type: Hard-water Walleye

DUNBAR LAKE

Location: Township 148 Range 28, 29
Watershed: Mississippi Headwaters-
Size of lake: 254 acres
Shorelength: 4.5 miles
Secchi disk (water clarity): 6.5 ft.
Water color: Brown
Cause of water color: Bog stain
Maximum depth: 30. 0 ft.
Median depth: 15.0 ft.
Accessibility: County-owned public access on southwest shore
Boat Ramp: Carry-down
Parking: Limited
Accommodations: Resort
Shoreland zoning classif.: Rec. Dev.
Dominant forest/soil type: Decid/Loam
Management class: Walleye-Centrarchid
Ecological type: Centrarchid

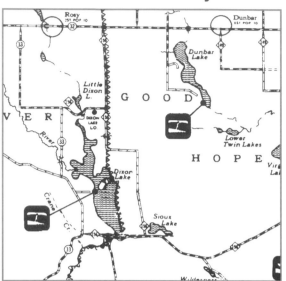

DIXON LAKE

DNR COMMENTS:
Lake experienced partial winterkill in 1993-94. Walleye numbers low; length range 8.5 to 24 inches; natural reproduction variable. Northern Pike population stable and above lake class median; age 2 and 3 fish compose 78 percent of sample. Black Crappie numbers fairly low, but size structure is very good; mean length 10.6 inches. Yellow Perch numbers above lake class median; mean length 8.1 inches; natural reproduction good. Largemouth Bass numbers low. Cisco present.

FISH STOCKING DATA

year	species	size	# released
90	Walleye	Fry	700,000
92	Walleye	Fry	700,000

NET CATCH DATA

survey date: 7/28/97

	Gill Nets		Trap Nets	
species	# per net	avg fish wt. (lbs)	# per set	avg fish wt. (lbs)
Black Bullhead	6.3	0.33	2.3	0.30
Black Crappie	0.1	1.01	0.8	0.71
Brown Bullhead	4.7	0.41	8.4	0.54
Northern Pike	6.4	1.39	1.0	0.77
Pumpkin. Sunfish	0.6	0.21	4.0	0.29
Rock Bass	0.3	0.27	trace	0.91
Tullibee (Cisco)	0.1	1.49	-	-
Walleye	1.4	0.91	0.7	1.06
White Sucker	2.7	1.88	1.0	2.50
Yellow Bullhead	-	-	0.4	0.36
Yellow Perch	23.2	0.27	5.0	0.32

LENGTH OF SELECTED SPECIES SAMPLED FROM ALL GEAR
Number of fish caught for the following length categories (inches):

species	0-5	6-8	9-11	12-14	15-19	20-24	25-29	>30	Total
Black Bullhead	7	69	19	-	-	-	-	-	95
Black Crappie	-	-	10	1	-	-	-	-	11
Brown Bullhead	1	68	61	22	-	-	-	-	152
Northern Pike	-	-	1	23	39	9	4	2	78
Pumpkin. Sunfish	12	42	-	-	-	-	-	-	54
Rock Bass	-	3	1	-	-	-	-	-	4
Tullibee (Cisco)	-	-	-	-	1	-	-	-	1
Walleye	-	3	11	3	5	1	-	-	23
Yellow Bullhead	-	3	2	-	-	-	-	-	5
Yellow Perch	44	155	108	-	-	-	-	-	307

DUNBAR LAKE

FISH STOCKING DATA: NO RECORD OF STOCKING

NET CATCH DATA

survey date: 7/15/96

	Gill Nets		Trap Nets	
species	# per net	avg fish wt. (lbs)	# per set	avg fish wt. (lbs)
Black Bullhead	0.2	1.03	-	-
Black Crappie	1.7	0.16	4.8	0.40
bluegill	0.2	0.66	0.9	0.51
Brown Bullhead	-	-	0.8	1.04
Northern Pike	6.2	1.67	0.3	1.72
Pumpkin. Sunfish	-	-	0.9	0.15
Trout-Perch	0.2	0.01	-	-
Walleye	3.0	1.29	0.3	3.01
White Sucker	0.8	0.69	-	-
Yellow Perch	17.3	0.16	2.2	0.22

LENGTH OF SELECTED SPECIES SAMPLED FROM ALL GEAR
Number of fish caught for the following length categories (inches):

species	0-5	6-8	9-11	12-14	15-19	20-24	25-29	>30	Total
Black Bullhead	-	-	1	-	-	-	-	-	1
Black Crappie	21	1	31	-	-	-	-	-	53
Bluegill	-	8	1	-	-	-	-	-	9
Brown Bullhead	-	-	1	6	-	-	-	-	7
Northern Pike	-	-	-	-	19	19	1	-	39
Pumpkin. Sunfish	5	3	-	-	-	-	-	-	8
Walleye	-	7	3	2	6	-	3	-	21
Yellow Perch	47	63	9	-	-	-	-	-	119

DNR COMMENTS:
Walleye numbers highest on record for this lake, despite cessation of stocking; length range 6.3 to 29 inches; mean weight 1.3 lb.; natural reproduction very good, and stocking is unnecessary. Northern Pike numbers also highest on record for lake; length range 15.2 to 28 inches; average weight 1.7 lb. Black Bullhead numbers down dramatically. Black Crappies up to 11.3 inches and Bluegills up to 9 inches sampled; anglers report fishing can be good at times for these species.

FISHING INFORMATION: Access to Dixon Lake and Dunbar Lake can be difficult. Which, of course, helps to ease fishing pressure. Jack at Squaw Lake Sports Center warns that the roads into the public launches (classified as "carry-down" by the DNR) are very poor. Anglers with four-wheel drive vehicles and winches which enable them to slosh through the mud and those who gain access at the resorts, are rewarded, though, with good Crappie fishing on both lakes. **Dixon** is notorious for its slab Crappies in the 1- to 2-pound class. Plate-size Bluegills are also present with some 1 1/2-pounders' being registered in the Blue Book each year. **Dunbar** receives much less pressure than Dixon and produces some 3/4-pound-plus Crappies and decent Walleyes. There are also some decent Bluegills and Pumpkinseeds in Dunbar. When Third River is open, spawning Walleyes from Big Winnie make their way into Dixon and get hammered by anglers crowded boat-to-boat. Dixon also gives up 5-pound-class Northerns with some frequency.

NOT FOR NAVIGATION

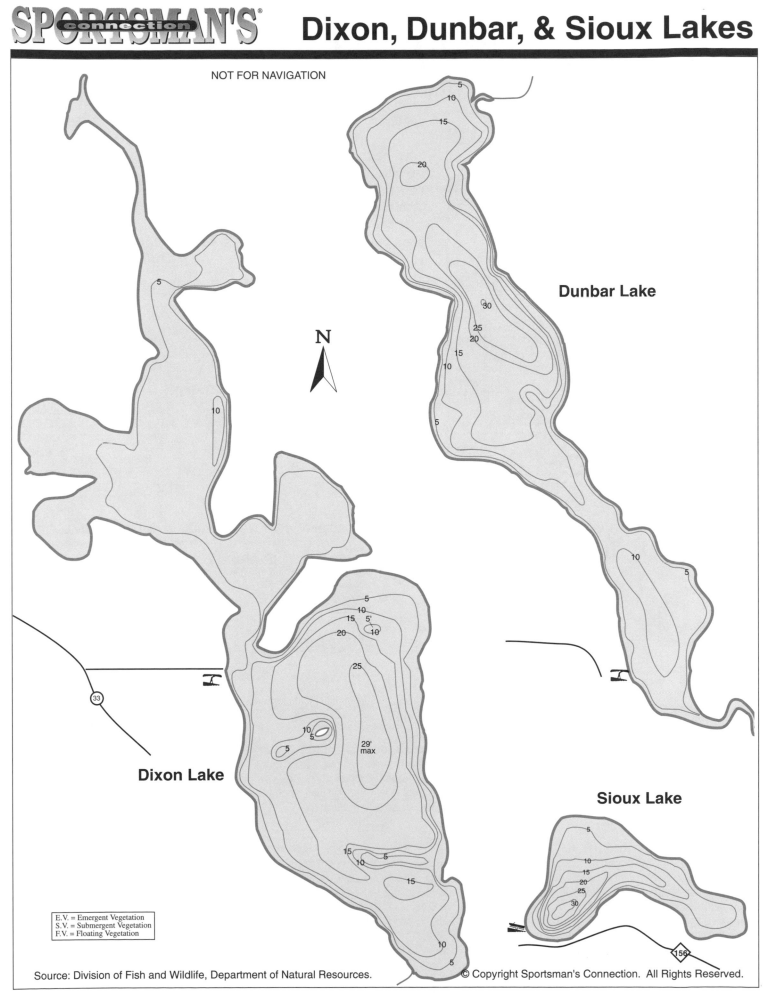

Dunbar Lake

N

Dixon Lake

Sioux Lake

E.V. = Emergent Vegetation
S.V. = Submergent Vegetation
F.V. = Floating Vegetation

Source: Division of Fish and Wildlife, Department of Natural Resources.

ROUND LAKE
Itasca County

Location: Township 148 Range 27, 28
Watershed: Big Fork
Size of lake: 2,828 acres
Shorelength: 8.2 miles
Secchi disk (water clarity): 6.5 ft.
Water color: Light brown
Cause of water color: Bog stain

Maximum depth: 24.0 ft.
Median depth: 12.0 ft.
Accessibility: State-owned public access on southeast and northeast shores
Boat Ramp: Concrete (both)
Parking: Limited
Accommodations: Resorts

Shoreland zoning classification: Recreational Development
Dominant forest/soil type: No Tree/Wet
Management class: Walleye
Ecological type: Hard-water Walleye

FISH STOCKING DATA

year	species	size	# released
90	Walleye	Fry	3,000,000
92	Walleye	Fry	3,000,000
96	Walleye	Fry	2,548,350

NET CATCH DATA

survey date: 6/24/96

species	Gill Nets # per net	Gill Nets avg fish wt. (lbs.)	Trap Nets # per set	Trap Nets avg fish wt. (lbs.)
Black Crappie	1.6	0.26	0.4	0.13
Bluegill	trace	0.29	0.4	0.14
Bowfin (Dogfish)	trace	4.41	-	-
Brown Bullhead	1.6	0.98	4.1	0.79
Burbot	0.1	2.62	-	-
Northern Pike	16.9	1.88	0.1	1.56
Pumpkin. Sunfish	-	-	0.4	0.16
Rock Bass	-	-	0.1	0.11
Tullibee (Cisco)	0.9	0.48	-	-
Walleye	6.1	1.48	1.2	4.29
White Sucker	4.2	2.32	0.1	2.20
Yellow Perch	38.4	0.32	8.2	0.10

LENGTH OF SELECTED SPECIES SAMPLED FROM ALL GEAR
Number of fish caught for the following length categories (inches):

species	0-5	6-8	9-11	12-14	15-19	20-24	25-29	>30	Total
Black Crappie	4	19	4	-	-	-	-	-	27
Bluegill	3	2	-	-	-	-	-	-	5
Brown Bullhead	1	1	34	24	-	-	-	-	60
Northern Pike	-	-	-	-	89	138	9	1	237
Pumpkin. Sunfish	3	1	-	-	-	-	-	-	4
Rock Bass	1	-	-	-	-	-	-	-	1
Tullibee (Cisco)	-	6	1	5	-	-	-	-	12
Walleye	-	4	21	6	46	18	1	-	96
Yellow Perch	112	132	205	1	-	-	-	-	450

DNR COMMENTS: Walleye population above lake class median, despite reduction in stocking; average length 15.7 inches; strong 1991 and 1994 year classes. Northern Pike continue to be abundant; average length 20.7 inches, with fish as large as 30 inches being captured; strong natural reproduction due to excellent spawning habitat. Black Crappies sampled in gill net at numbers above lake class median; length range 5.9 to 10.8 inches. Yellow Perch numbers down but still well above lake class median values; quality size structure for this species; average length 8.6 inches, with fish up to 12 inches being sampled.

FISHING INFORMATION: Round Lake, located within the Leech Lake Indian Reservation and Chippewa National Forest, is well known for its jumbo Perch. These attract anglers from Wisconsin as well as the rest of Minnesota every year. Winter fishing can be fast and furious, with 100-fish catches not being uncommon. Both Jack at Squaw Lake Sports Center and George of The Bait Shop in Deer River told us that 10- to 12-inch Perch in the 3/4-pound to 1-pound range have been hitting well. Jack also told us that the Walleyes in Round are nice when they're on the bite; fish up to 9 pounds have been landed. The Crappies are few but nice-size. Round's 3,000 acres warm up fairly quickly after ice out, due to dark, relatively shallow water. This makes it a good opener lake. Round Lake is connected by a channel to Squaw Lake. This provides spawning habitat and produces a spring Walleye migration. Not surprisingly, anglers get some good catches early in the season. Hunters take note: Squaw Lake's wild rice attracts not only fish, but good duck flights in the fall.

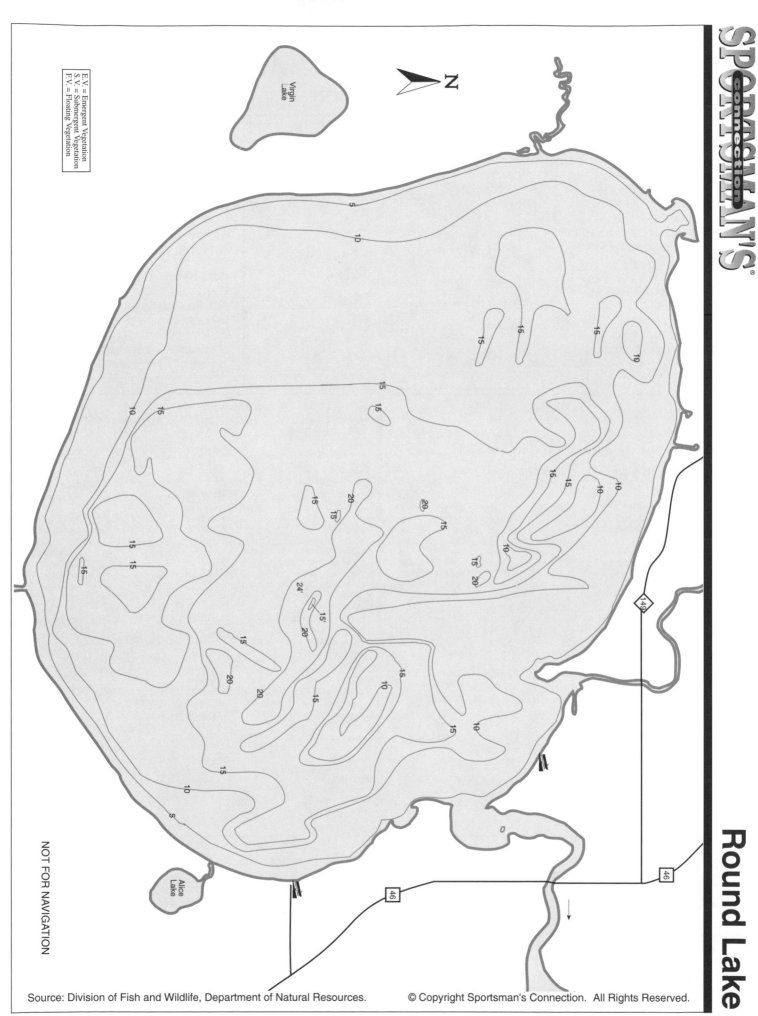

SPORTSMAN'S connection®

Virgin Lake

Alice Lake

N

E.V. = Emergent Vegetation
S.V. = Submergent Vegetation
F.V. = Floating Vegetation

NOT FOR NAVIGATION

Source: Division of Fish and Wildlife, Department of Natural Resources.

© Copyright Sportsman's Connection. All Rights Reserved.

ISLAND LAKE

MOOSE LAKE

Itasca County

Location: Township 150 Range 28
Watershed: Big Fork
Size of lake: 3,088 acres
Shorelength: 11.3 miles
Secchi disk (water clarity): 6.0 ft.
Water color: Light green
Cause of water color: Algae
Maximum depth: 35.0 ft.
Median depth: 17.0 ft.
Accessibility: State-owned public access on northwest shore off Hwy. 46
Boat Ramp: Concrete
Parking: Ample
Accommodations: Camping (on Elmwood Island); Resorts
Shoreland zoning classif.: Gen. Dev.
Dominant forest/soil type: NA
Management class: Walleye
Ecological type: Hard-water Walleye

Location: Township 150 Range 28
Watershed: Big Fork
Size of lake: 357 acres
Shorelength: 6.2 miles
Secchi disk (water clarity): 9.0 ft.
Water color: Clear
Cause of water color: NA
Maximum depth: 52.0 ft.
Median depth: 26.0 ft.
Accessibility: Federal-owned public access on south shore; from Hwy. 46, E on Co. Rd. 31, N on Forest Road 3335
Boat Ramp: Metal
Parking: Limited
Accommodations: None
Shoreland zoning classif.: Rec. Dev.
Dominant forest/soil type: Decid./Loam
Management class: Walleye
Ecological type: Hard-water Walleye

DNR COMMENTS (Island Lake):

Walleye population within the expected range for lake class; mean length 18.5 inches; mean weight of 2.4 lb. exceeds expected range. Northern Pike numbers above average for lake class; mean size 24 inches and 2.8 lb. Yellow Perch fairly numerous; mean length 6.5 inches for all gear. Bluegill stocking in 1984 has established a naturally reproducing population; numbers are within expected range, but size is small at 3.4 to 5.7 inches. Cisco numbers high.

FISH STOCKING DATA (Island Lake)

year	species	size	# released
90	Walleye	Fry	3,000,000
92	Walleye	Fry	3,000,000
96	Walleye	Fry	2,730,000

survey date: 6/23/97

NET CATCH DATA (Island Lake)

	Gill Nets		Trap Nets	
species	# per net	avg fish wt. (lbs)	# per set	avg fish wt. (lbs)
Black Bullhead	0.1	0.06	0.2	0.08
Black Crappie	-	-	0.2	1.04
Bluegill	trace	0.07	11.5	0.07
Brown Bullhead	-	-	0.3	0.99
Hybrid Sunfish	-	-	0.9	0.06
Northern Pike	8.7	2.79	trace	1.61
Pumpkin. Sunfish	0.3	0.16	39.2	0.09
Rock Bass	3.8	0.38	0.9	0.32
Tullibee (Cisco)	8.6	0.84	-	-
Walleye	4.2	2.37	0.3	0.27
White Sucker	1.8	2.23	-	-
Yellow Bullhead	-	-	0.2	1.00
Yellow Perch	64.0	0.14	40.5	0.12

LENGTH OF SELECTED SPECIES SAMPLED FROM ALL GEAR (Island Lake)

Number of fish caught for the following length categories (inches):

species	0-5	6-8	9-11	12-14	15-19	20-24	25-29	>30	Total
Black Bullhead	4	-	-	-	-	-	-	-	4
Black Crappie	-	-	1	2	-	-	-	-	3
Bluegill	151	-	-	-	-	-	-	-	151
Brown Bullhead	-	2	-	2	-	-	-	-	4
Hybrid Sunfish	12	-	-	-	-	-	-	-	12
Northern Pike	-	-	-	2	37	66	15	11	131
Pumpkin. Sunfish	335	25	-	-	-	-	-	-	360
Rock Bass	-	51	14	44	20	-	-	-	129
Tullibee (Cisco)	-	51	14	44	20	-	-	-	129
Walleye	1	5	-	19	17	18	7	-	67
Yellow Bullhead	-	-	1	1	-	-	-	-	2
Yellow Perch	631	588	96	1	-	-	-	-	1,316

FISH STOCKING DATA (Moose Lake)

year	species	size	# released
89	Walleye	Fry	700,000
91	Walleye	Fry	375,000
94	Walleye	Fry	375,000
97	Walleye	Fry	375,000

survey date: 08/24/92

NET CATCH DATA (Moose Lake)

	Gill Nets		Trap Nets	
species	# per net	avg fish wt. (lbs)	# per set	avg fish wt. (lbs)
Yellow Perch	102.6	0.31	1.6	0.13
Yellow Bullhead	0.3	0.63	0.1	1.00
White Sucker	1.3	1.86	-	-
Walleye	10.7	1.86	0.1	8.60
Rock Bass	1.4	0.36	-	-
Pumpkin. Sunfish	1.4	0.32	2.6	0.25
Northern Pike	4.3	2.58	0.7	1.27
Largemouth Bass	0.7	0.83	1.0	0.11
Bowfin (Dogfish)	0.2	2.30	-	-
Black Crappie	2.9	0.63	0.3	0.30
Black Bullhead	0.2	0.70	-	-

LENGTH OF SELECTED SPECIES SAMPLED FROM ALL GEAR (Moose Lake)

Number of fish caught for the following length categories (inches):

species	0-5	6-8	9-11	12-14	15-19	20-24	25-29	>30	Total
Yellow Perch	1	31	89	1	-	-	-	-	122
Yellow Bullhead	-	-	3	1	-	-	-	-	4
Walleye	-	-	4	7	72	9	5	-	97
Rock Bass	-	11	3	-	-	-	-	-	14
Pumpkin. Sunfish	-	13	2	-	-	-	-	-	15
Northern Pike	-	-	-	-	8	21	7	1	37
Largemouth Bass	-	2	1	3	-	-	-	-	6
Black Crappie	-	4	18	5	-	-	-	-	27
Black Bullhead	-	-	2	1	-	-	-	-	3

DNR COMMENTS (Moose Lake):

Northern Pike population down sharply from last sampling, but still nearly average for lake class. Walleyes very numerous, with population being above third-quartile values. Black Crappie gillnet sampling above third-quartile values. Rock Bass numerous. Yellow Perch numbers very high, with sampling at 102.5/set. Bullhead population low. Other species present in about average numbers.

FISHING INFORMATION: **Island Lake**'s structure provides excellent habitat for its high Walleye population. It is normally a late starter, according to Jim at Cedar Hill Resort on the lake. From Memorial weekend through the first three weeks in June, it produces some nice fish. At that time of year, Walleyes are found near the rocky points and other spawning areas in 5 to 10 feet of water. The underwater islands and deeper points produce better during the summer months. Jim said he knows of at least 25 good structure areas that usually hold Walleye – some in the 5- to 8-pound class. The lake also holds its fair share of "cigars," but you can usually count on some 2-pound fish. Average Perch size has also been increasing in recent years, with some pounders being taken. When you can find the Crappies, they run 3/4 pound-plus. Northerns are plentiful, but count on finding more hammerhandles than large ones. To the east of Island Lake on County Road 159 lies **Moose Lake**. Unlike Island's structure, Moose's is fairly simple, with relatively steep shoreline dropoffs. Jim told us to work the secondary breakline for Walleyes, which average in the 2-pound range. Largemouth Bass up to 3 and 4 pounds are caught by anglers willing to learn the lake. Walleye anglers have reported catching some 1-pound Crappies along the breaklines.

Island & Moose Lakes

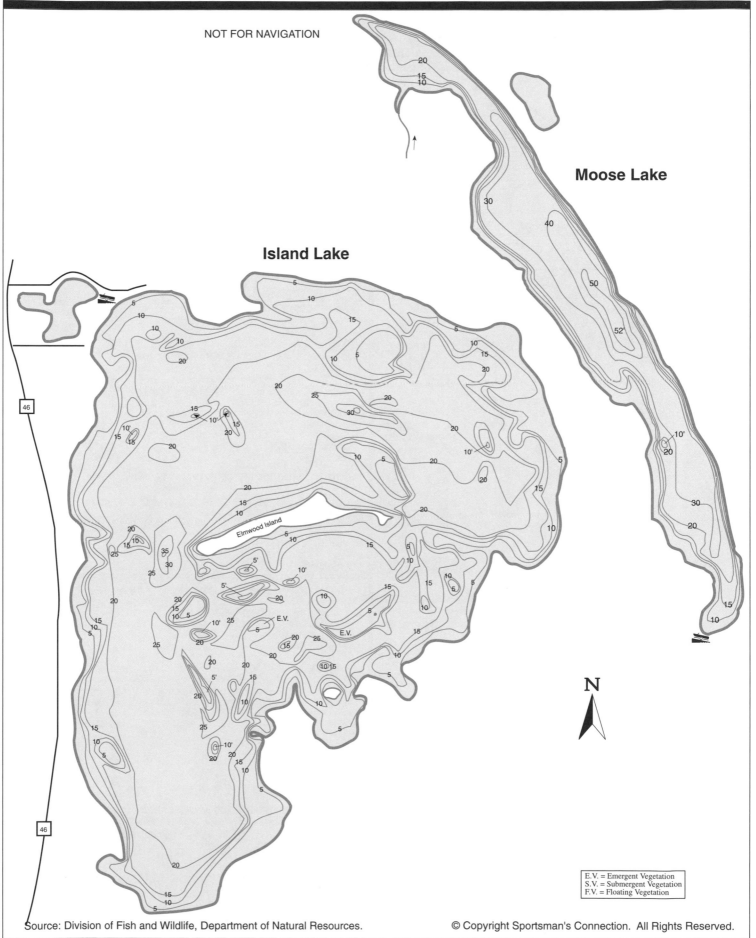

NOT FOR NAVIGATION

Moose Lake

Island Lake

Elmwood Island

E.V.

E.V.

46

N

| E.V. = Emergent Vegetation |
| S.V. = Submergent Vegetation |
| F.V. = Floating Vegetation |

Location: Township 149, 150   Range 26, 27
Watershed: Big Fork

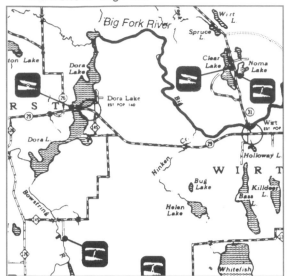

	DORA LAKE	CLEAR LAKE	NOMA LAKE
		Itasca County	
Size of lake:	735 acres	132 acres	55 acres
Shorelength:	10.3 miles	3.3 miles	1.3 miles
Secchi disk (water clarity):	8.0 ft.	8.0 ft.	12.0 ft.
Water color:	Brown	Clear	Clear
Cause of water color:	Bog stain	NA	NA
Maximum depth:	18.0 ft.	29.0 ft.	47.0 ft.
Median depth:	12.0 ft.	17.0 ft.	14.5 ft.
Accessibility:	USFS-owned public access on east shore by Cty. Rd. 29 bridge	Public access on east shore, off #27	USFS-owned public access on south shore
Boat Ramp:	Concrete	Earth	Carry-down
Parking:	Limited	Limited	Ample
Accommodations:	Resort	Resort	Campground
Shoreland zoning classif.:	Rec. Dev.	Rec. Dev.	Nat. Envt.
Dominant forest/soil type:	No tree/Wet	NA	NA
Management class:	Walleye	Walleye-Centrarchid	Centrarchid
Ecological type:	Hard-water Walleye	Centrarchid	Centrarchid

Dora Lake

DNR COMMENTS: Walleye numbers are lower than expected, although the gill netting information could be biased because of weed growth that prevented effective netting. All other species are within normal limits for this type of lake.

FISH STOCKING DATA

year	species	size	# released
89	Walleye	Fry	4,000,000
90	Walleye	Fry	750,000
93	Walleye	Fry	750,000
95	Walleye	Fry	750,000

survey date: 06/10/91

NET CATCH DATA

	Gill Nets		Trap Nets	
		avg fish		avg fish
species	# per net	wt. (lbs)	# per set	wt. (lbs)
Yellow Perch	45.9	0.25	2.9	0.27
White Sucker	9.0	1.93	0.6	1.68
Walleye	1.9	1.38	0.3	4.10
Silver Redhorse	2.1	3.47	0.1	2.50
Shorthead Red.	1.1	1.48	1.1	2.00
Pumpkin. Sunfish	0.3	0.45	0.1	0.60
Northern Pike	3.4	2.63	0.6	0.78
Hybrid Sunfish	0.1	0.80	0.1	0.80
Brown Bullhead	8.1	0.54	0.8	0.67
Black Crappie	0.1	0.90	0.8	0.80
Black Bullhead	4.3	0.38	1.3	0.25
Yellow Bullhead	-	-	1.0	0.46

LENGTH OF SELECTED SPECIES SAMPLED FROM ALL GEAR
Number of fish caught for the following length categories (inches):

species	0-5	6-8	9-11	12-14	15-19	20-24	25-29	>30	Total
Yellow Perch	-	71	27	-	-	-	-	-	98
Walleye	-	-	1	7	7	1	-	-	16
Pumpkin. Sunfish	-	2	-	-	-	-	-	-	2
Northern Pike	-	-	1	8	10	2	3	-	24
Hybrid Sunfish	-	1	-	-	-	-	-	-	1
Brown Bullhead	-	-	49	8	-	-	-	-	57
Black Crappie	-	-	-	1	-	-	-	-	1
Black Bullhead	-	12	18	-	-	-	-	-	30

Clear Lake

FISH STOCKING DATA

year	species	size	# released
89	Walleye	Fingerling	1,404
91	Walleye	Fingerling	459
96	Walleye	Fingerling	728

survey date: 08/22/83

NET CATCH DATA

	Gill Nets		Trap Nets	
		avg fish		avg fish
species	# per net	wt. (lbs)	# per set	wt. (lbs)
Yellow Perch	39.3	0.16	2.3	0.17
Walleye	3.8	1.57	-	-
Northern Pike	5.3	1.90	0.5	1.00
Bluegill	2.0	0.13	6.5	0.11
Pumpkin. Sunfish	-	-	1.5	0.20
Black Crappie	-	-	1.0	0.38

LENGTH OF SELECTED SPECIES SAMPLED FROM ALL GEAR
Number of fish caught for the following length categories (inches):

species	0-5	6-8	9-11	12-14	15-19	20-24	25-29	>30	Total
Black Crappie	-	1	3	-	-	-	-	-	4
Bluegill	4	30	-	-	-	-	-	-	34
Northern Pike	-	-	1	2	4	16	1	-	23
Pumpkin. Sunfish	2	4	-	-	-	-	-	-	6
Walleye	-	-	-	3	6	5	1	-	15
Yellow Perch	-	79	27	3	-	-	-	-	109

DNR COMMENTS: Northern Pike numbers have declined slightly but are still quite high. There has been a substantial decline in Perch abundance, but numbers are still higher than local medians. Walleye numbers have increased substantially since the last survey. Bluegill numbers have declined, while Pumpkinseed and Crappie abundance remains low.

Noma Lake

FISH STOCKING DATA

year	species	size	# released
90	Walleye	Yearling	54
96	Walleye	Fingerling	390

survey date: 7/19/93

NET CATCH DATA

	Gill Nets		Trap Nets	
		avg fish		avg fish
species	# per net	wt. (lbs)	# per set	wt. (lbs)
Black Crappie	-	-	0.1	0.30
Bluegill	6.7	0.26	20.0	0.25
Hybrid Sunfish	-	-	0.6	0.24
Largemouth Bass	-	-	0.1	0.72
Northern Pike	1.0	5.22	-	-
Pumpkin. Sunfish	-	-	0.5	0.11
Walleye	1.0	3.42	0.3	3.09
Yellow Perch	21.3	0.13	-	-

LENGTH OF SELECTED SPECIES SAMPLED FROM ALL GEAR
Number of fish caught for the following length categories (inches):

species	0-5	6-8	9-11	12-14	15-19	20-24	25-29	>30	Total
Black Crappie	-	1	-	-	-	-	-	-	1
Bluegill	24	156	-	-	-	-	-	-	180
Hybrid Sunfish	1	4	-	-	-	-	-	-	5
Largemouth Bass	-	-	1	-	-	-	-	-	1
Northern Pike	-	-	-	-	1	1	1	-	3
Pumpkin. Sunfish	3	1	-	-	-	-	-	-	4
Walleye	-	-	-	3	2	-	-	-	5
Yellow Perch	8	55	1	-	-	-	-	-	64

DNR COMMENTS: Walleyes scarce, but fish are generally in the 15- to 24-inch range. Northern Pike scarce, but mean weight is 5.2 lb. Largemouth Bass sample too small for accurate population assessment. Black Crappie numbers low. Bluegill population very strong; mean length 6.8 inches. Yellow Perch abundant but small, with average length being 6.6 inches. Pumpkinseed and Hybrid Sunfish numbers low.

FISHING INFORMATION: Dora Lake is a part of the Big Fork flowage that provides some excellent early-season Walleye fishing in the narrows, according to Joe at the River Rat Trading Post in Cohasset. Some Northerns also are pulled from Dora, but the lake is basically known for its Walleye. **Clear Lake** gives up some nice 2- to 3-pound Walleyes, along with a few larger ones, every season. Twenty-pound-class Northern Pike also lurk in these waters, feeding on the heavy Perch population. **Noma Lake** has a good Bluegill population and some decent Northerns. The DNR has been stocking Walleye over the last several years which should be taking hold. Noma also has a nice campground.

NOT FOR NAVIGATION

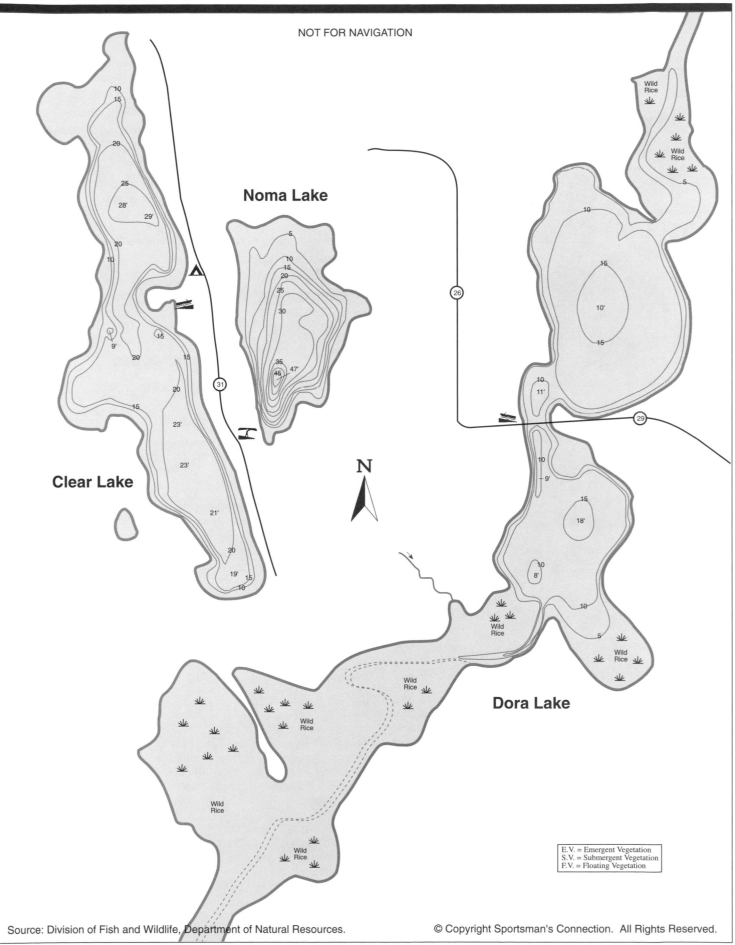

Noma Lake

Clear Lake

N

Dora Lake

Wild Rice

| E.V. = Emergent Vegetation |
| S.V. = Submergent Vegetation |
| F.V. = Floating Vegetation |

Source: Division of Fish and Wildlife, Department of Natural Resources.

© Copyright Sportsman's Connection. All Rights Reserved.

21

SAND LAKE
Itasca County

Location: Township 147, 148 Range 26
Watershed: Big Fork
Size of lake: 4,328 acres
Shorelength: 19.9 miles
Secchi disk (water clarity): 9.5 ft.
Water color: Light brown
Cause of water color: Bog stain

Maximum depth: 70.0 ft.
Median depth: 17.0 ft.
Accessibility: State-owned public access on southeast shore of southeast bay
Boat Ramp: Concrete
Parking: Ample
Accommodations: Resorts

Shoreland zoning classification: Recreational Development
Dominant forest/soil type: Decid/Loam
Management class: Walleye
Ecological type: Hard-water Walleye

FISH STOCKING DATA

year	species	size	# released
90	Walleye	Fry	3,800,000
92	Walleye	Fry	3,800,000

survey date:

7/15/96

NET CATCH DATA

	Gill Nets		Trap Nets	
species	# per net	avg fish wt. (lbs.)	# per set	avg fish wt. (lbs.)
Black Bullhead	-	-	0.4	0.80
Black Crappie	trace	0.80	0.7	0.85
Bluegill	trace	0.54	0.9	0.44
Bowfin (Dogfish)	-	-	0.8	4.15
Brown Bullhead	0.8	1.22	1.4	1.00
Northern Pike	10.1	1.14	0.4	1.12
Pumpkin. Sunfish	0.3	0.61	0.6	0.43
Rock Bass	0.6	0.77	0.1	0.80
Shorthead Redhorse	1.0	2.03	2.3	2.04
Silver Redhorse	trace	3.55	2.1	4.30
Tullibee (Cisco)	0.9	0.60	-	-
Walleye	3.9	0.93	trace	0.11
White Sucker	1.3	2.07	0.1	2.76
Yellow Bullhead	-	-	trace	0.62
Yellow Perch	11.1	0.28	1.6	0.19

LENGTH OF SELECTED SPECIES SAMPLED FROM ALL GEAR
Number of fish caught for the following length categories (inches):

species	0-5	6-8	9-11	12-14	15-19	20-24	25-29	>30	Total
Black Bullhead	-	-	4	1	-	-	-	-	5
Black Crappie	-	-	8	3	-	-	-	-	11
Bluegill	-	13	-	-	-	-	-	-	13
Brown Bullhead	-	-	7	25	-	-	-	-	32
Northern Pike	-	-	-	5	132	15	5	-	157
Pumpkin. Sunfish	1	12	-	-	-	-	-	-	13
Rock Bass	-	3	8	-	-	-	-	-	11
Tullibee (Cisco)	-	9	-	4	1	-	-	-	14
Walleye	-	13	20	7	19	-	1	-	60
Yellow Bullhead	-	-	1	-	-	-	-	-	1
Yellow Perch	33	110	45	-	-	-	-	-	188

DNR COMMENTS: Walleye numbers down somewhat, but 1994 and 1995 year classes should provide good angling; size range for species 6.7 to 26 inches; average weight .9 lb.; natural reproduction capable of supporting population. Northern Pike abundant, but smaller fish dominate the population; average size only 17.9 inches; fish to 27.2 inches captured; good natural reproduction in excellent spawning habitat. Black Crappie numbers near lake-class median; quality size structure present, with mean length of captured fish being 11.2 inches. Yellow Perch numbers down and below lake-class median values.

FISHING INFORMATION: Sand Lake's rolling structure provides anglers plenty of good areas to fish for its good numbers of Walleye, Crappie, jumbo Perch, and Largemouth Bass. Brian Krecklau, of the Pole Bender Guide Service, says you can expect Walleyes to average in the 1 1/2- to 2-pound range; Crappies around 3/4 pound, and Perch 10 inches-plus. Hammerhandle Northerns infest the lake. Brian says he likes Sand, because he can usually count on a mixed bag of fish. Crappies are taken consistently throughout the year; a 2-pounder is occasionally mixed in with the more-typical, 3/4-pound fish. If the Walleye fishing is slow, Perch are almost always active, and a good percentage of them are keepers. Largemouth Bass numbers are good, but be prepared to catch several small fish for every decent one. Most Bass caught are released, and more anglers are now releasing large female Walleyes. This will help natural reproduction of this important species.

SPORTSMAN'S Connection®

Sand Lake

NOT FOR NAVIGATION

N

Bird's Eye Lake

Portage Lake

Bowstring River

E.V. = Emergent Vegetation
S.V. = Submergent Vegetation
F.V. = Floating Vegetation

Source: Division of Fish and Wildlife, Department of Natural Resources.

BOWSTRING LAKE
Itasca County

Location: Township 146, 147
Range 25, 26
Watershed: Big Fork
Size of lake: 9,220 acres
Shorelength: 21.0 miles
Secchi disk (water clarity): 6.0 ft.
Water color: Green
Cause of water color: Algae

Maximum depth: 30.0 ft.
Median depth: 15.0 ft.
Accessibility: Accesses on northwest shore (1), northeast shore (1), and south shore (1)
Boat Ramp: Concrete (all)
Parking: Ample
Accommodations: Resorts, picnic grounds, campground.

Shoreland zoning classification: Recreational Development
Dominant forest/soil type: NA
Management class: Walleye
Ecological type: Hard-water Walleye

FISH STOCKING DATA

year	species	size	# released
85	Walleye	Fry	8,900,000
87	Walleye	Fry	8,900,000
89	Walleye	Fry	8,900,000
91	Walleye	Fry	8,900,000

survey date: **NET CATCH DATA**

8/5/96

	Gill Nets		Trap Nets	
species	# per net	avg fish wt. (lbs.)	# per set	avg fish wt. (lbs.)
Black Crappie	1.6	0.26	0.6	0.34
Bluegill	-	-	trace	0.87
Bowfin (Dogfish)	-	-	0.1	4.41
Brown Bullhead	-	-	0.9	1.20
Burbot	-	-	trace	2.04
Hybrid Sunfish	-	-	trace	0.62
Northern Pike	10.1	1.50	1.5	0.96
Pumpkin. Sunfish	-	-	0.3	0.16
Rock Bass	trace	0.34	0.5	0.81
Shorthead Redhorse	trace	2.76	0.8	2.39
Silver Redhorse	-	-	3.3	5.03
Tullibee (Cisco)	2.4	1.52	-	-
Walleye	15.0	0.58	trace	2.76
White Sucker	5.1	0.70	0.5	1.46
Yellow Bullhead	-	-	trace	0.25
Yellow Perch	15.7	0.37	1.0	0.21

LENGTH OF SELECTED SPECIES SAMPLED FROM ALL GEAR

Number of fish caught for the following length categories (inches):

species	0-5	6-8	9-11	12-14	15-19	20-24	25-29	>30	Total
Black Crappie	11	11	4	2	-	-	-	-	28
Bluegill	-	-	1	-	-	-	-	-	1
Brown Bullhead	1	-	2	11	-	-	-	-	14
Hybrid Sunfish	-	1	-	-	-	-	-	-	1
Northern Pike	-	1	-	11	96	31	2	2	143
Pumpkin. Sunfish	2	2	-	-	-	-	-	-	4
Rock Bass	-	3	6	-	-	-	-	-	9
Tullibee (Cisco)	-	4	2	6	16	1	-	-	29
Walleye	-	53	96	9	15	7	-	-	180
Yellow Bullhead	-	1	-	-	-	-	-	-	1
Yellow Perch	27	60	115	-	-	-	-	-	202

DNR COMMENTS: Walleye sampled at highest rate on record and well above expected range for lake class; most fish smaller, with mean length being 11 inches; fish to 22.3 inches captured; growth good; natural reproduction maintaining the population of this species. Northern Pike numbers lowest on record for lake, but still above expected range; average size 19 inches and 1.5 lb., but fish to 30.9 inches captured. Black Crappie numbers above expected range; growth good. Yellow Perch numbers the lowest on record but still within expected range; mean length 8.9 inches. Only one Bluegill captured, in part because conditions made trapnetting difficult; population of this species is low, however.

FISHING INFORMATION: Bowstring is a classic Walleye fishery, being relatively large, shallow, wind-swept and sandy in character. Its dark waters warm up quickly, making it a good early lake. The DNR's stocking efforts, along with good natural reproduction, provide excellent Walleye fishing. The lake is also fairly easy to fish, because its sandbars and rock piles are magnets for Walleye and Crappie. The Northern end of the lake is full of weedbeds, which attract Northern Pike, Crappie and Perch. Northern average around 3 pounds, and some reach the 20-pound class. In addition to the weedbed area, Inger Bay, on the east side by the Bowstring River outlet, is good for large Pike. Perch – some being jumbos 9 inches and larger – are found throughout the lake. The Crappie fishing in Bowstring can be phenomenal. Good numbers of slabs, in the 1- to 2-pound range, are caught throughout the year. Rarely do you catch a papermouth that isn't a keeper. Fishing pressure for them seems to be at its peak during the winter. The eastern shoreline of the lake has a relatively steep dropoff and is rocky. The north side's bottom structure is primarily sand, mixed with areas of rock.

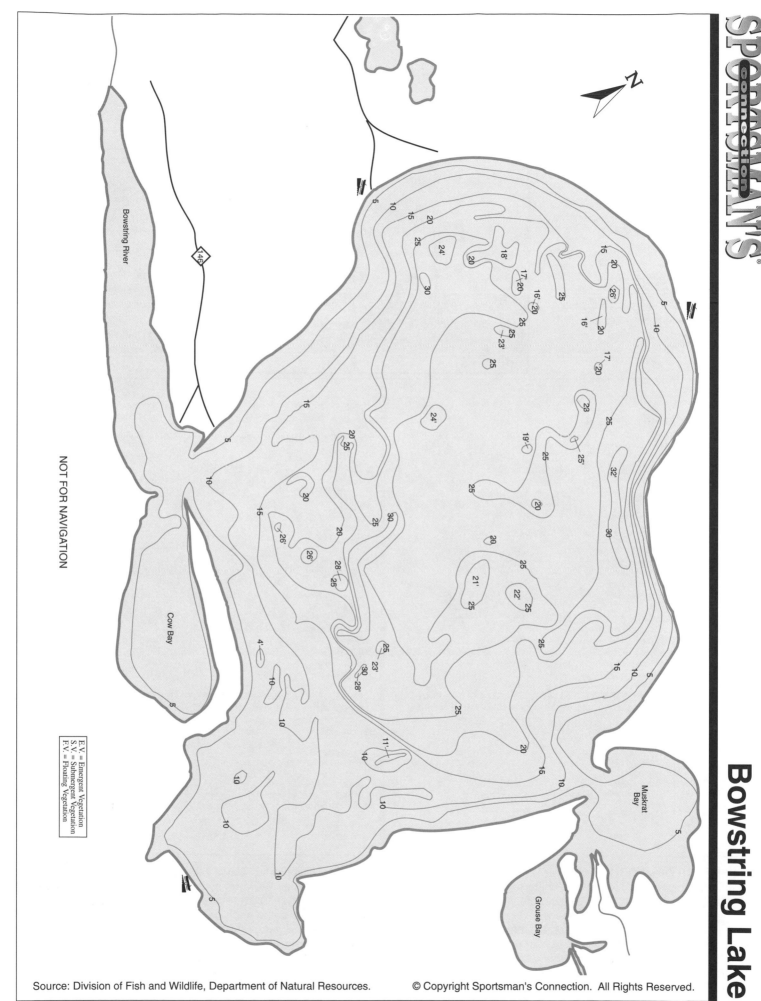

NOT FOR NAVIGATION

Bowstring River

Cow Bay

Bowstring Lake

MusKrat Bay

Grouse Bay

E.V. = Emergent Vegetation
S.V. = Submergent Vegetation
F.V. = Floating Vegetation

JESSIE LAKE   LITTLE JESSIE LAKE
Itasca County

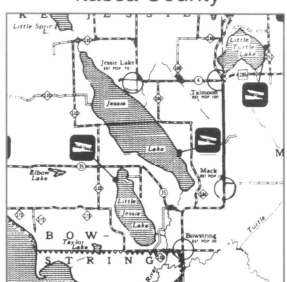

Location: Township 147, 148 Range 25
Watershed: Big Fork
Size of lake: 1,753 acres
Shorelength: 9.2 miles
Secchi disk (water clarity): 6.2 ft.
Water color: Green
Cause of water color: Algae
Maximum depth: 42.0 ft.
Median depth: 22.0 ft.
Accessibility: State-owned public access on southeast shore
Boat Ramp: Concrete
Parking: Ample
Accommodations: Resorts
Shoreland zoning classif.: Rec. Dev.
Dominant forest/soil type: Decid/Sand
Management class: Walleye
Ecological type: Hard-water Walleye

Location: Township 147, 148 Range 25
Watershed: Big Fork
Size of lake: 637 acres
Shorelength: 4.7 miles
Secchi disk (water clarity): 12.0 ft.
Water color: Light blue-green
Cause of water color: Calcium
Maximum depth: 49.0 ft.
Median depth: 28.0 ft.
Accessibility: State-owned public access on northwest corner
Boat Ramp: Concrete
Parking: Ample
Accommodations: Resort
Shoreland zoning classif.: Rec. Dev.
Dominant forest/soil type: Decid/Sand carbonate
Management class: Walleye-Centrarchid
Ecological type: Centrarchid-Walleye

DNR COMMENTS:
Walleye population about average for lake class; most fish between 10 and 28 inches; average weight 1.7 lb; some natural reproduction taking place. Northern Pike numbers low, but size is large: 18 to 33 inches; average weight 3.4 lb. Yellow Perch abundant; length range 4.5 to 11 inches. Black Crappies numerous; size good, with 82 percent of sample measuring 10 to 12 inches.

FISH STOCKING DATA

year	species	size	# released
89	Walleye	Fry	1,800,000
91	Walleye	Fry	1,800,000
93	Walleye	Fry	1,800,000
96	Walleye	Fry	1,592,850

NET CATCH DATA
survey date: 8/30/93

	Gill Nets		Trap Nets	
species	# per net	avg fish wt. (lbs)	# per set	avg fish wt. (lbs)
Black Crappie	-	-	2.3	0.72
Bluegill	trace	0.68	trace	0.45
Bowfin (Dogfish)	trace	2.98	0.4	4.38
Brown Bullhead	0.1	0.89	trace	1.26
Common Shiner	-	-	0.4	0.07
Hybrid Sunfish	-	-	trace	0.09
Largemouth Bass	0.1	0.87	trace	0.22
Northern Pike	2.5	3.40	0.2	2.09
Pumpkin. Sunfish	0.3	0.21	2.1	0.16
Rock Bass	3.7	0.51	0.3	0.32
Tullibee (Cisco)	5.7	1.19	-	-
Walleye	6.4	1.74	-	-
White Sucker	8.5	2.15	trace	1.94
Yellow Bullhead	trace	0.64	-	-
Yellow Perch	86.6	0.16	16.7	0.09

LENGTH OF SELECTED SPECIES SAMPLED FROM ALL GEAR
Number of fish caught for the following length categories (inches):

species	0-5	6-8	9-11	12-14	15-19	20-24	25-29	>30	Total
Black Crappie	-	6	28	-	-	-	-	-	34
Bluegill	-	1	1	-	-	-	-	-	2
Brown Bullhead	-	-	1	2	-	-	-	-	3
Hybrid Sunfish	1	-	-	-	-	-	-	-	1
Largemouth Bass	-	2	-	1	-	-	-	-	3
Northern Pike	-	-	-	1	4	24	8	4	41
Pumpkin. Sunfish	20	16	-	-	-	-	-	-	36
Rock Bass	7	32	20	-	-	-	-	-	59
Tullibee (Cisco)	1	14	2	46	22	-	-	-	85
Walleye	-	2	28	14	34	16	2	-	96
Yellow Bullhead	-	-	1	-	-	-	-	-	1
Yellow Perch	232	234	46	-	-	-	-	-	512

FISH STOCKING DATA

year	species	size	# released
90	Walleye	Fingerling	11,554
92	Walleye	Fingerling	9,270
94	Walleye	Fry	5,428

NET CATCH DATA
survey date: 7/29/96

	Gill Nets		Trap Nets	
species	# per net	avg fish wt. (lbs)	# per set	avg fish wt. (lbs)
Black Crappie	0.2	0.86	-	-
Bluegill	-	-	2.7	0.21
Bowfin (Dogfish)	-	-	0.1	5.62
Common Shiner	-	-	0.4	0.11
Hybrid Sunfish	-	-	0.1	0.07
Largemouth Bass	0.8	0.75	0.6	0.13
Northern Pike	3.3	2.87	0.5	0.46
Pumpkin. Sunfish	0.9	0.19	2.3	0.07
Rock Bass	3.6	0.59	7.3	0.24
Smallmouth Bass	0.3	2.01	-	-
Tullibee (Cisco)	4.3	0.66	-	-
Walleye	10.8	1.62	0.5	1.27
White Sucker	3.7	0.74	0.7	0.62
Yellow Bullhead	0.1	2.11	-	-
Yellow Perch	48.2	0.13	11.6	0.13

LENGTH OF SELECTED SPECIES SAMPLED FROM ALL GEAR
Number of fish caught for the following length categories (inches):

species	0-5	6-8	9-11	12-14	15-19	20-24	25-29	>30	Total
Black Crappie	-	-	2	-	-	-	-	-	2
Bluegill	9	20	-	-	-	-	-	-	29
Hybrid Sunfish	1	-	-	-	-	-	-	-	1
Largemouth Bass	6	2	5	1	-	-	-	-	14
Northern Pike	-	3	1	-	11	13	5	2	35
Pumpkin. Sunfish	25	8	-	-	-	-	-	-	33
Rock Bass	35	54	23	-	-	-	-	-	112
Smallmouth Bass	-	-	-	2	1	-	-	-	3
Tullibee (Cisco)	-	13	3	22	-	-	-	-	38
Walleye	-	-	17	11	61	14	-	-	103
Yellow Bullhead	-	-	-	1	-	-	-	-	1
Yellow Perch	139	394	19	-	-	-	-	-	552

DNR COMMENTS:
Walleye population in upper-quartile range for lake class; mean length 16.4 inches; growth normal. Northern Pike numbers down but still within expected range; mean size 22 inches and 2.9 lb. Yellow Perch numbers highest since 1958 and above expected range; length range 5.4 to 10.8 inches. Cisco numbers within expected range; less than half the sample was infested with worms. Black Crappie, Largemouth Bass and Smallmouth Bass sampled in low numbers, but these species may not be accurately assessed with standard sampling gear.

FISHING INFORMATION: Jessie and Little Jessie Lakes are located within the Chippewa National Forest, which provides a picturesque setting for anglers and recreational boaters. Both lakes give up some nice 2- to 3-pound Walleyes and an occasional trophy. Walleye can be found around the sunken islands, reefs and bars in **Big Jessie**. Joe at the River Rat Trading Post in Cohasset says Crappies averaging around 3/4 pound can provide fast action on spring evenings. Try the inlet area of the north bay of Big Jessie after ice out through early summer, and move out to the sandflats and deeper-water dropoffs later in the year. Northerns don't receive much pressure on either lake, but average sizes are good; there are plenty of 10-pound-class fish present. A good forage base of Ciscoes and Perch contribute to the rapid growth rate of this voracious predator. **Little Jessie**'s fishery is similar to that of its larger namesake, but it receives less attention. Its smaller size makes it easier to locate structure. Smallmouth Bass have been caught with some frequency on Little Jessie in recent years. Largemouth Bass are present in both lakes and are virtually unfished.

SPORTSMAN'S connection®

NOT FOR NAVIGATION

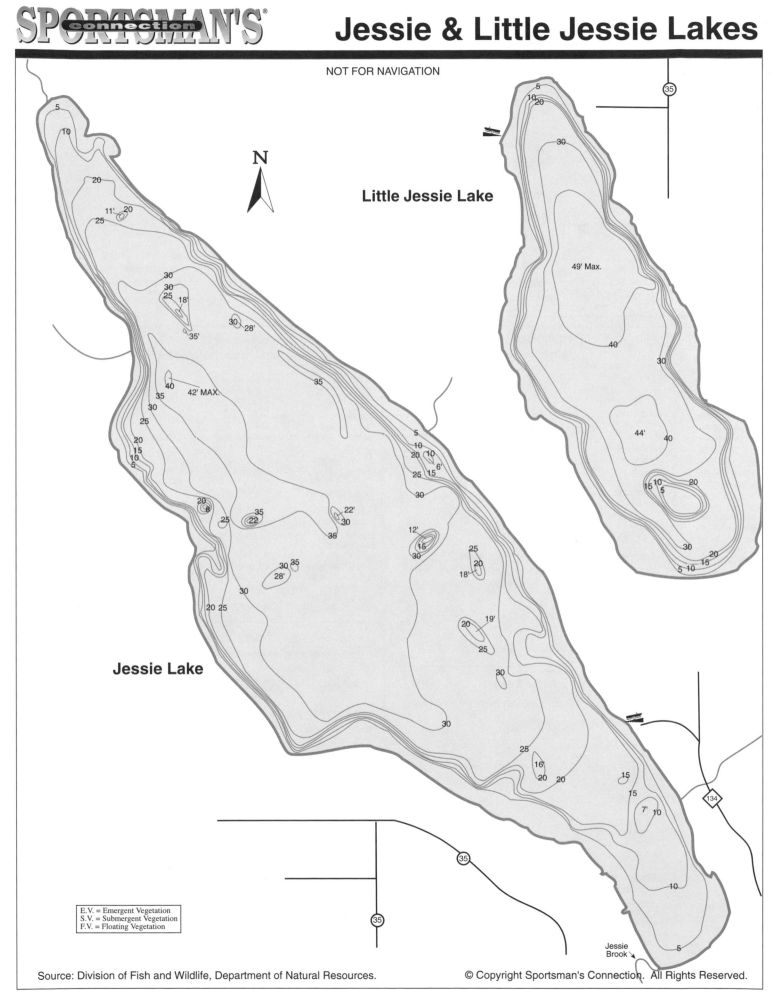

Little Jessie Lake

49' Max.

Jessie Lake

42' MAX.

N

E.V. = Emergent Vegetation
S.V. = Submergent Vegetation
F.V. = Floating Vegetation

Jessie Brook

Source: Division of Fish and Wildlife, Department of Natural Resources.

Location: Township 149   Range 25
Watershed: Big Fork

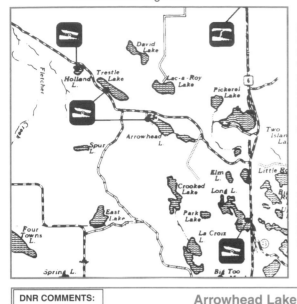

	ARROWHEAD (SAND) LAKE	LONG LAKE	TRESTLE LAKE	HOLLAND LAKE
	Itasca County			
Size of lake:	86 acres	121 acres	96 acres	19 acres
Shorelength:	2.0 miles	3.3 miles	2.0 miles	0.6 miles
Secchi disk (water clarity):	8.0 ft.	13.0 ft.	14.0 ft.	15.0 ft.
Water color:	Light green	Clear	Clear	Brown-green
Cause of water color:	Algae bloom	NA	NA	Algae/bog stain
Maximum depth:	30.0 ft.	75.0 ft.	30.0 ft.	45.0 ft.
Median depth:	15.0 ft.	27.0 ft.	18.1 ft.	18.1 ft.
Accessibility:	USFS-owned public access on west shore	Public access on southeast shore, off Hwy 6	Public access on northwest shore, off USFS Rd. 2187	Public access on northwest corner off USFS Rd. 2187
Boat Ramp:	Earth	Gravel	Concrete	Earth
Parking:	Ample	Ample	Ample	Limited
Accommodations:	NA	Campground	NA	NA
Shoreland zoning classif.:	Nat. Envt.	Nat. Envt.	Nat. Envt.	Nat. Envt.
Dominant forest/soil type:	NA	NA	NA	NA
Management class:	Walleye-Centrarchid	Centrarchid	Centrarchid	Centrarchid
Ecological type:	Centrarchid	Centrarchid	Centrarchid	Centrarchid

---

DNR COMMENTS:
Walleye numbers low. Northern Pike numbers average; size large. Yellow Perch numerous and small. LM Bass numbers about normal. Black Crappie numbers down but within expected range. Bluegill numbers normal.

FISHING INFO:
Arrowhead (aka Sand) is an excellent spring Crappie lake, says Joe at the River Rat Trading Post, providing 40 to 45 fish on a good evening. Plump Bluegills, Walleyes, and Northerns round out the fishery.

Arrowhead Lake
FISH STOCKING DATA

year	species	size	# released
89	Walleye	Fry	200,000
90	Walleye	Yearling	24
91	Walleye	Fry	90,000

NET CATCH DATA
survey date: 8/22/94

	Gill Nets		Trap Nets	
		avg fish		avg fish
species	# per net	wt. (lbs)	# per set	wt. (lbs)
Black Crappie	0.5	0.19	0.7	0.27
Bluegill	2.5	0.22	19.8	0.10
Golden Shiner	-	-	0.1	0.04
Largemouth Bass	0.3	2.20	0.6	1.08
Northern Pike	5.8	4.05	0.1	0.77
Pumpkin. Sunfish	-	-	0.4	0.11
Walleye	0.3	4.94	0.1	5.29
Yellow Perch	99.8	0.11	8.9	0.11

LENGTH OF SELECTED SPECIES SAMPLED FROM ALL GEAR
Number of fish caught for the following length categories (inches):

species	0-5	6-8	9-11	12-14	15-19	20-24	25-29	>30	Total
Black Crappie	-	7	1	-	-	-	-	-	8
Bluegill	127	51	-	-	-	-	-	-	178
Largemouth Bass	1	-	1	3	1	-	-	-	6
Northern Pike	-	-	-	-	2	12	8	2	24
Pumpkin. Sunfish	4	-	-	-	-	-	-	-	4
Walleye	-	-	-	-	-	-	2	-	2
Yellow Perch	58	112	1	-	-	-	-	-	171

DNR COMMENTS:
Northern Pike and Bluegill numbers are much higher than state and local catch medians. The abundance of other fish is within normal limits for this type of lake.

FISHING INFO:
Trestle (aka Fox) is a good Northern Pike lake holding with some 20-pound-class fish.

Trestle Lake
FISH STOCKING DATA: NO RECORD OF STOCKING

NET CATCH DATA
survey date: 06/22/83

	Gill Nets		Trap Nets	
		avg fish		avg fish
species	# per net	wt. (lbs)	# per set	wt. (lbs)
Yellow Perch	4.8	0.10	4.3	0.12
White Sucker	0.5	1.75	-	-
Northern Pike	17.5	1.53	1.5	0.23
Bluegill	3.5	0.10	79.3	0.09
Pumpkin. Sunfish	-	-	1.5	0.23
Golden Shiner	-	-	0.3	0.20
Black Crappie	-	-	2.8	0.39
Black Bullhead	-	-	0.5	1.25

LENGTH OF SELECTED SPECIES SAMPLED FROM ALL GEAR
Number of fish caught for the following length categories (inches):

species	0-5	6-8	9-11	12-14	15-19	20-24	25-29	>30	Total
Black Bullhead	-	-	-	2	-	-	-	-	2
Black Crappie	-	3	5	3	-	-	-	-	11
Bluegill	23	57	5	-	-	-	-	-	85
Northern Pike	-	-	1	1	30	36	5	-	73
Pumpkin. Sunfish	-	6	-	-	-	-	-	-	6
Yellow Perch	-	33	3	-	-	-	-	-	36

Holland Lake
FISH STOCKING DATA: NO RECORD OF STOCKING

NET CATCH DATA
survey date: 07/05/79

	Gill Nets		Trap Nets	
		avg fish		avg fish
species	# per net	wt. (lbs)	# per set	wt. (lbs)
Yellow Perch	45.5	0.11	1.8	0.21
Northern Pike	11.5	2.37	0.8	0.83
Bluegill	1.0	0.10	57.8	0.18
Black Crappie	0.5	0.20	7.0	0.05
Pumpkin. Sunfish	-	-	2.3	0.28
Largemouth Bass	-	-	0.8	0.27
Brown Bullhead	-	-	0.3	1.00

LENGTH OF SELECTED SPECIES SAMPLED FROM ALL GEAR
Number of fish caught for the following length categories (inches):

species	0-5	6-8	9-11	12-14	15-19	20-24	25-29	>30	Total
Black Crappie	-	2	25	-	-	-	-	-	27
Bluegill	-	29	3	-	-	-	-	-	32
Brown Bullhead	-	-	-	1	-	-	-	-	1
Largemouth Bass	-	3	-	-	-	-	-	-	3
Northern Pike	-	-	-	1	3	19	3	-	26
Pumpkin. Sunfish	-	8	1	-	-	-	-	-	9
Yellow Perch	-	30	4	-	-	-	-	-	34

DNR COMMENTS:
Northern Pike, Perch and Bluegill populations are at fairly high levels. All other fish populations appear to be within normal limits for this type of lake.

FISHING INFO:
Holland, tiny but deep, holds some 1/2- to 3/4-pound Crappies and lots of Bluegills. Largemouth Bass, averaging 2 pounds, can also be found. Catch and release of the Bass is highly recommended to help preserve the resource.

Long Lake
FISH STOCKING DATA: NO RECORD OF STOCKING

NET CATCH DATA
survey date: 08/03/83

	Gill Nets		Trap Nets	
		avg fish		avg fish
species	# per net	wt. (lbs)	# per set	wt. (lbs)
White Sucker	0.3	4.00	-	-
Tullibee (incl. Cisco)	13.3	0.48	0.5	0.75
Northern Pike	8.8	1.70	0.5	0.75
Largemouth Bass	0.3	0.50	0.3	0.50
Bluegill	1.0	0.18	12.8	0.15
Black Bullhead	0.3	0.20	-	-
Yellow Perch	-	-	1.0	0.10
Yellow Bullhead	-	-	0.3	0.80
Rock Bass	-	-	0.5	0.25
Pumpkin. Sunfish	-	-	1.3	0.12
Black Crappie	-	-	3.6	0.27

LENGTH OF SELECTED SPECIES SAMPLED FROM ALL GEAR
Number of fish caught for the following length categories (inches):

species	0-5	6-8	9-11	12-14	15-19	20-24	25-29	>30	Total
Black Crappie	-	8	6	-	-	-	-	-	14
Bluegill	13	42	-	-	-	-	-	-	55
Largemouth Bass	-	-	1	1	-	-	-	-	2
Northern Pike	-	-	-	1	20	11	4	1	37
Pumpkin. Sunfish	2	3	1	-	-	-	-	-	5
Rock Bass	-	1	1	-	-	-	-	-	2
Tullibee (incl. Cisco)	-	2	29	15	7	-	-	-	53
Yellow Perch	-	1	3	-	-	-	-	-	4

DNR COMMENTS:
Cisco and Northern Pike population are well above state and local medians. All other fish numbers seem to be within normal limits for this type of lake.

FISHING INFO:
Long Lake, deep and clear, is another good panfish lake. It has a nice campground and a good gravel boat landing. Northerns and Largemouth Bass are present, but Crappies and Bluegills provide most of the action.

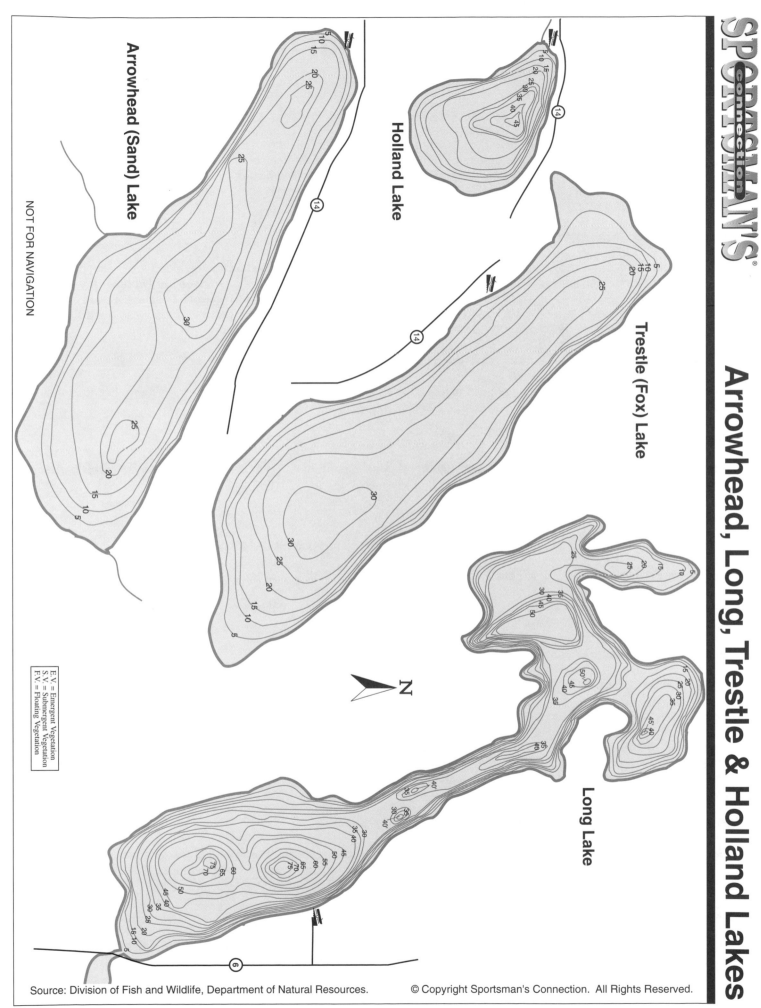

SPORTMAN'S
Connection

Arrowhead, Long, Trestle & Holland Lakes

Holland Lake

Arrowhead (Sand) Lake

NOT FOR NAVIGATION

Trestle (Fox) Lake

Long Lake

N

E.V. = Emergent Vegetation
S.V. = Submergent Vegetation
F.V. = Floating Vegetation

Source: Division of Fish and Wildlife, Department of Natural Resources.

© Copyright Sportsman's Connection. All Rights Reserved.

LAKE WINNIBIGOSHISH

(Continued from page 6)

Auger: One- to 2-pounders. In the fall and midsummer off of Bena Bar you catch a lot of 5- and 6-pounders. Up toward the top, past Big Bend where the bar starts breaking northwest, you can find some nice ones in late summer. Tamarack Point is good early spring in around 7 to 12 feet of water. Straight out from the satellite dishes there is a submerged point that gives up some fish in 8 to 12 feet of water. There's a pretty good breakline there with some weeds; pretty much a mixed bottom which seems to work pretty good.

Sportsman's Connection: How's the area off of Third River Flowage?

Auger: Again, the fish seem to follow a regular migratory pattern; coming out of the flowage up along the north shore, out on Stony Point and onto the Humps. The Humps are good all year once the fish get there – a week or two after the opener. If there are a lot of boats don't be afraid to go a little bit deeper and right along the edge. The Rock Piles are a good spot to fish with sand bottom changing to rock, back to sand and back to rock again. Out from The Gap there are weed humps that come up in the middle of summer. You can go out and cast them for Walleyes late in the evening.

Sportsman's Connection: So you can actually see the weeds; they're up above the water?

Auger: Right. They're pencil reeds right out of The Gap toward Tamarack Point. You can't miss them, because they are ringed with buoys. Some of the best fishing is right along the buoys.

Sportsman's Connection: How about Crappies?

Auger: Some in Sugar Lake but not a lot. McAvity Bay is good in the winter. Bena Bar, Highbanks, and Horseshoe Bar are good for Perch in the winter.

Sportsman's Connection: What are the sizes of the Perch?

Auger: Some years are better than others. A good year will yield some up to about 14 inches – about a pound and a half.

Sportsman's Connection: Do they get a lot of Muskies here?

Auger: Not a lot of Muskie. One about 46 pounds was caught recently with a Walleye rig. Seeley Point on Cut Foot Sioux is a good early- and late-season spot.

Sportsman's Connection: How deep?

Auger: Run the breakline from 10 to 17 feet.

Sportsman's Connection: Big Northerns?

Auger: Out of the Winnie/Cut Foot area? Not really. A lot of 4- to 10-pounders mixed in with snakes. There's not really enough cover for them. Sugar Lake has some. As far as the Perch go, fish the top of the Bena Bar with a jig and chub. Fish Highbanks and Bowlen in about 7 feet of water with jigs and chubs too. Winter or summer. Instead of fishing the breakline, fish the top or bottom of the bars.

Sportsman's Connection: How about the Third River Flowage itself?

Auger: I know they get a lot of Northerns and some Walleyes. Down on the opposite end of the lake around the "Reclaim" you can find some Walleyes that move in early to spawn. They call it the "Reclaim," because they're reclaiming the shore there, putting in huge rocks to cut down erosion. The fish are in about 7 to 12 feet in spring.

Sportsman's Connection: How about in the summer; are they still lying in there?

Auger: They go deeper as the summer progresses, or as boat traffic increases. As in any lake, the Walleyes shy away from light or other disturbances. Adjust the depth that you fish for them accordingly.

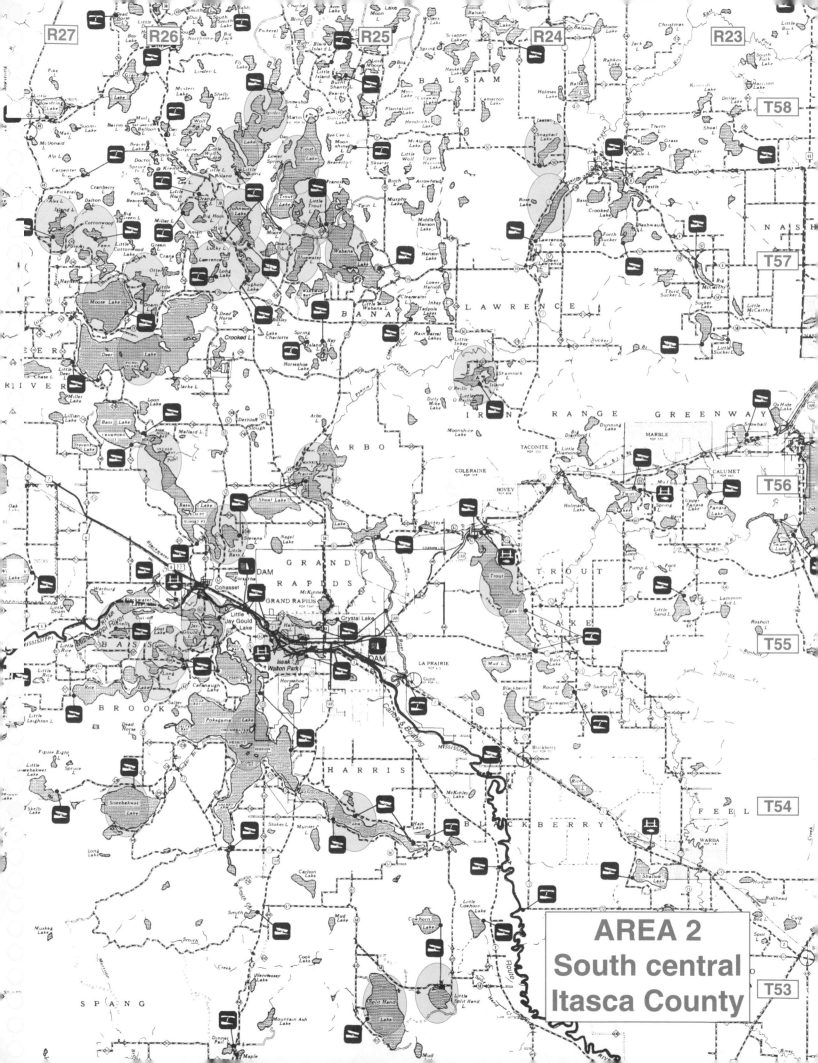

AREA 2
South central
Itasca County

DEER LAKE
Itasca County

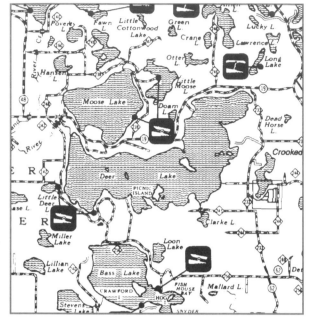

Location: Township 56, 57
Range 26, 27
Watershed: Mississippi Headwaters
Size of lake: 3,691 acres
Shorelength: 22.3 miles
Secchi disk (water clarity): 11.0 ft.
Water color: Green
Cause of water color: Algae

Maximum depth: 120.0 ft.
Median depth: NA
Accessibility: County-owned public access, with ramp and dock, on southwest bay
Boat Ramp: Concrete
Parking: Ample
Accommodations: Resorts

Shoreland zoning classification: Recreational Development
Dominant forest/soil type: Decid/Loam
Management class: Walleye-Centrarchid
Ecological type: Hard-water Walleye

FISH STOCKING DATA

year	species	size	# released
89	Walleye	Adult	9
89	Walleye	Fingerling	1,074
89	Walleye	Yearling	3,693
91	Walleye	Yearling	1,271
93	Walleye	Fingerling	6,229
97	Walleye	Fingerling	11,951

NET CATCH DATA

survey date: 7/24/95

	Gill Nets		Trap Nets	
species	# per net	avg fish wt. (lbs.)	# per set	avg fish wt. (lbs.)
Black Crappie	-	-	0.2	0.04
Bluegill	0.7	0.17	25.6	0.18
Bowfin (Dogfish)	-	-	trace	6.06
Hybrid Sunfish	trace	0.07	0.5	0.23
Lake Whitefish	0.2	1.10	-	-
Largemouth Bass	0.5	0.61	0.9	0.61
Muskellunge	0.3	2.68	-	-
Northern Pike	0.7	3.74	trace	5.95
Pumpkin. Sunfish	-	-	1.6	0.18
Rock Bass	30.2	0.27	8.7	0.24
Smallmouth Bass	4.1	1.57	-	-
Tullibee (Cisco)	0.3	0.21	-	-
Walleye	7.5	1.33	0.4	4.68
White Sucker	1.5	1.51	-	-
Yellow Bullhead	-	-	trace	1.34
Yellow Perch	18.3	0.20	0.3	0.14

LENGTH OF SELECTED SPECIES SAMPLED FROM ALL GEAR

Number of fish caught for the following length categories (inches):

species	0-5	6-8	9-11	12-14	15-19	20-24	25-29	>30	Total
Black Crappie	3	-	-	-	-	-	-	-	3
Bluegill	78	142	1	-	-	-	-	-	221
Hybrid Sunfish	3	5	-	-	-	-	-	-	8
Lake Whitefish	-	-	-	-	2	1	-	-	3
Largemouth Bass	8	2	6	2	2	-	-	-	20
Muskellunge	-	-	-	-	1	2	1	-	4
Northern Pike	-	-	-	-	1	4	5	1	11
Pumpkin. Sunfish	10	13	-	-	-	-	-	-	23
Rock Bass	78	311	13	-	-	-	-	-	402
Smallmouth Bass	1	-	10	29	22	-	-	-	62
Tullibee (Cisco)	-	1	4	-	-	-	-	-	5
Walleye	-	-	14	40	50	8	5	-	117
Yellow Bullhead	-	-	-	1	-	-	-	-	1
Yellow Perch	14	157	40	-	-	-	-	-	211

DNR COMMENTS: Walleye numbers above lake class median; average size 15.5 inches and 1.3 lb.; strong 1991 and 1993 year classes; most fish from stocked years. Northern Pike not abundant but of quality size, with mean weight being 3.7 lb.; fish range in length from 18.3 to 34.3 inches. Muskellunge population excellent; size structure good, with 76 percent of fish sampled being larger than 36 inches. Smallmouth Bass population good; average size of 1.6 lb. is largest on record for lake. Yellow Perch population stable. Rock Bass and Bluegill numbers up substantially; reason unclear.

FISHING INFORMATION: Brian Krecklau of Pole Bender Guide Service says he guides regularly on Deer Lake for Muskie, Walleye and Bass and sends his clients home happy. Walleye average about 1 3/4 pounds here, though some fish up to 11 pounds have been hauled out. Krecklau suggests fishing with Lindy rigs and minnows around the points and sunken islands found throughout the middle of the lake, including the area near Battleship Island, in 18 to 23 feet of water. Slip bobber setups rigged with minnows or leeches over the underwater islands produce well at night, too, says Krecklau. Floating Rapalas trolled over the mid-lake bars and shoreline structure also yield some Walleyes. Smallmouth Bass, averaging around 2 pounds are also found around some of these same areas. Some 20-pound-class Northerns are caught in Deer, usually by anglers chasing Muskies, which is what the lake is best-known for. Weekend fishing can be relatively crowded with Muskie fishermen, but early in the week is fairly quiet. Krecklau told us that an average Deer Lake Muskie runs about 37 inches (40 inches is the legal minimum), but he said he has seen 40-pound-class fish. The best time to chase Muskies in Deer, according to Krecklau, is from opening in late June into early July and again in September through early November. Krecklau said he has good success on light colored bucktails tossed near the cabbage weeds. Jerkbaits also will raise some fish, but follows outnumber strikes on wood. Trolling crankbaits through schools of Ciscoes can also produce some nice fish. A knowledgeable guide can increase your Muskie fishing success and improve your knowledge immensely.

Deer Lake

N

NOT FOR NAVIGATION

E.V. = Emergent Vegetation
S.V. = Submergent Vegetation
F.V. = Floating Vegetation

Battleship Island

Picnic Island

142

256

Source: Division of Fish and Wildlife, Department of Natural Resources.

MOOSE LAKE

Itasca County

LITTLE MOOSE LAKE

Location: Township 57   Range 26, 27
Watershed: Mississippi Headwaters
Size of lake: 1,265 acres
Shorelength: 6.7 miles
Secchi disk (water clarity): 9.0 ft.
Water color: Clear
Cause of water color: NA
Maximum depth: 61.0 ft.
Median depth: 30.0 ft.
Accessibility: State-owned public access on east shore
Boat Ramp: Concrete
Parking: Ample
Accommodations: Resorts, campground
Shoreland zoning classif.: Rec. Dev.
Dominant forest/soil type: Decid/Loam
Management class: Walleye
Ecological type: Hard-water Walleye

Location: Township 57   Range 26, 27
Watershed: Mississippi Headwaters-
Size of lake: 271 acres
Shorelength: 4.1 miles
Secchi disk (water clarity): 5.2 ft.
Water color: NA
Cause of water color: NA
Maximum depth: 23.0 ft.
Median depth: NA
Accessibility: County-owned public access on west shore, off Cty. Rd. 238
Boat Ramp: Earth
Parking: Limited
Accommodations: None
Shoreland zoning classif.: Rec. Dev.
Dominant forest/soil type: Decid/Loam
Management class: Walleye-Centrarchid
Ecological type: Centrarchid-Walleye

DNR COMMENTS:
Muskellunge population excellent, with excellent natural reproduction. Walleye population one of largest on record and largely the result of natural reproduction; length range 9.5 to 27 inches, and average weight 1.6 lb. Northern Pike numbers stable and low; length range 12.7 to 29.4 inches; average weight 2.2 lb. Cisco numbers highest on record for this lake. Modest numbers of Bluegill, Pumpkinseed and Largemouth Bass present.

FISH STOCKING DATA

year	species	size	# released
89	Walleye	Fry	1,100,000
91	Walleye	Fry	1,100,000

survey date: 8/19/96

NET CATCH DATA

	Gill Nets		Trap Nets	
species	# per net	avg fish wt. (lbs)	# per set	avg fish wt. (lbs)
Bluegill	-	-	1.2	0.21
Hybrid Sunfish	-	-	trace	0.13
Largemouth Bass	-	-	0.2	2.43
Muskellunge	0.3	6.78	-	-
Northern Pike	2.9	2.15	0.2	2.69
Pumpkin. Sunfish	-	-	0.2	0.31
Rock Bass	2.0	0.66	1.6	0.27
Tullibee (Cisco)	24.5	0.67	-	-
Walleye	8.8	1.57	1.2	1.14
White Sucker	0.8	1.46	-	-
Yellow Perch	52.0	0.15	2.3	0.18

LENGTH OF SELECTED SPECIES SAMPLED FROM ALL GEAR
Number of fish caught for the following length categories (inches):

species	0-5	6-8	9-11	12-14	15-19	20-24	25-29	>30	Total
Bluegill	8	6	-	-	-	-	-	-	14
Hybrid Sunfish	1	-	-	-	-	-	-	-	1
Largemouth Bass	-	1	-	-	1	-	-	-	2
Muskellunge	-	-	-	-	-	2	-	2	4
Northern Pike	-	-	-	1	9	24	3	-	37
Pumpkin. Sunfish	-	2	-	-	-	-	-	-	2
Rock Bass	9	17	17	-	-	-	-	-	43
Tullibee (Cisco)	-	24	127	138	2	-	-	-	291
Walleye	-	-	13	47	36	20	4	-	120
Yellow Perch	144	464	25	-	-	-	-	-	633

FISH STOCKING DATA: NO RECORD OF STOCKING

survey date: 8/19/96

NET CATCH DATA

	Gill Nets		Trap Nets	
species	# per net	avg fish wt. (lbs)	# per set	avg fish wt. (lbs)
Black Crappie	0.3	0.54	1.3	0.21
Bluegill	1.5	0.51	2.6	0.14
Common Shiner	-	-	0.1	0.08
Muskellunge	0.2	2.67	-	-
Northern Pike	5.0	2.94	0.8	2.66
Pumpkin. Sunfish	-	-	0.4	0.03
Rock Bass	0.2	0.31	0.4	0.08
Walleye	2.7	2.03	0.2	2.16
White Sucker	0.8	1.76	-	-
Yellow Perch	43.8	0.13	0.8	0.10

LENGTH OF SELECTED SPECIES SAMPLED FROM ALL GEAR
Number of fish caught for the following length categories (inches):

species	0-5	6-8	9-11	12-14	15-19	20-24	25-29	>30	Total
Black Crappie	6	3	4	-	-	-	-	-	13
Bluegill	17	13	2	-	-	-	-	-	32
Muskellunge	-	-	-	-	-	1	-	-	1
Northern Pike	-	-	-	-	3	25	6	1	35
Pumpkin. Sunfish	3	-	-	-	-	-	-	-	3
Rock Bass	4	1	-	-	-	-	-	-	5
Walleye	-	-	-	1	15	2	-	-	18
Yellow Perch	92	87	10	-	-	-	-	-	189

DNR COMMENTS:
Lake supports a good Muskellunge population; this species under represented in trapnetting assessment. Walleye numbers within expected range for lake class; mean size 18.2 inches and 2 lb; growth and natural reproduction good. Northern Pike numbers about normal; mean size 23.7 inches and 2.9 lb. Black Crappie numbers normal; size range 4.9 to 9.3 inches. Bluegill numbers low; size range 3.5 to 8.5 inches. Yellow Perch numbers slightly above normal; length range 5.3 to 10 inches.

FISHING INFORMATION: Moose Lake and Little Moose Lake are Muskie waters that also produce some nice Northern Pike. Brian Krecklau of Pole Bender Guide Service says he believes that he has the best success with jerkbaits on Moose, while Deer Lake's Muskies generally prefer bucktails. **Moose** has a lot of shoreline cabbage weeds running out into about 14 feet of water. These are best fished by casting parallel to the breaklines. Krecklau told us that Moose has a reputation for larger numbers of Muskies than Deer. Some of these are in the 30- to 40-pound class. **Little Moose** produces some Muskies for anglers working the shoreline cabbage weeds and the bar in the north bay just off the creek to Moose. Northern Pike provide some excitement on both lakes between Muskie strikes (which, as any Muskie hunter knows, can be few and far between). The lakes' forage bases and general ecological makeup seem to provide conditions for large fish sizes. Walleye anglers fare well on Moose by working its numerous underwater islands, bars and points. Nice Largemouth Bass, some reaching the 4-pound category, are also caught. Little Moose also offers some Walleyes, but its Crappies – mostly in the 3/4-pound to 1 1/2-pound class – provide the best action, especially right after ice out.

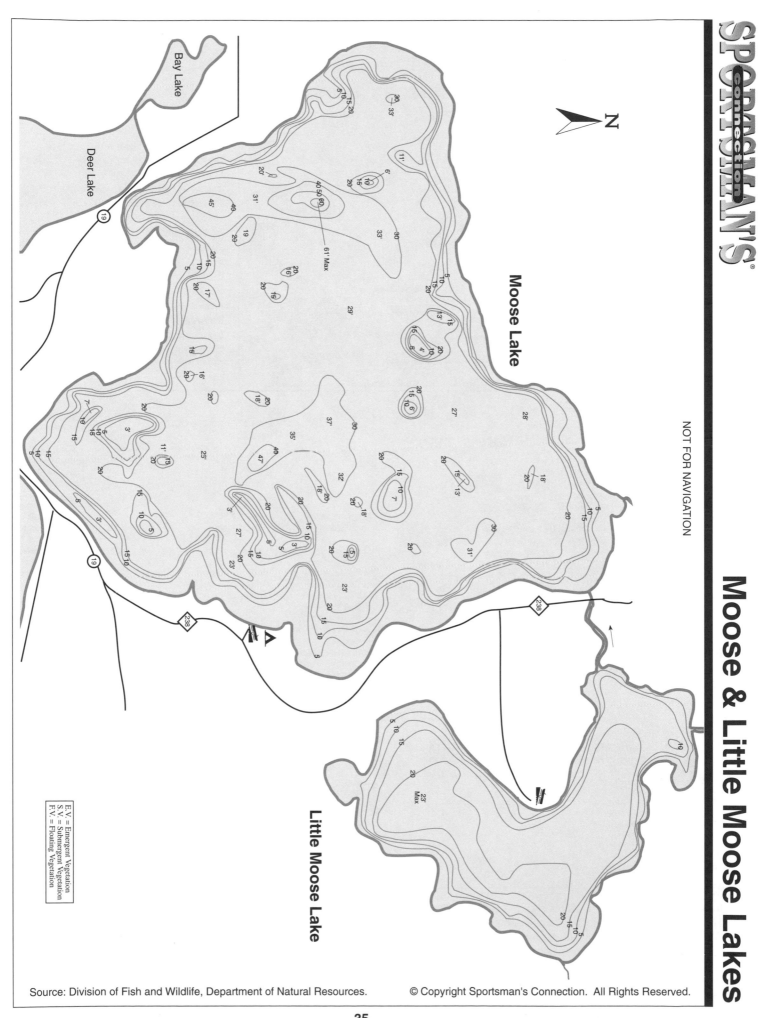

Moose & Little Moose Lakes

NOT FOR NAVIGATION

Moose Lake

Little Moose Lake

Bay Lake

Deer Lake

N

E.V. = Emergent Vegetation
S.V. = Submergent Vegetation
F.V. = Floating Vegetation

Source: Division of Fish and Wildlife, Department of Natural Resources.

COTTONWOOD LAKE   ISLAND LAKE

Itasca County

Location: Township 57 Range 26, 27
Watershed: Mississippi Headwaters
Size of lake: 105 acres
Shorelength: 2.5 miles
Secchi disk (water clarity): 10.0 ft.
Water color: Light brown
Cause of water color: Bog stain
Maximum depth: 40.0 ft.
Median depth: 15.0 ft.
Accessibility: State-owned public access at campground on south shore
Boat Ramp: Concrete
Parking: Ample
Accommodations: Campground
Shoreland zoning classif.: Nat. Envt.
Dominant forest/soil type: NA
Management class: Centrarchid
Ecological type: Centrarchid

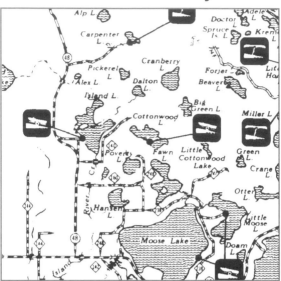

Location: Township 57 Range 26, 27
Watershed: Mississippi Headwaters
Size of lake: 283 acres
Shorelength: 5.2 miles
Secchi disk (water clarity): 5.5 ft.
Water color: Yellow-brown
Cause of water color: Swamp drainage
Maximum depth: 31.0 ft.
Median depth: 13.0 ft.
Accessibility: USFS-owned public access on southwest shore, off Co. Rd. #48
Boat Ramp: Earth
Parking: Ample
Accommodations: Resorts
Shoreland zoning classif.: Rec. Dev.
Dominant forest/soil type: Decid/Loam
Management class: Walleye-Centrarchid
Ecological type: Centrarchid-Walleye

DNR COMMENTS:
Northern Pike abundance is at a high level while Perch numbers are fairly low. Panfish numbers are typical for this type of lake.

FISH STOCKING DATA: NO RECORD OF STOCKING

NET CATCH DATA

survey date: 06/27/83

species	Gill Nets # per net	avg fish wt. (lbs)	Trap Nets # per set	avg fish wt. (lbs)
Yellow Perch	4.3	0.16	0.3	0.30
Yellow Bullhead	0.3	0.70	1.5	0.58
Rock Bass	2.0	0.14	0.3	0.10
Northern Pike	16.8	1.66	1.3	0.52
Brown Bullhead	0.5	0.35	0.8	0.50
Bowfin (Dogfish)	0.3	1.80	0.8	4.73
Bluegill	0.5	0.35	5.8	0.15
Black Crappie	1.0	0.93	2.8	0.22
Pumpkin. Sunfish	-	-	2.8	0.13

LENGTH OF SELECTED SPECIES SAMPLED FROM ALL GEAR
Number of fish caught for the following length categories (inches):

species	0-5	6-8	9-11	12-14	15-19	20-24	25-29	>30	Total
Black Crappie	1	12	6	-	-	-	-	-	19
Bluegill	12	9	4	-	-	-	-	-	25
Brown Bullhead	-	2	2	1	-	-	-	-	5
Northern Pike	-	-	1	10	40	15	3	3	72
Pumpkin. Sunfish	6	5	-	-	-	-	-	-	11
Rock Bass	2	2	1	-	-	-	-	-	5
Yellow Bullhead	-	1	3	3	-	-	-	-	7
Yellow Perch	6	5	-	-	-	-	-	-	11

FISH STOCKING DATA

year	species	size	# released
91	Walleye	Fry	285,000
93	Walleye	Fry	296,400

NET CATCH DATA

survey date: 08/26/91

species	Gill Nets # per net	avg fish wt. (lbs)	Trap Nets # per set	avg fish wt. (lbs)
Yellow Perch	102.2	0.17	11.7	0.13
Yellow Bullhead	0.8	0.68	0.3	0.50
White Sucker	1.0	1.94	-	-
Walleye	1.0	3.10	0.2	0.80
Northern Pike	11.0	3.36	1.3	0.90
Brown Bullhead	1.4	1.19	0.2	1.60
Bowfin (Dogfish)	0.4	4.45	1.0	5.20
Bluegill	1.0	0.98	1.8	0.65
Black Bullhead	4.2	0.83	0.2	1.30
Pumpkin. Sunfish	-	-	0.8	0.28
Largemouth Bass	-	-	0.2	0.20
Hybrid Sunfish	-	-	0.2	0.40
Black Crappie	-	-	1.5	0.81

LENGTH OF SELECTED SPECIES SAMPLED FROM ALL GEAR
Number of fish caught for the following length categories (inches):

species	0-5	6-8	9-11	12-14	15-19	20-24	25-29	>30	Total
Yellow Perch	-	134	11	-	-	-	-	-	145
Yellow Bullhead	-	3	1	-	-	-	-	-	4
Walleye	-	-	-	2	-	2	1	-	5
Northern Pike	-	-	-	-	3	39	9	4	55
Brown Bullhead	-	-	1	6	-	-	-	-	7
Bluegill	-	5	-	-	-	-	-	-	5
Black Bullhead	-	3	9	9	-	-	-	-	21

DNR COMMENTS:
Northern Pike increasing in both numbers and size, due to large forage base. Walleye population near median for lake class; natural reproduction poor; growth slow. Good natural reproduction taking place among Largemouth Bass. Bluegills scarce, but numbers are normal for Island Lake. Black Crappie numbers near lake class median. Roughfish populations remain stable near lake class median.

FISHING INFORMATION: Just north of the big popular waters of Deer and Moose Lakes lie two small bodies of water that you don't hear much about. **Cottonwood** has a small campground that is well secluded and doesn't get much use. The lake is basically a Bass, panfish, Northern Pike fishery, with some decent-size Crappie and Bluegill thrown in. Blowdowns and brush piles provide exciting Largemouth and Northern fishing when bait fish are in shallow. The Bass aren't large, typically around the 1 1/2-pound class, but there are a lot of them. Northern Pike are also numerous, with some reaching the 8- to 10-pound class. **Island Lake** is larger than Cottonwood and has some Walleye in it. Prior to DNR stocking efforts, Northern Pike and Perch were about the only species caught with any regularity.

SPORTSMAN'S connection

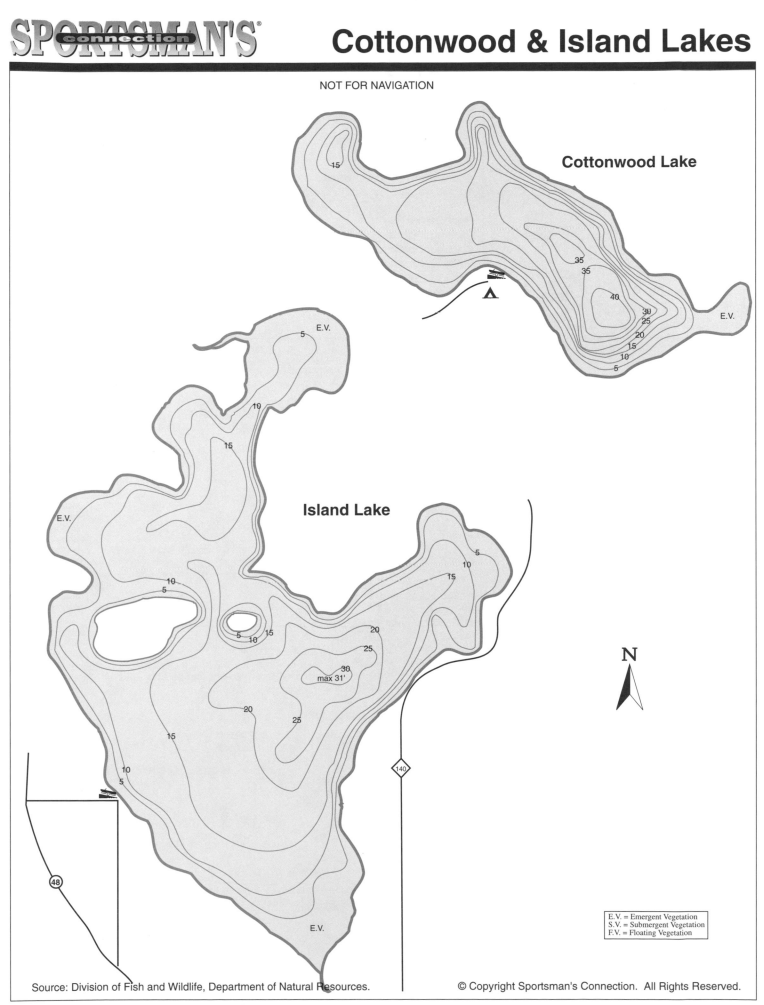

Cottonwood Lake

Island Lake

max 31'

E.V. = Emergent Vegetation
S.V. = Submergent Vegetation
F.V. = Floating Vegetation

N

Source: Division of Fish and Wildlife, Department of Natural Resources.

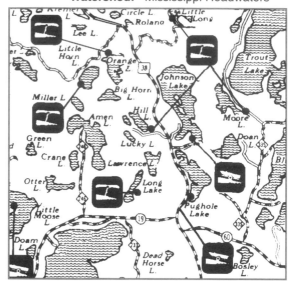

PUGHOLE LAKE   LONG LAKE   ORANGE LAKE
Itasca County

	PUGHOLE LAKE	LONG LAKE	ORANGE LAKE
Size of lake:	152 acres	48 acres	86 acres
Shorelength:	2.4 miles	1.5 miles	1.8 miles
Secchi disk (water clarity):	9.0 ft.	4.0	14.5 ft.
Water color:	Brown	Light brown	Clear
Cause of water color:	Bog stain	Bog stain	NA
Maximum depth:	20.0 ft.	48.0 ft.	30.0 ft.
Median depth:	8.0 ft.	10.0 ft.	11.0 ft.
Accessibility:	State-owned public access off state Hwy. 38	Public access on south shore, off Cty. Rd. 19	USFS carry-down on north shore, from Orange Lake Road
Boat Ramp:	Earth	Carry-down	Carry-down
Parking:	Ample	Side of road	Lot down on Hwy 38
Accommodations:	Wayside Rest	None	Campsite
Shoreland zoning classif.:	Rec. Dev.	Nat. Envt.	Rec. Dev.
Dominant forest/soil type:	NA	NA	NA
Management class:	Walleye-Centrarchid	Centrarchid	Centrarchid
Ecological type:	Centrarchid-Walleye	Centrarchid	Centrarchid

DNR COMMENTS:
Northern Pike numbers down but still within expected range for lake class; mean size 22.2 inches and 2.2 lb. Black Crappie population slightly low; mean length 8 inches; growth slow. Largemouth Bass not adequately sampled. Walleye numbers low. Yellow Perch population below expected range; length range 5.5 to 9.1 inches. Pumpkinseed also present.

Pughole Lake

FISH STOCKING DATA

year	species	size	# released
91	Walleye	Adult	366
94	Walleye	Fingerling	2,115

survey date: 7/8/96

NET CATCH DATA

	Gill Nets		Trap Nets	
species	# per net	avg fish wt. (lbs)	# per set	avg fish wt. (lbs)
Black Crappie	0.3	0.34	2.6	0.30
Bluegill	2.7	0.15	17.4	0.19
Golden Shiner	-	-	0.2	0.06
Largemouth Bass	-	-	0.1	trace
Northern Pike	4.0	2.82	0.7	3.44
Pumpkin. Sunfish	-	-	1.9	0.19
Walleye	0.3	1.44	0.2	3.13
Yellow Perch	3.5	0.14	0.6	0.07

LENGTH OF SELECTED SPECIES SAMPLED FROM ALL GEAR
Number of fish caught for the following length categories (inches):

species	0-5	6-8	9-11	12-14	15-19	20-24	25-29	>30	Total
Black Crappie	5	9	11	-	-	-	-	-	25
Bluegill	68	83	-	-	-	-	-	-	151
Largemouth Bass	1	-	-	-	-	-	-	-	1
Northern Pike	-	-	-	1	14	4	5	4	28
Pumpkin. Sunfish	11	6	-	-	-	-	-	-	17
Walleye	-	-	1	-	2	1	-	-	4
Yellow Perch	12	13	1	-	-	-	-	-	26

Long Lake

FISH STOCKING DATA: NO RECORD OF STOCKING

survey date: 07/01/91

NET CATCH DATA

	Gill Nets		Trap Nets	
species	# per net	avg fish wt. (lbs)	# per set	avg fish wt. (lbs)
Yellow Perch	13.3	0.18	2.8	0.26
White Sucker	0.3	2.50	-	-
Largemouth Bass	0.5	0.25	0.5	0.10
Bluegill	0.8	0.23	1.8	0.09
Black Crappie	-	-	0.5	0.10

LENGTH OF SELECTED SPECIES SAMPLED FROM ALL GEAR
Number of fish caught for the following length categories (inches):

species	0-5	6-8	9-11	12-14	15-19	20-24	25-29	>30	Total
Yellow Perch	-	35	20	-	-	-	-	-	55
Largemouth Bass	-	-	2	-	-	-	-	-	2
Bluegill	-	3	-	-	-	-	-	-	3

DNR COMMENTS:
Muskellunge have not been sampled since 1980, and it appears that stockings failed to produce a self-sustaining population. LM Bass sampling slightly below lake-class median; catch rates down since Muskellunge introduction. Bluegills well below lake-class medians. Yellow Perch present at above-median levels; however, population still reflects Muskellunge predation.

Orange Lake

FISH STOCKING DATA: NO RECORD OF STOCKING

survey date: 08/18/92

NET CATCH DATA

	Gill Nets		Trap Nets	
species	# per net	avg fish wt. (lbs)	# per set	avg fish wt. (lbs)
Yellow Perch	39.8	0.36	0.3	0.30
Muskellunge	0.3	8.50	-	-
Largemouth Bass	5.8	0.57	0.3	2.80
Bluegill	03	0.50	0.8	0.27
Black Crappie	0.3	0.10	-	-
White Sucker	-	-	0.3	4.20

LENGTH OF SELECTED SPECIES SAMPLED FROM ALL GEAR
Number of fish caught for the following length categories (inches):

species	0-5	6-8	9-11	12-14	15-19	20-24	25-29	>30	Total
Yellow Perch	-	6	89	10	-	-	-	-	105
Muskellunge	-	-	-	-	-	-	1	-	1
Largemouth Bass	-	-	3	18	-	-	-	-	21
Bluegill	-	2	-	-	-	-	-	-	2
Black Crappie	1	1	-	-	-	-	-	-	2

DNR COMMENTS:
Largemouth Bass population up sharply to values above those for 3rd quartile; lengths in 12-19" range. Smallmouth Bass sampled only by shoreline seining. Black Crappies scarce. Bluegills below 1st quartile values. This lake contains no Northern Pike or Walleyes.

FISHING INFORMATION: These three gems are located on either side of Highway 38 and have at least one thing in common: Muskies. Years ago, **Pughole** held some good Muskies, and locals claim they still roam the lake's dark waters. Pughole used to be regarded as an outstanding lake but has declined in recent years. Some good Crappies can still be found, and some nice Northerns are caught. One alligator, in fact was weighed in at 14 pounds by God's Country Outfitters. **Orange** is located in the Suomi Hills Recreation Area which is a semi-primitive, non-motorized area (SMA) that is off-limits to boat motors and motorized vehicles. Shoepack-strain Muskies are still quite abundant in this fascinating lake. Largemouth Bass up to 5 pounds and nice Smallmouth Bass are also found. Bluegills average around 1/2 pound. By canoeing down to the south end of the lake you can portage a short trail to Little Horn Lake for some more excellent Largemouth Bass fishing. **Long Lake**'s north end also is located in the SMA. It too has a history of producing Muskies, although these fish are rarely caught now. Largemouth fishing can be pretty good; decent numbers and sizes are caught.

NOT FOR NAVIGATION

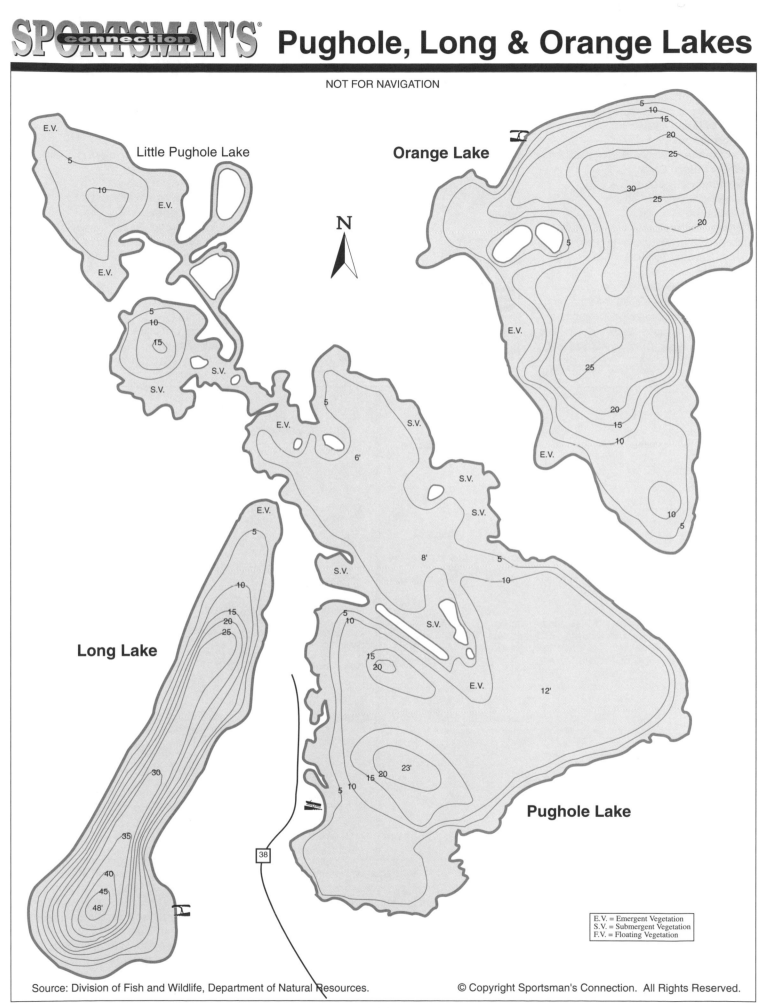

Little Pughole Lake

Orange Lake

N

Long Lake

Pughole Lake

E.V. = Emergent Vegetation
S.V. = Submergent Vegetation
F.V. = Floating Vegetation

Source: Division of Fish and Wildlife, Department of Natural Resources.

JOHNSON LAKE   LITTLE LONG LAKE

Itasca County

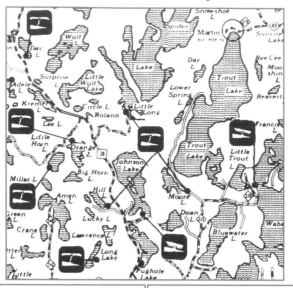

JOHNSON LAKE

Location: Township 57 Range 26
Watershed: Mississippi Headwaters
Size of lake: 492 acres
Shorelength: 5.1 miles
Secchi disk (water clarity): 13.0 ft.
Water color: Clear
Cause of water color: NA
Maximum depth: 88.0 ft.
Median depth: 20.5 ft.
Accessibility: State-owned public access on south shore, off Hwy. 38
Boat Ramp: Concrete
Parking: Ample
Accommodations: None
Shoreland zoning classif.: Rec. Dev.
Dominant forest/soil type: Decid/Loam
Management class: Walleye-Centrarchid
Ecological type: Centrarchid-Walleye

LITTLE LONG LAKE

Location: Township 57 Range 26
Watershed: Mississippi Headwaters
Size of lake: 253 acres
Shorelength: 7.4 miles
Secchi disk (water clarity): 13.0
Water color: Clear
Cause of water color: NA
Maximum depth: 61.0 ft.
Median depth: NA
Accessibility: State-owned public access on southwest shore
Boat Ramp: Carry-down
Parking: Limited
Accommodations: None
Shoreland zoning classif.: Rec. Dev.
Dominant forest/soil type: Decid/Loam
Management class: Centrarchid
Ecological type: Centrarchid

DNR COMMENTS: Walleye population within expected range for lake class, despite termination of stocking in 1990; mean length 13.6 inches; growth at or above statewide mean for all ages. Northern Pike numerous; mean length 18.9 inches; growth near statewide mean rate. Largemouth Bass numbers below expected range for lake class; length range 5.1 to 11.6 inches. Smallmouth Bass numbers within expected range; length range 17 to 18.6 inches; growth near statewide average. Bluegill and Black Crappie numbers below expected range. Yellow Perch scarce.

FISH STOCKING DATA

year	species	size	# released
90	Walleye	Fingerling	3,010

NET CATCH DATA

survey date: 6/23/97

	Gill Nets		Trap Nets	
species	# per net	avg fish wt. (lbs)	# per set	avg fish wt. (lbs)
Black Crappie	-	-	0.4	0.38
Bluegill	0.3	0.32	7.0	0.25
Largemouth Bass	0.1	1.83	0.2	0.11
Northern Pike	7.8	1.49	0.8	1.53
Pumpkin. Sunfish	-	-	1.3	0.29
Rock Bass	0.2	0.57	2.1	0.26
Smallmouth Bass	0.4	3.04	-	-
Walleye	1.7	1.02	-	-
White Sucker	1.8	2.75	0.1	4.78
Yellow Perch	2.3	0.18	0.8	0.15

LENGTH OF SELECTED SPECIES SAMPLED FROM ALL GEAR

Number of fish caught for the following length categories (inches):

species	0-5	6-8	9-11	12-14	15-19	20-24	25-29	>30	Total
Black Crappie	-	3	1	-	-	-	-	-	4
Bluegill	10	56	-	-	-	-	-	-	66
Largemouth Bass	-	2	-	1	-	-	-	-	3
Northern Pike	-	-	3	9	27	32	1	1	73
Pumpkin. Sunfish	-	12	-	-	-	-	-	-	12
Rock Bass	6	12	3	-	-	-	-	-	21
Smallmouth Bass	-	-	-	-	4	-	-	-	4
Walleye	-	3	3	5	2	2	-	-	15
Yellow Perch	3	21	3	-	-	-	-	-	27

FISH STOCKING DATA: NO RECORD OF STOCKING

NET CATCH DATA

survey date: 7/6/92

	Gill Nets		Trap Nets	
species	# per net	avg fish wt. (lbs)	# per set	avg fish wt. (lbs)
Yellow Perch	21.5	0.11	2.8	0.10
White Sucker	1.0	2.97	-	-
Walleye	0.8	3.46	0.1	7.50
Rock Bass	2.2	0.18	1.2	0.33
Pumpkin. Sunfish	1.5	0.17	9.8	0.17
Northern Pike	8.5	2.10	0.8	2.73
Largemouth Bass	0.3	1.55	0.3	1.43
Hybrid Sunfish	0.3	0.40	2.7	0.17
Bluegill	12.2	0.17	49.1	0.14
Black Crappie	1.5	0.37	1.3	0.41
Golden Shiner	-	-	0.1	0.10

LENGTH OF SELECTED SPECIES SAMPLED FROM ALL GEAR

Number of fish caught for the following length categories (inches):

species	0-5	6-8	9-11	12-14	15-19	20-24	25-29	>30	Total
Yellow Perch	-	110	3	-	-	-	-	-	113
Walleye	-	-	-	-	5	-	-	5
Rock Bass	2	12	-	-	-	-	-	-	14
Pumpkin. Sunfish	-	10	-	-	-	-	-	-	10
Northern Pike	-	-	-	9	39	3	-	51
Largemouth Bass	-	-	-	2	-	-	-	-	2
Hybrid Sunfish	-	2	1	-	-	-	-	-	3
Bluegill	1	30	2	-	-	-	-	-	33
Black Crappie	-	6	1	1	-	-	-	-	8

DNR COMMENTS: Northern Pike fairly numerous at third-quartile level; good natural reproduction and good growth. Some Walleyes sampled. Largemouth Bass sample not believed reliable. Black Crappies present in near-average numbers; growth about average for lake class. Bluegills relatively numerous at third-quartile values; growth poor, however. Yellow Perch population at third-quartile level.

FISHING INFORMATION: Walleye fishing has taken off in **Johnson,** with some 4-pound fish caught right into the summer months. Try working the north end with a jig and minnow early in the year, and move onto the secondary breakline in about 15 to 20 feet with a leech as summer progresses. Muskies are rumored to be present but not in targetable numbers. The Northerns are respectable, with 3-pound fish being common. Pokegama Sports weighed a 5-pound, 12-ounce Largemouth Bass a few seasons ago, and Smallmouth numbers and size are good. Early in the year anglers in boats congregate on the north end of the lake to fish for 1/2- to 3/4-pound Crappies. **Little Long Lake** used to be a Muskie-rearing pond years ago, and some fish remain. The lake, though, is better known for its Northern Pike fishing. The average alligator is 3 pounds, and there are some 15-pound-class fish present. Largemouth Bass are also fairly abundant and have good spawning habitat.

NOT FOR NAVIGATION

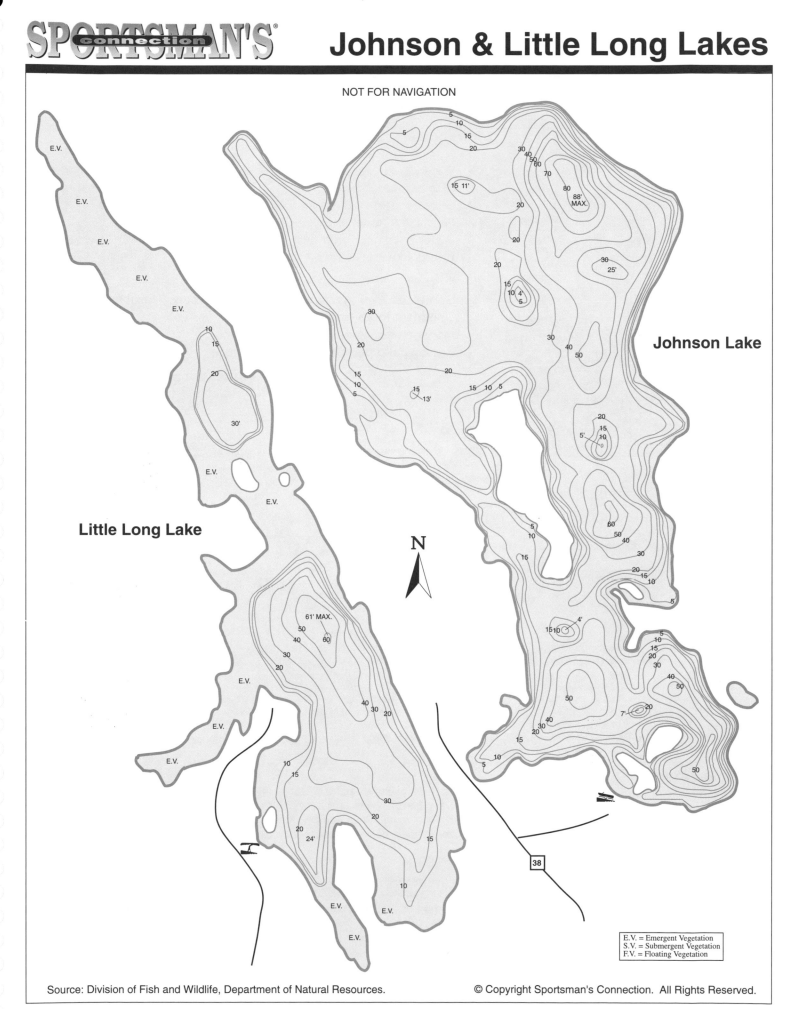

Johnson Lake

Little Long Lake

N

E.V. = Emergent Vegetation
S.V. = Submergent Vegetation
F.V. = Floating Vegetation

Source: Division of Fish and Wildlife, Department of Natural Resources.

SPIDER LAKE

Itasca County

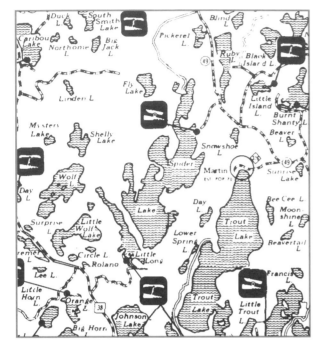

Location: Township 58 Range 25,26

Watershed: Mississippi Headwaters
Size of lake: 1,349 acres
Shorelength: 16.0 miles
Secchi disk (water clarity): 7.4 ft.
Water color: Green-brown
Cause of water color: Algae

Maximum depth: 35.0 ft.
Median depth: 12.1 ft.
Accessibility: USFS-owned public access on northeast shore
Boat Ramp: Concrete
Parking: Ample
Accommodations: Resorts

Shoreland zoning classification: Recreational Development
Dominant forest/soil type: Decid/Loam
Management class: Walleye-Centrarchid
Ecological type: Centrarchid-Walleye

FISH STOCKING DATA

year	species	size	# released
89	Walleye	Adult	4
89	Walleye	Fingerling	5,275
89	Walleye	Yearling	548
90	Walleye	Fry	1,500,000
91	Walleye	Fingerling	1,494
91	Walleye	Yearling	1,478
92	Walleye	Fry	1,400,000
96	Walleye	Fry	1,350,000

NET CATCH DATA

survey date: 8/8/94

species	Gill Nets # per net	Gill Nets avg fish wt. (lbs.)	Trap Nets # per set	Trap Nets avg fish wt. (lbs.)
Black Bullhead	0.4	0.50	-	-
Black Crappie	0.5	0.48	0.6	0.44
Bluegill	22.5	0.21	32.0	0.18
Brown Bullhead	0.3	1.04	trace	1.46
Golden Shiner	0.2	0.09	0.3	0.08
Hybrid Sunfish	trace	0.11	-	-
Largemouth Bass	-	-	0.2	0.30
Muskellunge	trace	2.16	-	-
Northern Pike	2.5	4.00	0.2	1.24
Pumpkin. Sunfish	4.3	0.24	3.6	0.18
Rock Bass	0.4	0.37	0.5	0.19
Smallmouth Bass	1.5	1.06	-	-
Walleye	2.9	2.94	trace	4.16
White Sucker	4.8	1.69	0.4	2.86
Yellow Perch	63.8	0.14	4.0	0.13

LENGTH OF SELECTED SPECIES SAMPLED FROM ALL GEAR

Number of fish caught for the following length categories (inches):

species	0-5	6-8	9-11	12-14	15-19	20-24	25-29	>30	Total
Black Bullhead	-	1	4	-	-	-	-	-	5
Black Crappie	1	4	8	-	-	-	-	-	13
Bluegill	125	364	-	-	-	-	-	-	489
Brown Bullhead	1	-	-	3	-	-	-	-	4
Hybrid Sunfish	-	1	-	-	-	-	-	-	1
Largemouth Bass	1	-	1	-	-	-	-	-	2
Muskellunge	-	-	-	-	-	1	-	-	1
Northern Pike	-	-	-	1	4	15	10	2	32
Pumpkin. Sunfish	21	73	-	-	-	-	-	-	94
Rock Bass	3	8	-	-	-	-	-	-	11
Smallmouth Bass	-	2	6	8	2	-	-	-	18
Walleye	-	-	-	4	15	13	4	-	36
Yellow Perch	36	306	3	-	-	-	-	-	345

DNR COMMENTS: Walleye numbers down to below lake-class median levels; average size, however, is excellent. Northern Pike numbers down and below median level for lake class; average size excellent at approximately 4 lb. Muskellunge last stocked in 1979; natural reproduction is occurring, and species was sampled in low numbers; anglers report fish larger than 40 inches present. Bluegill numbers stable; average size about 6.5 inches for all sampling gear. Smallmouth Bass numbers down but still above third-quartile values for lake class; average size 12.3 inches. Largemouth Bass and Black Crappie numbers moderate.

FISHING INFORMATION: Spider Lake has a long history of being an all-around good-fishing lake holding good numbers and sizes of Walleye, Bass, Northern, Muskie and Panfish. Brian Krecklau of Pole Bender Guide Service says fishing is usually either on or off, depending upon when you're there. He says he has guided parties that filled out on 1 1/2- to 6-pound Walleyes and others that couldn't buy a bite. When Walleye fishing is slow, the plump Crappies and Bluegills can usually be enticed into biting. Crappies in the 1-pound class are relatively abundant. Smallies are real nice, and Largemouth are also caught, although less frequently than smallies. Spider is a designated Muskie lake. There are some of impressive size present, along with some pretty fair Northern Pike. In fact, there are many Pike in the 5- to 10-pound class and even some 20-pounders to provide steady action.

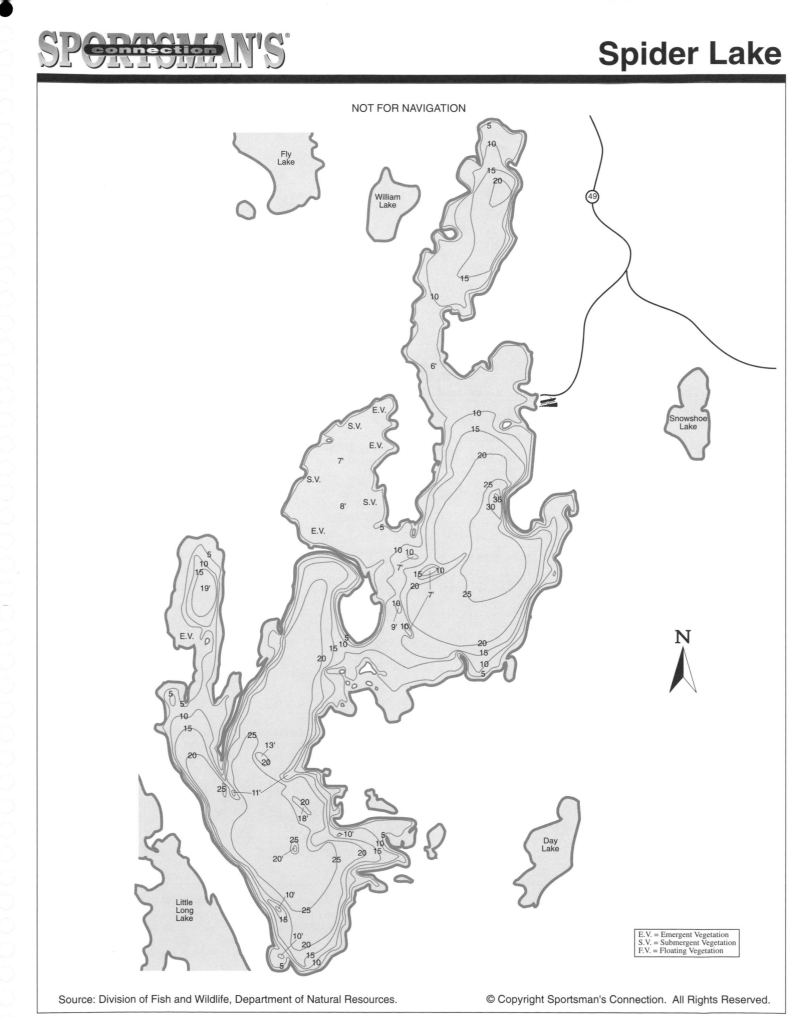

NOT FOR NAVIGATION

E.V. = Emergent Vegetation
S.V. = Submergent Vegetation
F.V. = Floating Vegetation

TROUT LAKE   LITTLE TROUT LAKE

Itasca County

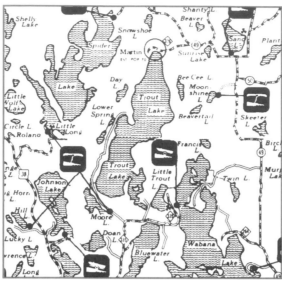

Location: Township 57, 58 Range 25
Watershed: Prairie-Willow
Size of lake: 1,753 acres
Shorelength: 13.1 miles
Secchi disk (water clarity): 12.0 ft.
Water color: Blue-green
Cause of water color: Carbonates
Maximum depth: 157.0 ft.
Median depth: 48.0 ft.
Accessibility: County-owned public access on north shore at resort
Boat Ramp: Earth
Parking: Toll on parking
Accommodations: Resort, 3 Chippewa Natl. Forest campsites
Shoreland zoning classif.: Rec. Dev.
Dominant forest/soil type: Decid/Loam
Management class: Lake Trout
Ecological type: Trout

Location: Township 57, 58 Range 25
Watershed: Prairie-Willow
Size of lake: 74 acres
Shorelength: 1.6 miles
Secchi disk (water clarity): 20.0 ft.
Water color: Clear
Cause of water color: NA
Maximum depth: 90.0 ft.
Median depth: 33.0 ft.
Accessibility: Access from road over inlet; access from Wabana Lake through inlet
Boat Ramp: Carry-down; ramps on Wabana
Parking: Limited
Accommodations: None
Shoreland zoning classif.: Rec. Dev.
Dominant forest/soil type: NA
Management class: Centrarchid
Ecological type: Centrarchid

DNR COMMENTS:
Lake is stocked with Lake Trout biennially, but some natural reproduction is taking place; species sampled at rate of .9/gillnet set; length range 8.8 to 34.3 inches; mean weight 2.9 lb. Splake stocking ongoing; this species sampled in low numbers; quality size range for this species at 14.3 to 26.2 inches; mean weight 4.8 lb. Northern Pike scarce but large; numbers of this species limited by poor spawning habitat. Ciscoes present. Largemouth Bass, Smallmouth Bass, Black Crappies and Sunfish also sampled in survey.

FISH STOCKING DATA

year	species	size	# released
92	Splake	Fingerling	45,000
93	Lake Trout	Yearling	8,874
93	Splake	Fingerling	30,640
94	Splake	Fingerling	43,820
95	Lake Trout	Yearling	8,742
96	Splake	Fingerling	43,565
97	Lake Trout	Yearling	8,765

NET CATCH DATA
survey date: 8/12/96

	Gill Nets		Trap Nets	
		avg fish		avg fish
species	# per net	wt. (lbs)	# per set	wt. (lbs)
Black Crappie	-	-	0.3	0.18
Bluegill	-	-	29.7	0.14
Green Sunfish	-	-	3.1	0.13
Hybrid Sunfish	-	-	0.2	0.26
Lake Trout	0.9	2.85	-	-
Largemouth Bass	-	-	1.6	0.27
Northern Pike	1.0	3.74	0.5	1.75
Pumpkin. Sunfish	-	-	2.3	0.09
Rock Bass	-	-	5.9	0.10
Smallmouth Bass	-	-	0.1	0.21
Splake	0.3	4.85	-	-
Tullibee (Cisco)	9.8	0.09	-	-
Yellow Perch	0.2	0.17	1.1	0.19

LENGTH OF SELECTED SPECIES SAMPLED FROM ALL GEAR
Number of fish caught for the following length categories (inches):

species	0-5	6-8	9-11	12-14	15-19	20-24	25-29	>30	Total
Black Crappie	-	5	-	-	-	-	-	-	5
Bluegill	127	121	-	-	-	-	-	-	248
Green Sunfish	11	20	-	-	-	-	-	-	31
Hybrid Sunfish	1	2	-	-	-	-	-	-	3
Lake Trout	-	1	3	3	3	2	-	2	14
Largemouth Bass	3	8	3	2	-	-	-	-	16
Northern Pike	-	-	-	-	4	8	9	-	21
Pumpkin. Sunfish	7	9	-	-	-	-	-	-	16
Rock Bass	8	27	-	-	-	-	-	-	35
Smallmouth Bass	1	1	-	-	-	-	-	-	2
Splake	-	-	-	1	-	2	1	-	4
Tullibee (Cisco)	-	145	1	-	-	-	-	-	146
Yellow Perch	2	10	6	-	-	-	-	-	18

FISH STOCKING DATA: NO RECORD OF STOCKING

NET CATCH DATA
survey date: 07/13/81

	Gill Nets		Trap Nets	
		avg fish		avg fish
species	# per net	wt. (lbs)	# per set	wt. (lbs)
Yellow Perch	0.5	0.15	-	-
White Sucker	0.5	2.10	-	-
Tullibee (incl. Cisco)	34.3	0.22	-	-
Splake	0.3	0.50	-	-
Rock Bass	0.3	0.10	4.0	0.22
Northern Pike	0.3	4.50	0.3	1.50
Largemouth Bass	0.3	0.20	2.0	0.43
Lake Trout	0.3	5.60	-	-
Pumpkin. Sunfish	-	-	4.0	0.18
Bluegill	-	-	48.5	0.13

LENGTH OF SELECTED SPECIES SAMPLED FROM ALL GEAR
Number of fish caught for the following length categories (inches):

species	0-5	6-8	9-11	12-14	15-19	20-24	25-29	>30	Total
Bluegill	26	109	1	-	-	-	-	-	136
Lake Trout	-	-	-	-	1	-	-	-	1
Largemouth Bass	-	7	-	2	-	-	-	-	9
Northern Pike	-	-	-	-	1	1	-	-	2
Pumpkin. Sunfish	-	16	-	-	-	-	-	-	16
Rock Bass	3	13	1	-	-	-	-	-	17
Splake	-	-	-	1	-	-	-	-	1
Tullibee (incl. Cisco)	-	21	113	3	-	-	-	-	137
Yellow Perch	-	2	-	-	-	-	-	-	2

DNR COMMENTS:
Little Trout has a very good population of Cisco. Bluegill numbers are well over state and local averages. Northern Pike numbers are under medians. Bass population good.

FISHING INFORMATION: Trout Lake, located within the Trout Lake Semi-primitive Non-motorized Area (SNA), is one of the prettiest lakes in the Chippewa National Forest, with very little development and clear, blue water. It is accessible by motorized vehicles on the north end, but a four-wheel-drive vehicle and small boats are recommended, due to steep ramp and sugar sand landing. Or you can access the lake by launching at one of Wabana Lake's landings and traveling through Little Trout. During the summer months, Lake Trout and Splake are caught in Trout Lake by anglers using downriggers with spoons and floating Rapalas. Earlier in the year, when the Lakers' preferred water temperature is still near the surface, jigging dead smelt or trolling Rapalas and spoons behind planer boards works well. Brian at the Forest Lake Motel told us that Trout can be easy to locate in the winter through the ice by jigging or live bait-fishing with Shiners. Walleyes don't receive much attention, but they average 2 to 3 pounds, and there are some trophy-size fish around. Northerns average 5 to 6 pounds, but there are some in the 20-pound class. Northerns taken occasionally. **Little Trout Lake** also gives up some Lakers and Splake. Largemouth Bass and panfish are plentiful.

Trout & Little Trout Lakes

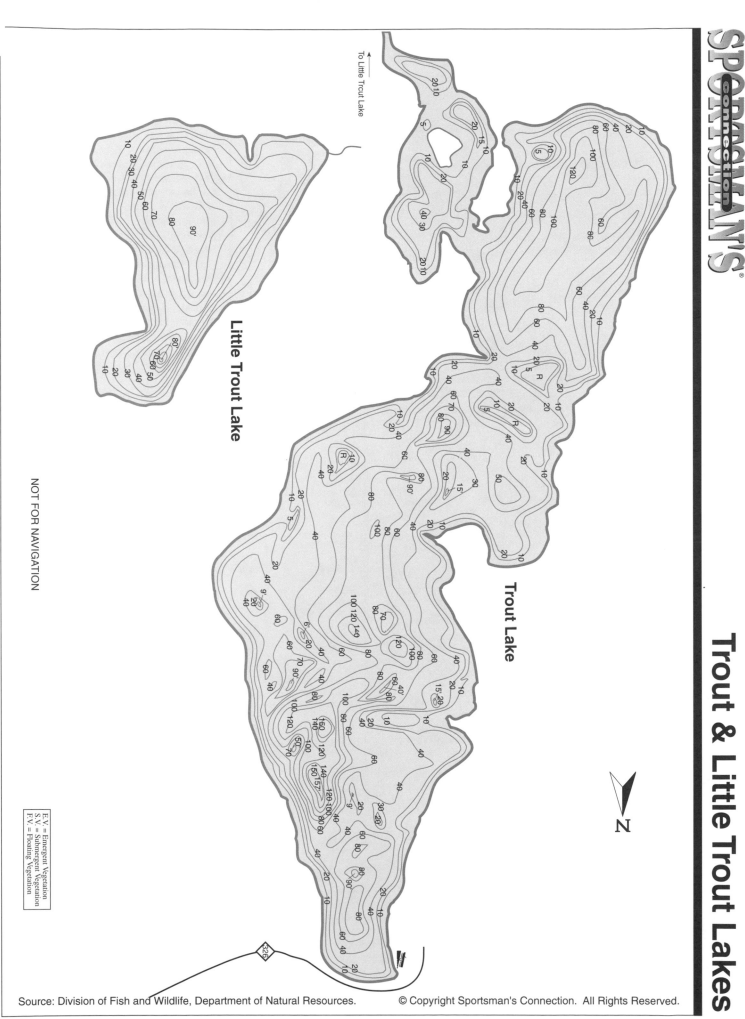

To Little Trout Lake

Little Trout Lake

Trout Lake

NOT FOR NAVIGATION

N

E.V. = Emergent Vegetation
S.V. = Submergent Vegetation
F.V. = Floating Vegetation

Source: Division of Fish and Wildlife, Department of Natural Resources.

WABANA LAKE

Location: Township 57 Range 25
Watershed: Prairie-Willow
Size of lake: 2,215 acres
Shorelength: 23.2 miles
Secchi disk (water clarity): 19.0 ft.
Water color: Clear
Cause of water color: NA
Maximum depth: 115.0 ft.
Median depth: 26.0 ft.
Accessibility: State-owned public access on northwest and southeast corners
Boat Ramp: Concrete (both)
Parking: SE: 6-8 vehicles
　　　　　　NW: 3-4 vehicles
Accommodations: Resorts
Shoreland zoning classif.: Rec. Dev.
Dominant forest/soil type: Decid/Loam
Management class: Walleye-Centrarchid
Ecological type: Centrarchid-Walleye

BLUEWATER LAKE

Itasca County

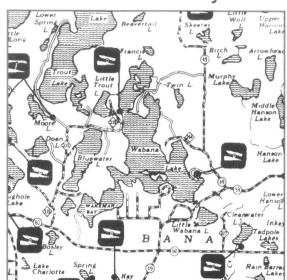

Location: Township 57 Range 25
Watershed: Prairie-Willow
Size of lake: 364 acres
Shorelength: 4.2 miles
Secchi disk (water clarity): 18.0 ft.
Water color: Clear
Cause of water color: NA
Maximum depth: 120.0 ft.
Median depth: 54.2 ft.
Accessibility: From Wakeman Bay, Wabana Lake
Boat Ramp: On Wabana Lake
Parking: At Wabana Lake
Accommodations: Resort
Shoreland zoning classif.: Rec. Dev.
Dominant forest/soil type: Decid/Loam
Management class: Lake Trout
Ecological type: Trout

DNR COMMENTS:
Walleye stocking appears to have created a strong fishery; numbers of this species are within expected range for lake class; mean size 18.4 inches and 2.4 lb.; growth good; some natural reproduction taking place. Northern Pike population largest on record for lake; mean weight 2.7 lb. Smallmouth Bass numbers high; mean size 15.7 inches and 2.3 lb. Black Crappie numbers within expected range, but fish are small. Bluegill numbers up sharply and well above expected range; length range 3.9 to 8.3 inches. Yellow Perch numbers low; length range 4.6 to 9.1 inches.

FISH STOCKING DATA

year	species	size	# released
90	Walleye	Fingerling	1,413
90	Walleye	Yearling	1,541
92	Walleye	Fingerling	22,813
92	Walleye	Yearling	16
94	Walleye	Fingerling	9,620
97	Walleye	Fingerling	12,628

survey date: 7/10/95

NET CATCH DATA

	Gill Nets		Trap Nets	
species	# per net	avg fish wt. (lbs)	# per set	avg fish wt. (lbs)
Black Crappie	-	-	1.0	0.11
Bluegill	4.3	0.19	71.7	0.18
Golden Shiner	-	-	trace	0.04
Green Sunfish	-	-	5.7	0.18
Hybrid Sunfish	trace	0.15	4.2	0.22
Largemouth Bass	0.6	1.03	0.4	0.45
Northern Pike	4.4	2.68	0.2	0.66
Pumpkin. Sunfish	0.6	0.22	2.0	0.21
Rock Bass	5.4	0.32	7.2	0.26
Smallmouth Bass	1.1	2.29	0.2	0.20
Tullibee (Cisco)	4.2	0.66	-	-
Walleye	4.5	2.35	0.4	3.29
White Sucker	0.7	2.06	-	-
Yellow Perch	9.1	0.12	1.0	0.20

LENGTH OF SELECTED SPECIES SAMPLED FROM ALL GEAR
Number of fish caught for the following length categories (inches):

species	0-5	6-8	9-11	12-14	15-19	20-24	25-29	>30	Total
Black Crappie	10	-	2	-	-	-	-	-	12
Bluegill	117	237	2	-	-	-	-	-	356
Green Sunfish	25	43	-	-	-	-	-	-	68
Hybrid Sunfish	12	39	-	-	-	-	-	-	51
Largemouth Bass	1	1	7	4	1	-	-	-	14
Northern Pike	-	-	-	9	26	17	11	5	68
Pumpkin. Sunfish	8	25	-	-	-	-	-	-	33
Rock Bass	31	131	4	-	-	-	-	-	166
Smallmouth Bass	1	1	3	4	9	-	-	-	18
Tullibee (Cisco)	-	11	22	27	3	-	-	-	63
Walleye	-	1	2	19	15	32	4	-	73
Yellow Perch	21	127	1	-	-	-	-	-	149

FISH STOCKING DATA

year	species	size	# released
89	Lake Trout	Yearling	808
90	Lake Trout	Yearling	700
91	Lake Trout	Yearling	1,000
93	Lake Trout	Yearling	1,820
95	Lake Trout	Yearling	1,820
97	Lake Trout	Yearling	1,809

survey date: 8/5/96

NET CATCH DATA

	Gill Nets		Trap Nets	
species	# per net	avg fish wt. (lbs)	# per set	avg fish wt. (lbs)
Black Bullhead	-	-	0.4	0.64
Bluegill	-	-	29.1	0.14
Creek Chub	-	-	0.1	0.09
Green Sunfish	-	-	13.1	0.17
Hybrid Sunfish	-	-	1.6	0.20
Lake Trout	3.3	2.13	-	-
Largemouth Bass	-	-	2.6	0.29
Rock Bass	-	-	5.9	0.17
Smallmouth Bass	0.7	2.22	0.2	1.01
Tullibee (Cisco)	0.4	0.10	-	-
White Sucker	0.1	3.35	-	-
Yellow Perch	-	-	1.3	0.19

LENGTH OF SELECTED SPECIES SAMPLED FROM ALL GEAR
Number of fish caught for the following length categories (inches):

species	0-5	6-8	9-11	12-14	15-19	20-24	25-29	>30	Total
Black Bullhead	-	2	1	1	-	-	-	-	4
Bluegill	98	68	-	-	-	-	-	-	166
Green Sunfish	45	73	-	-	-	-	-	-	118
Hybrid Sunfish	5	9	-	-	-	-	-	-	14
Lake Trout	-	2	8	4	7	3	6	-	30
Largemouth Bass	1	17	4	1	-	-	-	-	23
Rock Bass	19	34	-	-	-	-	-	-	53
Smallmouth Bass	-	-	1	4	3	-	-	-	8
Tullibee (Cisco)	-	4	-	-	-	-	-	-	4
Yellow Perch	1	6	5	-	-	-	-	-	12

DNR COMMENTS:
Lake is managed primarily for Lake Trout and stocked biennially with this species; length range 8.3 to 28.9 inches; mean weight 2.1 lb. Ciscoes scarce and small. Bluegill, Green Sunfish and Rock Bass dominated trapnet catch but were generally small. Largemouth and Smallmouth Bass also sampled; both species tend to run small.

FISHING INFORMATION: Wabana's deep, clear waters make the lake difficult to fish but hold a wide variety of fish to catch. Anglers have their best success by fishing Walleyes in low-light conditions and at night. Wabana's Bass fishing is excellent; there are good numbers and sizes of both Largemouth and Smallmouth. Underwater islands and other structure on the lake can be overwhelming. You can save yourself a lot of time by hiring a guide the first time or two on the lake. **Bluewater**, meanwhile, can be reached via the channel from Wabana's Wakeman Bay. Lake Trout can be found by following the species' preferred water temperature range of around 50 degrees progressively deeper as the season progresses. Early in the season, when area lakes' Walleyes may still be in their post-spawn funk, Lake Trout are often still in shallow water, where they can be fairly easily located. Later in the season, getting down deep is the key to catching them. Two-ounce jigs on braided line or downriggers rigged with spoons, floating Rapalas and other attractants can be effective.

Wabana & Bluewater Lakes

NOT FOR NAVIGATION

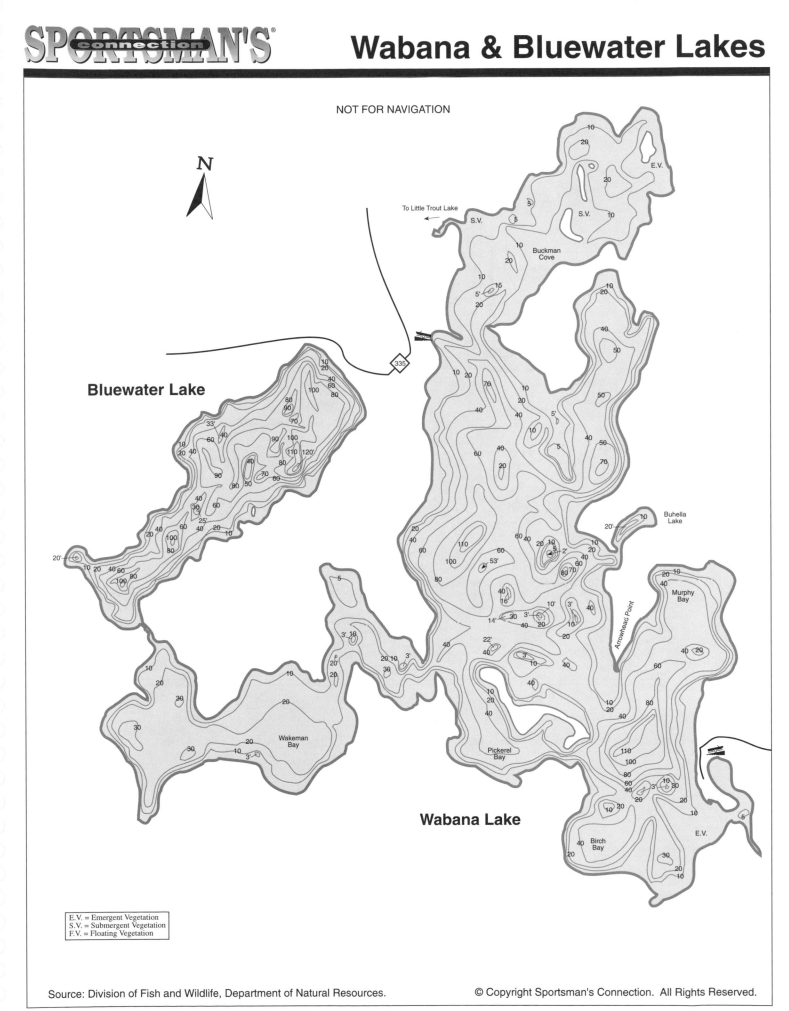

N

To Little Trout Lake

Bluewater Lake

335

Wabana Lake

Buckman Cove

S.V.

E.V.

S.V.

Buhella Lake

Murphy Bay

Arrowhead Point

Wakeman Bay

Pickerel Bay

Birch Bay

E.V.

E.V. = Emergent Vegetation
S.V. = Submergent Vegetation
F.V. = Floating Vegetation

Source: Division of Fish and Wildlife, Department of Natural Resources.

Location: Township 56, 57, 58 Range 24
Watershed: Prairie-Willow

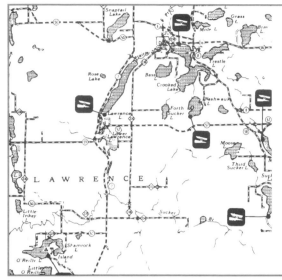

	LAWRENCE LAKE	**SNAPTAIL LAKE**	**O'REILLY LAKE**
	Itasca County		
Size of lake:	395 acres	146 acres	202 acres
Shorelength:	5.7 miles	5.0 miles	3.1 miles
Secchi disk (water clarity):	5.0 ft.	12.5 ft.	16.5 ft.
Water color:	Brown	Light brown	Clear
Cause of water color:	Bog drainage	Bog stain	NA
Maximum depth:	32.0 ft.	68.0 ft.	79.0 ft.
Median depth:	NA	28.0 ft.	22.0 ft.
Accessibility:	State-owned public access on southeast corner, 9 miles N of Taconite, MN	State-owned public access on south shore off Cty. Rd. 50	State-owned public access on south shore off Hwy. 7
Boat Ramp:	Earth	Earth	Earth
Parking:	Ample	Side of road	Ample
Accommodations:	Resort	None	Park
Shoreland zoning classif.:	Rec. Dev.	Rec. Dev.	Rec. Dev.
Dominant forest/soil type:	Decid/Wet	NA	Decid/Loam
Management class:	Walleye-Centrarchid	Walleye-Centrarchid	Centrarchid
Ecological type:	Centrarchid-Walleye	Centrarchid	Centrarchid

DNR COMMENTS:
The Northern Pike net catch is below first-quartile range. Yellow Bullhead and Pumpkinseed populations below first quartile. Bluegill population low as well, and previous samplings show a low and stable population for this species.

Lawrence Lake

FISH STOCKING DATA

year	species	size	# released
90	Walleye	Fingerling	3,875
92	Walleye	Fingerling	17,979
92	Walleye	Yearling	120

survey date: 07/15/91

NET CATCH DATA

	Gill Nets		Trap Nets	
species	# per net	avg fish wt. (lbs)	# per set	avg fish wt. (lbs)
Yellow Perch	10.5	0.11	1.5	0.17
Walleye	1.5	1.00	0.1	2.50
Rock Bass	0.2	0.90	-	-
Northern Pike	2.5	2.12	0.6	2.00
Bluegill	0.2	0.20	3.8	0.23
Black Crappie	2.8	0.21	5.0	0.22
Yellow Bullhead	-	-	0.1	1.10
Pumpkin. Sunfish	-	-	0.3	0.15
Hybrid Sunfish	-	-	0.1	0.60

LENGTH OF SELECTED SPECIES SAMPLED FROM ALL GEAR
Number of fish caught for the following length categories (inches):

species	0-5	6-8	9-11	12-14	15-19	20-24	25-29	>30	Total
Yellow Perch	-	58	5	-	-	-	-	-	63
Walleye	-	-	1	6	1	1	-	-	9
Rock Bass	-	-	1	-	-	-	-	-	1
Northern Pike	-	-	-	-	4	9	2	-	15
Bluegill	-	1	-	-	-	-	-	-	1
Black Crappie	-	15	2	-	-	-	-	-	17

Snaptail Lake

FISH STOCKING DATA

year	species	size	# released
90	Walleye	Yearling	165
92	Walleye	Fingerling	2,700

survey date: 6/21/93

NET CATCH DATA

	Gill Nets		Trap Nets	
species	# per net	avg fish wt. (lbs)	# per set	avg fish wt. (lbs)
Black Crappie	0.3	0.05	2.6	0.26
Bluegill	0.3	0.08	80.9	0.12
Largemouth Bass	0.2	0.35	0.4	0.24
Northern Pike	1.7	4.33	0.4	0.58
Pumpkin. Sunfish	-	-	3.4	0.12
Rock Bass	-	-	0.1	0.22
Walleye	0.2	2.65	0.3	5.07
Yellow Perch	8.8	0.11	0.8	0.10

LENGTH OF SELECTED SPECIES SAMPLED FROM ALL GEAR
Number of fish caught for the following length categories (inches):

species	0-5	6-8	9-11	12-14	15-19	20-24	25-29	>30	Total
Black Crappie	4	19	2	-	-	-	-	-	25
Bluegill	340	196	-	-	-	-	-	-	536
Largemouth Bass	-	3	2	-	-	-	-	-	5
Northern Pike	-	-	1	2	3	3	2	3	14
Pumpkin. Sunfish	23	8	-	-	-	-	-	-	31
Rock Bass	-	1	-	-	-	-	-	-	1
Walleye	-	-	-	-	-	2	2	-	4
Yellow Perch	24	34	-	-	-	-	-	-	58

DNR COMMENTS:
Walleye numbers low, despite periodic stocking; poor survival and recruitment rate for stocked fish. Northern Pike abundant, and average size is large. Largemouth Bass, Bluegill and Black Crappies abundant but slow-growing.

O'Reilly Lake

FISH STOCKING DATA: No record of stocking since 1988.

LENGTH OF SELECTED SPECIES SAMPLED FROM ALL GEAR
Number of fish caught for the following length categories (inches):

species	0-5	6-8	9-11	12-14	15-19	20-24	25-29	>30	Total
Yellow Perch	2	-	-	-	-	-	-	-	2
Walleye	-	-	-	1	-	-	-	-	1
Tullibee (incl. Cisco)	-	-	4	-	-	-	-	-	4
Smallmouth Bass	-	-	-	1	-	-	-	-	1
Rock Bass	1	21	9	-	-	-	-	-	31
Pumpkin. Sunfish	2	-	-	-	-	-	-	-	2
Northern Pike	-	-	-	-	6	8	-	-	14
Largemouth Bass	-	2	4	1	2	-	-	-	9
Hybrid Sunfish	-	1	1	-	-	-	-	-	2
Bluegill	24	4	-	-	-	-	-	-	28
Black Crappie	-	14	5	-	-	-	-	-	19

survey date: 08/31/92

NET CATCH DATA

	Gill Nets		Trap Nets	
species	# per net	avg fish wt. (lbs)	# per set	avg fish wt. (lbs)
Yellow Perch	0.2	0.10	0.3	0.40
Walleye	0.2	1.80	-	-
Tullibee (incl. Cisco)	0.8	0.28	-	-
Smallmouth Bass	0.2	1.00	-	-
Rock Bass	6.2	0.38	2.5	0.15
Pumpkin. Sunfish	0.2	0.10	-	-
Northern Pike	2.8	3.61	0.3	3.00
Largemouth Bass	1.4	0.90	1.3	0.76
Hybrid Sunfish	0.2	0.50	-	-
Bluegill	5.4	0.07	12.5	0.11
Black Crappie	3.4	0.21	1.0	0.20
Common Shiner	-	-	0.3	1.20

DNR COMMENTS:
No. Pike population is below median for lake class; average weight of 3.6 lb. Walleye population marginal even though fry were stocked in 1986, '88; low Yellow Perch population may be limiting Walleye forage and viability. Tullibee population low.

FISHING INFORMATION: Lawrence Lake has been receiving significant plantings of fry, fingerling, and yearling Walleye over the last several years, and these are providing anglers with some steady, if not spectacular, Walleye fishing. One- to 2-pounders are the norm. Crappies average about 1/2 pound and some of the Bluegills run to 3/4 pound. The lake's structure is fairly basic; most anglers work the subtle points and dropoffs. **Snaptail** is beginning to produce a few Walleyes. Crappies run about 3 to the pound. Northern fishing can be pretty good with good numbers of 3-pound-plus fish being taken. Bass might also be worth trying. **O'Reilly** is a pretty lake with some good Largemouth and Northern Pike. The folks at Hollywood Bait in Coleraine told us the lake's heavy Cisco population keeps the fish well fed and tough to catch. Try fishing early in the morning before the gamefish have had a chance to gorge themselves.

Lawrence, Snaptail, & O'Reilly Lakes

NOT FOR NAVIGATION

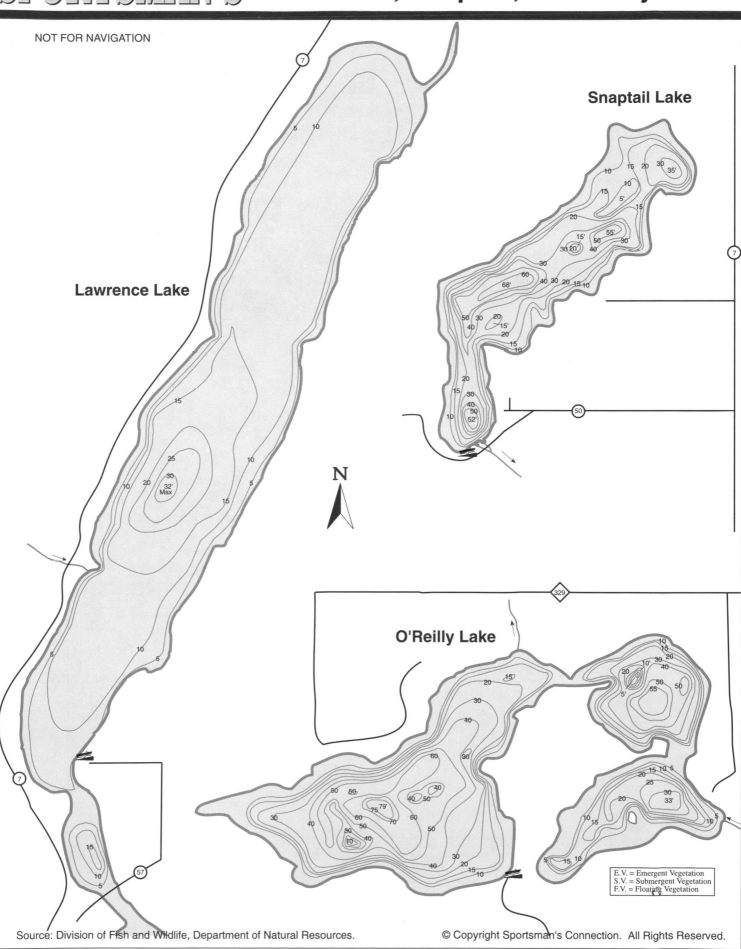

Lawrence Lake

Snaptail Lake

O'Reilly Lake

N

E.V. = Emergent Vegetation
S.V. = Submergent Vegetation
F.V. = Floating Vegetation

Source: Division of Fish and Wildlife, Department of Natural Resources.

BASS LAKE LITTLE BASS LAKE

Itasca County

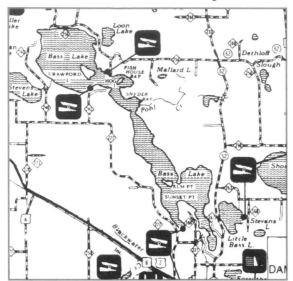

Location: Township 55, 56 Range 26
Watershed: Mississippi Headwaters
Size of lake: 2,407 acres
Shorelength: 14.5 miles
Secchi disk (water clarity): 16.0 ft.
Water color: Clear
Cause of water color: NA
Maximum depth: 76.0 ft.
Median depth: NA
Accessibility: Access on northeast shore in Fish House Bay; access on south shore of north basin; access on south shore
Boat Ramps: Earth (2); Concrete (1)
Parking: Ample
Accommodations: Resorts
Shoreland zoning classif.: Rec. Dev.
Dominant forest/soil type: Decid/Loam
Management class: Walleye-Centrarchid
Ecological type: Centrarchid-Walleye

Location: Township 55, 56 Range 26
Watershed: Mississippi Headwaters
Size of lake: 158 acres
Shorelength: 2.4 miles
Secchi disk (water clarity): NA
Water color: Green
Cause of water color: Algae
Maximum depth: 62.0 ft.
Median depth: 35.0 ft.
Accessibility: Public access on east shore
Boat Ramp: Earth
Parking: Ample
Accommodations: Resorts
Shoreland zoning classif.: Rec. Dev.
Dominant forest/soil type: Decid/Loam
Management class: Centrarchid
Ecological type: Centrarchid

DNR COMMENTS:
Walleye numbers about average for lake class; average size 16 inches and 1.7 lb.; some natural reproduction taking place. Northern Pike numbers normal; average size 18 inches and 1.4 lb., but fish to 35 inches present. Bluegill numbers up, and stunting is occurring; catch-and-release of larger individuals is recommended. Largemouth Bass sampled in low numbers. Yellow Perch numbers about average for lake class. Black Crappies scarce. Rock Bass not uncommon and average .5 lb.

FISH STOCKING DATA

year	species	size	# released
89	Walleye	Fry	3,000,000
91	Walleye	Fry	3,000,000
93	Walleye	Fry	2,496,000
96	Walleye	Fry	1,250,000

NET CATCH DATA
survey date: 7/12/93

	Gill Nets		Trap Nets	
species	# per net	avg fish wt. (lbs)	# per set	avg fish wt. (lbs)
Black Bullhead	trace	0.83	-	-
Black Crappie	trace	0.29	-	-
Bluegill	0.3	0.44	5.1	0.29
Bowfin (Dogfish)	trace	6.17	trace	4.63
Brown Bullhead	0.4	1.16	0.3	1.07
Hybrid Sunfish	-	-	0.2	0.38
Largemouth Bass	-	-	0.1	1.74
Northern Pike	6.9	1.37	0.6	0.70
Pumpkin. Sunfish	0.2	0.25	1.6	0.29
Rock Bass	2.1	0.52	1.8	0.46
Tullibee (Cisco)	0.6	1.03	-	-
Walleye	3.6	1.67	0.3	3.13
White Sucker	0.1	1.60	-	-
Yellow Bullhead	0.6	0.81	0.9	0.84
Yellow Perch	15.5	0.12	0.5	0.08

LENGTH OF SELECTED SPECIES SAMPLED FROM ALL GEAR
Number of fish caught for the following length categories (inches):

species	0-5	6-8	9-11	12-14	15-19	20-24	25-29	>30	Total
Black Bullhead	-	-	1	-	-	-	-	-	1
Black Crappie	-	1	-	-	-	-	-	-	1
Bluegill	30	44	7	-	-	-	-	-	81
Brown Bullhead	-	-	2	9	-	-	-	-	11
Hybrid Sunfish	-	3	-	-	-	-	-	-	3
Largemouth Bass	-	1	-	-	1	-	-	-	2
Northern Pike	-	-	13	3	75	20	1	1	113
Pumpkin. Sunfish	5	21	1	-	-	-	-	-	27
Rock Bass	16	23	20	-	-	-	-	-	59
Tullibee (Cisco)	-	-	2	5	2	-	-	-	9
Walleye	-	1	6	18	26	7	1	-	59
Yellow Bullhead	-	1	17	3	1	-	-	-	22
Yellow Perch	127	77	6	-	-	-	-	-	210

FISH STOCKING DATA

year	species	size	# released
93	Black Crappie	Adult	373

NET CATCH DATA
survey date: 06/25/90

	Gill Nets		Trap Nets	
species	# per net	avg fish wt. (lbs)	# per set	avg fish wt. (lbs)
Yellow Perch	9.7	0.10	0.3	0.10
White Sucker	1.0	2.30	-	-
Walleye	1.0	3.47	0.3	0.10
Tullibee (incl. Cisco)	2.7	1.91	-	-
Northern Pike	4.7	2.02	0.3	3.00
Yellow Bullhead	-	-	1.3	0.64
Rock Bass	-	-	2.3	0.23
Pumpkin. Sunfish	-	-	3.3	0.18
Largemouth Bass	-	-	0.5	2.00
Bluegill	-	-	31.8	0.15

LENGTH OF SELECTED SPECIES SAMPLED FROM ALL GEAR
Number of fish caught for the following length categories (inches):

species	0-5	6-8	9-11	12-14	15-19	20-24	25-29	>30	Total
Yellow Perch	-	29	-	-	-	-	-	-	29
Walleye	-	-	-	1	-	1	1	-	3
Tullibee (incl. Cisco)	-	-	-	4	3	1	-	-	8
Northern Pike	-	-	-	-	6	8	-	-	14

DNR COMMENTS:
Northern Pike decreasing from historically high numbers; age classes 2-6 represented; growth good till age 4. Walleyes scarce; natural reproduction appears to be occurring. Bluegills present in above-average numbers. Cisco about average in numbers, with a wide range of sizes being sampled. Yellow Perch population stable.

FISHING INFORMATION: Bass Lake holds some Largemouth Bass, but its big Walleyes, Northerns and Sunfish get most of the attention. Brian Krecklau of Pole Bender Guide Service in Grand Rapids says stringers of 1 1/2- to 2-pound Walleyes will often include some 3- to 6-pounders. Northern Pike up to 20 pounds are also found, although 3- to 4-pound fish are the norm. The north and south lobes of the lake are separated by a large, long, shallow, weedy stretch that produces some plate-size Bluegills and large Pumpkinseeds. The Bass, Northerns and Walleyes are fished primarily off the points and underwater islands in the north and south lobes. **Little Bass Lake** holds some good Largemouth Bass and lots of Northern Pike. Walleye fishing can be spotty but average size is good. Panfish run small.

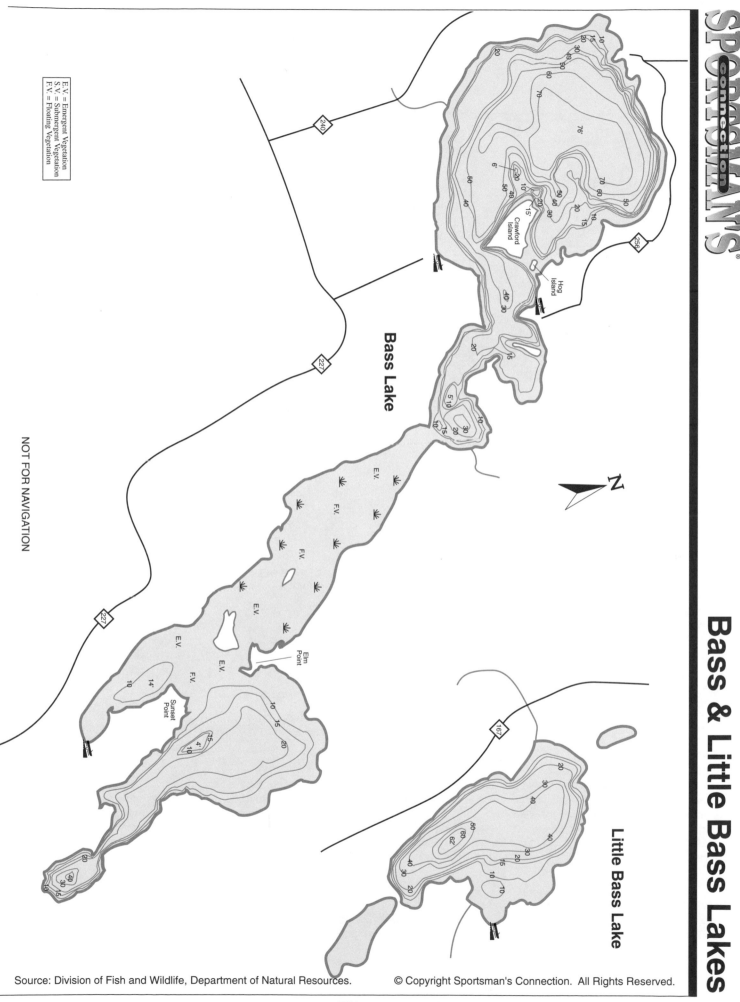

Bass & Little Bass Lakes

Bass Lake

Little Bass Lake

E.V. = Emergent Vegetation
S.V. = Submergent Vegetation
F.V. = Floating Vegetation

NOT FOR NAVIGATION

PRAIRIE LAKE

Itasca County

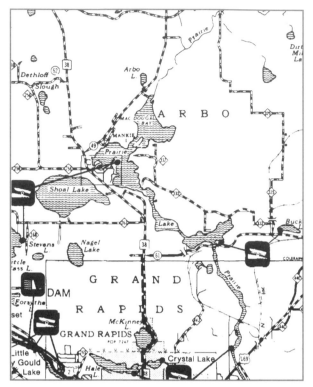

Location: Township 56
Range 25
Watershed: Prairie-Willow
Size of lake: 1,064 acres
Shorelength: 16.6 miles
Secchi disk (water clarity): 6.3 ft.
Water color: Brown
Cause of water color: Bog stain and suspended silt

Maximum depth: 31.0 ft.
Median depth: 12.0 ft.
Accessibility: Access on west shore, off Millard Pt. Road; access can also be gained on lower Prairie Lake
Boat Ramp: Concrete (both)
Parking: Ample
Accommodations: Resorts, Campground

Shoreland zoning classification: Recreational Development
Dominant forest/soil type: Decid/Loam
Management class: Walleye-Centrarchid
Ecological type: Centrarchid-Walleye

FISH STOCKING DATA

year	species	size	# released
89	Walleye	Fry	2,000,000
90	Walleye	Fingerling	11,044
91	Walleye	Fry	2,000,000
92	Walleye	Fingerling	7,087
92	Walleye	Yearling	81
92	Walleye	Fingerling	3,479
92	Walleye	Yearling	2
92	Walleye	Adult	78
97	Walleye	Fry	835,000

NET CATCH DATA

survey date: 7/24/95

species	Gill Nets # per net	Gill Nets avg fish wt. (lbs.)	Trap Nets # per set	Trap Nets avg fish wt. (lbs.)
Black Crappie	5.5	0.25	1.9	0.16
Bluegill	0.5	0.19	10.2	0.18
Bowfin (Dogfish)	-	-	0.4	5.49
Brown Bullhead	-	-	0.1	0.94
Golden Redhorse	-	-	0.4	7.73
Northern Pike	3.6	1.56	0.4	1.93
Pumpkin. Sunfish	-	-	1.0	0.11
Rock Bass	0.5	0.33	0.3	0.26
Shorthead Redhorse	0.7	2.08	-	-
Silver Redhorse	trace	4.41	trace	3.97
Smallmouth Bass	trace	1.37	-	-
Walleye	2.4	1.35	-	-
White Sucker	1.1	1.51	0.7	2.62
Yellow Bullhead	0.1	0.88	0.2	0.79
Yellow Perch	12.0	0.09	1.9	0.08

LENGTH OF SELECTED SPECIES SAMPLED FROM ALL GEAR

Number of fish caught for the following length categories (inches):

species	0-5	6-8	9-11	12-14	15-19	20-24	25-29	>30	Total
Black Crappie	17	82	10	-	-	-	-	-	109
Bluegill	64	86	-	-	-	-	-	-	150
Brown Bullhead	-	-	1	1	-	-	-	-	2
Northern Pike	-	-	-	6	30	22	2	-	60
Pumpkin. Sunfish	12	2	-	-	-	-	-	-	14
Rock Bass	3	7	1	-	-	-	-	-	11
Smallmouth Bass	-	-	-	1	-	-	-	-	1
Walleye	-	1	5	12	15	2	1	-	36
Yellow Bullhead	-	-	4	1	-	-	-	-	5
Yellow Perch	107	54	-	-	-	-	-	-	161

DNR COMMENTS: Walleye population relatively stable and within expected range for lake class; length range 8.5 to 28.7 inches; average size 15.4 inches and 1.4 lb.; growth average; stocking supplements natural reproduction. Northern Pike numbers stable and within expected range; mean size 19 inches and 1.9 lb.; Black Crappie population within expected range; length range 3.7 to 10.1 inches. Bluegill population likewise within expected range; length range 4.3 to 8.1 inches. Yellow Perch numbers about what can be expected in lakes of this type; length range 5.3 to 8.6 inches. Largemouth Bass, Smallmouth Bass, Rock Bass, Pumpkinseed and Yellow and Brown Bullheads also sampled, along with Redhorse, Bowfin and White Sucker.

FISHING INFORMATION: Prairie Lake was created when the river of the same name was dammed for hydroelectric power generation. Its relatively shallow, bog-stained waters teem with Crappies which provide steady action year around. Good numbers of Northerns and Largemouth Bass also are found in the reservoir, and Walleyes averaging about 1 1/2 pounds have resulted from DNR stocking.

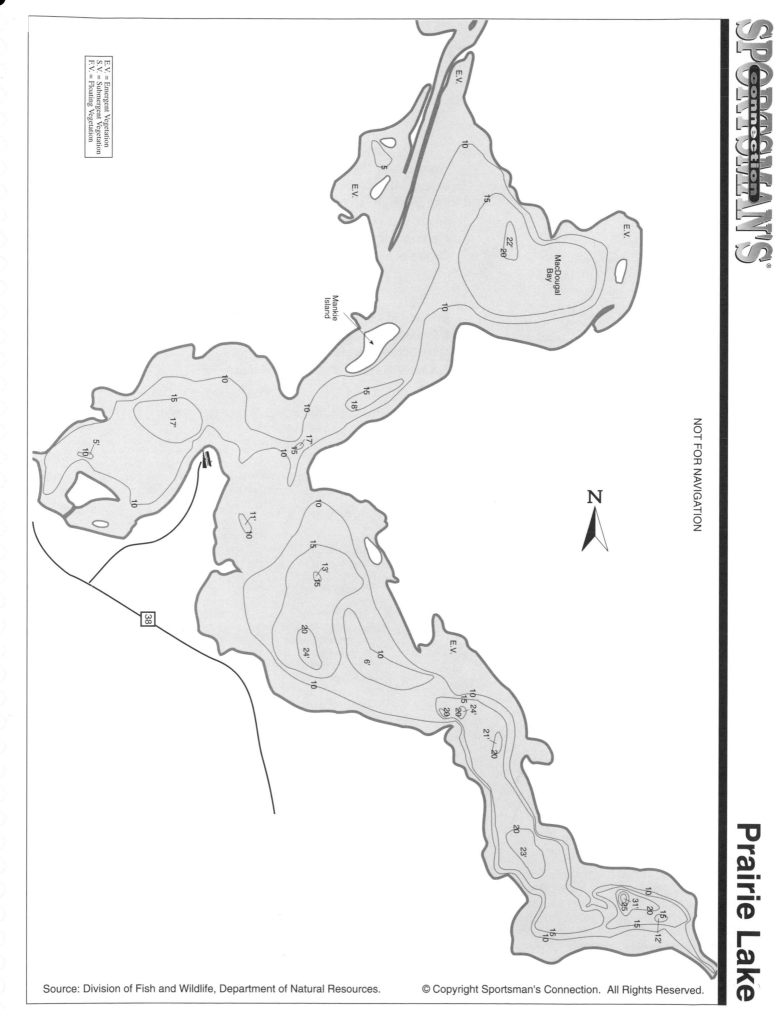

NOT FOR NAVIGATION

N

Prairie Lake

E.V. = Emergent Vegetation
S.V. = Submergent Vegetation
F.V. = Floating Vegetation

MacDougal Bay

Mankie Island

38

TROUT LAKE
Itasca County

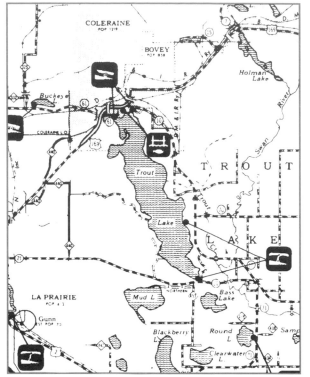

Location: Township 55, 56 Range 24
Watershed: Prairie-Willow
Size of lake: 1,890 acres
Shorelength: 13.0 miles
Secchi disk (water clarity): 20.0 ft.
Water color: Clear
Cause of water color: NA

Maximum depth: 115.0 ft.
Median depth: NA
Accessibility: Two city-owned accesses with concrete ramps on north shore; also at Komenen Park and on south shore
Boat Ramp: Concrete (2), carry-down (2)
Parking: Ample
Accommodations: Park

Shoreland zoning classification: Recreational Development
Dominant forest/soil type: Decid/Loam
Management class: Walleye
Ecological type: Hard-water Walleye

FISH STOCKING DATA

year	species	size	# released
89	Walleye	Fry	2,000,000
91	Walleye	Fry	2,000,000
93	Walleye	Fry	2,085,200

survey date: 8/16/93

NET CATCH DATA

	Gill Nets		Trap Nets	
species	# per net	avg fish wt. (lbs.)	# per set	avg fish wt. (lbs.)
Black Crappie	-	-	0.3	0.58
Bluegill	0.2	0.47	0.5	0.03
Bowfin (Dogfish)	-	-	0.7	6.15
Brown Bullhead	-	-	trace	2.01
Burbot	trace	1.36	-	-
Common Shiner	-	-	trace	0.08
Hybrid Sunfish	-	-	0.1	0.24
Largemouth Bass	0.2	3.56	trace	2.65
Northern Pike	7.4	3.01	0.2	2.94
Pumpkin. Sunfish	0.5	0.23	0.9	0.17
Rock Bass	4.1	0.46	0.7	0.39
Smallmouth Bass	0.3	1.29	-	-
Tullibee (Cisco)	0.3	1.03	-	-
Walleye	7.9	1.67	0.4	3.30
White Sucker	1.0	1.78	0.3	2.14
Yellow Bullhead	-	-	trace	1.15
Yellow Perch	78.1	0.11	8.8	0.12

LENGTH OF SELECTED SPECIES SAMPLED FROM ALL GEAR

Number of fish caught for the following length categories (inches):

species	0-5	6-8	9-11	12-14	15-19	20-24	25-29	>30	Total
Black Crappie	1	-	3	-	-	-	-	-	4
Bluegill	7	3	-	-	-	-	-	-	10
Brown Bullhead	-	-	-	-	1	-	-	-	1
Hybrid Sunfish	-	2	-	-	-	-	-	-	2
Largemouth Bass	-	-	-	1	2	1	-	-	4
Northern Pike	-	-	-	-	10	86	16	2	114
Pumpkin. Sunfish	13	9	-	-	-	-	-	-	22
Rock Bass	11	45	15	-	-	-	-	-	71
Smallmouth Bass	-	1	-	3	-	-	-	-	4
Tullibee (Cisco)	-	-	-	5	-	-	-	-	5
Walleye	-	1	32	17	62	11	2	-	125
Yellow Bullhead	-	-	-	1	-	-	-	-	1

DNR COMMENTS: Walleye population remains high with strong 1989 and 1991 year classes; mean length of sampled fish 15.9 inches; natural reproduction evident, but supplemented by stocking. Northern Pike numbers good; average size 22.8 inches; 1991 year class accounted for 50 percent of sample. Yellow Perch abundant. Smallmouth Bass and Black Crappie numbers low.

FISHING INFORMATION: In the 1930s to 1950s Trout Lake (near Coleraine) was filled with Lake Trout, many in the 30- to 35-pound range. The folks at Hollywood Bait near the lake told us of stories about Lakers' being so plentiful that you could walk across their backs when they were spawning in the shallower bays in the autumn. However, those days have passed; years of silt buildup essentially destroyed the spawning areas. The lake has been managed for Walleyes in more recent times and is receiving regular fry stocking by the DNR. Walleyes can be found along the underwater islands and points throughout the lake. Northern Pike appear to be fattening up on Ciscoes and Perch. In fact, there have been reports of 20-pound fish being caught. Bass, both Largemouth and Smallmouth, are also found around the sunken islands and other irregular structure. Crappies up to 1 1/2 pounds are successfully fished in the winter and spring but virtually disappear in the summer. Electronic fish-finding gear is a must in locating the structure on Trout. You don't hear much about Lakers on Trout Lake these days, but some spear fishermen have reported seeing them swim past their holes.

NOT FOR NAVIGATION

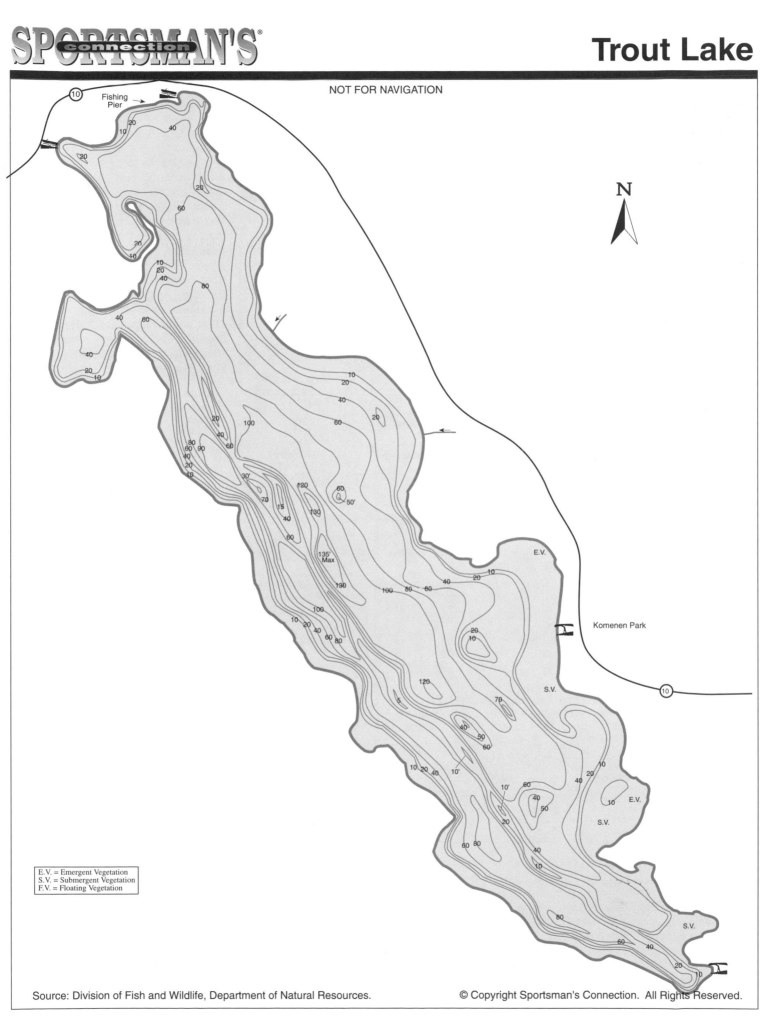

Fishing Pier

N

E.V.

Komenen Park

S.V.

E.V.

S.V.

S.V.

135' Max

E.V. = Emergent Vegetation
S.V. = Submergent Vegetation
F.V. = Floating Vegetation

Source: Division of Fish and Wildlife, Department of Natural Resources.

SPLIT HAND LAKE   LITTLE SPLIT HAND LAKE

Itasca County

Location: Township 53 Range 24, 25
Watershed: Prairie-Willow
Size of lake: 1,420 acres
Shorelength: 7.1 miles
Secchi disk (water clarity): 6.5 ft.
Water color: Green
Cause of water color: Algae bloom
Maximum depth: 34.0 ft.
Median depth: NA
Accessibility: State-owned public access on west shore
Boat Ramp: Concrete
Parking: Ample
Accommodations: Resort
Shoreland zoning classif.: Rec. Dev.
Dominant forest/soil type: Decid/Wet
Management class: Walleye
Ecological type: Hard-water Walleye

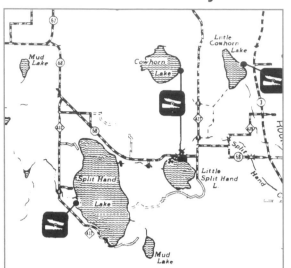

Location: Township 53 Range 24, 25
Watershed: Prairie-Willow
Size of lake: 223 acres
Shorelength: 2.5 miles
Secchi disk (water clarity): 7.0 ft.
Water color: Brown-green
Cause of water color: Suspended silt and algae bloom
Maximum depth: 23.0 ft.
Median depth: 13.0 ft.
Accessibility: State-owned public access on north shore off #68
Boat Ramp: Concrete
Parking: Ample
Accommodations: Resorts
Shoreland zoning classif.: Rec. Dev.
Dominant forest/soil type: No tree/Wet
Management class: Centrarchid
Ecological type: Centrarchid

DNR COMMENTS:
Walleye population about normal for lake class; average size 15.6 inches and 1.8 lb. Northern Pike numbers slightly below normal; average size 23.5 inches and 3.1 lb. Black Crappie numbers typical for lake class; average length 8.8 inches. Bluegill population below normal; average length 7.3 inches. Lake is subject to algae blooms as a result of high phosphorus levels. Exact cause of high phosphorus content unknown.

FISH STOCKING DATA

year	species	size	# released
89	Walleye	Fry	1,300,000
91	Walleye	Fry	1,300,000
93	Walleye	Fry	1,398,880

survey date: 8/2/93

NET CATCH DATA

| | Gill Nets | | Trap Nets | |
| | | avg fish | | avg fish |
species	# per net	wt. (lbs)	# per set	wt. (lbs)
Black Crappie	0.6	0.16	0.5	0.42
Bluegill	trace	0.57	2.1	0.36
Bowfin (Dogfish)	trace	0.11	1.2	6.61
Brown Bullhead	trace	1.96	0.4	1.46
Buffalo	-	-	0.1	11.46
Common Shiner	-	-	0.1	0.07
Northern Pike	2.0	3.13	0.6	2.67
Pumpkin. Sunfish	-	-	2.7	0.28
Rock Bass	-	-	0.4	0.57
Tullibee (Cisco)	1.2	0.77	-	-
Walleye	5.2	1.77	0.3	1.76
White Sucker	3.3	1.95	0.2	2.76
Yellow Bullhead	-	-	0.3	1.87
Yellow Perch	43.1	0.13	4.7	0.12

LENGTH OF SELECTED SPECIES SAMPLED FROM ALL GEAR
Number of fish caught for the following length categories (inches):

species	0-5	6-8	9-11	12-14	15-19	20-24	25-29	>30	Total
Black Crappie	1	8	3	-	-	-	-	-	12
Bluegill	2	22	-	-	-	-	-	-	24
Brown Bullhead	-	-	-	5	-	-	-	-	5
Northern Pike	-	-	-	1	4	19	6	1	31
Pumpkin. Sunfish	9	21	-	-	-	-	-	-	30
Rock Bass	1	1	2	-	-	-	-	-	4
Tullibee (Cisco)	-	1	8	3	2	-	-	-	14
Walleye	-	1	25	7	15	15	2	-	65
Yellow Bullhead	-	-	-	3	-	-	-	-	3
Yellow Perch	137	222	10	-	-	-	-	-	369

FISH STOCKING DATA

year	species	size	# released
90	Walleye	Yearling	392
92	Walleye	Yearling	52
92	Walleye	Fingerling	200
92	Walleye	Yearling	227
92	Walleye	Adult	114
96	Walleye	Fingerling	3,770

survey date: 6/17/96

NET CATCH DATA

| | Gill Nets | | Trap Nets | |
| | | avg fish | | avg fish |
species	# per net	wt. (lbs)	# per set	wt. (lbs)
Black Crappie	1.0	0.60	0.9	0.30
Bluegill	-	-	0.9	0.42
Bowfin (Dogfish)	0.7	4.97	0.9	3.77
Brown Bullhead	0.2	0.08	0.8	1.05
Largemouth Bass	-	-	0.1	0.07
Northern Pike	11.8	2.13	0.7	1.03
Pumpkin. Sunfish	0.3	0.29	3.3	0.21
Rock Bass	-	-	0.6	0.53
Shorthead Redhorse	0.3	1.19	-	-
Walleye	0.7	3.91	-	-
White Sucker	4.2	1.73	0.1	2.43
Yellow Bullhead	0.7	0.78	1.6	0.91
Yellow Perch	39.2	0.12	1.7	0.10

LENGTH OF SELECTED SPECIES SAMPLED FROM ALL GEAR
Number of fish caught for the following length categories (inches):

species	0-5	6-8	9-11	12-14	15-19	20-24	25-29	>30	Total
Black Crappie	4	2	8	-	-	-	-	-	14
Bluegill	2	6	-	-	-	-	-	-	8
Brown Bullhead	2	-	-	6	-	-	-	-	8
Largemouth Bass	1	-	-	-	-	-	-	-	1
Northern Pike	-	-	-	4	38	28	4	2	76
Pumpkin. Sunfish	13	19	-	-	-	-	-	-	32
Rock Bass	1	2	2	-	-	-	-	-	5
Walleye	-	-	-	-	-	3	1	-	4
Yellow Bullhead	-	2	11	5	-	-	-	-	18
Yellow Perch	69	97	1	-	-	-	-	-	167

DNR COMMENTS:
Walleye numbers within expected range for lake class; length range 20.5 to 25.5 inches. Northern Pike fairly abundant; mean size 20.3 inches and 2.1 lb. Largemouth Bass sample inadequate for accurate population assessment. Black Crappie numbers within expected range; mean length 10 inches in gillnets, 6.8 inches in trapnets. Bluegill numbers low; mean length 7.5 inches. Yellow Perch numerous; length range 5 to 9.6 inches. Yellow and Brown Bullhead, Pumpkinseed Sunfish and Rock Bass also present.

FISHING INFORMATION: Mike Auger of the Blue Horizon Guide Service out of Ken's Pokegama Sports, fishes **Splithand Lake** regularly and offered several tips. Crappie fishing is excellent, he says, with typical fish running from 1/2 pound on up to 1 3/4 pounds. The east end of the lake between the creeks is good in the winter. Start on the north end of this area after ice up and move down to the south beds as winter progresses on into spring. The 20-foot bar in the middle of the lake actually comes up to about 18 feet and is good for Walleyes. Auger says Splithand's relatively murky waters can be productive all day for Walleyes. The 10-foot island off of the center bar comes up to about 7 feet and is good for Crappie off the deep sides. Move up into the shallower water over the island as night falls. Fish the edges for Walleyes also. The north bay is good for spring Crappie. Bluegills in the 1/2-pound to 1-pound range can also be found around 10 to 15 feet down in this area, a little shallower than the Crappies. Fish the shoreline weeds in the spring and summer for Northerns, many in the 8-12 pound range. **Little Splithand** has some good early Walleye and Crappie fishing. Recent years' Walleye stockings of fingerlings and older fish seem to be successful.

SPORTSMAN'S Connection

NOT FOR NAVIGATION

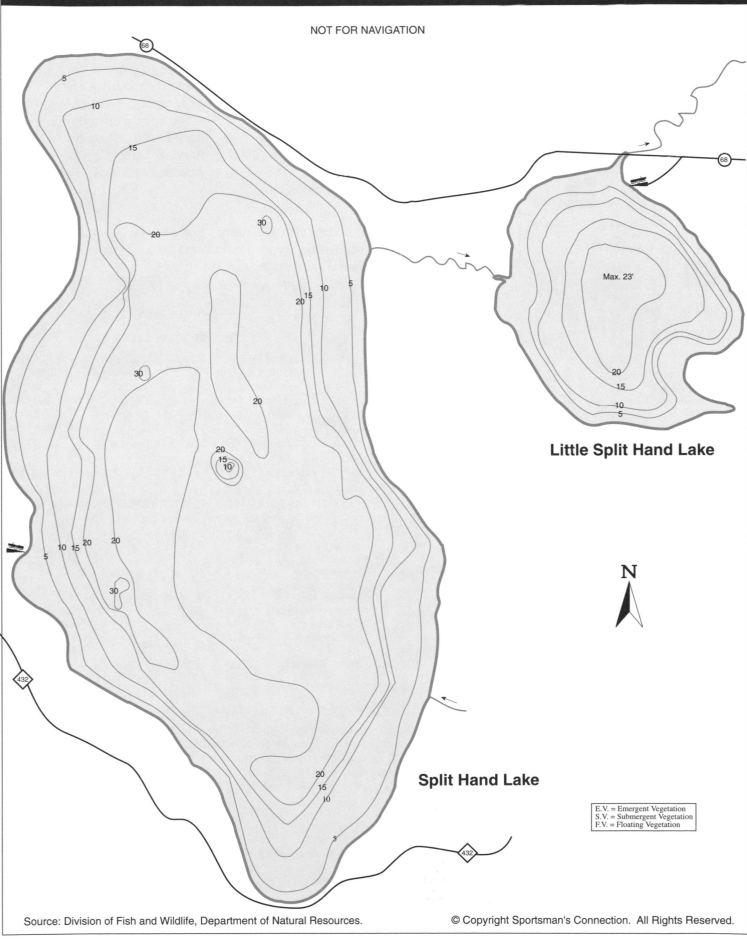

Max. 23'

Little Split Hand Lake

N

Split Hand Lake

E.V. = Emergent Vegetation
S.V. = Submergent Vegetation
F.V. = Floating Vegetation

Source: Division of Fish and Wildlife, Department of Natural Resources.

SISEEBAKWET (Sugar) LAKE
Itasca County

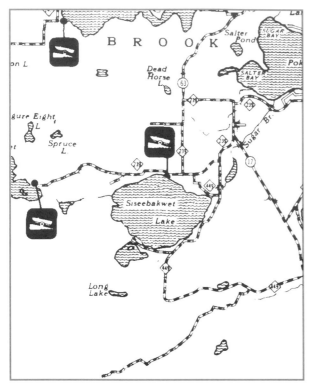

Location: Township 54
Range 26
Watershed: Mississippi Headwaters
Size of lake: 1,306 acres
Shorelength: 7.7 miles
Secchi disk (water clarity): 10.5 ft.
Water color: Clear
Cause of water color: NA

Maximum depth: 105.0 ft.
Median depth: NA
Accessibility: County-owned
public access on north shore
Boat Ramp: Concrete
Parking: Ample
Accommodations: Resort

Shoreland zoning classification: Recreational Development
Dominant forest/soil type: Decid/Loam
Management class: Walleye
Ecological type: Hard-water Walleye

FISH STOCKING DATA

year	species	size	# released
89	Walleye	Fry	1,300,000
90	Walleye	Yearling	1,138
91	Walleye	Fry	1,300,000
92	Walleye	Fingerling	4,964
94	Walleye	Fry	1,300,000
96	Walleye	Fingerling	3,823

NET CATCH DATA

survey date: 8/29/94

	Gill Nets		Trap Nets	
species	# per net	avg fish wt. (lbs.)	# per set	avg fish wt. (lbs.)
Black Crappie	-	-	trace	0.77
Bluegill	-	-	3.2	0.29
Common Shiner	0.1	0.14	-	-
Hybrid Sunfish	0.3	0.44	trace	0.48
Largemouth Bass	0.3	1.61	-	-
Northern Pike	1.7	2.33	trace	0.17
Pumpkin. Sunfish	0.8	0.29	0.5	0.34
Rock Bass	15.8	0.54	2.1	0.28
Tullibee (Cisco)	1.2	0.49	-	-
Walleye	11.1	1.93	trace	0.78
White Sucker	2.4	1.44	0.2	2.97
Yellow Bullhead	-	-	trace	1.19
Yellow Perch	16.0	0.20	1.1	0.21

LENGTH OF SELECTED SPECIES SAMPLED FROM ALL GEAR

Number of fish caught for the following length categories (inches):

species	0-5	6-8	9-11	12-14	15-19	20-24	25-29	>30	Total
Black Crappie	-	-	1	-	-	-	-	-	1
Bluegill	2	36	-	-	-	-	-	-	38
Hybrid Sunfish	-	4	-	-	-	-	-	-	4
Largemouth Bass	-	-	1	1	1	-	-	-	3
Northern Pike	-	1	2	1	3	6	3	-	16
Pumpkin. Sunfish	2	11	-	-	-	-	-	-	13
Rock Bass	20	64	64	-	-	-	-	-	148
Tullibee (Cisco)	-	1	6	4	-	-	-	-	11
Walleye	-	-	13	37	25	22	4	-	101
Yellow Bullhead	-	-	-	1	-	-	-	-	1
Yellow Perch	8	105	44	-	-	-	-	-	157

DNR COMMENTS: Walleye population strong and well above median value for lake class; mean size 16.6 inches and 1.9 lb.; fish to 28.7 inches captured. Northern Pike numbers below median value for lake class; mean size 19.9 inches and 2.3 lb. Largemouth Bass and Black Crappie captured in low numbers; samples too small for accurate population assessments. Yellow Perch numbers near lake class median; mean length 7.8 inches. Bluegills scarce, but mean size good at 7.2 inches. Rock Bass sampled in high numbers, and anglers report good catches with live bait. Ciscoes, White Suckers, Pumpkinseed and hybrid Sunfish also sampled, along with several minnow species.

FISHING INFORMATION: Siseebakwet Lake, also known as Sugar Lake, is one of the best Walleye lakes in the entire region. Its clear water holds some plump fish, including wall hangers. The key to catching marble eyes in Sugar, according to Ken Patterson, owner of Pokegama Sports in Grand Rapids, is night fishing. Shad Raps and other shallow-running crankbaits trolled along the shoreline or across the sunken islands can be very productive. Sugar's notoriety as a good night-fishing lake is creating some traffic after dark, so be sure that your boat's lights are in good working order. Daytime fishing for Walleye can be tough, but light line with small hooks and weights will produce fish; especially in low-light conditions and choppy water. Serious Bass anglers pull some nice Largemouth out of the lake. Pan-fish don't receive much attention, though.

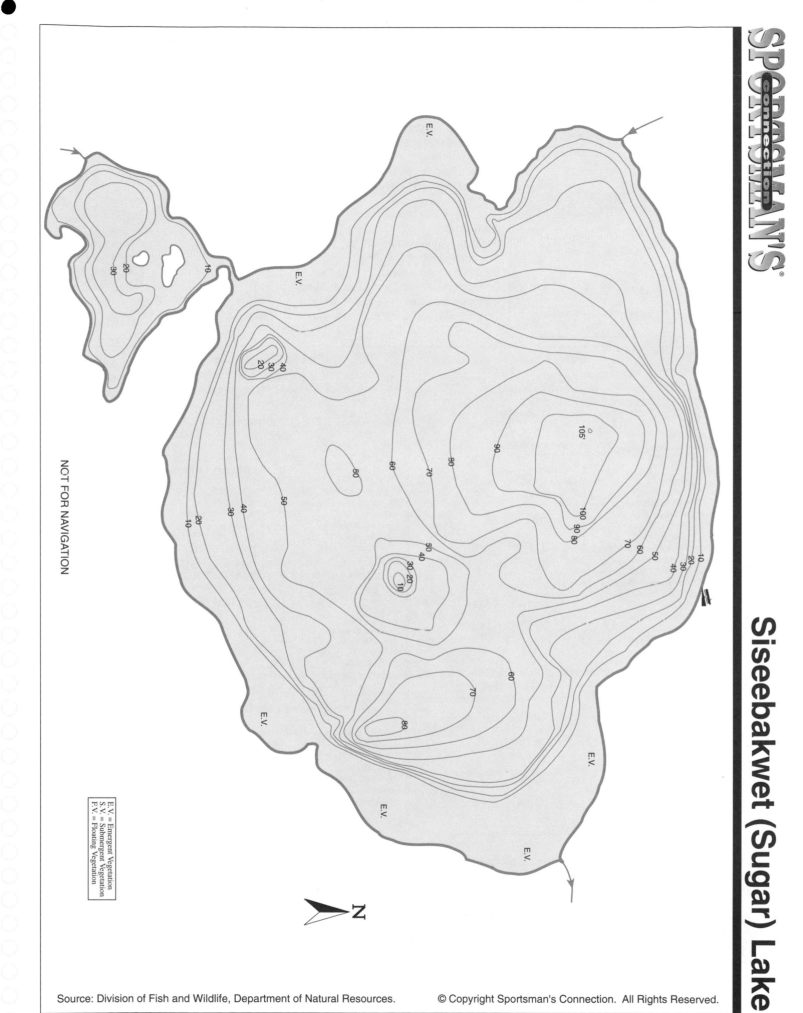

Siseebakwet (Sugar) Lake

NOT FOR NAVIGATION

E.V. = Emergent Vegetation
S.V. = Submergent Vegetation
F.V. = Floating Vegetation

N

Source: Division of Fish and Wildlife, Department of Natural Resources.

Location: Township 55 Range 26
Watershed: Mississippi Headwaters

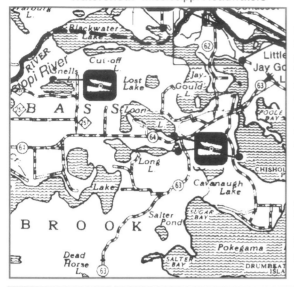

	LOON LAKE	SNELLS LAKE	LONG LAKE
	Itasca County		
Size of lake:	235 acres	86 acres	121 acres
Shorelength:	3.5 miles	1.1 miles	1.1 miles
Secchi disk (water clarity):	14.0 ft.	NA	13.0 ft.
Water color:	Clear	Green	Clear
Cause of water color:	NA	Algae bloom	NA
Maximum depth:	69.0 ft.	50.0 ft.	75.0 ft.
Median depth:	35.0 ft.	NA	9.0 ft.
Accessibility:	County-owned public access on east shore	County-owned access on the north-east shore	Public access on extreme east arm off Cty. Rd. 63
Boat Ramp:	Earth	Earth	Earth
Parking:	Adequate	Adequate	Adequate
Accommodations:	NA	NA	NA
Shoreland zoning classif.:	Rec. Dev.	Rec. Dev.	Nat. Envt.
Dominant forest/soil type:	Decid/Sand	NA	NA
Management class:	Walleye-Centrarchid	Centrarchid	Centrarchid
Ecological type:	Centrarchid	Centrarchid	Centrarchid

DNR COMMENTS: Northern Pike population near median levels. Walleyes scarce but increasing in number; Yellow Perch population could increase the numbers of Walleyes. Bluegill and Pumpkinseed populations above lake-class medians; growth slow. Largemouth Bass population increasing; many Bass seen in shallows during assessment. Yellow Perch population up to twice third-quartile values. Ciscoes well above lake class third-quartile levels. Bowfin more numerous, as well.

Loon Lake

FISH STOCKING DATA

year	species	size	# released
90	Walleye	Yearling	319

survey date: 06/08/92

NET CATCH DATA

	Gill Nets		Trap Nets	
		avg fish		avg fish
species	# per net	wt. (lbs)	# per set	wt. (lbs)
Yellow Perch	30.7	0.09	0.3	0.17
Yellow Bullhead	0.5	0.67	0.9	0.65
White Sucker	0.2	2.50	-	-
Walleye	0.3	1.70	-	-
Tullibee (incl. Cisco)	7.5	1.20	-	-
Rock Bass	0.5	0.23	0.9	0.28
Pumpkin. Sunfish	0.3	0.10	10.3	0.16
Northern Pike	4.0	2.33	-	-
Largemouth Bass	0.7	1.73	0.3	1.13
Brown Bullhead	0.2	0.40	0.2	0.30
Bluegill	2.5	0.07	57.3	0.13
Black Crappie	0.2	0.30	0.7	0.40
Hybrid Sunfish	-	-	1.0	0.13
Bowfin (Dogfish)	-	-	1.2	4.65

LENGTH OF SELECTED SPECIES SAMPLED FROM ALL GEAR
Number of fish caught for the following length categories (inches):

species	0-5	6-8	9-11	12-14	15-19	20-24	25-29	>30	Total
Yellow Perch	-	89	-	-	-	-	-	-	89
Yellow Bullhead	-	-	3	-	-	-	-	-	3
Walleye	-	-	-	1	-	1	-	-	2
Tullibee (incl. Cisco)	-	-	-	7	38	-	-	-	45
Rock Bass	2	2	2	-	-	-	-	-	6
Pumpkin. Sunfish	1	-	-	-	-	-	-	-	1
Northern Pike	-	-	-	5	16	3	-	-	24
Largemouth Bass	1	1	-	-	1	1	-	-	4
Brown Bullhead	-	-	1	-	-	-	-	-	1
Bluegill	14	1	-	-	-	-	-	-	15
Black Crappie	-	-	1	-	-	-	-	-	1

Snells (Giles) Lake

FISH STOCKING DATA: NO RECORD OF STOCKING

survey date: 07/19/89

NET CATCH DATA

	Gill Nets		Trap Nets	
		avg fish		avg fish
species	# per net	wt. (lbs)	# per set	wt. (lbs)
Walleye	0.3	5.90	-	-
Northern Pike	10.5	3.06	0.5	2.00
Largemouth Bass	0.3	3.90	-	-
Brown Bullhead	0.5	1.85	-	-
Bluegill	27.5	0.17	15.5	0.15
Black Crappie	0.3	0.30	-	-
Yellow Perch	-	-	0.5	0.20
Pumpkin. Sunfish	-	-	4.5	0.09

LENGTH OF SELECTED SPECIES SAMPLED FROM ALL GEAR
Number of fish caught for the following length categories (inches):

species	0-5	6-8	9-11	12-14	15-19	20-24	25-29	>30	Total
Walleye	-	-	-	-	-	-	1	-	1
Northern Pike	-	-	-	-	20	22	-	-	42
Largemouth Bass	-	-	-	1	-	-	-	-	1
Brown Bullhead	-	-	2	-	-	-	-	-	2
Bluegill	1	82	-	-	-	-	-	-	83
Black Crappie	-	1	-	-	-	-	-	-	1

DNR COMMENTS: Yellow Perch numbers have decreased drastically. Northern Pike much more numerous. Bluegill numbers up as well.

Long Lake

FISH STOCKING DATA: NO RECORD OF STOCKING

survey date: 08/03/77

NET CATCH DATA

	Gill Nets		Trap Nets	
		avg fish		avg fish
species	# per net	wt. (lbs)	# per set	wt. (lbs)
Yellow Bullhead	6.0	0.54	4.5	0.58
Pumpkin. Sunfish	5.7	0.13	7.3	0.41
Northern Pike	10.3	1.48	1.5	1.33
Largemouth Bass	0.7	1.50	0.3	4.00
Crappie	0.7	0.10	0.8	0.33
Brown Bullhead	2.3	0.57	2.0	0.53
Bowfin (Dogfish)	0.3	4.50	2.3	5.06
Bluegill	6.0	0.18	22.3	0.31
Rock Bass	-	-	0.3	0.50

LENGTH OF SELECTED SPECIES SAMPLED FROM ALL GEAR
Number of fish caught for the following length categories (inches):

species	0-5	6-8	9-11	12-14	15-19	20-24	25-29	>30	Total
Bluegill	3	83	4	-	-	-	-	-	90
Brown Bullhead	-	2	9	4	-	-	-	-	15
Crappie	-	4	1	-	-	-	-	-	5
Largemouth Bass	-	-	-	1	1	1	-	-	3
Northern Pike	-	-	-	1	20	12	1	-	34
Pumpkin. Sunfish	6	40	1	-	-	-	-	-	47
Rock Bass	-	-	1	-	-	-	-	-	1
Yellow Bullhead	-	2	23	11	-	-	-	-	36

DNR COMMENTS: Northern Pike and Bluegill populations at quite high levels. All other fish populations within normal limits for this type of lake.

FISHING INFORMATION: Mike Auger of Blue Horizon Guide Service says **Loon** and **Long Lake**s have Largemouth Bass in the 2- to 3-pound range and Crappies averaging about 1/2 to 3/4 pound. Crappie fishing is best from ice out until mid-July, he says, especially just before nightfall. Loon has been receiving Walleye stockings in even-numbered years, but we haven't heard about any being caught yet. **Snells**, aka Giles, yields good numbers and average sizes of Northern Pike, along with a few big Largemouth. Bluegills are thick, but most are small. Crappies are better, but less plentiful. There are some lunker Walleyes hiding out there somewhere, too.

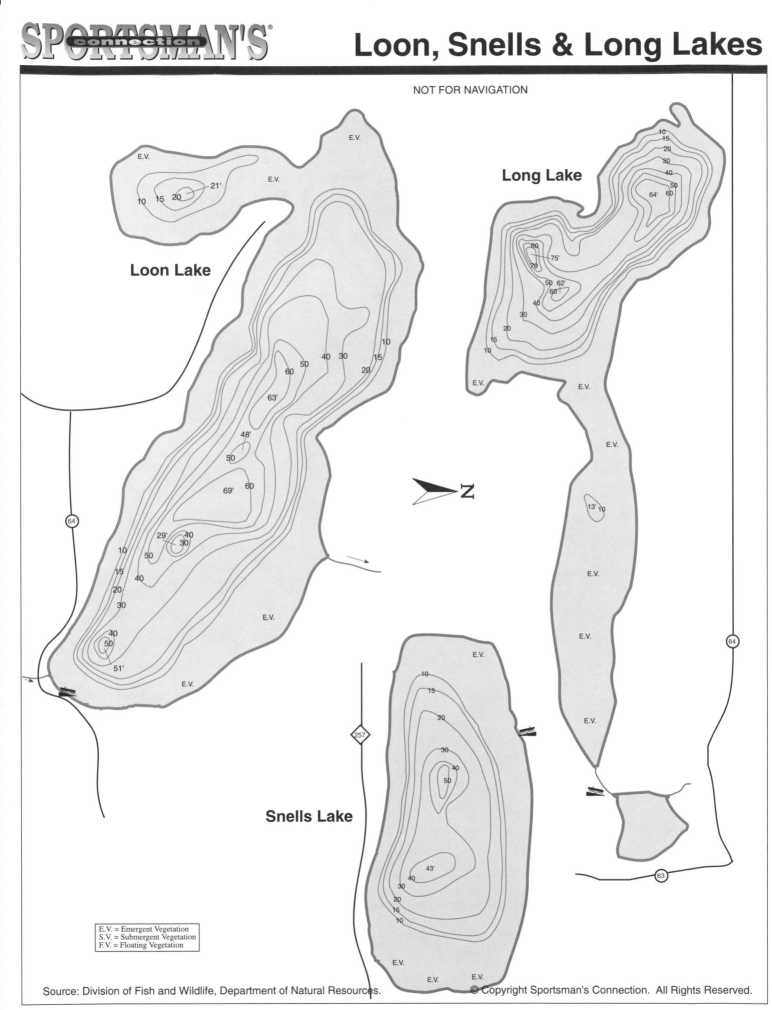

NOT FOR NAVIGATION

Long Lake

Loon Lake

N

Snells Lake

E.V. = Emergent Vegetation
S.V. = Submergent Vegetation
F.V. = Floating Vegetation

Source: Division of Fish and Wildlife, Department of Natural Resources.

BLANDIN RESERVOIR   JAY GOULD LAKE
Itasca County

Location: Township 55 Range 25, 26
Watershed: Prairie-Willow
Size of lake: 449 acres
Shorelength: 7.0 miles
Secchi disk (water clarity): 9.6 ft.
Water color: Amber
Cause of water color: Slight bog stain
Maximum depth: 44.0 ft.
Median depth: 20.0 ft.
Accessibility: County-owned public access on south shore, off CSAH #63 near bridge, also access on SE shore at Sylvan Bay
Boat Ramp: Earth; Concrete
Parking: Ample
Accommodations: County park
Shoreland zoning classif.: Gen. Dev.
Dominant forest/soil type: No tree/loam
Management class: Walleye-Centrarchid
Ecological type: Centrarchid

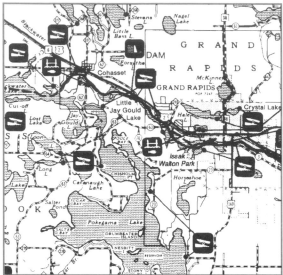

Location: Township 55 Range 25, 26
Watershed: Prairie-Willow
Size of lake: 426 acres
Shorelength: 5.0 miles
Secchi disk (water clarity): 10.0 ft.
Water color: Light green
Cause of water color: Algae
Maximum depth: 33.0 ft.
Median depth: NA
Accessibility: New access on south shore; access also on north shore of Blackwater Bay
Boat Ramp: Concrete (both)
Parking: Adequate
Accommodations: None
Shoreland zoning classif.: Rec. Dev.
Dominant forest/soil type: Decid/Sand
Management class: Walleye-Centrarchid
Ecological type: Centrarchid-Walleye

DNR COMMENTS:
Walleye population modest; stocking has had little impact on numbers of this species, as non-stocked year classes made up 64 percent of sample; good 1994 and 1995 year classes; average length 14 inches. Lake supports modest population of Leech Lake strain Muskellunge. Northern Pike numbers low; average weight 1.4 lb. Black Crappie, Bluegill and Largemouth Bass sampled in low numbers; Bluegill length range 3.5 to 8.3 inches.

FISH STOCKING DATA

year	species	size	# released
89	Walleye	Fingerling	6,088
89	Walleye	Yearling	699
91	Walleye	Fingerling	1,916
91	Walleye	Yearling	551
91	Walleye	Adult	31
91	Muskellunge	Fingerling	366
93	Walleye	Fingerling	8,264
94	Muskellunge	Fingerling	400

NET CATCH DATA
survey date: 8/13/96

	Gill Nets		Trap Nets	
species	# per net	avg fish wt. (lbs)	# per set	avg fish wt. (lbs)
Black Crappie	0.2	0.28	0.4	0.31
Bluegill	0.1	0.04	1.2	0.28
Bowfin (Dogfish)	0.3	5.02	0.2	3.36
Largemouth Bass	0.1	2.27	0.1	0.05
Northern Pike	1.6	1.37	1.0	0.76
Pumpkin. Sunfish	0.7	0.20	1.0	0.15
Rock Bass	4.8	0.28	0.2	0.64
Shorthead Redhorse	0.6	2.30	-	-
Silver Redhorse	0.2	2.81	-	-
Walleye	1.8	1.37	0.1	0.49
White Sucker	1.0	1.99	-	-
Yellow Bullhead	0.2	0.70	0.4	0.81
Yellow Perch	5.1	0.12	0.6	0.14

LENGTH OF SELECTED SPECIES SAMPLED FROM ALL GEAR
Number of fish caught for the following length categories (inches):

species	0-5	6-8	9-11	12-14	15-19	20-24	25-29	>30	Total
Black Crappie	-	6	-	-	-	-	-	-	6
Bluegill	5	7	-	-	-	-	-	-	12
Largemouth Bass	1	-	-	-	1	-	-	-	2
Northern Pike	-	-	2	4	13	2	-	1	22
Pumpkin. Sunfish	7	7	-	-	-	-	-	-	14
Rock Bass	21	15	9	-	-	-	-	-	45
Walleye	-	3	7	2	1	3	1	-	17
Yellow Bullhead	-	-	5	1	-	-	-	-	6
Yellow Perch	25	22	2	-	-	-	-	-	49

FISH STOCKING DATA

year	species	size	# released
90	Walleye	Fry	500,000
92	Walleye	Fry	425,000
94	Walleye	Fry	425,000

NET CATCH DATA
survey date: 8/4/97

	Gill Nets		Trap Nets	
species	# per net	avg fish wt. (lbs)	# per set	avg fish wt. (lbs)
Black Crappie	0.4	1.27	0.1	0.84
Bluegill	3.9	0.52	11.9	0.23
Brown Bullhead	3.1	1.58	0.4	1.03
Largemouth Bass	0.3	1.23	0.7	0.72
Muskellunge	0.1	4.40	-	-
Northern Pike	9.8	1.09	1.4	1.23
Pumpkin. Sunfish	0.5	0.09	3.7	0.14
Rock Bass	0.5	0.60	1.7	0.68
Smallmouth Bass	0.1	1.65	-	-
Tullibee (Cisco)	1.4	1.00	-	-
Walleye	4.6	1.63	-	-
Yellow Bullhead	0.1	0.89	3.4	0.98
Yellow Perch	22.9	0.15	7.3	0.22

LENGTH OF SELECTED SPECIES SAMPLED FROM ALL GEAR
Number of fish caught for the following length categories (inches):

species	0-5	6-8	9-11	12-14	15-19	20-24	25-29	>30	Total
Black Crappie	-	-	2	2	-	-	-	-	4
Bluegill	41	68	5	-	-	-	-	-	114
Brown Bullhead	-	1	1	26	-	-	-	-	28
Largemouth Bass	4	-	1	1	1	-	-	-	7
Muskellunge	-	-	-	-	-	-	1	-	1
Northern Pike	-	-	6	19	50	7	4	1	87
Pumpkin. Sunfish	23	6	-	-	-	-	-	-	29
Rock Bass	2	6	8	-	-	-	-	-	16
Smallmouth Bass	-	-	-	1	-	-	-	-	1
Tullibee (Cisco)	-	-	7	3	1	-	-	-	11
Walleye	-	1	4	12	12	7	1	-	37
Yellow Bullhead	2	-	11	12	-	-	-	-	25
Yellow Perch	115	84	25	1	-	-	-	-	225

DNR COMMENTS:
Walleye numbers up and above the typical range for lake class; mean size 15.9 inches and 1.6 lb.; growth rates above average for younger fish and near average for fish ages 3 and older; natural reproduction is apparently producing most of the population. Northern Pike numbers up but still within expected range; mean size 16.9 inches and 1.1 lb. Largemouth Bass numbers within expected range; size range 4.5 to 19.6 inches. Bluegill numbers typical for lake class; length range 3.1 to 9.1 inches.

FISHING INFORMATION: Blandin Reservoir, better known as Paper Mill Reservoir, has a reputation for big Muskies, according to Brian Krecklau of Pole Bender Guide Service and Mike Auger of Blue Horizon Guide Service. While the Muskies reach the 30- to 40-pound class, over-all Muskie numbers are low, compared to the populations of other Muskie waters in the area. Ken's Pokegama Sports weighed in a 33-pounder recently. Patrons talked about some excellent Largemouth Bass fishing on the reservoir. Walleye have been stocked with some success, and anglers' catches appear to be improving. Early ice is excellent for Crappie fishing, especially in Sylvan Bay, where some 1- to 1 1/2-pounders are taken. **Jay Gould** is also part of the Mississippi River flowage. Krecklau says he has caught some 15-pound-class Northerns and some decent Muskies there. Walleye are caught with some regularity, and Crappies run in the pound-plus range. Largemouth and Smallmouth can also be found.

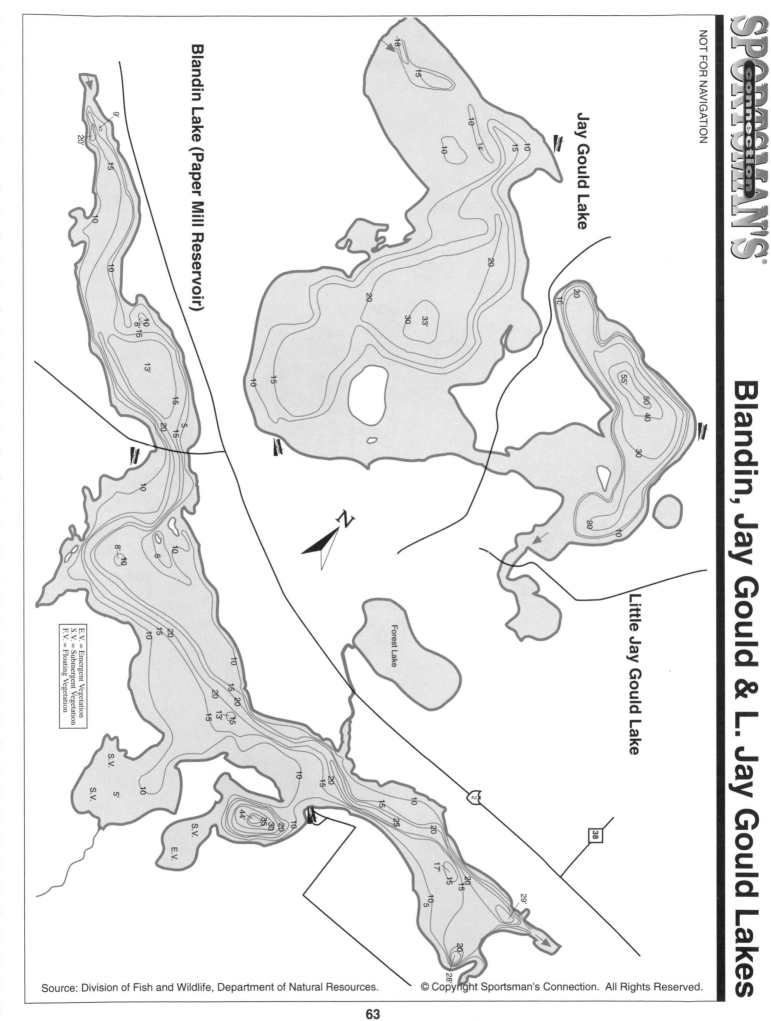

Blandin, Jay Gould & L. Jay Gould Lakes

Jay Gould Lake

Little Jay Gould Lake

Blandin Lake (Paper Mill Reservoir)

Forest Lake

E.V. = Emergent Vegetation
S.V. = Submergent Vegetation
F.V. = Floating Vegetation

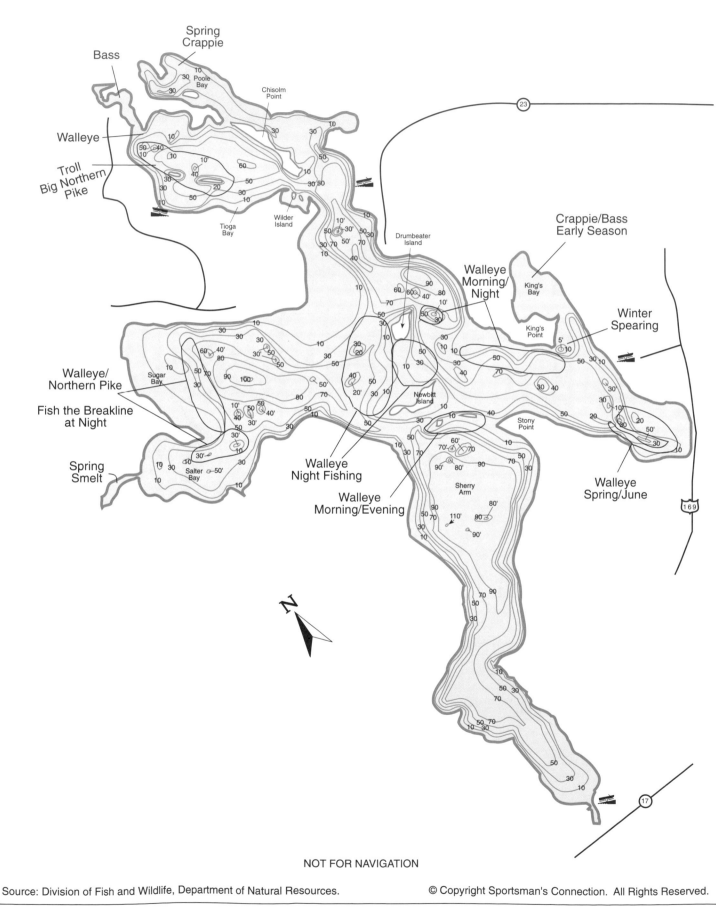

Spring Crappie

Bass

Walleye

Troll Big Northern Pike

Poole Bay

Chisolm Point

Tioga Bay

Wilder Island

Drumbeater Island

Crappie/Bass Early Season

King's Bay

Walleye Morning/ Night

King's Point

Winter Spearing

Walleye/ Northern Pike

Sugar Bay

Fish the Breakline at Night

Spring Smelt

Salter Bay

Newbitt Island

Walleye Night Fishing

Walleye Morning/Evening

Sherry Arm

Stony Point

Walleye Spring/June

N

NOT FOR NAVIGATION

Source: Division of Fish and Wildlife, Department of Natural Resources.

NOT FOR NAVIGATION

FISHING INFORMATION: Mike Auger, who operates the Blue Horizon Guide Service out of Ken's Pokegama Sports, lives on the lake and knows it like the back of his hand. He shared some of Pokegama's fish-holding hot spots with us while marking our map. The lake is full of steep drops with more structure than any other lake in the area and weeds just about

the west of the island (see map - "Walleye summer 17-ft. breakline") that is good for summer Walleye. The flat between Nesbitt Island and Drumbeater Island is poor during the day because of recreational boat traffic, but night fishing with a weedless jig and minnow or a Rapala can be very productive. Walleyes can be found just about anywhere along

caught. Fish the weedlines throughout the lake, trolling Rapalas or using bright jigs in the afternoon. Some big Pike are caught downrigging to 30 feet, where the thermocline and Smelt can be found. Sometimes, Lakers in the 8- to12-pound range are picked up while Northern fishing this way. Crappies are nice with some 1 1/2-

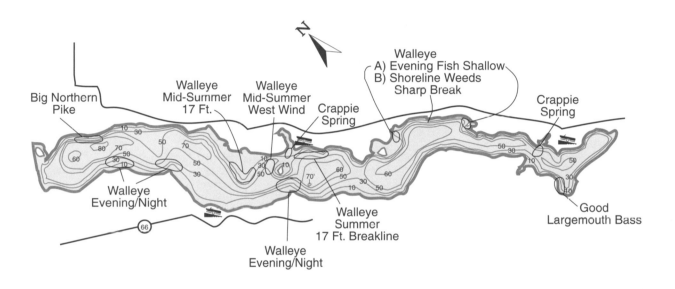

everywhere. The Walleyes seem to key on the 17-foot depth, according to Mike, because that is where the weedline breaks. Due to the lake's clear water and recreational boating, night fishing is best. Fish the shallows in the evenings. The island down in Wendigo Arm is good when there is a west wind, especially in the summer. The maps don't show it but there is a 17-foot breakline in the deep water to

the whole shoreline but the steep breaks are tough. Find the gradual breaklines and start out in the evening in about 17 to 18 feet, moving up into the flats as night falls. A lot of the Walleyes you catch at night run between 2 and 4 pounds. There are also some lunkers taken then. Mike says he caught a 12 1/2-pounder a while back. Northern Pike in the 10-pound class are not uncommon, and some 20- to 25-pounders are

pound slabs being present. Pokegama has a good Smallmouth population and is underestablished as a Largemouth Bass fishery. There are many fish in the 3- to 6-pound range. Try the Largemouth in the evening by working the cabbage beds at 17 feet with jigs and worms or spinnerbaits. Pokegama even has an annual Smelt run up from Salter Bay.

(Please turn page for lake data).

POKEGAMA LAKE
Itasca County

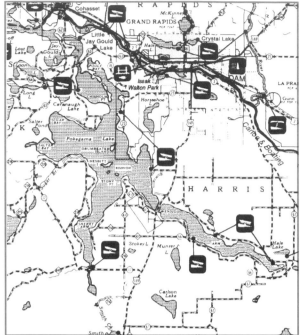

Location: Township 54, 55
Range 25, 26
Watershed: Mississippi Headwaters
Size of lake: 6,612 acres
Shorelength: 50.8 miles
Secchi disk (water clarity): 14.8 ft.
Water color: Clear
Cause of water color: NA

Maximum depth: 110.0 ft.
Median depth: NA
Accessibility: See below (*)
Boat Ramps: Concrete; Earth
Parking: Ample
Accommodations: Resorts, campground

*Accessibility: Access off Hwy. 17 on south shore; off Hwy. 23 on east shore; off Hwy. 169 on east shore; at Tioga Beach on northwest shore; also three accesses on Wendigo Arm

Shoreland zoning classification: General Development
Dominant forest/soil type: NA
Management class: Walleye-Centrarchid
Ecological type: Centrarchid-Walleye

FISH STOCKING DATA

year	species	size	# released
90	Walleye	Fingerling	7,395
90	Walleye	Yearling	6,235
91	Lake Trout	Yearling	25,000
92	Walleye	Fingerling	36,814
92	Walleye	Yearling	54
94	Walleye	Fingerling	15,098
97	Lake Trout	Yearling	1,529
97	Lake Trout	Adult	342

NET CATCH DATA

survey date: 7/31/95

species	Gill Nets # per net	Gill Nets avg fish wt. (lbs.)	Trap Nets # per set	Trap Nets avg fish wt. (lbs.)
Black Crappie	trace	0.57	0.2	0.08
Bluegill	0.9	0.21	15.3	0.20
Bowfin (Dogfish)	trace	5.35	0.5	6.14
Brown Bullhead	0.1	1.04	trace	1.06
Lake Whitefish	trace	2.43	-	-
Largemouth Bass	0.1	0.32	0.4	1.70
Northern Pike	6.6	2.67	0.7	3.02
Pumpkin. Sunfish	1.8	0.13	1.9	0.14
Rainbow Smelt	0.3	0.05	-	-
Rock Bass	8.4	0.36	5.5	0.27
Smallmouth Bass	0.6	2.09	-	-
Tullibee (Cisco)	trace	1.10	-	-
Walleye	9.2	2.81	0.4	1.83
White Sucker	0.9	2.14	0.2	1.29
Yellow Bullhead	2.2	0.70	0.7	0.52
Yellow Perch	37.8	0.10	6.7	0.12

LENGTH OF SELECTED SPECIES SAMPLED FROM ALL GEAR
Number of fish caught for the following length categories (inches):

species	0-5	6-8	9-11	12-14	15-19	20-24	25-29	>30	Total
Black Crappie	3	-	1	-	-	-	-	-	4
Bluegill	60	121	-	-	-	-	-	-	181
Brown Bullhead	-	-	-	3	-	-	-	-	3
Lake Whitefish	-	-	-	-	1	-	-	-	1
Largemouth Bass	2	3	1	-	2	-	-	-	8
Northern Pike	-	-	1	6	25	47	20	4	103
Pumpkin. Sunfish	41	12	-	-	-	-	-	-	53
Rock Bass	40	113	21	1	-	-	-	-	175
Smallmouth Bass	-	-	-	5	4	-	-	-	9
Tullibee (Cisco)	-	-	-	1	-	-	-	-	1
Walleye	1	5	3	8	66	47	5	-	135
Yellow Bullhead	-	9	29	3	1	-	-	-	42
Yellow Perch	149	191	13	-	-	-	-	-	353

DNR COMMENTS: Walleye gill net catch rate the highest on record for this lake, but still within expected range for lake class; mean size large at 19.1 inches and 2.8 lb.; growth good; some natural reproduction is taking place. Northern Pike numbers within expected range for lake class; length range from 11.3 to 35.9 inches; growth good. Smallmouth Bass numbers typical of lake class; good average size of 15 inches and 1.3 lb.; growth good. Largemouth Bass sampled in low numbers; length range 12.2 to 18.7 inches; growth good. Black Crappie numbers continue to be low. Bluegill population up considerably for no apparent reason; length range 3.9 to 8.4 inches. Yellow Perch numbers slightly above expected range for lake class. Cisco numbers have been failing in recent years, and the 1995 catch rate is lowest on record for this lake; competition from Smelt could be harming the population. Other species sampled include Bowfin, Brown and Yellow Bullhead, Lake Whitefish, Pumpkinseed, Rock Bass, White Sucker and Smelt.

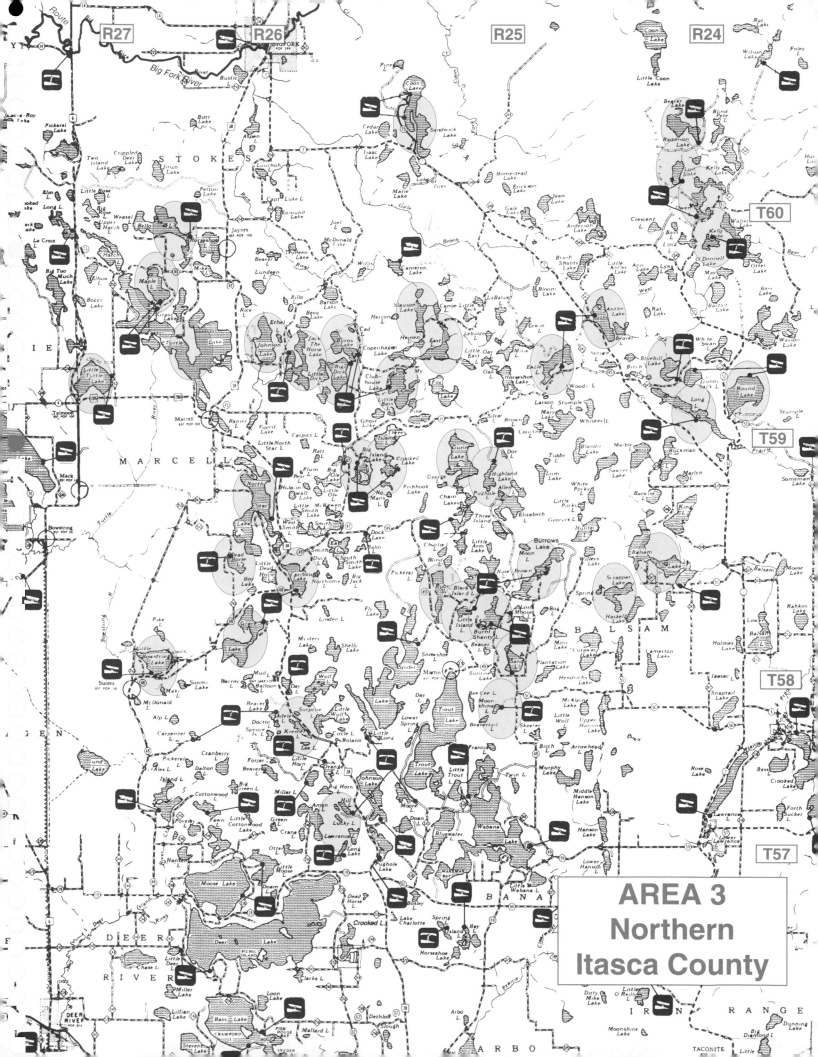

AREA 3
Northern
Itasca County

GRAVE LAKE   LITTLE BOWSTRING LAKE

Itasca County

Location: Township 58 Range 27
Watershed: Big Fork
Size of lake: 500 acres
Shorelength: 7.5 miles
Secchi disk (water clarity): 8.5 ft.
Water color: Greenish-brown
Cause of water color: Algae
Maximum depth: 39.0 ft.
Median depth: 16.2 ft.
Accessibility: State-owned public access on east shore of north basin
Boat Ramp: Concrete
Parking: Ample
Accommodations: None
Shoreland zoning classif.: Rec./Dev.
Dominant forest/soil type: Decid/Loam
Management class: Walleye-Centrarchid
Ecological type: Centrarchid-Walleye

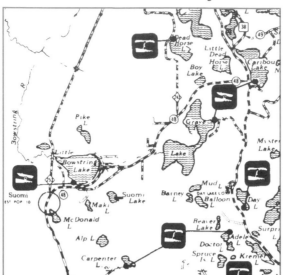

Location: Township 58 Range 27
Watershed: Big Fork
Size of lake: 319 acres
Shorelength: 2.5 miles
Secchi disk (water clarity): 3.9 ft.
Water color: Brownish
Cause of water color: Bog stain and algae bloom
Maximum depth: 33.0 ft.
Median depth: 20.0 ft.
Accessibility: County-owned public access on south shore, off Cty. Rd. 48
Boat Ramp: Earth
Parking: Ample
Accommodations: Resort
Shoreland zoning classif.: Rec/Dev
Dominant forest/soil type: Decid/Loam
Management class: Walleye
Ecological type: Hard-water Walleye

DNR COMMENTS:
Walleye numbers about typical for lake class; mean size 16.7 inches and 1.7 lb.; some natural reproduction of this species. Northern Pike numbers above average for lake class, but mean size below average. Largemouth Bass numbers appear low. Bluegill numbers below mean for lake class; mean length 6.2 inches; growth good. Yellow perch numbers above average for lake class; mean length 6.3 inches.

FISH STOCKING DATA

year	species	size	# released
89	Walleye	Fingerling	3,814
91	Walleye	Fingerling	2,318
97	Walleye	Fry	500,000

NET CATCH DATA

survey date: 8/15/94

	Gill Nets		Trap Nets	
		avg fish		avg fish
species	# per net	wt. (lbs)	# per set	wt. (lbs)
Black Crappie	0.3	0.52	0.1	0.06
Bluegill	4.4	0.32	3.2	0.20
Bowfin (Dogfish)	0.2	7.69	0.2	5.40
Brown Bullhead	0.3	1.26	0.2	1.08
Hybrid Sunfish	0.4	0.57	0.1	0.45
Largemouth Bass	0.1	1.68	-	-
Northern Pike	9.3	1.45	1.6	1.35
Pumpkin. Sunfish	0.2	0.28	0.3	0.26
Rock Bass	1.1	0.59	0.8	0.15
Tullibee (Cisco)	0.3	1.03	-	-
Walleye	3.4	1.74	-	-
White Sucker	0.2	1.55	-	-
Yellow Perch	33.9	0.11	3.6	0.11

LENGTH OF SELECTED SPECIES SAMPLED FROM ALL GEAR
Number of fish caught for the following length categories (inches):

species	0-5	6-8	9-11	12-14	15-19	20-24	25-29	>30	Total
Black Crappie	2	-	2	-	-	-	-	-	4
Bluegill	23	44	2	-	-	-	-	-	69
Brown Bullhead	-	1	1	3	-	-	-	-	5
Hybrid Sunfish	-	5	-	-	-	-	-	-	5
Largemouth Bass	-	-	-	1	-	-	-	-	1
Northern Pike	-	-	1	10	52	34	1	-	98
Pumpkin. Sunfish	1	4	-	-	-	-	-	-	5
Rock Bass	7	6	4	-	-	-	-	-	17
Tullibee (Cisco)	-	1	-	1	1	-	-	-	3
Walleye	1	-	-	6	20	4	-	-	31
Yellow Perch	117	127	3	-	-	-	-	-	247

FISH STOCKING DATA

year	species	size	# released
89	Walleye	Fry	350,000
91	Walleye	Fry	960,000
93	Walleye	Fry	960,000
95	Walleye	Fry	960,000
97	Walleye	Fry	960,000

NET CATCH DATA

survey date: 8/28/95

	Gill Nets		Trap Nets	
		avg fish		avg fish
species	# per net	wt. (lbs)	# per set	wt. (lbs)
Black Crappie	0.1	0.05	0.6	0.08
Bluegill	0.1	0.68	1.6	0.36
Bowfin (Dogfish)	-	-	0.4	4.03
Brown Bullhead	-	-	0.8	1.08
Hybrid Sunfish	-	-	0.1	0.57
Northern Pike	6.1	1.78	0.6	1.03
Pumpkin. Sunfish	-	-	0.7	0.15
Rock Bass	-	-	0.8	0.36
Tullibee (Cisco)	2.5	1.04	-	-
Walleye	6.4	1.26	0.4	1.07
White Sucker	3.9	1.55	1.6	2.03
Yellow Bullhead	-	-	0.1	0.44
Yellow Perch	95.3	0.26	4.4	0.17

LENGTH OF SELECTED SPECIES SAMPLED FROM ALL GEAR
Number of fish caught for the following length categories (inches):

species	0-5	6-8	9-11	12-14	15-19	20-24	25-29	>30	Total
Black Crappie	6	-	-	-	-	-	-	-	6
Bluegill	2	11	2	-	-	-	-	-	15
Brown Bullhead	-	-	2	5	-	-	-	-	7
Hybrid Sunfish	-	1	-	-	-	-	-	-	1
Northern Pike	-	-	-	4	27	21	2	-	54
Pumpkin. Sunfish	3	3	-	-	-	-	-	-	6
Rock Bass	2	4	1	-	-	-	-	-	7
Tullibee (Cisco)	-	1	2	14	3	-	-	-	20
Walleye	-	-	22	10	15	8	-	-	55
Yellow Bullhead	-	1	-	-	-	-	-	-	1
Yellow Perch	50	152	52	-	-	-	-	-	254

DNR COMMENTS:
Walleye population above expected range for lake class; mean length 14.6 inches; growth about average. Northern Pike numbers within expected range; mean size 20.1 inches and 1.8 lb.; growth average. Largemouth Bass sampled during shoreline seining. Black Crappie and Bluegill numbers low; Bluegill mean size good, however, at 7.2 inches. Yellow Perch numerous; mean length 7.9 inches. Cisco numbers highest on record for this lake, but still within expected range for lake class.

FISHING INFORMATION: Grave Lake (sometimes referred to as Graves Lake) is home of the 2-pound Bluegill, according to Don Wendt, owner of Rapids Tackle in Grand Rapids. Several pound-plus 'gills take honors in the Fisherman's Blue Book every year. Walleye are also caught with some regularity; 1 1/2- to 2-pounders are typical. As with most of the lakes in the area, Northern Pike and Largemouth Bass are present in Grave, although the majority of those caught run on the small side. **Little Bowstring** doesn't receive much attention, but it also has some nice 'gills and Crappies. And it's a good lake to try for lunker Largemouth Bass. Walleye fishing can be good, if not spectacular, with average sizes being similar to those in Grave. Little Bowstring is somewhat bowl-shaped without a lot of structure, but there are some underwater islands and steep drops worth trying.

NOT FOR NAVIGATION

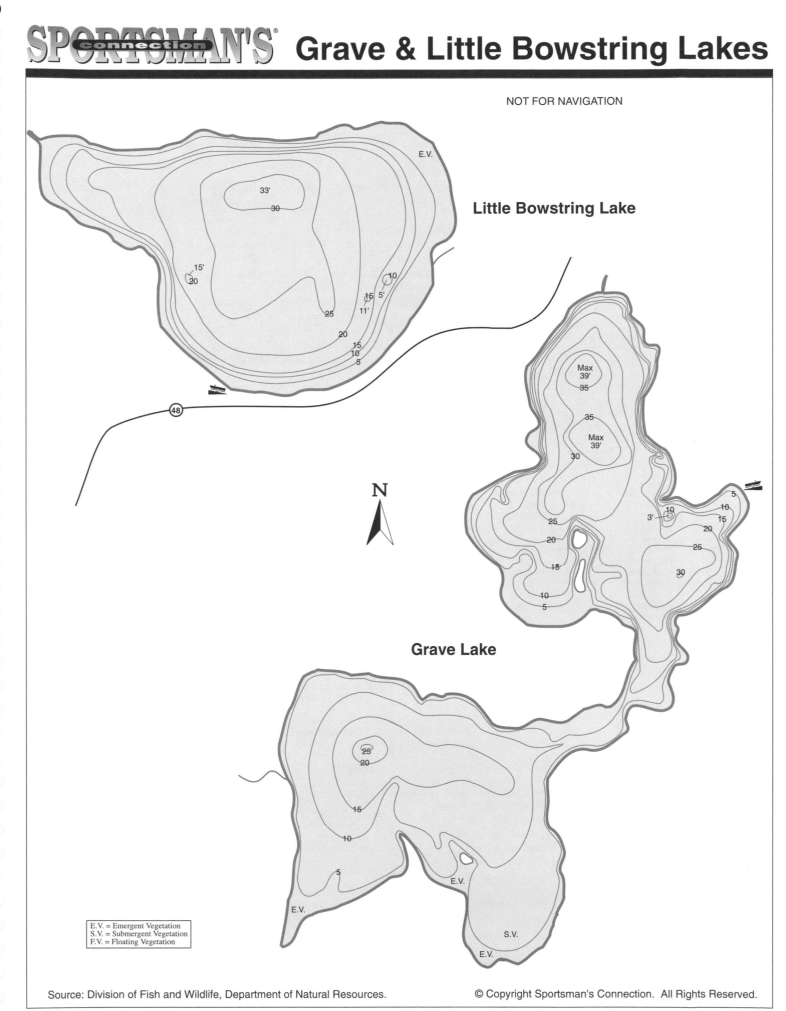

Little Bowstring Lake

Grave Lake

E.V. = Emergent Vegetation
S.V. = Submergent Vegetation
F.V. = Floating Vegetation

Source: Division of Fish and Wildlife, Department of Natural Resources.

Location: Township 58   Range 25
Watershed: Bigfork

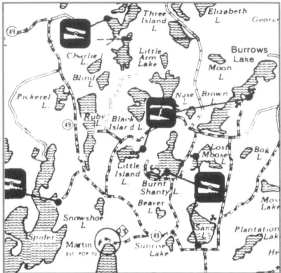

Itasca County

	RUBY LAKE	LITTLE ISLAND LAKE	BURNT SHANTY LAKE
Size of lake:	243 acres	61 acres	182 acres
Shorelength:	3.8 miles	1.9 miles	3.3 miles
Secchi disk (water clarity):	21.0 ft.	15.0 ft.	13.5 ft.
Water color:	Clear	Blue-green	Light green
Cause of water color:	NA	Algae	Algae bloom
Maximum depth:	88.0 ft.	35.0 ft.	33.0 ft.
Median depth:	25.0 ft.	7.0 ft.	15.0 ft.
Accessibility:	USFS-owned public access on east shore	State-owned access on east shore	State-owned access on south shore, off Cty. Rd. 49
Boat Ramp:	Carry-down	Carry-down	Concrete
Parking:	Limited	Limited	Adequate
Accommodations:	None	Resort	Outhouses
Shoreland zoning classif.:	Rec. Dev.	Nat. Envt.	Rec. Dev.
Dominant forest/soil type:	Decid/Loam	NA	Decid/Loam
Management class:	Walleye-Centrarchid	Centrarchid	Centrarchid
Ecological type:	Centrarchid-Walleye	Centrarchid	Centrarchid

DNR COMMENTS:
Walleye population highest on record and above expected range for lake class; mean size 15.8 inches and 1.5 lb.; growth above average; natural reproduction contributing the majority of population. Smallmouth Bass captured in low numbers. Largemouth Bass numbers within expected range; length range 7 to 20.1 inches. Northern Pike numbers above expected range; mean size 24 inches and 3.5 lb.; fish to 39.4 inches present. Bluegill numbers within expected range. Black Crappies Rock Bass, and Ciscoes present.

Ruby Lake

FISH STOCKING DATA

year	species	size	# released
91	Walleye	Fingerling	17
91	Walleye	Adult	98
93	Walleye	Fingerling	900
95	Walleye	Fingerling	330
97	Walleye	Fingerling	800

NET CATCH DATA
survey date: 6/17/96

	Gill Nets		Trap Nets	
		avg fish		avg fish
species	# per net	wt. (lbs)	# per set	wt. (lbs)
Bluegill	0.3	0.13	9.1	0.19
Largemouth Bass	0.3	0.30	1.0	0.86
Northern Pike	9.0	3.49	1.9	1.03
Rock Bass	0.8	0.23	0.7	0.16
Smallmouth Bass	0.3	3.96	-	-
Tullibee (Cisco)	6.5	0.41	-	-
Walleye	7.8	1.54	-	-
White Sucker	5.2	2.25	-	-
Yellow Perch	5.0	0.15	1.6	0.17

LENGTH OF SELECTED SPECIES SAMPLED FROM ALL GEAR
Number of fish caught for the following length categories (inches):

species	0-5	6-8	9-11	12-14	15-19	20-24	25-29	>30	Total
Bluegill	31	46	-	-	-	-	-	-	77
Largemouth Bass	-	7	3	-	-	1	-	-	11
Northern Pike	-	-	7	7	7	26	13	7	67
Rock Bass	3	8	-	-	-	-	-	-	11
Smallmouth Bass	-	-	-	-	2	-	-	-	2
Tullibee (Cisco)	-	11	11	10	-	-	-	-	32
Walleye	-	2	5	18	11	11	-	-	47
Yellow Perch	9	31	3	-	-	-	-	-	43

Little Island Lake

FISH STOCKING DATA: NO RECORD OF STOCKING

NET CATCH DATA
survey date: 06/25/79

	Gill Nets		Trap Nets	
		avg fish		avg fish
species	# per net	wt. (lbs)	# per set	wt. (lbs)
Yellow Perch	49.0	0.12	0.3	0.20
Yellow Bullhead	5.0	0.30	12.8	0.25
White Sucker	0.5	3.00	-	-
Pumpkin. Sunfish	3.0	0.13	46.0	0.11
Northern Pike	5.5	3.09	0.5	0.75
Bluegill	14.5	0.10	136.8	0.12
Black Crappie	3.5	0.46	12.5	0.18
Largemouth Bass	-	-	2.3	0.50

LENGTH OF SELECTED SPECIES SAMPLED FROM ALL GEAR
Number of fish caught for the following length categories (inches):

species	0-5	6-8	9-11	12-14	15-19	20-24	25-29	>30	Total
Black Crappie	-	29	14	1	-	-	-	-	44
Bluegill	1	53	-	-	-	-	-	-	54
Largemouth Bass	-	1	5	2	-	-	-	-	8
Northern Pike	-	-	-	3	7	3	1	-	14
Pumpkin. Sunfish	8	25	-	-	-	-	-	-	33
Yellow Bullhead	-	9	33	-	-	-	-	-	42
Yellow Perch	-	26	-	-	-	-	-	-	26

DNR COMMENTS:
Perch, Bluegill and Crappie populations are considerably higher than state and local medians. All other fish populations are within normal limits for this type of lake.

Burnt Shanty Lake

FISH STOCKING DATA: NO RECORD OF STOCKING

NET CATCH DATA
survey date: 08/30/89

	Gill Nets		Trap Nets	
		avg fish		avg fish
species	# per net	wt. (lbs)	# per set	wt. (lbs)
Yellow Perch	1.0	0.28	-	-
Yellow Bullhead	92.0	0.27	5.8	0.34
Pumpkin. Sunfish	6.5	0.18	1.5	0.17
Northern Pike	12.5	2.88	0.3	1.00
Largemouth Bass	1.0	0.90	-	-
Bluegill	60.3	0.21	17.3	0.19
Black Crappie	9.5	0.36	0.5	0.30

LENGTH OF SELECTED SPECIES SAMPLED FROM ALL GEAR
Number of fish caught for the following length categories (inches):

species	0-5	6-8	9-11	12-14	15-19	20-24	25-29	>30	Total
Yellow Perch	-	2	2	-	-	-	-	-	4
Yellow Bullhead	-	45	54	1	-	-	-	-	100
Pumpkin. Sunfish	8	17	1	-	-	-	-	-	26
Northern Pike	-	-	-	12	16	18	2	-	48
Largemouth Bass	-	-	3	1	-	-	-	-	4
Bluegill	5	140	3	-	-	-	-	-	148
Black Crappie	-	17	20	1	-	-	-	-	38

DNR COMMENTS:
Extremely high numbers of Yellow Bullheads. Black Crappie and Bluegill are abundant. Northern Pike size and abundance are very good. Some 200,000 Walleye fry were stocked in 1986, but no Walleyes were caught in the nets, or reported taken by fishermen.

FISHING INFORMATION: If you want a change of pace from some of the larger, more famous lakes along Scenic Highway 38, drop your canoe or small boat into one of these gems. **Ruby** 's deep, clear water makes for tough fishing which, along with the Perch and Cisco forage base, contributes to the lake's large Northern and Walleye. Anglers can also find some nice Smallmouth and Largemouth Bass in Ruby. As in other clear-water lakes, early-morning and evening fishing with light line and small hooks work best. **Burnt Shanty** is a very good Largemouth Bass lake, according to Brian Krecklau of the Pole Bender Guide Service in Grand Rapids. He says there are good numbers and some 5-pound-class fish present. Decent-size Northern Pike and a healthy panfish population also provide good action. **Little Island Lake** is also a Bass, Northern, panfish lake that yields a few decent Largemouth.

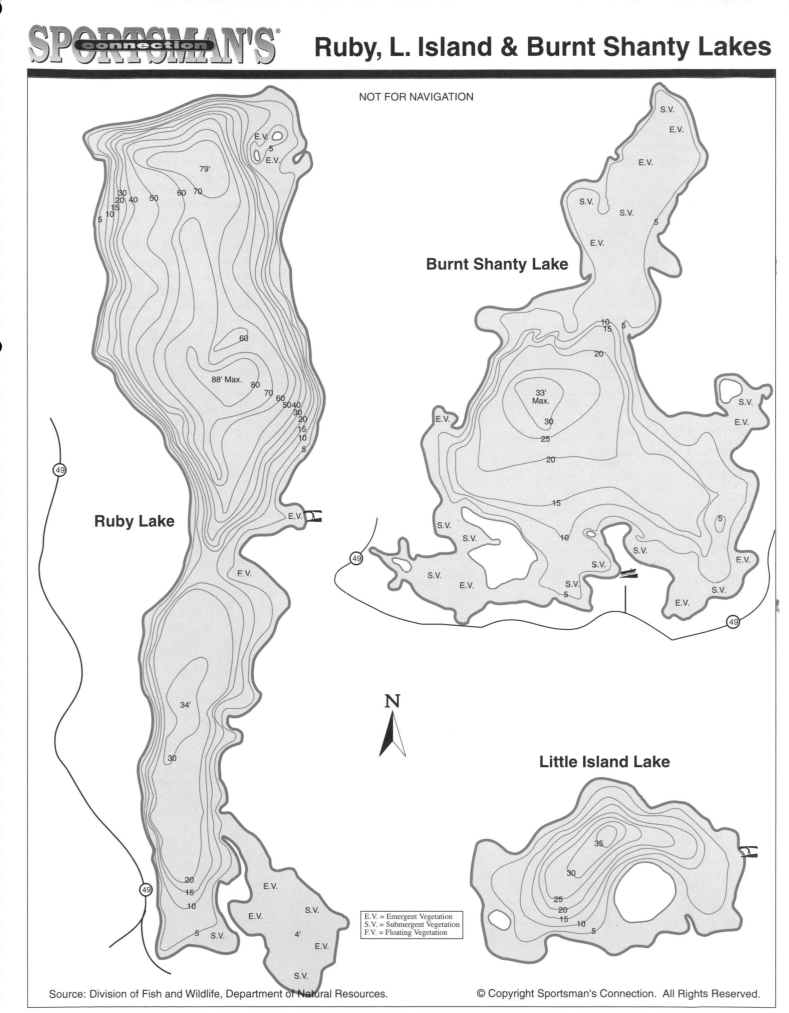

Ruby, L. Island & Burnt Shanty Lakes

NOT FOR NAVIGATION

Burnt Shanty Lake

Ruby Lake

Little Island Lake

E.V. = Emergent Vegetation
S.V. = Submergent Vegetation
F.V. = Floating Vegetation

BURROWS LAKE

Location: Township 58   Range 25
Watershed: Prairie-Willow
Size of lake: 291 acres
Shorelength: 6.4 miles
Secchi disk (water clarity): 12.9 ft.
Water color: Clear
Cause of water color: NA
Maximum depth: 36.0 ft.
Median depth: 15.0 ft.
Accessibility: State-owned public access on east shore, off Co. Rd. 53
Boat Ramp: Carry-down
Parking: Limited
Accommodations: None
Shoreland zoning classif.: Rec. Dev.
Dominant forest/soil type: NA
Management class: Walleye-Centrarchid
Ecological type: Centrarchid-Walleye

Itasca County

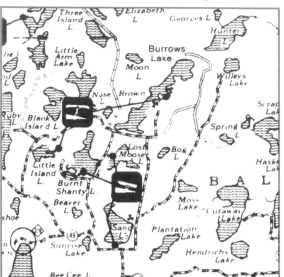

SAND LAKE

Location: Township 58   Range 25
Watershed: Prairie-Willow
Size of lake: 157 acres
Shorelength: 2.6 miles
Secchi disk (water clarity): 16.0 ft.
Water color: Clear
Cause of water color: NA
Maximum depth: 53.0 ft.
Median depth: 20.0 ft.
Accessibility: State-owned public access on south shore
Boat Ramp: Earth
Parking: Limited
Accommodations: None
Shoreland zoning classif.: Rec. Dev.
Dominant forest/soil type: Decid/Loam
Management class: Centrarchid
Ecological type: Centrarchid

DNR COMMENTS:
Walleye population highest since 1975; most fish from stocked year classes. Largemouth Bass number down; sample included only a few young-of-year fish. Black Crappie catch rate lowest on record for this lake; mean length 7.1 inches. Bluegill numbers moderate, but mean length only 5.7 inches. Yellow Perch population stable; mean length 6.5 inches.

FISH STOCKING DATA

year	species	size	# released
90	Walleye	Fingerling	5,200
96	Walleye	Fry	225,000

NET CATCH DATA

survey date: 7/11/94

	Gill Nets		Trap Nets	
species	# per net	avg fish wt. (lbs)	# per set	avg fish wt. (lbs)
Black Crappie	-	-	0.6	0.21
Bluegill	0.2	0.33	12.0	0.13
Golden Shiner	0.2	0.07	-	-
Northern Pike	7.0	1.77	0.9	0.99
Walleye	3.7	1.56	0.4	1.71
White Sucker	3.3	1.47	0.3	3.14
Yellow Perch	7.8	0.10	0.2	0.11

LENGTH OF SELECTED SPECIES SAMPLED FROM ALL GEAR
Number of fish caught for the following length categories (inches):

species	0-5	6-8	9-11	12-14	15-19	20-24	25-29	>30	Total
Black Crappie	1	4	-	-	-	-	-	-	5
Bluegill	73	35	-	-	-	-	-	-	108
Northern Pike	-	-	6	14	10	14	4	1	49
Walleye	-	2	1	4	17	2	-	-	26
Yellow Perch	6	42	-	-	-	-	-	-	48

DNR COMMENTS:
Northern Pike population at very high levels and Perch numbers are low.

FISH STOCKING DATA

year	species	size	# released
90	Walleye	Fry	175,000

NET CATCH DATA

survey date: 07/23/86

	Gill Nets		Trap Nets	
species	# per net	avg fish wt. (lbs)	# per set	avg fish wt. (lbs)
Yellow Perch	3.4	0.17	-	-
White Sucker	1.6	1.53	-	-
Walleye	2.2	2.32	-	-
Rock Bass	2.4	1.08	2.3	0.67
Pumpkin. Sunfish	0.8	0.35	-	-
Northern Pike	12.4	1.71	1.3	1.00
Largemouth Bass	0.2	1.10	0.3	0.20
Bluegill	2.6	0.32	11.3	0.18
Black Crappie	0.2	0.30	0.3	0.40

LENGTH OF SELECTED SPECIES SAMPLED FROM ALL GEAR
Number of fish caught for the following length categories (inches):

species	0-5	6-8	9-11	12-14	15-19	20-24	25-29	>30	Total
Black Crappie	-	2	-	-	-	-	-	-	2
Bluegill	26	30	3	-	-	-	-	-	59
Largemouth Bass	-	1	-	1	-	-	-	-	2
Northern Pike	-	-	2	11	30	24	1	1	69
Pumpkin. Sunfish	-	4	-	-	-	-	-	-	4
Rock Bass	1	4	12	5	-	-	-	-	22
Walleye	-	-	2	1	5	2	1	-	11
Yellow Perch	-	16	1	-	-	-	-	-	17

FISHING INFORMATION: Burrows Lake is off the beaten path and doesn't receive a lot of pressure. Some of the locals do pull some plump 2- to 3-pound Walleyes from the lake which has been receiving regular stocking in even-numbered years. Northern Pike and Largemouth Bass fishing can be very good at times. Panfish tend to run on the small side. **Sand Lake** received Walleye fry via DNR stocking in 1990. This effort has provided anglers with some catches. Largemouth Bass fishing is pretty good, and if you can get past the hammerhandles, there are some good-size Northern Pike to be had. Panfish are plentiful, but most are small.

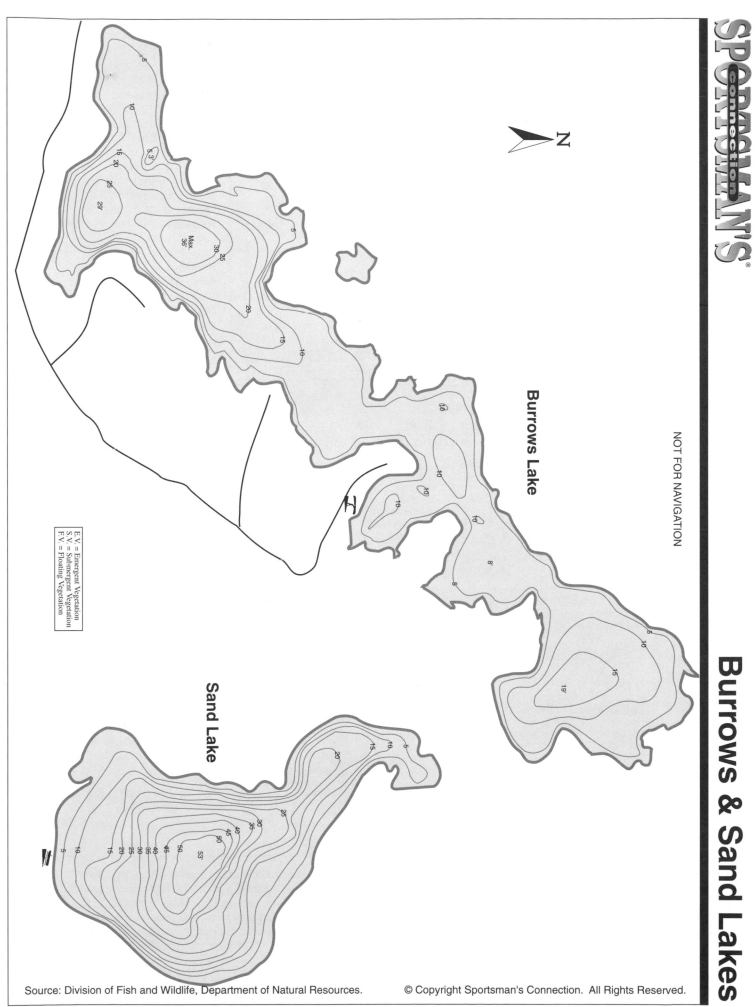

Burrows & Sand Lakes

N

NOT FOR NAVIGATION

Burrows Lake

Sand Lake

E.V. = Emergent Vegetation
S.V. = Submergent Vegetation
F.V. = Floating Vegetation

Max. 36'

29'

19'

53'

BALSAM LAKE

SCRAPPER LAKE

Itasca County

Location: Township 58, 59 Range 24, 25
Watershed: Prairie-Willow
Size of lake: 710 acres
Shorelength: 9.1 miles
Secchi disk (water clarity): 7.5 ft.
Water color: Light green
Cause of water color: Light algae bloom
Maximum depth: 37.0 ft.
Median depth: 16.0 ft.
Accessibility: State-owned access two miles west of Hwy. 7 on Cty. Rd. 51
Boat Ramp: Earth
Parking: Ample
Accommodations: Resorts
Shoreland zoning classif.: Rec. Dev.
Dominant forest/soil type: Decid/Sand
Management class: Walleye-Centrarchid
Ecological type: Centrarchid-Walleye

Location: Township 58, 59 Range 24, 25
Watershed: Prairie-Willow
Size of lake: 153 acres
Shorelength: 5.0 miles
Secchi disk (water clarity): 7.0
Water color: Brown
Cause of water color: Swamp drainage
Maximum depth: 28.0 ft.
Median depth: 15.0 ft.
Accessibility: Balsam and Brandon Lake Creeks
Boat Ramp: Carry-down access only
Parking: At Balsam Lake
Accommodations: None
Shoreland zoning classif.: Nat. Envt.
Dominant forest/soil type: Decid/Loam
Management class: Centrarchid
Ecological type: Centrarchid

DNR COMMENTS:
Northern Pike present in about average numbers; growth average, as well. Walleyes scarce; growth appears about average, but sample numbers too small for reliable estimate. Largemouth Bass found during shoreline seining. Black Crappie population above third-quartile values; Yellow Perch scarce. Ciscoes numerous at above-third-quartile numbers.

FISH STOCKING DATA

year	species	size	# released
90	Walleye	Fingerling	2,153
92	Walleye	Fingerling	7,790
92	Walleye	Yearling	660
97	Walleye	Fingerling	2,766

NET CATCH DATA
survey date: 06/29/92

	Gill Nets		Trap Nets	
		avg fish		avg fish
species	# per net	wt. (lbs)	# per set	wt. (lbs)
Yellow Perch	0.8	0.09	0.7	0.09
White Sucker	1.5	2.67	-	-
Walleye	1.0	3.18	-	-
Tullibee (incl. Cisco)	9.1	0.73	-	-
Rock Bass	0.4	0.48	0.9	0.39
Pumpkin. Sunfish	0.2	0.10	2.8	0.18
Northern Pike	5.7	1.80	0.6	2.64
Largemouth Bass	0.1	2.50	0.2	1.65
Brown Bullhead	1.1	0.66	0.8	1.04
Bluegill	1.2	0.14	13.1	0.20
Black Crappie	7.9	0.28	1.6	0.25

LENGTH OF SELECTED SPECIES SAMPLED FROM ALL GEAR
Number of fish caught for the following length categories (inches):

species	0-5	6-8	9-11	12-14	15-19	20-24	25-29	>30	Total
Yellow Perch	-	9	-	-	-	-	-	-	9
Walleye	-	-	-	2	3	5	2	-	12
Tullibee (incl. Cisco)	-	25	25	25	34	-	-	-	109
Rock Bass	-	3	1	1	-	-	-	-	5
Pumpkin. Sunfish	1	1	-	-	-	-	-	-	2
Northern Pike	-	-	-	2	22	37	6	1	68
Largemouth Bass	-	-	-	-	1	-	-	-	1
Brown Bullhead	-	-	6	7	-	-	-	-	13
Bluegill	8	8	-	-	-	-	-	-	16
Black Crappie	5	45	43	1	-	-	-	-	94

FISH STOCKING DATA: NO RECORD OF STOCKING

NET CATCH DATA
survey date: 08/13/80

	Gill Nets		Trap Nets	
		avg fish		avg fish
species	# per net	wt. (lbs)	# per set	wt. (lbs)
White Sucker	0.8	1.93	-	-
Tullibee (incl. Cisco)	0.6	1.50	-	-
Pumpkin. Sunfish	0.2	0.25	0.8	0.27
Northern Pike	10.4	1.45	1.3	1.50
Largemouth Bass	1.6	1.50	-	-
Brown Bullhead	7.2	0.58	6.0	0.52
Bluegill	3.6	0.15	6.0	0.15
Black Crappie	10.4	0.25	0.5	0.75
Rock Bass	-	-	0.3	0.30

LENGTH OF SELECTED SPECIES SAMPLED FROM ALL GEAR
Number of fish caught for the following length categories (inches):

species	0-5	6-8	9-11	12-14	15-19	20-24	25-29	>30	Total
Black Crappie	-	16	19	-	-	-	-	-	35
Bluegill	9	33	-	-	-	-	-	-	42
Brown Bullhead	-	-	38	14	-	-	-	-	52
Largemouth Bass	-	-	-	7	1	-	-	-	8
Northern Pike	-	-	-	7	29	15	6	-	57
Pumpkin. Sunfish	-	4	-	-	-	-	-	-	4
Rock Bass	-	1	-	-	-	-	-	-	1
Tullibee (incl. Cisco)	-	-	-	-	3	-	-	-	3

DNR COMMENTS:
Crappie and Northern Pike populations are quite high. Other fish populations are normal for this type of lake.

FISHING INFORMATION: Big Northern Pike and Largemouth Bass roam **Balsam Lake**'s nine miles of shoreline. Tony at the Balsam Store, along Scenic Highway 7, told us that the Crappie and Sunfish average about 1/2 pound and can be found throughout the lake. Walleye stocked by the DNR in recent years are starting to take hold, with 1- to 1 1/2- pound fish being hooked more frequently. Reports of 3-pound-plus Walleye are also heard at various times throughout the season. Balsam has some nice fish-holding structure with its numerous underwater points and sunken islands. The shallow water connecting the southeast bay with the rest of the lake provides excellent spawning habitat for the Bass, which reach 5 pounds. The Balsam River and creek to Scrapper Lake are good Northern Pike spawning grounds. **Scrapper Lake** can be reached from the creek to Balsam and also has good numbers of Northerns, Bass, and panfish. The Northerns run small, but some of the Crappies run a little larger than those at Balsam. The Largemouth Bass are pretty nice. There are some scrappy 2- to 3-pounders out there for the taking.

SPORTSMAN'S connection®

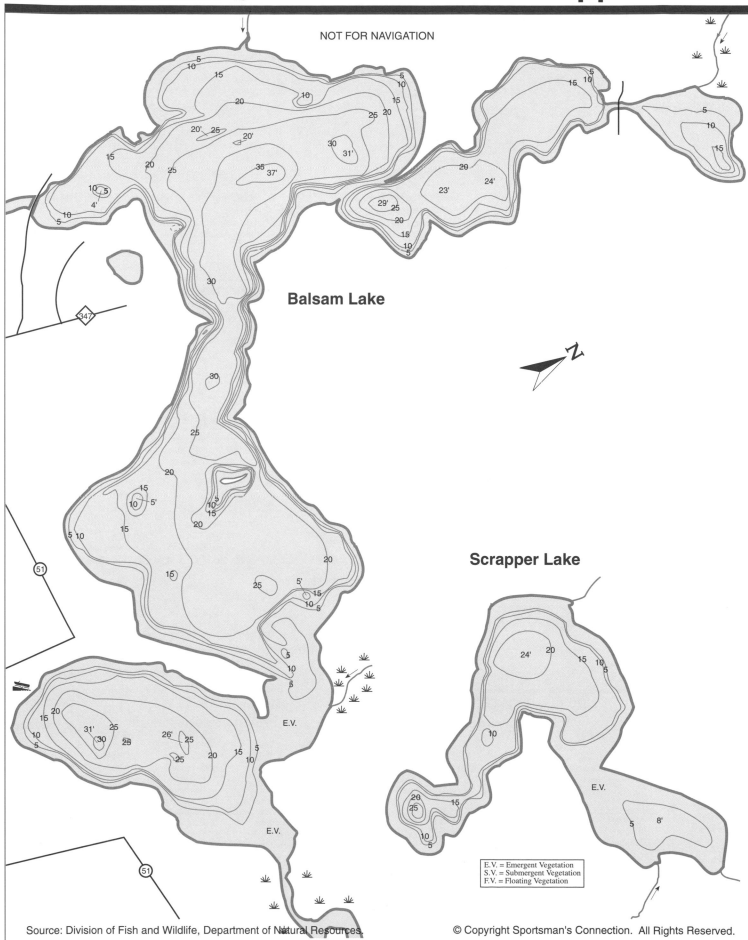

NOT FOR NAVIGATION

Balsam Lake

Scrapper Lake

E.V. = Emergent Vegetation
S.V. = Submergent Vegetation
F.V. = Floating Vegetation

E.V.

E.V.

E.V.

Source: Division of Fish and Wildlife, Department of Natural Resources.

Location: Township 57, 58   Range 25, 26
Watershed: Big Fork

Itasca County

	CARIBOU LAKE	KREMER LAKE	LUCKY LAKE	MOONSHINE LAKE
Size of lake:	240 acres	72 acres	12 acres	25 acres
Shorelength:	3.4 miles	2.1 miles	0.6 miles	0.7 miles
Secchi disk (water clarity):	24.0 ft.	18.0 ft.	9.0 ft.	9.0 ft.
Water color:	Clear	Clear	Clear	Green
Cause of water color:	NA	NA	NA	Algae bloom
Maximum depth:	152.0 ft.	85.0 ft.	44.0 ft.	68.0 ft.
Median depth:	47.0 ft.	34.2 ft.	10.0 ft.	25.0 ft.
Accessibility:	USFS-owned public access off Hwy. 38 on southwest corner	Northeast shore of lake	Federal-owned access trail off state Hwy. 38	East shore, off Co. Rd. 49.
Boat Ramp:	Gravel	Carry-down	Carry-down	Carry-down
Parking:	Limited	None	None	None
Accommodations:	Resort, 3-4 campground sites	Campsite	None	None
Shoreland zoning classif.:	Rec. Dev.	Nat. Envt.	Nat. Envt.	Nat. Envt.
Dominant forest/soil type:	Conifer/Sand	NA	NA	NA
Management class:	Lake Trout	Centrarchid	Stream Trout	Trout
Ecological type:	Trout	Centrarchid	Unclassified	Centrarchid

DNR COMMENTS:
Lake Trout numbers down from those of 1992 assessment but still high; length range 9.2 to 27.4 inches; average weight 1.8 lb. Yellow Perch present. Bluegill numerous but small. Smallmouth Bass scarce. Rock Bass present.

FISHING INFO:
Caribou holds nice Lake Trout, Splake, and Rainbows. It also holds nice Smallmouth and a few monster Northerns. Terry of Frontier Sports in Marcell, said the lake receives a fair amount of pressure in the winter, when folks catch 3- to 4-pound Splake and some decent Lakers through the ice.

Caribou Lake

FISH STOCKING DATA

year	species	size	# released
87	Rainbow Trout	Yearling	3,250
87	Brook Trout	Fingerling	5,130
88	Rainbow Trout	Yearling	1,391
89	Lake Trout	Yearling	2,896
89	Rainbow Trout	Fingerling	6,256
89	Rainbow Trout	Yearling	1,200
90	Lake Trout	Yearling	3,000
91	Lake Trout	Yearling	3,000
93	Lake Trout	Yearling	1,200
95	Lake Trout	Yearling	1,200
97	Lake Trout	Yearling	1,197

survey date: 7/8/96

NET CATCH DATA

	Gill Nets		Trap Nets	
species	# per net	avg fish wt. (lbs)	# per set	avg fish wt. (lbs)
Bluegill	-	-	16.0	0.15
Lake Trout	2.7	1.78	-	-
Rock Bass	-	-	5.9	0.16
Smallmouth Bass	-	-	0.2	0.13
Yellow Perch	2.8	0.15	-	-

LENGTH OF SELECTED SPECIES SAMPLED FROM ALL GEAR
Number of fish caught for the following length categories (inches):

species	0-5	6-8	9-11	12-14	15-19	20-24	25-29	>30	Total
Bluegill	87	57	-	-	-	-	-	-	144
Lake Trout	-	-	9	2	2	2	1	-	16
Rock Bass	37	15	1	-	-	-	-	-	53
Smallmouth Bass	-	2	-	-	-	-	-	-	2
Yellow Perch	-	14	3	-	-	-	-	-	17

Kremer Lake

FISH STOCKING DATA

year	species	size	# released
89	Rainbow Trout	Fingerling	6,392
89	Rainbow Trout	Yearling	4,690
90	Rainbow Trout	Fingerling	6,392
90	Rainbow Trout	Yearling	3,200
91	Rainbow Trout	Fingerling	6,368
91	Rainbow Trout	Yearling	3,202
92	Rainbow Trout	Yearling	3,200
92	Rainbow Trout	Fingerling	6,400
93	Rainbow Trout	Yearling	3,200
93	Rainbow Trout	Fingerling	6,400
94	Rainbow Trout	Fingerling	5,500
94	Rainbow Trout	Yearling	2,600
95	Rainbow Trout	Yearling	3,100
96	Brown Trout	Yearling	3,600
97	Splake	Yearling	3,676

survey date: 10/16/89

NET CATCH DATA

	Gill Nets		Trap Nets	
species	# per net	avg fish wt. (lbs)	# per set	avg fish wt. (lbs)
Rainbow Trout	5.5	0.72	0.8	0.64
White Sucker	-	-	1.1	0.25
Golden Shiner	-	-	1.6	trace
Brook Trout	-	-	trace	0.80

LENGTH OF SELECTED SPECIES SAMPLED FROM ALL GEAR
Number of fish caught for the following length categories (inches):

species	0-5	6-8	9-11	12-14	15-19	20-24	25-29	>30	Total
Rainbow Trout	-	-	2	9	-	-	-	-	11

DNR COMMENTS:
White Sucker have become established in Kremer Lake since the last reclamation in November, 1973. This assessment sampled a trapnet CPUE of 1.1 compared to 1.3 in 1981. Past studies on Trout lakes in Minnesota indicated a CPUE in heavily fished lakes of 1-5 Trout in fall trapnetting. Growth rates of the Rainbow Trout are comparable to those in other trout lakes.

FISHING INFO:
Twelve-inch Rainbows, with some larger ones, are taken. Moderately heavy fishing pressure.

DNR COMMENTS:

NOT AVAILABLE

FISHING INFO:
Lucky holds some nice Brown Trout for those willing to walk the mile or so to get into it. Darwin, of God's Country Outfitters on Highway 38, said some 4- to 5-pound Browns are caught every year, along with good numbers of 1- to 2-pound fish.

Lucky Lake

FISH STOCKING DATA

year	species	size	# released
88	Brown Trout	Yearling	1,081
90	Brown Trout	Yearling	600
92	Brown Trout	Yearling	600
94	Brown Trout	Yearling	1,149
96	Brown Trout	Yearling	600

survey date: 10/18/88

NET CATCH DATA

	Gill Nets		Trap Nets	
species	# per net	avg fish wt. (lbs)	# per set	avg fish wt. (lbs)
Brown Trout	-	-	2.2	1.17

LENGTH OF SELECTED SPECIES SAMPLED FROM ALL GEAR
Number of fish caught for the following length categories (inches):

species	0-5	6-8	9-11	12-14	15-19	20-24	25-29	>30	Total
Brown Trout	-	2	16	41	34	-	-	-	93

Moonshine Lake

FISH STOCKING DATA

year	species	size	# released
88	Rainbow Trout	Fingerling	1,275
89	Rainbow Trout	Fingerling	2,516
90	Rainbow Trout	Fingerling	2,539
91	Rainbow Trout	Fingerling	2,500
92	Rainbow Trout	Fingerling	2,500
93	Rainbow Trout	Fingerling	2,653
94	Rainbow Trout	Fingerling	2,598
95	Rainbow Trout	Fingerling	2,576
96	Rainbow Trout	Fingerling	1,553
97	Rainbow Trout	Fingerling	2,629

NET CATCH DATA NOT AVAILABLE

LENGTH OF SELECTED SPECIES NOT AVAILABLE

DNR COMMENTS:

NOT AVAILABLE

FISHING INFO:
Moonshine is another pothole that holds some nice Trout. Stocked Rainbows, reaching 5 to 6 pounds, are caught. Most of the fish run smaller in size and are fished fairly hard by area and visiting anglers due to accessibility.

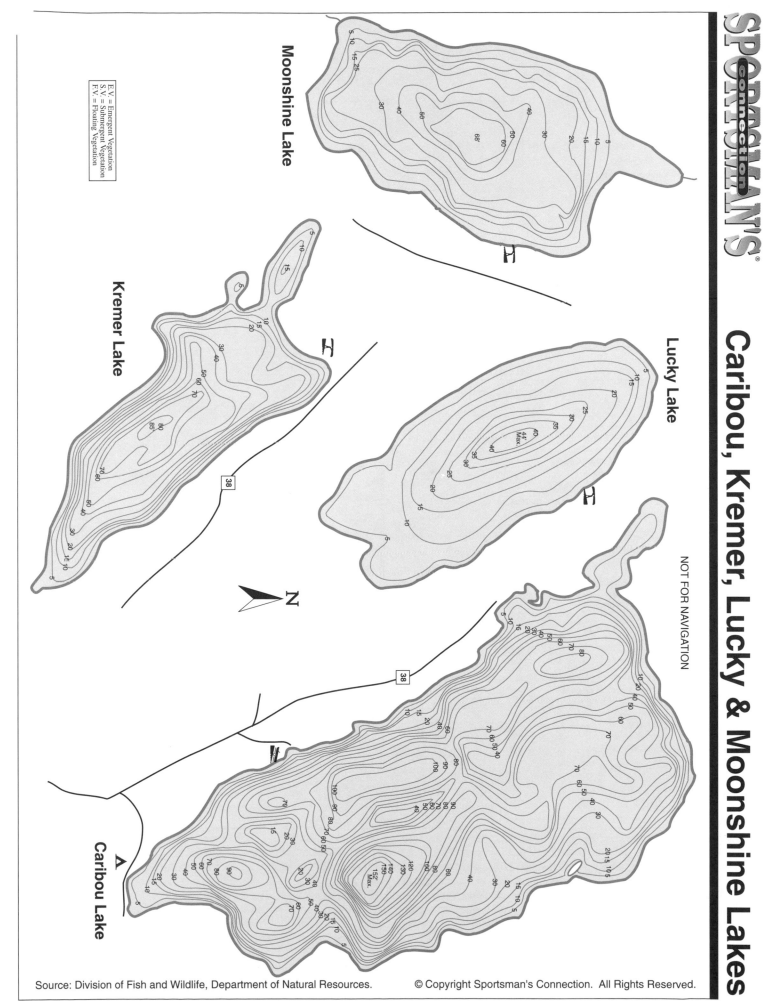

Caribou, Kremer, Lucky & Moonshine Lakes

Moonshine Lake

E.V. = Emergent Vegetation
S.V. = Submergent Vegetation
F.V. = Floating Vegetation

Kremer Lake

Lucky Lake

38

N

Caribou Lake

Source: Division of Fish and Wildlife, Department of Natural Resources.

NORTH STAR LAKE   DEAD HORSE LAKE

Itasca County

Location: Township 58, 59 Range 26
Watershed: Big Fork
Size of lake: 1,059 acres
Shorelength: 14.6 miles
Secchi disk (water clarity): 14.5 ft.
Water color: Light green
Cause of water color: Algae
Maximum depth: 80.0 ft.
Median depth: 26.7 ft.
Accessibility: Federal-owned public access on east shore, off Hwy. 38
Boat Ramp: Concrete
Parking: Ample
Accommodations: Resorts, Campground
Shoreland zoning classif.: Rec. Dev.
Dominant forest/soil type: Decid/Loam
Management class: Walleye-Centrarchid
Ecological type: Centrarchid-Walleye

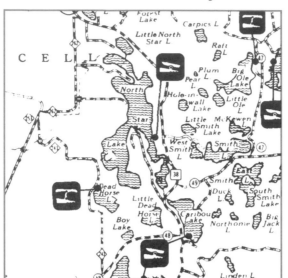

Location: Township 58, 59 Range 26
Watershed: Big Fork
Size of lake: 97 acres
Shorelength: 1.8 miles
Secchi disk (water clarity): 7.0 ft.
Water color: Light green
Cause of water color: Algae bloom
Maximum depth: 36.0 ft.
Median depth: 16.0 ft.
Accessibility: USFS-owned public access on north shore
Boat Ramp: Carry-down
Parking: Limited
Accommodations: None
Shoreland zoning classif.: Nat. Envt.
Dominant forest/soil type: NA
Management class: Walleye-Centrarchid
Ecological type: Centrarchid-Walleye

DNR COMMENTS:
Walleye numbers within range expected for lake class; mean size 18.3 inches and 2.2 lb. Northern Pike numbers continue to be below expected range; mean size 23.5 inches and 2.8 lb. Largemouth Bass sampled in low numbers. Black Crappie catch below expected range. Muskellunge sampled in survey. Smallmouth Bass numbers highest on record for this lake; mean weight 2.1 lb. Bluegill numbers within expected range. Yellow Perch numbers lowest on record; length range 6.1 to 8.6 inches. Cisco population within expected range.

FISH STOCKING DATA

year	species	size	# release
89	Muskellunge	Fingerling	314
89	Muskellunge	Fingerling	314
90	Walleye	Fingerling	346
90	Walleye	Yearling	1,798
91	Muskellunge	Fingerling	314
92	Walleye	Fingerling	20,535
94	Muskellunge	Fingerling	314

NET CATCH DATA
survey date: 8/26/96

	Gill Nets		Trap Nets	
species	# per net	avg fish wt. (lbs)	# per set	avg fish wt. (lbs)
Black Crappie	0.3	0.35	0.3	0.28
Bluegill	0.9	0.16	11.1	0.17
Hybrid Sunfish	-	-	0.2	0.36
Largemouth Bass	trace	0.81	0.2	0.02
Northern Pike	2.8	3.35	0.6	2.24
Pumpkin. Sunfish	-	-	1.8	0.20
Rock Bass	1.9	0.45	0.9	0.23
Smallmouth Bass	1.1	2.08	-	-
Tullibee (Cisco)	0.7	0.71	-	-
Walleye	3.1	2.17	-	-
Yellow Perch	2.0	0.10	0.9	0.23

LENGTH OF SELECTED SPECIES SAMPLED FROM ALL GEAR
Number of fish caught for the following length categories (inches):

species	0-5	6-8	9-11	12-14	15-19	20-24	25-29	>30	Total
Black Crappie	-	6	2	-	-	-	-	-	8
Bluegill	62	81	-	-	-	-	-	-	143
Hybrid Sunfish	-	2	-	-	-	-	-	-	2
Largemouth Bass	1	-	1	-	-	-	-	-	2
Northern Pike	-	-	-	-	13	15	7	4	39
Pumpkin. Sunfish	10	10	-	-	-	-	-	-	20
Rock Bass	8	18	8	-	-	-	-	-	34
Smallmouth Bass	-	1	11	2	8	-	-	-	12
Tullibee (Cisco)	-	2	2	3	1	-	-	-	8
Walleye	-	-	-	7	19	9	2	-	37
Yellow Perch	1	31	3	-	-	-	-	-	35

FISH STOCKING DATA

year	species	size	# released
89	Walleye	Fry	300,000
91	Walleye	Fry	100,000
93	Walleye	Fry	104,000

NET CATCH DATA
survey date: 7/6/93

	Gill Nets		Trap Nets	
species	# per net	avg fish wt. (lbs)	# per set	avg fish wt. (lbs)
Bluegill	62.8	0.15	115.0	0.14
Golden Shiner	4.8	0.07	0.9	0.09
Hybrid Sunfish	-	-	0.2	0.36
Largemouth Bass	0.8	1.82	0.2	2.81
Northern Pike	5.0	3.81	0.2	3.27
Pumpkin. Sunfish	0.8	0.17	10.7	0.16
Rock Bass	1.5	0.58	2.1	0.58
Walleye	3.0	2.49	0.4	3.03
White Sucker	1.3	3.32	-	-
Yellow Perch	18.5	0.15	1.2	0.19

LENGTH OF SELECTED SPECIES SAMPLED FROM ALL GEAR
Number of fish caught for the following length categories (inches):

species	0-5	6-8	9-11	12-14	15-19	20-24	25-29	>30	Total
Bluegill	226	159	-	-	-	-	-	-	385
Largemouth Bass	-	-	1	1	3	-	-	-	5
Northern Pike	-	-	-	-	-	12	9	1	22
Pumpkin. Sunfish	83	16	-	-	-	-	-	-	99
Rock Bass	4	12	9	-	-	-	-	-	25
Walleye	-	-	-	4	5	6	1	-	16
Yellow Perch	22	53	10	-	-	-	-	-	85

DNR COMMENTS:
Lake subject to occasional winterkill, most recently in 1978. Walleye population low, but average weight good at 2.5 lb.; population appears to be maintained by stocking. Northern Pike numbers decreasing, but size is good, with 3.8-lb. average weight. Bluegills very numerous; population is slow-growing.

FISHING INFORMATION: Terry of Frontier Sports in Marcell says some huge Northerns roam **North Star Lake**, and the Walleye are chunky, averaging 2 pounds or better. Northerns can be found near the weedbeds throughout the lake. Try the underwater islands, points, and shoreline structure for Walleye. North Star also provides some good Bass fishing, according to Terry, with Largemouth providing more action than Smallmouth. Spinnerbaits, worms, and other Bass baits give good results off the shallow reeds and cabbage patches. Along with Walleyes, the DNR has been stocking Muskies and has designated North Star as a Muskie lake. Muskies seem to be taking hold, as anglers fishing for Northerns have reported hooking and releasing some small ones (check the current regs for minimum length). Bluegills run on the small side, and Crappies are average. North Star is fairly clear and has some steep dropoffs. Fishing pressure is relatively heavy in the summer, because of easy accessibility (good concrete ramp and ample parking). **Little North Star** is accessible through a channel from North Star and provides some 3/4-pound to 1-pound Crappies, plus Northerns, and an occasional Walleye. **Dead Horse Lake**, meanwhile, has an abundance of Northerns, some Largemouth, and Walleyes. Weed growth is fairly heavy, providing good cover. Terry says if you do find the Walleyes, you can count on nice ones. Pressure is minimal due, in part, to a primitive access.

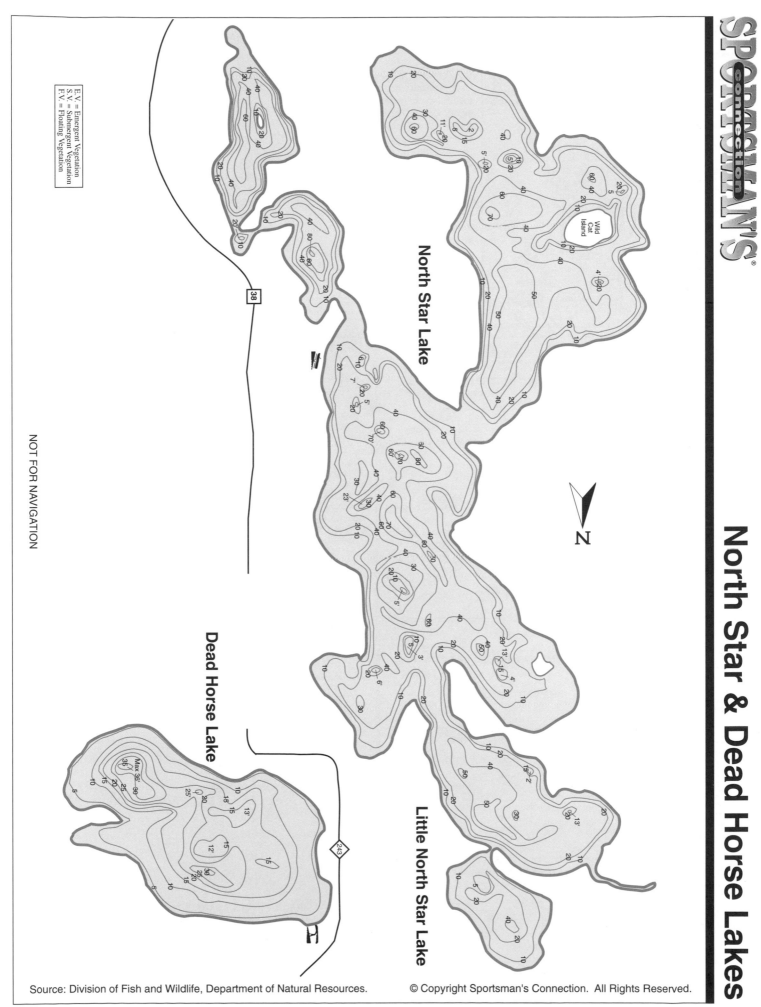

North Star Lake

Wild Cat Island

Little North Star Lake

Dead Horse Lake

N

Max 36'

NOT FOR NAVIGATION

E.V. = Emergent Vegetation
S.V. = Submergent Vegetation
F.V. = Floating Vegetation

North Star & Dead Horse Lakes

Location: Township 59   Range 25, 26
Watershed: Big Fork

BIG ISLAND LAKE   HIGHLAND LAKE   GUNN LAKE   CROOKED LAKE

Itasca County

	BIG ISLAND LAKE	HIGHLAND LAKE	GUNN LAKE	CROOKED LAKE
Size of lake:	220 acres	102 acres	342 acres	115 acres
Shorelength:	4.1 miles	2.8 miles	5.1 miles	3.7 miles
Secchi disk (water clarity):	11.3 ft.	12.0 ft.	11.3 ft.	8.0
Water color:	Brown-green	Amber	Brown	Brown
Cause of water color:	Bog stain, algae	Bog stain, algae	Bog stain	Swamp stain
Maximum depth:	44.0 ft.	38.0 ft.	39.0 ft.	46.0 ft.
Median depth:	6.5 ft.	13.0 ft.	10.1 ft.	8.0 ft.
Accessibility:	USFS-owned public access off Cty. Rd. #47 on the west shore	County-owned earthen access on north shore, off Co. Rd. 45	Access by Lake #6 of the Gunn Lake Chain	Itasca Cty. Land Dept. access on southeast shore
Boat Ramp:	Earth	Carry-down	Concrete	Earth
Parking:	Ample	Limited	Ample	Ample
Accommodations:	None	None	Resort	None
Shoreland zoning classif.:	Rec. Dev.	Rec. Dev.	Rec. Dev.	Nat. Envt.
Dominant forest/soil type:	Decid/Loam	NA	Decid/Sand	NA
Management class:	Centrarchid	Centrarchid	Centrarchid	Centrarchid
Ecological type:	Centrarchid	Centrarchid	Centrarchid	Centrarchid

---

DNR COMMENTS:
N. Pike remain relatively abundant; good growth. No Walleye were sampled. Black Crappie numbers continue to decrease Only two LM Bass captured. Anglers, however, report good fishing for this species.

FISHING INFO:
Big Island holds some nice LM Bass, many in the 3- to 4-pound range. Also good numbers and sizes of N. Pike.

Big Island Lake

FISH STOCKING DATA: NO RECORD OF STOCKING

survey date: 7/22/90

NET CATCH DATA

	Gill Nets		Trap Nets	
species	# per net	avg fish wt. (lbs)	# per set	avg fish wt. (lbs)
Yellow Perch	3.0	0.13	-	-
White Sucker	0.2	3.20	-	-
Northern Pike	9.0	2.32	0.8	1.43
Largemouth Bass	0.4	1.05	-	-
Bluegill	9.6	0.19	9.0	0.25
Black Crappie	0.6	0.53	1.8	0.21

LENGTH OF SELECTED SPECIES SAMPLED FROM ALL GEAR
Number of fish caught for the following length categories (inches):

species	0-5	6-8	9-11	12-14	15-19	20-24	25-29	>30	Total
Yellow Perch	-	15	-	-	-	-	-	1	16
Northern Pike	-	-	-	1	13	25	5	-	44
Largemouth Bass	-	1	1	-	1	-	-	-	3
Bluegill	11	36	1	-	-	-	-	-	48
Black Crappie	-	-	2	-	-	-	-	-	2

DNR COMMENTS:
N Pike population below average LM Bass sampled in low numbers; however, local anglers report good success. Black Crappies sampled in near-average numbers and sizes.

FISHING INFO:
Gunn is the first of a chain of six lakes referred to as the Gunn Lake Chain. You can reach the other lakes through a series of narrow channels deep enough to get a boat and motor through. Each lake has good depth and a healthy LM Bass population. Northern and panfish are also abundant, but small. Scenery is spectacular.

Gunn Lake

FISH STOCKING DATA: NO RECORD OF STOCKING

survey date: 7/7/92

NET CATCH DATA

	Gill Nets		Trap Nets	
species	# per net	avg fish wt. (lbs)	# per set	avg fish wt. (lbs)
Yellow Perch	1.3	0.09	trace	0.10
Tullibee (Cisco)	3.6	0.39	-	-
Rock Bass	0.3	0.37	1.1	0.26
Pumpkin. Sunfish	trace	0.10	3.8	0.19
Northern Pike	2.3	2.73	0.3	1.10
Largemouth Bass	0.3	1.23	0.8	0.61
Hybrid Sunfish	trace	0.60	-	-
Bluegill	.1	0.13	61.7	0.16
Black Crappie	0.9	0.35	1.3	0.31

LENGTH OF SELECTED SPECIES SAMPLED FROM ALL GEAR
Number of fish caught for the following length categories (inches):

species	0-5	6-8	9-11	12-14	15-19	20-24	25-29	>30	Total
Yellow Perch	11	5	-	-	-	-	-	-	16
Tullibee (Cisco)	-	11	20	10	-	-	-	-	41
Rock Bass	-	3	-	-	-	-	-	-	3
Pumpkin. Sunfish	1	-	-	-	-	-	-	-	1
Northern Pike	-	-	-	-	9	13	4	2	28
Largemouth Bass	-	1	1	1	1	-	-	-	4
Hybrid Sunfish	-	1	-	-	-	-	-	-	1
Bluegill	9	4	-	-	-	-	-	-	13
Black Crappie	-	6	5	-	-	-	-	-	11

Highland Lake

FISH STOCKING DATA: NO RECORD OF STOCKING

survey date: 6/20/88

NET CATCH DATA

	Gill Nets		Trap Nets	
species	# per net	avg fish wt. (lbs)	# per set	avg fish wt. (lbs)
Tullibee (Cisco)	4.5	0.66	-	-
Pumpkin. Sunfish	0.5	0.15	4.0	0.08
Northern Pike	9.5	2.98	1.0	1.48
Bluegill	0.5	0.20	39.0	0.17
Black Crappie	0.3	0.20	2.8	0.30
Rock Bass	-	-	1.5	0.30
Largemouth Bass	-	-	1.0	0.55
Hybrid Sunfish	-	-	1.3	0.32
Black Bullhead	-	-	0.3	0.20

LENGTH OF SELECTED SPECIES SAMPLED FROM ALL GEAR
Number of fish caught for the following length categories (inches):

species	0-5	6-8	9-11	12-14	15-19	20-24	25-29	>30	Total
Tullibee (Cisco)	-	2	3	13	-	-	-	-	18
Pumpkin. Sunfish	-	2	-	-	-	-	-	-	2
Northern Pike	-	-	-	-	10	19	6	3	38
Bluegill	-	2	-	-	-	-	-	-	2
Black Crappie	-	1	-	-	-	-	-	-	1

DNR COMMENTS:
N. Pike abundant and of good average size, probably due to good Cisco population Bluegill abundance above normal. No Yellow Perch nets but 36 young-of-year were caught in shoreline seining. All other species appear to be present in average numbers.

FISHING INFO:
Highland Lake has a primitive access classified as "carry-in," although it's possible to back a small boat in. Bass are plentiful, but run small. Northerns are also plentiful and nice-size.

Crooked Lake

FISH STOCKING DATA: NO RECORD OF STOCKING

survey date: 9/3/82

NET CATCH DATA

	Gill Nets		Trap Nets	
species	# per net	avg fish wt. (lbs)	# per set	avg fish wt. (lbs)
Yellow Perch	1.0	0.17	0.4	0.25
White Sucker	0.3	3.00	-	-
Northern Pike	5.3	2.11	-	-
Bluegill	23.0	0.20	7.4	0.17
Black Crappie	1.0	0.40	0.6	0.53

LENGTH OF SELECTED SPECIES SAMPLED FROM ALL GEAR
Number of fish caught for the following length categories (inches):

species	0-5	6-8	9-11	12-14	15-19	20-24	25-29	>30	Total
Black Crappie	-	2	-	-	-	-	-	-	6
Bluegill	29	77	-	-	-	-	-	-	106
Northern Pike	-	-	-	-	2	8	4	-	14
Yellow Perch	-	4	1	-	-	-	-	-	5

DNR COMMENTS:
Northern Pike and Bluegill populations are good. Perch and Crappie numbers are below medians. It does not appear that past stockings of Muskie were successful.

FISHING INFO:
A truck is recommended for accessing this lake via a rocky, minimum-maintenance road (see area map inset). The access has a steep dropoff. Bass and Northerns run small, but some nice ones are mixed in.

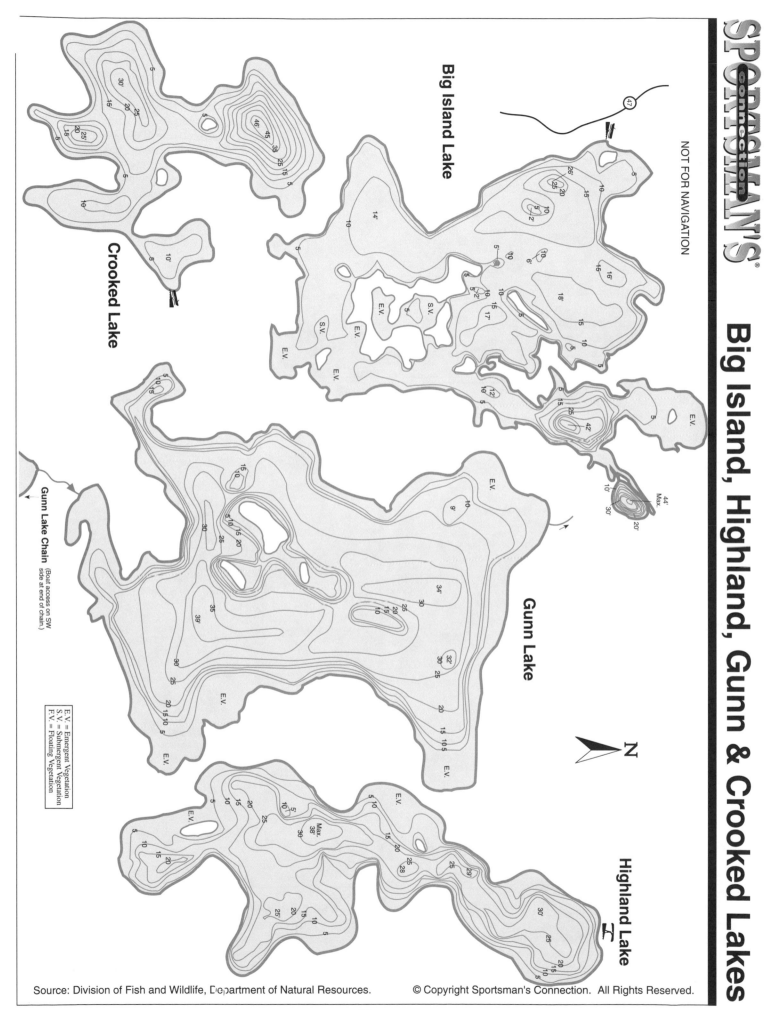

Big Island, Highland, Highland, Gunn & Crooked Lakes

NOT FOR NAVIGATION

Big Island Lake

Crooked Lake

Gunn Lake

Highland Lake

Gunn Lake Chain
(Boat access on SW
side at end of chain.)

E.V. = Emergent Vegetation
S.V. = Submergent Vegetation
F.V. = Floating Vegetation

N

Source: Division of Fish and Wildlife, Department of Natural Resources.

ANTLER LAKE

EAGLE LAKE

Itasca County

Location: Township 59, 60 Range 24, 25
Watershed: Prairie-Willow
Size of lake: 306 acres
Shorelength: 3.3 miles
Secchi disk (water clarity): 16.0 ft.
Water color: Green
Cause of water color: Algae bloom
Maximum depth: 90.0 ft.
Median depth: 30.0 ft.
Accessibility: State-owned public access on northwest shore, off County Road 341
Boat Ramp: Earth
Parking: Ample
Accommodations: Resort
Shoreland zoning classif.: Rec. Dev.
Dominant forest/soil type: Decid/Loam
Management class: Walleye-Centrarchid
Ecological type: Centrarchid

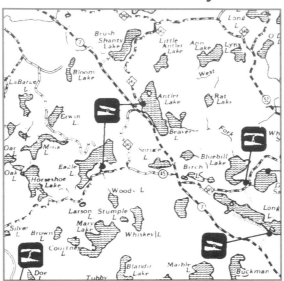

Location: Township 59, 60 Range 24, 25
Watershed: Prairie-Willow
Size of lake: 279 acres
Shorelength: 4.5 miles
Secchi disk (water clarity): 7.1 ft.
Water color: Brown
Cause of water color: Bog stain
Maximum depth: 35.0 ft.
Median depth: 18.0 ft.
Accessibility: State-owned public access on southeast corner, off County Road 45
Boat Ramp: Gravel
Parking: Ample
Accommodations: None
Shoreland zoning classif.: Rec. Dev.
Dominant forest/soil type: Decid/Loam
Management class: Walleye-centrarchid
Ecological type: Centrarchid

DNR COMMENTS:
Northern Pike population low and typical for this lake at below-first-quartile values. Walleye population between first and third quartiles; all from stocked age classes; growth normal for lake class. Largemouth Bass scarce. Bluegills slightly above average in numbers; growth good. Black Crappies average in number; growth good. Cisco, White Sucker and Rock Bass numbers near lake class median levels.

FISH STOCKING DATA

year	species	size	# released
90	Walleye	Yearling	223

NET CATCH DATA

survey date: 07/27/92

	Gill Nets		Trap Nets	
species	# per net	avg fish wt. (lbs)	# per set	avg fish wt. (lbs)
Yellow Perch	0.2	0.10	0.2	0.10
White Sucker	0.8	2.19	-	-
Walleye	1.3	2.10	0.1	1.70
Tullibee (incl. Cisco)	1.6	0.16	-	-
Rock Bass	0.6	0.26	-	-
Northern Pike	1.3	3.37	0.1	2.00
Largemouth Bass	0.2	1.25	0.04	0.28
Bluegill	0.2	0.10	25.3	0.09
Black Crappie	0.9	0.25	1.0	0.18
Yellow Bullhead	-	-	1.2	0.73
Pumpkin. Sunfish	-	-	1.1	0.19
Hybrid Sunfish	-	-	0.6	0.22
Brown Bullhead	-	-	0.3	0.73

LENGTH OF SELECTED SPECIES SAMPLED FROM ALL GEAR
Number of fish caught for the following length categories (inches):

species	0-5	6-8	9-11	12-14	15-19	20-24	25-29	>30	Total
Yellow Perch	-	3	-	-	-	-	-	-	3
Walleye	-	-	-	9	2	1	-	-	12
Tullibee (incl. Cisco)	-	7	7	-	-	-	-	-	14
Rock Bass	-	5	1	-	-	-	-	-	6
Northern Pike	-	-	-	2	5	3	-	-	10
Largemouth Bass	-	-	-	1	1	-	-	-	2
Bluegill	2	1	-	-	-	-	-	-	3
Black Crappie	-	4	3	-	-	-	-	-	7

FISH STOCKING DATA

year	species	size	# released
90	Walleye	Yearling	473
93	Walleye	Fingerling	2,940
96	Walleye	Fingerling	561

NET CATCH DATA

survey date: 8/11/97

	Gill Nets		Trap Nets	
species	# per net	avg fish wt. (lbs)	# per set	avg fish wt. (lbs)
Black Bullhead	-	-	0.1	0.13
Black Crappie	1.5	0.60	0.9	0.49
Bluegill	5.5	0.26	5.2	0.20
Hybrid Sunfish	0.2	0.15	0.3	0.37
Largemouth Bass	0.2	0.62	-	-
Northern Pike	5.0	1.64	0.3	0.66
Pumpkin. Sunfish	0.7	0.22	1.4	0.21
Rock Bass	1.0	0.44	1.1	0.26
Walleye	5.3	1.60	0.1	4.08
White Sucker	0.3	2.77	-	-
Yellow Perch	3.3	0.12	1.0	0.12

LENGTH OF SELECTED SPECIES SAMPLED FROM ALL GEAR
Number of fish caught for the following length categories (inches):

species	0-5	6-8	9-11	12-14	15-19	20-24	25-29	>30	Total
Black Bullhead	1	-	-	-	-	-	-	-	1
Black Crappie	1	3	13	-	-	-	-	-	17
Bluegill	17	62	-	-	-	-	-	-	79
Hybrid Sunfish	1	3	-	-	-	-	-	-	4
Largemouth Bass	-	-	1	-	-	-	-	-	1
Northern Pike	-	-	-	3	21	6	3	-	33
Pumpkin. Sunfish	10	7	-	-	-	-	-	-	17
Rock Bass	7	6	3	-	-	-	-	-	16
Walleye	1	-	4	5	18	5	-	-	33
Yellow Perch	11	16	1	-	-	-	-	-	28

DNR COMMENTS:
Walleye numbers above expected range for lake class; mean length 16 inches; growth rates exceed statewide mean for ages 1-3. Northern Pike numbers within expected range; mean size 19.3 inches and 1.6 lb.. Black Crappie population typical of lake class; mean length 8.9 inches. Bluegill numbers low; mean length 6.3 inches. Yellow Perch numbers within expected range; length range 5.6 to 9.1 inches. Black Bullhead, hybrid Sunfish, Pumpkin-seed Sunfish, Rock Bass, and White Sucker also present.

FISHING INFORMATION: Walleye averaging 1 to 1 1/2 pounds have taken hold in **Antler Lake** off Scenic Highway 7. The DNR also stocked some Lake Trout in this deep, clear lake several years ago, but there haven't been any reports of their showing up in anglers' creels or the DNR's nets. Northerns are good-size, with 5-pound fish being about average. Largemouth Bass fishing can be very good at times. Antler's access is very shallow, with a loose gravel surface. **Eagle Lake**'s Crappies are of the slab variety with some 2- to 3-pound fish being caught occasionally. Walleye have been receiving a boost from DNR stocking and average 1 1/2 to 2 pounds. Most of the fishing pressure on the lake comes from spring and winter Crappie anglers.

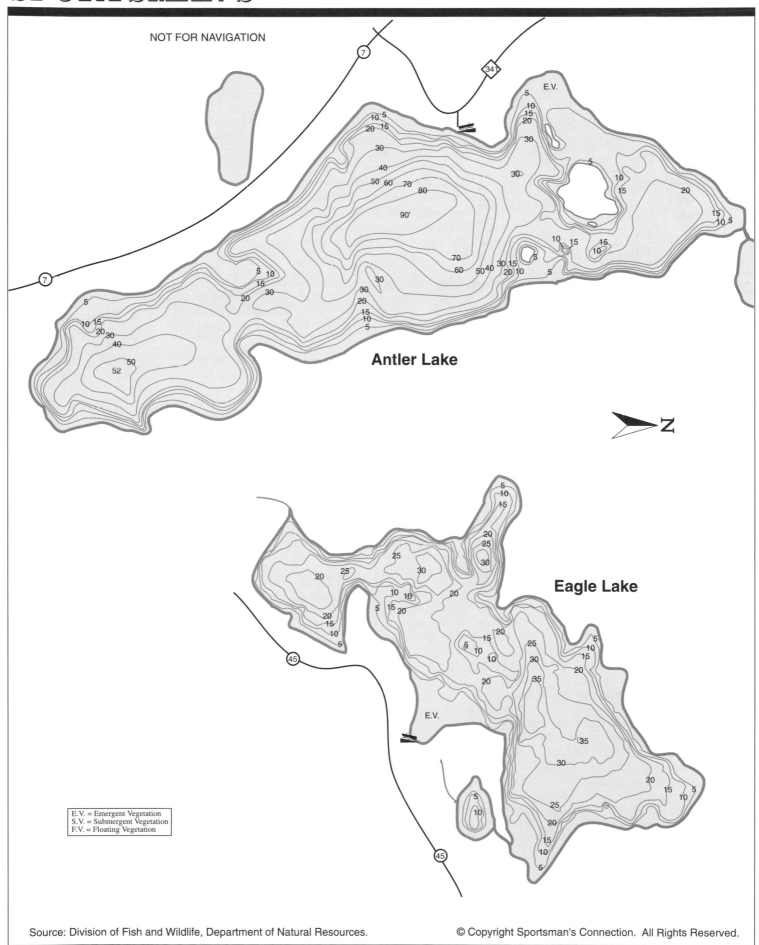

NOT FOR NAVIGATION

Antler Lake

Eagle Lake

E.V. = Emergent Vegetation
S.V. = Submergent Vegetation
F.V. = Floating Vegetation

Source: Division of Fish and Wildlife, Department of Natural Resources.

Location: Township 59 Range 24
Watershed: Prairie-Willow

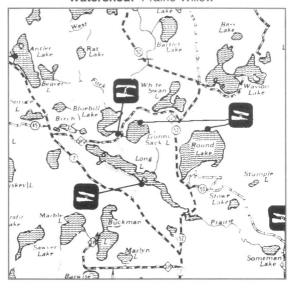

	LONG LAKE	ROUND LAKE	BLUEBILL LAKE
		Itasca County	
Size of lake:	353 acres	502 acres	136 acres
Shorelength:	9.0 miles	5.0 miles	2.8 miles
Secchi disk (water clarity):	6.0 ft.	9.0 ft.	3.0 ft.
Water color:	Brown	Clear	Brown
Cause of water color:	Bog stain	NA	Bog stain
Maximum depth:	34.0 ft.	40.0 ft.	14.0 ft.
Median depth:	17.0 ft.	16.0 ft.	NA
Accessibility:	State-owned access on south shore, off Highway 7 (Section 16)	Access on north shore off Tabour Rd.	From feeder creek off Cty. Rd. 345
Boat Ramp:	Concrete	Concrete	Carry-down
Parking:	Adequate	Ample	Limited
Accommodations:	Resorts	Resorts	None
Shoreland zoning classif.:	Rec. Dev.	Rec. Devel.	Natural Environment
Dominant forest/soil type:	Decid/Sand	Decid/Sand	NA
Management class:	Walleye-Centrarchid	Walleye-Centrarchid	Walleye-Centrarchid
Ecological type:	Centrarchid	Centrarchid	Centrarchid-Walleye

Long Lake

DNR COMMENTS: NOT AVAILABLE

FISH STOCKING DATA

year	species	size	# released
91	Walleye	Fingerling	1,692

NET CATCH DATA

survey date: 7/5/89

	Gill Nets		Trap Nets	
		avg fish		avg fish
species	# per net	wt. (lbs)	# per set	wt. (lbs)
Yellow Perch	5.4	0.11	1.9	0.10
White Sucker	0.4	1.75	-	-
Walleye	0.6	2.80	-	-
Rock Bass	2.0	0.33	0.9	0.42
Pumpkin. Sunfish	0.6	0.17	9.6	0.12
Northern Pike	13.6	2.22	0.9	1.50
Largemouth Bass	0.4	1.35	-	-
Golden Shiner	0.2	0.10	-	-
Bluegill	0.2	0.30	32.9	0.11
Black Crappie	4.2	0.16	5.0	0.19

LENGTH OF SELECTED SPECIES SAMPLED FROM ALL GEAR
Number of fish caught for the following length categories (inches):

species	0-5	6-8	9-11	12-14	15-19	20-24	25-29	>30	Total
Yellow Perch	-	27	-	-	-	-	-	-	27
Walleye	-	-	-	1	1	-	1	-	3
Rock Bass	-	8	2	-	-	-	-	-	10
Pumpkin. Sunfish	-	3	-	-	-	-	-	-	3
Northern Pike	-	-	-	2	27	24	14	1	68
Largemouth Bass	-	-	-	2	-	-	-	-	2
Bluegill	-	1	-	-	-	-	-	-	1
Black Crappie	5	13	3	-	-	-	-	-	21

Round Lake

FISH STOCKING DATA

year	species	size	# released
89	Walleye	Fingerling	7,080
91	Walleye	Fingerling	3,841
94	Walleye	Fingerling	3,945

NET CATCH DATA

survey date: 6/28/93

	Gill Nets		Trap Nets	
		avg fish		avg fish
species	# per net	wt. (lbs)	# per set	wt. (lbs)
Black Crappie	0.1	0.40	-	-
Bluegill	3.1	0.22	28.3	0.13
Largemouth Bass	0.7	1.39	0.1	0.37
Northern Pike	7.9	2.21	0.2	5.18
Pumpkin. Sunfish	-	-	0.3	0.20
Rock Bass	0.2	0.16	1.2	0.44
Walleye	6.3	1.65	-	-
Yellow Perch	5.0	0.08	-	-

LENGTH OF SELECTED SPECIES SAMPLED FROM ALL GEAR
Number of fish caught for the following length categories (inches):

species	0-5	6-8	9-11	12-14	15-19	20-24	25-29	>30	Total
Black Crappie	-	1	-	-	-	-	-	-	1
Bluegill	111	68	1	-	-	-	-	-	180
Largemouth Bass	-	1	-	6	-	-	-	-	7
Northern Pike	-	-	-	34	31	6	2	-	73
Pumpkin. Sunfish	1	2	-	-	-	-	-	-	3
Rock Bass	1	10	2	-	-	-	-	-	13
Walleye	-	-	11	7	32	7	-	-	57
Yellow Perch	35	10	-	-	-	-	-	-	45

DNR COMMENTS: Lake contains an excellent Walleye fishery; some natural reproduction taking place, but the dominant year classes appear to be from stocked years. Northern Pike numbers good, with mean weight of 2.2 lb. Good populations of Largemouth Bass and Bluegill present. Lake is known for good Black Crappie angling.

Bluebill Lake

FISH STOCKING DATA: NO RECORD OF STOCKING

NET CATCH DATA

survey date: 7/11/83

	Gill Nets		Trap Nets	
		avg fish		avg fish
species	# per net	wt. (lbs)	# per set	wt. (lbs)
Yellow Perch	8.3	0.16	0.5	0.25
Walleye	3.3	0.93	-	-
Rock Bass	0.3	0.30	-	-
Northern Pike	5.5	0.79	0.5	0.60
Black Crappie	5.8	0.32	-	-
Pumpkin. Sunfish	-	-	0.8	0.47
Bluegill	-	-	0.5	0.60

LENGTH OF SELECTED SPECIES SAMPLED FROM ALL GEAR
Number of fish caught for the following length categories (inches):

species	0-5	6-8	9-11	12-14	15-19	20-24	25-29	>30	Total
Black Crappie	-	18	4	1	-	-	-	-	23
Bluegill	-	1	1	-	-	-	-	-	2
Northern Pike	-	-	2	3	13	6	-	-	24
Pumpkin. Sunfish	-	3	-	-	-	-	-	-	3
Rock Bass	-	1	-	-	-	-	-	-	1
Walleye	-	2	-	4	7	-	-	-	13
Yellow Perch	-	30	5	-	-	-	-	-	35

DNR COMMENTS: Walleye are reproducing naturally and numbers are above the local median. Abundance of other species within limits for this type of lake.

FISHING INFORMATION: Long, Round, and Bluebill Lakes can be found by traveling up Scenic Highway 7. **Round Lake** is the largest of the three at 437 acres and consistently produces 1 1/2- to 2-pound Walleyes, along with a few 9- to 10-pounders each year. Bev Truman at the Scenic Pines Store, near Round Lake, told us that the sunnies, Bluegills and Crappies are average-size and provide good action for the kids. Some nice Northerns and Largemouth Bass also roam the lake. Tony, owner and operator at the Balsam Store on Highway 7, says he has weighed several 10- to 15-pound Northerns from **Long Lake**. Walleye are also caught; a few chunky 3- to 4-pounders show up now and then. Largemouth Bass anglers have reported good catches of 2- to 3-pound fish. **Bluebill Lake** doesn't get much pressure. Anglers can access the lake from the creek that adjoins Bluebill and Gunny Sack Lake (which has an access, but hasn't been mapped by the DNR). Bluebill has some nice Pumpkinseed and Bluegill Sunfish, decent Crappies, and Walleyes.

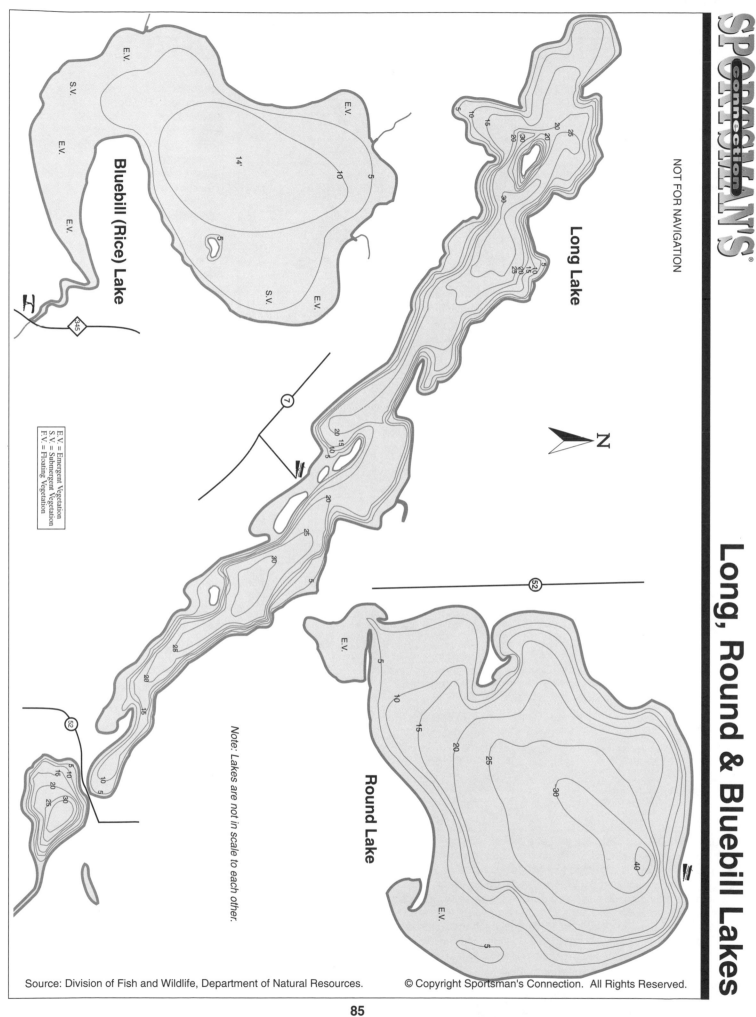

Long, Round & Bluebill Lakes

Long Lake

Bluebill (Rice) Lake

Round Lake

NOT FOR NAVIGATION

N

E.V. = Emergent Vegetation
S.V. = Submergent Vegetation
F.V. = Floating Vegetation

Note: Lakes are not in scale to each other.

TURTLE LAKE   LITTLE TURTLE LAKE
Itasca County

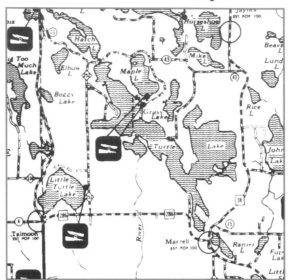

Location: Township 59, 60 Range 26, 27
Watershed: Big Fork
Size of lake: 2,052 acres
Shorelength: 21.8 miles
Secchi disk (water clarity): 12.0 ft.
Water color: Light green
Cause of water color: Bicarbonates
Maximum depth: 130.0 ft.
Median depth: 33.9 ft.
Accessibility: State-owned public access on northeast shore
Boat Ramp: Concrete
Parking: Ample
Accommodations: Resort
Shoreland zoning classif.: Rec. Dev.
Dominant forest/soil type: Decid/Loam
Management class: Walleye-Centrarchid
Ecological type: Centrarchid-Walleye

Location: Township 59, 60 Range 26, 27
Watershed: Big Fork
Size of lake: 475 acres
Shorelength: 3.8 miles
Secchi disk (water clarity): 10.0 ft.
Water color: Green
Cause of water color: Algae bloom
Maximum depth: 30.0 ft.
Median depth: 16.5 ft.
Accessibility: County-owned public access on east shore, off Co. Rd. 252
Boat Ramp: Earth
Parking: Adequate
Accommodations:
Shoreland zoning classif.: Rec. Dev.
Dominant forest/soil type: Decid/Wet
Management class: Walleye
Ecological type: Hard-water Walleye

DNR COMMENTS:
Walleye numbers up substantially; fish of quality size, averaging 20.3 inches and 3.1 lb.; some natural reproduction occurring, but stocking contributes substantially to the population. Northern Pike numbers down, but quality-size fish present; mean weight 3 lb. Smallmouth Bass population highest on record for this lake; mean length 12.8 inches. Yellow Perch numbers low. Black Crappie, Bluegill and Largemouth Bass populations about average for lake class.

FISH STOCKING DATA

year	species	size	# released
89	Walleye	Fingerling	4,429
89	Walleye	Yearling	12
91	Walleye	Fingerling	27
91	Walleye	Yearling	190
91	Walleye	Adult	992
97	Walleye	Fingerling	7,959

NET CATCH DATA
survey date: 8/7/95

	Gill Nets		Trap Nets	
species	# per net	avg fish wt. (lbs)	# per set	avg fish wt. (lbs)
Black Crappie	0.2	0.65	1.1	0.07
Bluegill	1.1	0.07	13.9	0.15
Common Shiner	-	-	trace	0.02
Hybrid Sunfish	-	-	0.4	0.22
Lake Whitefish	2.1	0.92	-	-
Largemouth Bass	0.5	0.77	0.6	0.09
Northern Pike	2.9	3.02	0.5	1.48
Pumpkin. Sunfish	0.3	0.11	1.9	0.16
Rock Bass	6.9	0.43	4.6	0.18
Smallmouth Bass	6.1	1.41	0.2	0.18
Tullibee (Cisco)	8.5	0.36	-	-
Walleye	3.9	3.15	-	-
Yellow Perch	3.5	0.17	2.6	0.12

LENGTH OF SELECTED SPECIES SAMPLED FROM ALL GEAR
Number of fish caught for the following length categories (inches):

species	0-5	6-8	9-11	12-14	15-19	20-24	25-29	>30	Total
Black Crappie	15	1	2	-	-	-	-	-	18
Bluegill	110	77	-	-	-	-	-	-	187
Hybrid Sunfish	1	4	-	-	-	-	-	-	5
Lake Whitefish	-	2	8	10	11	-	-	-	31
Largemouth Bass	7	4	2	2	-	-	-	-	15
Northern Pike	1	-	-	2	8	30	6	3	50
Pumpkin. Sunfish	24	7	-	-	-	-	-	-	31
Rock Bass	44	96	27	1	-	-	-	-	168
Smallmouth Bass	6	6	21	42	20	-	-	-	95
Tullibee (Cisco)	-	36	47	21	-	-	-	-	104
Walleye	-	-	-	-	33	20	6	-	59
Yellow Perch	28	51	8	-	-	-	-	-	87

FISH STOCKING DATA

year	species	size	# released
89	Walleye	Fry	500,000
91	Walleye	Fingerling	1,030
91	Walleye	Adult	49
93	Walleye	Fry	500,000
93	Walleye	Fry	100,000

NET CATCH DATA
survey date: 7/19/93

	Gill Nets		Trap Nets	
species	# per net	avg fish wt. (lbs)	# per set	avg fish wt. (lbs)
Black Crappie	-	-	0.6	1.00
Bluegill	1.4	0.20	5.3	0.25
Bowfin (Dogfish)	0.1	5.29	-	-
Largemouth Bass	0.1	1.01	0.1	1.54
Northern Pike	10.6	1.78	0.9	1.10
Pumpkin. Sunfish	2.1	0.19	4.6	0.21
Rock Bass	0.9	0.26	0.5	0.29
Shorthead Redhorse	0.1	2.31	-	-
Tullibee (Cisco)	3.9	0.58	-	-
Walleye	3.0	1.66	-	-
White Sucker	1.3	2.21	-	-
Yellow Bullhead	0.1	1.10	0.1	0.69
Yellow Perch	62.1	0.13	6.6	0.12

LENGTH OF SELECTED SPECIES SAMPLED FROM ALL GEAR
Number of fish caught for the following length categories (inches):

species	0-5	6-8	9-11	12-14	15-19	20-24	25-29	>30	Total
Black Crappie	-	-	2	3	-	-	-	-	5
Bluegill	25	28	2	-	-	-	-	-	55
Largemouth Bass	-	-	-	2	-	-	-	-	2
Northern Pike	-	-	4	4	55	34	4	1	102
Pumpkin. Sunfish	23	33	-	-	-	-	-	-	56
Rock Bass	3	9	-	-	-	-	-	-	12
Tullibee (Cisco)	-	9	19	4	3	-	-	-	35
Walleye	-	-	-	9	16	2	-	-	27
Yellow Bullhead	-	1	1	-	-	-	-	-	2
Yellow Perch	110	157	1	-	-	-	-	-	268

DNR COMMENTS:
Northern Pike abundant, with a good range of sizes available; average size 19.6 inches and 1.8 lb.; fish to 32.5 inches sampled. Walleye numbers typical of lake class; average size 16.4 inches and 1.7 lb.; natural reproduction may be contributing substantially to population. Black Crappie numbers not high, but size structure is very good; average weight about 1 lb. Largemouth Bass scarce. Bluegill numbers below average for lake class. Yellow Perch numerous; length range 5 to 8 inches.

FISHING INFORMATION: Turtle Lake, off of Highway 38, is a deep, relatively clear, pretty lake punctuated with numerous islands and bays. It has a reputation of giving up good-size Walleye, typically in the 2- to 4-pound range, as well as a few lunkers. According to Terry Schmitz, owner of Frontier Sport in Marcell, a half-limit (3) of 3-pound Walleyes is considered a good day on the lake. Turtle is a good choice for anglers seeking big Walleye and 5-pound-class Smallmouth Bass. Its rocky, underwater points and sunken islands are good holding areas for these species. Moose Bay, on the west side of the lake, holds Northerns in the 13- to 15-pound range. Panfish success seems to be confined to winter and early spring. Largemouth Bass, some in the 4- to 5-pound range, are also present. **Little Turtle Lake** is considerably smaller and shallower than Turtle, making it easier to fish. Schmitz told us that fishing pressure had taken its toll on the Walleye several years ago, but pressure has relaxed since, and the Walleye fishing is picking up again. Fish of 1 1/2 to 2 pounds sizes are now the norm. Most of the Walleye are caught in 8 to 10 feet of water early in the season; they move out a little as summer progresses. Five- to 6-pound Northerns are mixed in with the ubiquitous "snakes." Largemouth Bass are fairly scarce, but some 3- to 5-pounders can be found. Crappies and Bluegills are nice-size. In fact, the 'gills run up to a pound.

NOT FOR NAVIGATION

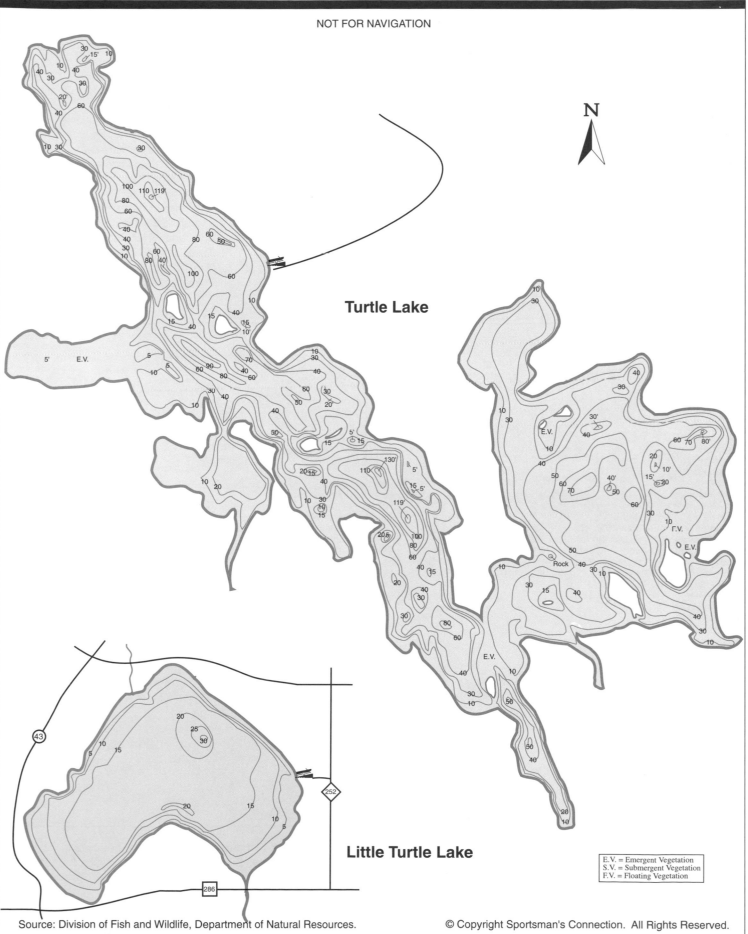

Turtle Lake

N

Little Turtle Lake

E.V. = Emergent Vegetation
S.V. = Submergent Vegetation
F.V. = Floating Vegetation

Source: Division of Fish and Wildlife, Department of Natural Resources.

BELLO LAKE

Itasca County

Location: Township 60   Range 26, 27
Watershed: Big Fork
Size of lake: 493 acres
Shorelength: 7.3 miles
Secchi disk (water clarity): 9.5 ft.
Water color: Brown
Maximum depth: 58.0 ft.
Median depth: 30.0 ft.
Accessibility: State-owned public access on southeast shore
Boat Ramp: Earth
Parking: Ample
Accommodations: Resort
Shoreland zoning classif.: Rec. /Dev.
Dominant forest/soil type: Decid/Loam
Cause of water color: Bog Stain
Management class: Walleye-Centrarchid
Ecological type: Centrarchid

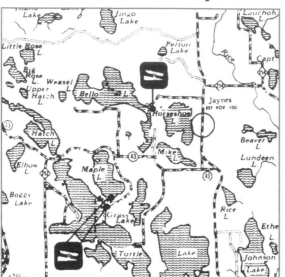

MAPLE LAKE

Location: Township 60   Range 26, 27
Watershed: Big Fork
Size of lake: 228 acres
Shorelength: 3.2 miles
Secchi disk (water clarity): 9.0 ft.
Water color: Green
Maximum depth: 35.0 ft.
Median depth: 20.0 ft.
Accessibility: State-owned public access on south shore
Boat Ramp: Concrete
Parking: Ample
Accommodations: Resorts
Shoreland zoning classif.: Rec./Dev.
Dominant forest/soil type: Decid/Loam
Cause of water color: Slight algae bloom
Management class: Walleye
Ecological type: Hard-water Walleye

DNR COMMENTS:
Northern Pike population above normal; size small, with most fish in 16- to 19-inch range; growth good. Walleyes scarce, below first-quartile values. Bowfin scarce as well. Largemouth Bass present in undetermined numbers. Many Black Crappies in 10-to12-inch range reported caught by local anglers; population appears about normal for lake class. Bluegills very numerous; growth slower than normal.

FISH STOCKING DATA: NO RECORD OF STOCKING

NET CATCH DATA

survey date: 7/29/91

	Gill Nets		Trap Nets	
		avg fish		avg fish
species	# per net	wt. (lbs)	# per set	wt. (lbs)
Yellow Perch	0.5	0.10	0.3	0.10
Walleye	0.8	2.76	-	-
Tullibee (Cisco)	4.8	1.42	-	-
Pumpkin. Sunfish	1.2	0.21	1.6	0.13
Northern Pike	10.7	1.32	0.4	1.10
Largemouth Bass	1.7	1.10	0.6	0.22
Bluegill	9.7	0.20	4.9	0.10
Black Crappie	1.2	0.46	0.8	0.15
Bowfin (Dogfish)	-	-	0.1	5.50

LENGTH OF SELECTED SPECIES SAMPLED FROM ALL GEAR
Number of fish caught for the following length categories (inches):

species	0-5	6-8	9-11	12-14	15-19	20-24	25-29	>30	Total
Walleye	-	-	-	-	2	3	-	-	5
Tullibee (Cisco)	-	7	-	3	19	-	-	-	29
Pumpkin. Sunfish	-	7	-	-	-	-	-	-	7
Northern Pike	-	-	-	47	10	5	2	-	64
Largemouth Bass	-	3	-	3	4	-	-	-	10
Bluegill	8	45	4	-	-	-	-	-	57
Black Crappie	-	3	1	2	-	-	-	-	6

FISH STOCKING DATA

year	species	size	# released
90	Walleye	Fingerling	693
92	Walleye	Fingerling	3,465

NET CATCH DATA

survey date: 8/25/97

	Gill Nets		Trap Nets	
		avg fish		avg fish
species	# per net	wt. (lbs)	# per set	wt. (lbs)
Black Crappie	0.7	0.38	0.8	0.46
Bluegill	4.0	0.28	7.9	0.26
Bowfin (Dogfish)	0.7	3.77	1.9	4.22
Hybrid Sunfish	-	-	0.1	0.07
Largemouth Bass	0.7	1.12	-	-
Northern Pike	9.8	2.05	0.7	0.64
Pumpkin. Sunfish	0.5	0.25	2.6	0.20
Rock Bass	3.8	0.43	1.0	0.24
Tullibee (Cisco)	12.5	0.87	-	-
Walleye	3.5	1.48	-	-
White Sucker	0.5	2.95	-	-
Yellow Bullhead	0.5	0.69	0.2	0.53
Yellow Perch	7.2	0.12	-	-

LENGTH OF SELECTED SPECIES SAMPLED FROM ALL GEAR
Number of fish caught for the following length categories (inches):

species	0-5	6-8	9-11	12-14	15-19	20-24	25-29	>30	Total
Black Crappie	2	3	6	-	-	-	-	-	11
Bluegill	14	80	-	-	-	-	-	-	94
Hybrid Sunfish	1	-	-	-	-	-	-	-	1
Largemouth Bass	-	-	1	3	-	-	-	-	4
Northern Pike	-	-	2	10	29	14	6	4	65
Pumpkin. Sunfish	16	9	-	-	-	-	-	-	25
Rock Bass	8	14	7	-	-	-	-	-	29
Tullibee (Cisco)	-	26	8	22	17	-	-	-	73
Walleye	-	-	4	10	3	-	-	-	21
Yellow Bullhead	-	2	2	1	-	-	-	-	5
Yellow Perch	17	22	1	-	-	-	-	-	40

DNR COMMENTS:
Walleye numbers within expected range for lake class; mean size 16 inches and 1.5 lb.; growth near statewide average after age 1. Northern Pike population within expected range; mean size 19.8 inches and 2 lb. Largemouth Bass sampled in low numbers, but population believed to be in expected range. Black Crappie population about average; mean length 8.1 inches. Bluegill numbers within expected range; good mean length of 6.9 inches. Yellow Perch numbers about average. Ciscoes abundant; numbers are well above lake class average.

FISHING INFORMATION: Bello Lake is regarded as one of the better panfish lakes in the area. It offers good numbers of 1/2- to 3/4-pound Crappies and Bluegills. Terry Schmitz of Frontier Sport in Marcell told us that Bello has some excellent Largemouth Bass, including some 2 1/2- to 3-pound fish. Walleye caught are typically on the large side, and the DNR has been stocking the lake in an attempt to increase numbers. Northerns are abundant, and some large ones are taken occasionally. **Maple Lake** is much smaller than Bello, and it produces some good Walleyes. Bluegill fishing is good – especially around the sunken island on the west side of the lake. Bass fishermen also catch some nice Largemouth. You don't hear a lot about the Crappies, but when you do locate a school, it's usually composed of slabs in the pound-plus range.

NOT FOR NAVIGATION

Bello & Maple Lakes

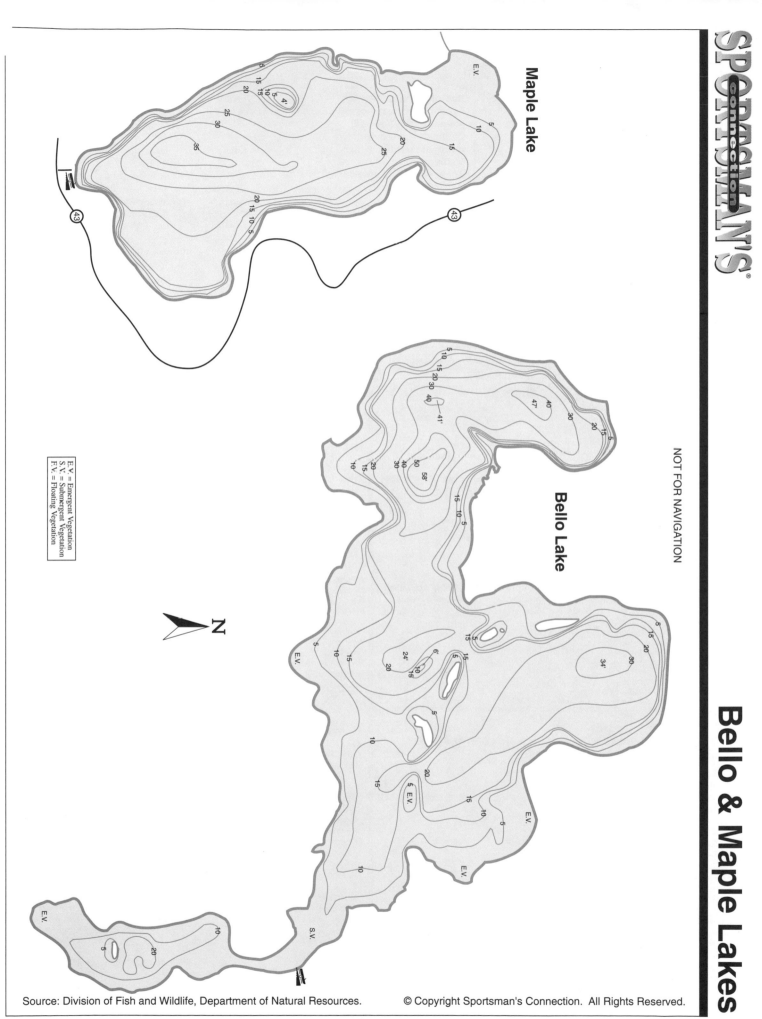

Maple Lake

Bello Lake

E.V. = Emergent Vegetation
S.V. = Submergent Vegetation
F.V. = Floating Vegetation

N

Location: Township 59, 60   Range 26
Watershed: Big Fork

	JOHNSON LAKE	JACK THE HORSE LAKE	BIG DICK LAKE	BURNS LAKE
	Itasca County			
Size of lake:	305 acres	383 acres	249 acres	144 acres
Shorelength:	3.7 miles	7.7 miles	2.6 miles	3.6 miles
Secchi disk (water clarity):	15.0 ft.	8.0 ft.	10.0 ft.	15.0 ft.
Water color:	Brown tint	NA	Clear	Clear
Cause of water color:	NA	NA	NA	NA
Maximum depth:	51.0 ft.	45.0 ft.	28.0 ft.	100.0 ft.
Median depth:	24.6 ft.	11.0 ft.	12.0 ft.	14.0 ft.
Accessibility:	Carry-down off Jack the Horse Road on south shore	Poorly developed public access; off USFS road from state Hwy. #38	USFS-owned access on east shore off USFS Rd. #2181	Federally-owned public access on SE bay off USFS Rd. 2181
Boat Ramp:	Carry-down	Carry-down	Concrete	Earth
Parking:	Limited; side of road	Limited	Limited	Ample
Accommodations:	Resort	Resort	None	None
Shoreland zoning classif.:	Rec. Dev.	Rec. Dev.	Rec. Dev.	Rec. Dev.
Dominant forest/soil type:	Decid/Loam	Decid/Loam	Decid/Loam	NA
Management class:	Walleye	Centrarchid	Centrarchid	Centrarchid
Ecological type:	Hard-water Walleye	Centrarchid	Centrarchid	Centrarchid

Johnson Lake

DNR COMMENTS:
Walleye numbers within expected range for lake class; mean weight 1.8 lb. Northern Pike abundant but small; average weight 1.5 lb.

FISHING INFO:
Johnson's Walleye fishing has been picking up. Some nice Crappies are present, but they're tough to locate, especially in the summer. The north end of the lake, where the creek flows out to Rice Lake, is a good spot to try early. Some lunker Largemouth provide exciting action. Northern Pike are easy to catch, but run small.

FISH STOCKING DATA

year	species	size	# released
90	Walleye	Fry	300,000
92	Walleye	Fry	100,000
94	Walleye	Fry	300,000
97	Walleye	Fry	300,000

NET CATCH DATA
survey date: 6/12/93

	Gill Nets		Trap Nets	
		avg fish		avg fish
species	# per net	wt. (lbs)	# per set	wt. (lbs)
Black Crappie	0.5	0.63	-	-
Bluegill	2.2	0.14	5.7	0.09
Largemouth Bass	0.3	1.30	0.1	0.16
Northern Pike	12.2	1.51	1.1	1.34
Pumpkin. Sunfish	0.3	0.31	3.1	0.09
Rock Bass	2.7	0.32	1.1	0.12
Tullibee (Cisco)	1.3	1.04	-	-
Walleye	3.3	1.85	0.1	3.31
Yellow Perch	22.5	0.11	4.2	0.09

LENGTH OF SELECTED SPECIES SAMPLED FROM ALL GEAR
Number of fish caught for the following length categories (inches):

species	0-5	6-8	9-11	12-14	15-19	20-24	25-29	>30	Total
Black Crappie	-	1	2	-	-	-	-	-	3
Bluegill	54	10	-	-	-	-	-	-	64
Largemouth Bass	-	1	1	-	1	-	-	-	3
Northern Pike	-	1	3	11	44	23	-	1	83
Pumpkin. Sunfish	22	8	-	-	-	-	-	-	30
Rock Bass	11	13	2	-	-	-	-	-	26
Tullibee (Cisco)	-	5	-	1	2	-	-	-	8
Walleye	-	1	-	4	13	3	-	-	21
Yellow Perch	70	101	2	-	-	-	-	-	173

Jack the Horse Lake

FISH STOCKING DATA: NO RECORD OF STOCKING

NET CATCH DATA
survey date: 7/23/82

	Gill Nets		Trap Nets	
		avg fish		avg fish
species	# per net	wt. (lbs)	# per set	wt. (lbs)
Yellow Perch	3.0	0.11	1.4	0.09
Tullibee (Cisco)	12.7	0.28	-	-
Rock Bass	1.0	0.27	3.1	0.27
Pumpkin. Sunfish	0.7	0.18	6.0	0.15
Northern Pike	6.0	1.82	0.1	0.30
Largemouth Bass	0.2	0.50	0.1	0.30
Bluegill	5.7	0.09	38.6	0.11
Black Crappie	0.5	0.23	1.8	0.40

LENGTH OF SELECTED SPECIES SAMPLED FROM ALL GEAR
Number of fish caught for the following length categories (inches):

species	0-5	6-8	9-11	12-14	15-19	20-24	25-29	>30	Total
Black Bullhead	-	3	-	-	1	-	-	-	4
Black Crappie	-	12	5	-	-	-	-	-	17
Bluegill	36	46	-	-	-	-	-	-	82
Largemouth Bass	-	1	-	1	-	-	-	-	2
Northern Pike	-	-	-	1	16	9	9	1	36
Pumpkin. Sunfish	26	38	1	-	-	-	-	-	65
Rock Bass	5	24	2	-	-	-	-	-	31
Tullibee (Cisco)	-	35	8	5	-	-	-	-	48
Yellow Perch	-	28	1	-	-	-	-	-	29

DNR COMMENTS:
High pop. of small Cisco, Northern Pike and Bluegill. Very low pop. of Yellow Perch, LM Bass, and Black Crappie.

FISHING INFO:
Jack the Horse's irregular bays are excellent habitat for Northern Pike and Largemouth Bass. Some of the Bass range in the 4 to 6 pound size. Plan on a good share of snaky Northerns for every keeper, but some 7 to 10 pounders can be found. Crappies aren't plentiful but the sizes are respectable.

Big Dick Lake

DNR COMMENTS:
Big Dick has high populations of Northern Pike and Panfish.

FISHING INFO:
Hefty Northerns, some in the 10- to 13-pound range, roam the lake's weedbeds. Largemouth Bass are also nice-size and numerous. The lake holds good numbers of sunnies and Crappies, but most are on the small side. Big Dick's primitive access and obscure location keep it fairly quiet.

FISH STOCKING DATA: NO RECORD OF STOCKING

NET CATCH DATA
survey date: 7/17/85

	Gill Nets		Trap Nets	
		avg fish		avg fish
species	# per net	wt. (lbs)	# per set	wt. (lbs)
Yellow Perch	3.2	0.11	1.3	0.14
Rock Bass	0.2	0.20	-	-
Pumpkin. Sunfish	0.4	0.10	1.5	0.22
Northern Pike	6.2	3.98	0.3	7.00
Largemouth Bass	1.8	0.47	0.3	1.50
Golden Shiner	0.4	0.13	-	-
Bluegill	8.4	0.04	26.3	0.07
Black Crappie	4.8	0.28	3.3	0.08

LENGTH OF SELECTED SPECIES SAMPLED FROM ALL GEAR
Number of fish caught for the following length categories (inches):

species	0-5	6-8	9-11	12-14	15-19	20-24	25-29	>30	Total
Black Crappie	1	29	5	2	-	-	-	-	37
Bluegill	118	25	4	-	-	-	-	-	147
Largemouth Bass	-	1	8	-	1	-	-	-	10
Northern Pike	-	-	-	-	16	11	4	-	31
Pumpkin. Sunfish	2	5	1	-	-	-	-	-	8
Rock Bass	-	1	-	-	-	-	-	-	1
Yellow Perch	-	16	4	1	-	-	-	-	21

Burns Lake

FISH STOCKING DATA: NO RECORD OF STOCKING

NET CATCH DATA
survey date: 6/23/86

	Gill Nets		Trap Nets	
		avg fish		avg fish
species	# per net	wt. (lbs)	# per set	wt. (lbs)
Yellow Perch	6.2	0.15	0.8	0.10
Rock Bass	2.4	0.33	1.8	0.26
Pumpkin. Sunfish	2.0	0.30	6.8	0.23
Northern Pike	8.4	3.15	0.3	2.50
Largemouth Bass	1.4	1.26	0.3	0.10
Bluegill	4.8	0.18	46.3	0.14
Black Crappie	6.2	0.28	1.5	0.50

LENGTH OF SELECTED SPECIES SAMPLED FROM ALL GEAR
Number of fish caught for the following length categories (inches):

species	0-5	6-8	9-11	12-14	15-19	20-24	25-29	>30	Total
Black Crappie	1	19	17	-	-	-	-	-	37
Bluegill	71	70	-	-	-	-	-	-	141
Largemouth Bass	1	-	2	5	-	-	-	-	8
Northern Pike	-	-	-	1	-	17	22	2	42
Pumpkin. Sunfish	5	32	-	-	-	-	-	-	37
Rock Bass	1	13	5	-	-	-	-	-	19
Yellow Perch	-	34	-	-	-	-	-	-	34

DNR COMMENTS:
Bluegill population very high but fish are small. N Pike population is a little above average. Other fish populations are near average.

FISHING INFO:
Deep, clear waters hold some excellent LM Bass and some good numbers of 5- to 6-pound Northern Pike. The underwater points and bars are most productive, especially in early morning and evening due to the clear water. Crappies are nice when you can find them.

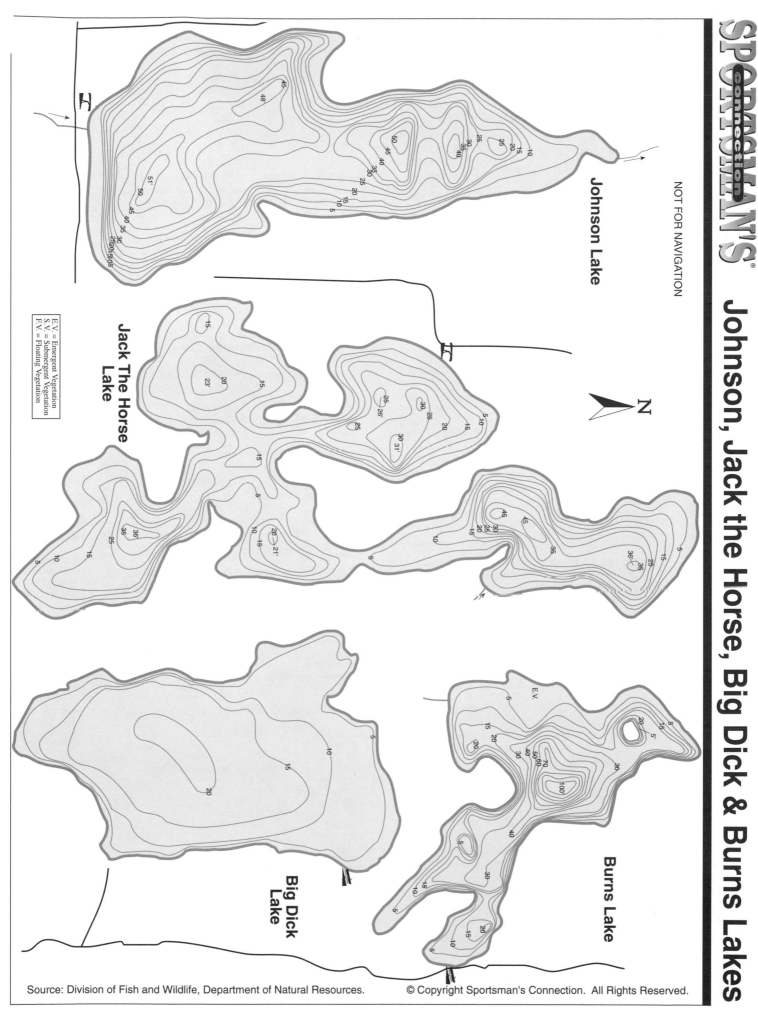

NOT FOR NAVIGATION

N

Johnson Lake

Jack The Horse Lake

E.V. = Emergent Vegetation
S.V. = Submergent Vegetation
F.V. = Floating Vegetation

Big Dick Lake

Burns Lake

Location: Township 59, 60 Range 25, 26
Watershed: Mississippi Headwaters

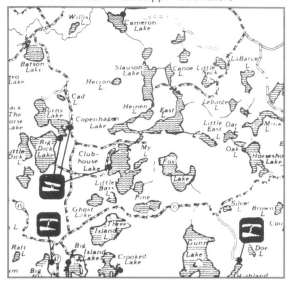

	SLAUSON LAKE	CLUBHOUSE LAKE	EAST LAKE
	Itasca County		
Size of lake:	106 acres	210 acres	160 acres
Shorelength:	1.9 miles	3.6 miles	4.0 miles
Secchi disk (water clarity):	14.0 ft.	22.5 ft.	14.0
Water color:	Clear	Clear	Clear-brown
Cause of water color:	NA	NA	Suspended silt
Maximum depth:	40.0 ft.	103.0 ft.	65.0 ft.
Median depth:	NA	35.0 ft.	19.0 ft.
Accessibility:	Via navigable channel from Clubhouse Lake	Federal-owned public access at campground, west shore	From Clubhouse Lake
Boat Ramp:	On Clubhouse Lake	Concrete	On Clubhouse Lake
Parking:	At Clubhouse Lake	Ample	None
Accommodations:	Resort	Campground	None
Shoreland zoning classif.:	Rec. Dev.	Rec. Dev.	Rec. Dev.
Dominant forest/soil type:	NA	Decid/Loam	Decid/Loam
Management class:	Centrarchid	Centrarchid	Centrarchid
Ecological type:	Centrarchid	Centrarchid	Centrarchid

DNR COMMENTS:
The fish population looks similar to that found in the last lake survey. Northern Pike are more numerous than both the state and local medians. Perch numbers rather low. Panfish population is close to state and local medians.

Slauson Lake

FISH STOCKING DATA: NO RECORD OF STOCKING

NET CATCH DATA

survey date: 9/4/84

	Gill Nets		Trap Nets	
		avg fish		avg fish
species	# per net	wt. (lbs)	# per set	wt. (lbs)
Yellow Perch	1.8	0.14	0.3	0.10
Tullibee (Cisco)	0.3	0.70	-	-
Silver Redhorse	0.3	2.00	-	-
Rock Bass	0.8	0.23	0.5	0.25
Pumpkin. Sunfish	3.0	0.21	0.3	0.30
Northern Pike	8.3	1.35	0.5	1.00
Largemouth Bass	0.8	0.67	-	-
Bluegill	21.3	0.06	1.3	0.14
Black Crappie	4.3	0.47	0.5	0.25
Silver Redhorse	-	-	0.3	4.00

LENGTH OF SELECTED SPECIES SAMPLED FROM ALL GEAR
Number of fish caught for the following length categories (inches):

species	0-5	6-8	9-11	12-14	15-19	20-24	25-29	>30	Total
Black Crappie	1	1	13	4	-	-	-	-	19
Bluegill	30	57	2	-	-	-	-	-	89
Brown Bullhead	-	-	2	1	-	-	-	-	3
Largemouth Bass	-	-	2	1	-	-	-	-	3
Northern Pike	-	-	-	3	27	3	1	1	35
Pumpkin. Sunfish	2	11	-	-	-	-	-	-	13
Rock Bass	1	4	-	-	-	-	-	-	5
Tullibee (Cisco)	-	-	-	1	-	-	-	-	1
Yellow Perch	-	7	-	-	-	-	-	-	7

Clubhouse Lake

FISH STOCKING DATA: NO RECORD OF STOCKING

NET CATCH DATA

survey date: 6/29/92

	Gill Nets		Trap Nets	
		avg fish		avg fish
species	# per net	wt. (lbs)	# per set	wt. (lbs)
Tullibee (Cisco)	2.8	0.36	-	-
Rock Bass	1.5	0.21	1.4	0.19
Pumpkin. Sunfish	1.2	0.23	3.0	0.15
Northern Pike	8.0	1.73	0.3	1.90
Bluegill	1.3	0.10	10.2	0.11
Black Crappie	1.0	0.67	0.3	0.20
Yellow Perch	-	-	0.1	0.10
Silver Redhorse	-	-	0.1	6.10
Largemouth Bass	-	-	0.1	0.20
Hybrid Sunfish	-	-	1.4	0.14

LENGTH OF SELECTED SPECIES SAMPLED FROM ALL GEAR
Number of fish caught for the following length categories (inches):

species	0-5	6-8	9-11	12-14	15-19	20-24	25-29	>30	Total
Tullibee (Cisco)	-	2	12	2	1	-	-	-	17
Rock Bass	6	3	5	-	-	-	-	-	14
Pumpkin. Sunfish	1	7	-	-	-	-	-	-	8
Northern Pike	-	-	-	-	30	10	6	1	47
Bluegill	10	3	-	-	-	-	-	-	13
Black Crappie	-	2	4	-	-	-	-	-	6

DNR COMMENTS:
Northern Pike numerous and the dominant species in this lake; growth average for lake class; mean weight 1.73 lb.; about 1/3 of sample exceeds 21inches. Black Crappie sample relatively small, but indications are the population is medium-size (7 to 9 inches), with average growth rates. Bluegills relatively numerous and small, with only 21 percent of population reaching 6 inches. Yellow Perch population very low. Tullibees and Bowfin both fairly numerous.

East Lake

FISH STOCKING DATA: NO RECORD OF STOCKING

NET CATCH DATA

survey date: 7/14/82

	Gill Nets		Trap Nets	
		avg fish		avg fish
species	# per net	wt. (lbs)	# per set	wt. (lbs)
Warmouth	0.2	0.10	-	-
Tullibee (Cisco)	8.4	0.38	-	-
Rock Bass	1.0	0.30	-	-
Northern Pike	7.2	2.22	0.3	1.50
Bluegill	0.6	0.10	13.8	0.13
Black Crappie	0.2	0.30	1.0	0.23
Yellow Perch	-	-	1.5	0.12
Redhorse	-	-	0.3	7.50
Pumpkin. Sunfish	-	-	0.8	0.10

LENGTH OF SELECTED SPECIES SAMPLED FROM ALL GEAR
Number of fish caught for the following length categories (inches):

species	0-5	6-8	9-11	12-14	15-19	20-24	25-29	>30	Total
Black Crappie	-	3	2	-	-	-	-	-	5
Bluegill	17	37	4	-	-	-	-	-	58
Northern Pike	-	-	-	1	12	17	5	2	37
Pumpkin. Sunfish	1	2	-	-	-	-	-	-	3
Rock Bass	1	2	2	-	-	-	-	-	5
Tullibee (Cisco)	-	-	8	24	-	-	-	-	32
Yellow Perch	-	4	2	-	-	-	-	-	6

DNR COMMENTS:
Cisco, Pumpkinseed and Crappie populations have declined since the 1974 survey. Northern Pike numbers have increased, while populations of other species have remained stable.

FISHING INFORMATION: Clubhouse, East and Slauson Lakes are part of the Rice River chain of lakes designated as the Rice River canoe route by the U.S. Forest Service. **Clubhouse Lake** has a nice campground and concrete boat landing. East Lake and Slauson Lake can be reached by traveling north (downstream) from Clubhouse (see area insert map above). There's beautiful stand of 200-year-old pine trees on East Lake, and the entire chain is very scenic. The Rice River area's virgin pine stands were logged from about 1890 to 1925, utilizing the Rice and Big Fork rivers to move the logs downstream to International Falls. For more information on the historical points of interest and other facts about this route, contact Chippewa National Forest, Marcell Ranger District, Box 155, Marcell, MN 56657, (218) 832-3161. Clubhouse Lake is a good Largemouth Bass lake that also holds some Smallmouth. Northerns and panfish are abundant, though not very large. **Slauson** and **East** Lakes are similar to Clubhouse with good populations of Northern, Bass and panfish. There are no motor restrictions on the chain, but a small boat or canoe is recommended for travel between the lakes.

SPORTSMAN'S Connection® Slauson, Clubhouse & East Lakes

NOT FOR NAVIGATION

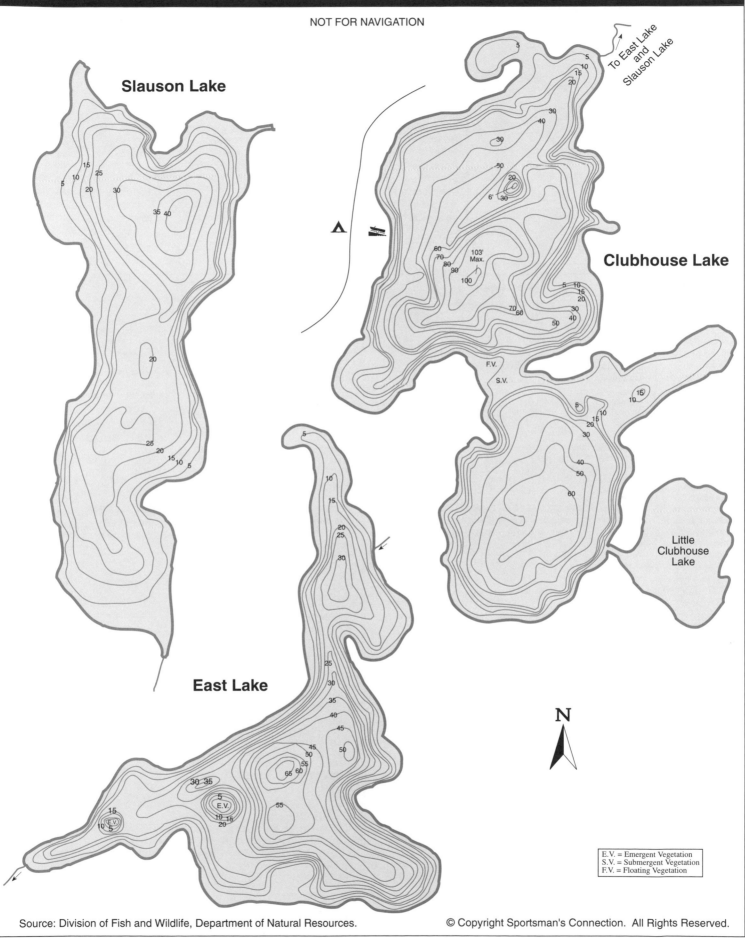

Slauson Lake

Clubhouse Lake

East Lake

Little Clubhouse Lake

To East Lake and Slauson Lake

103' Max.

6'

F.V.
S.V.

E.V.

N

E.V. = Emergent Vegetation
S.V. = Submergent Vegetation
F.V. = Floating Vegetation

Location: Township 60   Range 24
Watershed: Little Fork

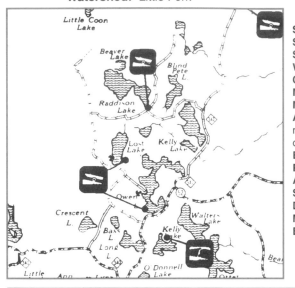

	OWEN LAKE	LOST LAKE	RADDISON LAKE	KELLY LAKE

Itasca County

	OWEN LAKE	LOST LAKE	RADDISON LAKE	KELLY LAKE
Size of lake:	257 acres	88 acres	197 acres	69 acres
Shorelength:	10.0 miles	1.6 miles	3.6 miles	2.2 miles
Secchi disk (water clarity):	14.0 ft.	9.5 ft.	5.9 ft.	7.0 ft.
Water color:	Clear	Amber	NA	Brown
Cause of water color:	NA	Slight bog stain	NA	Swamp stain
Maximum depth:	34.0 ft.	27.0 ft.	40.0 ft.	40.0 ft.
Median depth:	18.0 ft.	14.6 ft.	19.0 ft.	15.9 ft.
Accessibility:	USFS campground on north shore; state-owned public access on southwest shore	State-owned access on southeast shore	County-owned public access on south shore	Public access on north shore
Boat Ramp:	Concrete	Concrete	Concrete	Carry down
Parking:	Ample	Ample	Limited	Limited
Accommodations:	Campground	Campground	None	None
Shoreland zoning classif.:	Rec. Dev.	Nat. Envt.	Rec. Dev.	Rec. Dev.
Dominant forest/soil type:	Decid/Sand	NA	Decid/Sand	NA
Management class:	Walleye-Centrarchid	Centrarchid	Centrarchid	Unclassified
Ecological type:	Centrarchid	Centrarchid	Centrarchid	Unclassified

---

DNR COMMENTS:
Walleye population highest on record ; mean weight 1.8 lb. Northern Pike population largest on record; mean weight 2.4 lb.. Largemouth Bass present. Black Crappie population stable. Bluegills numerous but small. Yellow Perch numerous.

FISHING INFO:
Owen Lake has some nice Walleyes and big Northerns according to the folks at Scenic Pines Store on Highway 52, near Round Lake. Largemouth Bass and Crappie are plentiful.

Owen Lake

FISH STOCKING DATA

year	species	size	# released
90	Walleye	Fingerling	4,675
93	Walleye	Fingerling	6,275
96	Walleye	Fingerling	1,598

survey date: 6/28/94
NET CATCH DATA

	Gill Nets		Trap Nets	
species	# per net	avg fish wt. (lbs)	# per set	avg fish wt. (lbs)
Black Crappie	5.2	0.37	2.0	0.40
Bluegill	13.7	0.09	38.9	0.14
Golden Shiner	-	-	0.1	0.07
Largemouth Bass	1.7	1.29	0.3	0.72
Northern Pike	7.8	2.41	0.6	1.81
Pumpkin. Sunfish	0.5	0.12	1.2	0.20
Walleye	2.0	1.79	-	-
Yellow Perch	18.0	0.11	0.1	0.08

LENGTH OF SELECTED SPECIES SAMPLED FROM ALL GEAR
Number of fish caught for the following length categories (inches):

species	0-5	6-8	9-11	12-14	15-19	20-24	25-29	>30	Total
Black Crappie	2	24	21	-	-	-	-	-	47
Bluegill	130	108	-	-	-	-	-	-	238
Largemouth Bass	-	2	3	7	1	-	-	-	13
Northern Pike	-	1	3	5	13	15	13	2	52
Pumpkin. Sunfish	7	7	-	-	-	-	-	-	14
Walleye	-	-	-	3	6	3	-	-	12
Yellow Perch	41	66	1	-	-	-	-	-	108

Lost Lake

FISH STOCKING DATA

year	species	size	# released
90	Walleye	Fry	100,000

survey date: 6/21/89
NET CATCH DATA

	Gill Nets		Trap Nets	
species	# per net	avg fish wt. (lbs)	# per set	avg fish wt. (lbs)
Yellow Perch	3.0	0.10	-	-
White Sucker	0.5	2.10	-	-
Walleye	1.5	1.32	-	-
Rock Bass	1.8	0.43	1.5	0.42
Northern Pike	19.3	1.52	1.0	1.15
Bluegill	2.0	0.06	20.3	0.13
Black Crappie	0.5	0.10	6.8	0.25
Pumpkin. Sunfish	-	-	7.0	0.10

LENGTH OF SELECTED SPECIES SAMPLED FROM ALL GEAR
Number of fish caught for the following length categories (inches):

species	0-5	6-8	9-11	12-14	15-19	20-24	25-29	>30	Total
Yellow Perch	-	12	-	-	-	-	-	-	12
Walleye	-	-	-	-	5	1	-	-	6
Rock Bass	3	1	3	-	-	-	-	-	7
Northern Pike	-	-	-	-	42	34	-	1	77
Bluegill	8	-	-	-	-	-	-	-	8
Black Crappie	-	2	-	-	-	-	-	-	2

DNR COMMENTS:
N. Pike are very abundant at 19.3/gillnet, but growth is slow. Walleye abundance is low at only 1.5/gillnet. Five of the 6 Walleye sampled were age 3, and coincide with fry stocking in 1986. Bluegill and Black Crappie indices are above state and local means.

FISHING INFO:
This lake is small and picturesque with a lot of hammerhandle Northerns, small panfish and some Walleye. The campground only has a few sites.

DNR COMMENTS:
N. Pike abundant. Perch and LM Bass abundant; SM Bass have declined. Pumpkinseed and Bluegill abundance has increased. Natural reproduction seems adequate to maintain fish population.

FISHING INFO:
Raddison gives up nice Crappie. Late winter before ice out is a good time. Largemouth fishing is good; nice-size Smallmouth can also be found. Northerns and Bluegills are plentiful and found throughout.

Raddison Lake

FISH STOCKING DATA: NO RECORD OF STOCKING

survey date: 7/2/82
NET CATCH DATA

	Gill Nets		Trap Nets	
species	# per net	avg fish wt. (lbs)	# per set	avg fish wt. (lbs)
Yellow Perch	10.8	0.11	-	-
Smallmouth Bass	0.5	2.13	-	-
Pumpkin. Sunfish	2.0	0.09	12.8	0.18
Northern Pike	7.5	2.20	0.5	3.37
Largemouth Bass	0.3	0.20	2.5	0.69
Bluegill	2.8	0.11	73.2	0.19
Black Crappie	1.3	0.22	0.5	0.70

LENGTH OF SELECTED SPECIES SAMPLED FROM ALL GEAR
Number of fish caught for the following length categories (inches):

species	0-5	6-8	9-11	12-14	15-19	20-24	25-29	>30	Total
Black Crappie	1	2	4	1	-	-	-	-	8
Bluegill	9	106	3	-	-	-	-	-	118
Largemouth Bass	-	6	4	5	1	-	-	-	16
Northern Pike	-	-	-	1	7	15	9	-	32
Pumpkin. Sunfish	7	77	1	-	-	-	-	-	85
Smallmouth Bass	-	-	-	1	1	-	-	-	2
Yellow Perch	-	43	-	-	-	-	-	-	43

Kelly Lake

FISH STOCKING DATA: NO RECORD OF STOCKING

survey date: 8/13/82
NET CATCH DATA

	Gill Nets		Trap Nets	
species	# per net	avg fish wt. (lbs)	# per set	avg fish wt. (lbs)
Yellow Perch	5.3	0.09	3.0	0.11
White Sucker	0.7	2.15	-	-
Rock Bass	0.7	0.45	0.5	0.15
Pumpkin. Sunfish	4.0	0.08	3.0	0.09
Northern Pike	1.7	2.10	-	-
Bluegill	2.7	0.10	17.3	0.10
Black Crappie	6.3	0.14	0.8	0.27

LENGTH OF SELECTED SPECIES SAMPLED FROM ALL GEAR
Number of fish caught for the following length categories (inches):

species	0-5	6-8	9-11	12-14	15-19	20-24	25-29	>30	Total
Black Crappie	5	9	8	-	-	-	-	-	22
Bluegill	52	25	-	-	-	-	-	-	77
Northern Pike	-	-	-	-	2	3	-	-	5
Pumpkin. Sunfish	23	1	-	-	-	-	-	-	24
Rock Bass	1	2	1	-	-	-	-	-	4
Yellow Perch	-	27	-	-	-	-	-	-	27

DNR COMMENTS:
Abundance of Perch and Northern Pike is slightly below local catch medians. Bluegill abundance is moderately higher than local medians, while the numbers of other fish seem to be within normal limits. Natural reproduction for all fish except Northern Pike appears adequate for population maintenance.

FISHING INFO:
This is a Bass, panfish, Northern Pike lake. It's perhaps worth a try.

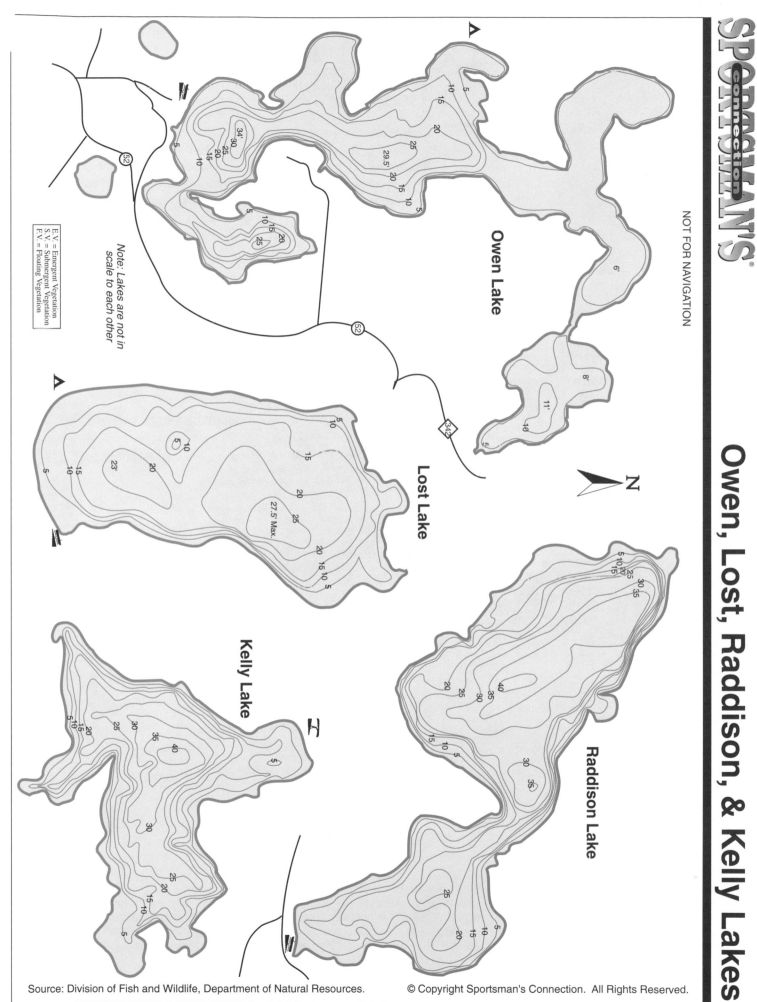

Owen, Lost, Raddison, & Kelly Lakes

NOT FOR NAVIGATION

Owen Lake

Lost Lake

Kelly Lake

Raddison Lake

Note: Lakes are not in scale to each other

E.V. = Emergent Vegetation
S.V. = Submergent Vegetation
F.V. = Floating Vegetation

COON LAKE
Itasca County

Location: Township 60, 61 Range 25

Watershed: Big Fork

Size of lake: 627 acres

Shorelength: 8.9 miles

Secchi disk (water clarity): 8.0 ft.

Water color: Clear

Cause of water color: NA

Maximum depth: 36.0 ft.

Median depth: NA

Accessibility: Two state-owned public accesses on west shore in Scenic State Park

Boat Ramp: Concrete (both)

Parking: Ample

Accommodations: Campground, State Park

Shoreland zoning classification: Natural Environment

Dominant forest/soil type: NA

Management class: Walleye-Centrarchid

Ecological type: Centrarchid-Walleye

FISH STOCKING DATA

year	species	size	# released
90	Walleye	Fingerling	20,380
96	Walleye	Fingerling	4,100

NET CATCH DATA

survey date: 7/9/84

	Gill Nets		Trap Nets	
species	# per net	avg fish wt. (lbs.)	# per set	avg fish wt. (lbs.)
Yellow Perch	16.6	0.14	0.9	0.21
White Sucker	0.1	2.50	-	-
Walleye	1.1	2.13	0.1	2.00
Pumpkin. Sunfish	3.1	0.09	9.5	0.13
Northern Pike	9.9	1.69	0.5	0.62
Bluegill	0.6	0.10	36.8	0.24
Black Crappie	0.3	0.37	0.4	0.33
Black Bullhead	0.3	0.10	-	-
Largemouth Bass	-	-	0.5	0.20
Brown Bullhead	-	-	0.1	1.50

LENGTH OF SELECTED SPECIES SAMPLED FROM ALL GEAR

Number of fish caught for the following length categories (inches):

species	0-5	6-8	9-11	12-14	15-19	20-24	25-29	>30	Total
Black Bullhead	-	3	-	-	-	-	-	-	3
Black Crappie	-	4	2	1	-	-	-	-	7
Bluegill	26	90	11	-	-	-	-	-	127
Brown Bullhead	-	-	-	1	-	-	-	-	1
Largemouth Bass	-	4	-	-	-	-	-	-	4
Northern Pike	-	-	4	15	52	15	3	5	94
Pumpkin. Sunfish	54	33	-	-	-	-	-	-	87
Walleye	-	-	-	-	7	4	-	-	11
Yellow Perch	-	100	20	3	-	-	-	-	123

DNR COMMENTS: Bluegill, Northern Pike, and Perch numbers above state and local medians.

FISHING INFORMATION: Coon Lake and Sandwick Lake are essentially one body of water contained in the Scenic State Park. Walleye fishing has improved substantially, according to local anglers, probably due in large part to the DNR's stocking program. Bluegill fishing provides the most action, and there are good numbers of fish in the half-pound range. Northern Pike and Largemouth Bass can also be found throughout the lake's weedbeds. Scenic State Park includes a nice campground and good boat launches. Good panfish action for the kids, combined with pristine surroundings, make this an excellent area for a family vacation. Bait, tackle, grub, and brew are all within a short distance.

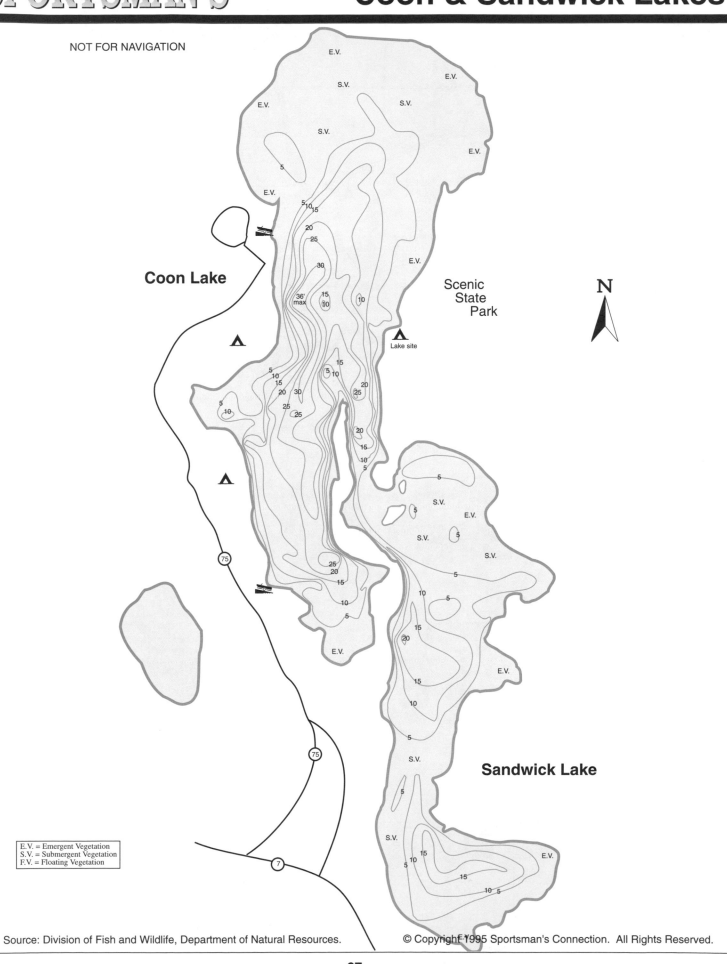

NOT FOR NAVIGATION

Coon Lake

Scenic
State
Park

N

Sandwick Lake

E.V. = Emergent Vegetation
S.V. = Submergent Vegetation
F.V. = Floating Vegetation

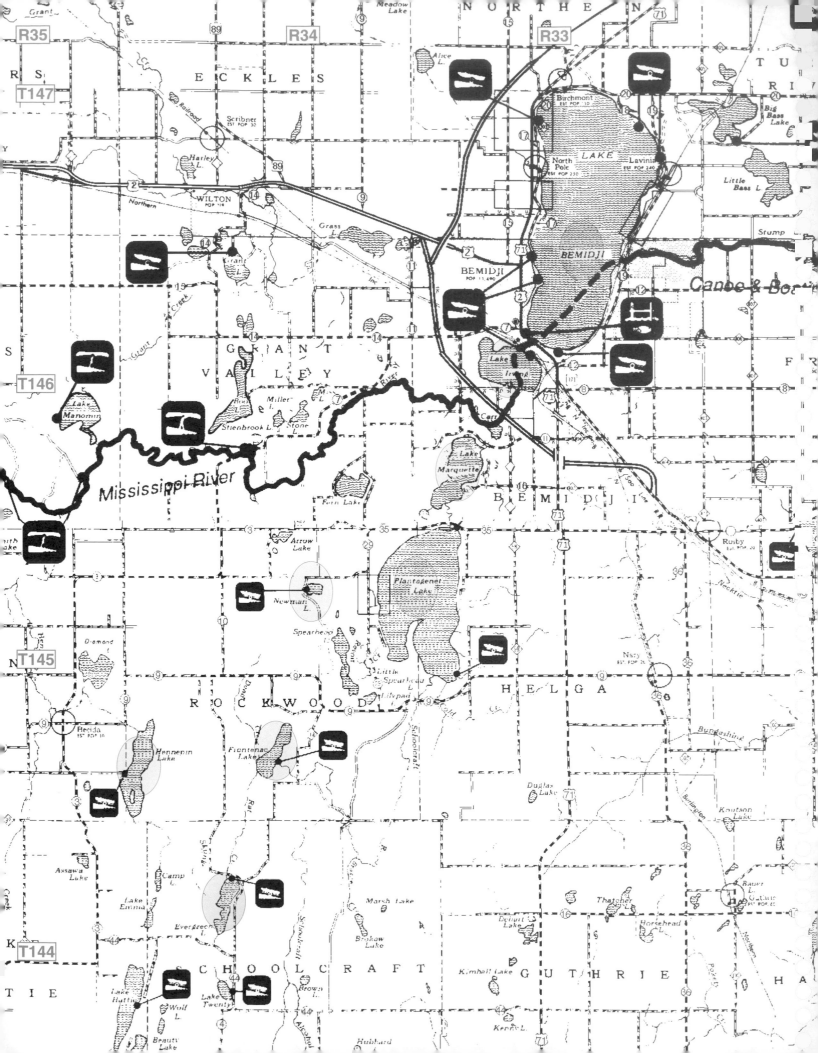

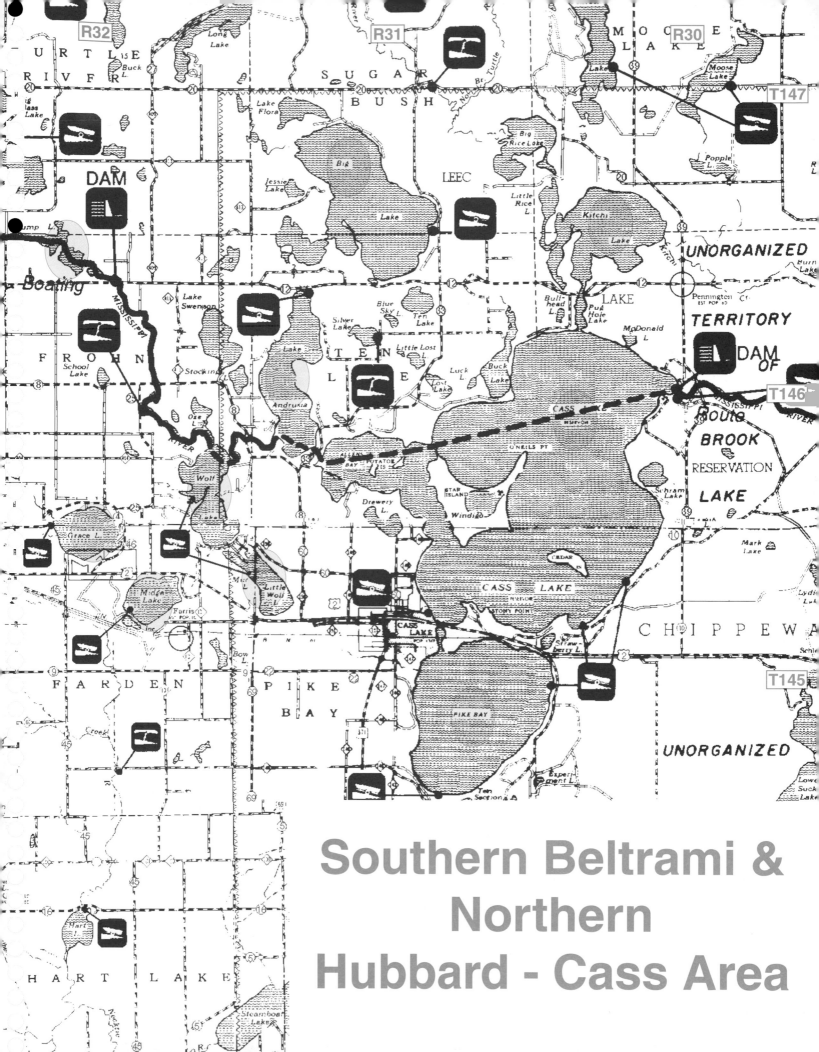

Southern Beltrami & Northern Hubbard - Cass Area

LAKE BEMIDJI
Beltrami County

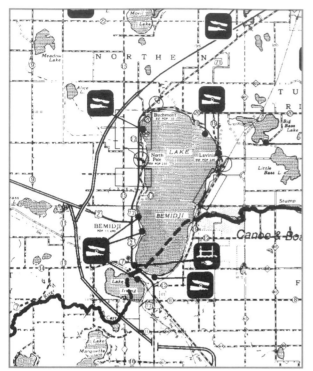

Location: Township 146,147
Range 32,33
Watershed: Mississippi Headwaters
Surface Water Area: 6,420 acres
Shorelength: 14.8 miles
Secchi disk (water clarity): 9.1 ft.
Water color: Grey-green
Cause of water color: Algae

Maximum depth: 76 ft.
Median depth: 34 ft.
Accessibility: One on south
shore; 2 on northeast shore;
2 on west shore (see map)
Boat Ramp: Concrete, metal
Accommodations: Parks, resort,
fishing, pier, swimming beach

Shoreland zoning classification: General Development
Dominant forest/soil type: Deciduous Sand
Management class: Walleye
Ecological type: Hard-water Walleye

FISH STOCKING DATA

year	species	size	# released
90	Muskellunge	Fingerling	1,820
92	Muskellunge	Fingerling	1,986
94	Muskellunge	Fingerling	2,850
96	Muskellunge	Fingerling	1,853

survey date: **NET CATCH DATA**

8/22/94

species	Gill Nets # per net	Gill Nets avg fish wt. (lbs.)	Trap Nets # per set	Trap Nets avg fish wt. (lbs.)
Black Crappie	0.1	0.72	0.2	0.60
Bluegill	-	-	trace	0.44
Common Shiner	-	-	0.3	0.08
Hybrid Sunfish	trace	0.64	0.7	0.45
Lake Whitefish	trace	1.10	-	-
Largemouth Bass	-	-	1.1	0.29
Muskellunge	trace	2.72	-	-
Northern Pike	2.5	3.39	0.7	2.10
Pumpkin. Sunfish	-	-	trace	0.43
Rock Bass	0.8	0.61	0.7	0.66
Tullibee (Cisco)	12.3	0.65	-	-
Walleye	10.7	1.46	0.7	1.15
Yellow Perch	103.7	0.21	42.7	0.17

LENGTH OF SELECTED SPECIES SAMPLED FROM ALL GEAR
Number of fish caught for the following length categories (inches):

species	0-5	6-8	9-11	12-14	15-19	20-24	25-29	>30	Total
Black Crappie	1	-	4	-	-	-	-	-	5
Bluegill	-	1	-	-	-	-	-	-	1
Hybrid Sunfish	-	10	1	-	-	-	-	-	11
Lake Whitefish	-	-	-	1	-	-	-	-	1
Largemouth Bass	15	-	-	1	1	-	-	-	17
Muskellunge	-	-	-	-	-	1	-	-	1
Northern Pike	-	1	4	-	6	26	8	3	48
Pumpkin. Sunfish	-	1	-	-	-	-	-	-	1
Rock Bass	2	11	10	-	-	-	-	-	23
Tullibee (Cisco)	-	35	23	126	1	-	-	-	185
Walleye	-	9	34	40	67	19	3	-	172
Yellow Perch	111	343	100	1	-	-	-	-	555

DNR COMMENTS: Walleye population above third-quartile levels for lake class; 58 percent of population exceeds 15 inches; fish to 27 inches present; average weight 1.5 lb. Northern Pike numbers down and in first-quartile range for lake class; average weight 3.4 lb.; 83 percent of Pike exceed 21 inches. Ciscoes numerous. One Muskellunge sampled; anglers report good numbers of sightings; fish to 52 inches have been caught. Largemouth Bass sampled during shoreline seining; few adult fish captured. Black Crappies, Bluegills, and Pumpkinseeds scarce. Lake Whitefish numbers low. Yellow Perch abundance down but numbers still above third-quartile range.

FISHING INFORMATION: This 6,400-acre lake is considered one of the best places in the region to fish year round for Walleyes and Perch. There are also a few big Northern Pike around. The lake is full of structure and has fertile weedbeds, along with holes as deep as 70 feet. Because Bemidji is bisected by a bar crossing west to east at Diamond Point, it's almost like two lakes. That impression is reinforced by the fact that the south end is swept by a weak current of the Mississippi River, while the north part – isolated by the long bar – is barely current-influenced at all. The long bars are good places to find Walleyes early in the season. Try the two bars north of Diamond Point, near Cameron Park by Highway 17. And check out the Clam Bar and the North Bar along the west shore. Rock Pile Bar at the center of the lake is considered one of the great Walleye spots in the spring, and the area surrounding it remains productive right through summer into fall. Crossing the Diamond Point Bar into the south part of the lake, head for the bar off the south shore at the swimming beach. Spring anglers do well there, using leeches or minnows and working the sides of sand bars rather than the tops. A favorite summer area is off the bar at the lake's northeast corner called Rocky Point. Other spots productive in summer include the sunken island nearly at mid lake in the north end; Lost Bar and Hook Bar in the south end, and the south end of the lake off the bar at the river's inlet. The cabbage along the east side is usually inhabited by lots of small Perch, and Walleyes should be there looking for them. Backtroll or just drift outside the weedbeds with a leech or minnow. Wagner's Point, near Cameron Park, on the west side of the lake, is a good Northern spot because of the thick offshore weeds. There are also good submerged weeds at the northwest corner of the lake. Other Pike locations include Rocky Point, in the northeast corner; the flats north of the big, lake-crossing bar; and the heavily weeded area at the outlet of the Mississippi River. You may turn out a few fair-size Largemouth Bass if you go into the weeds with weedless or topwater gear.

NOT FOR NAVIGATION

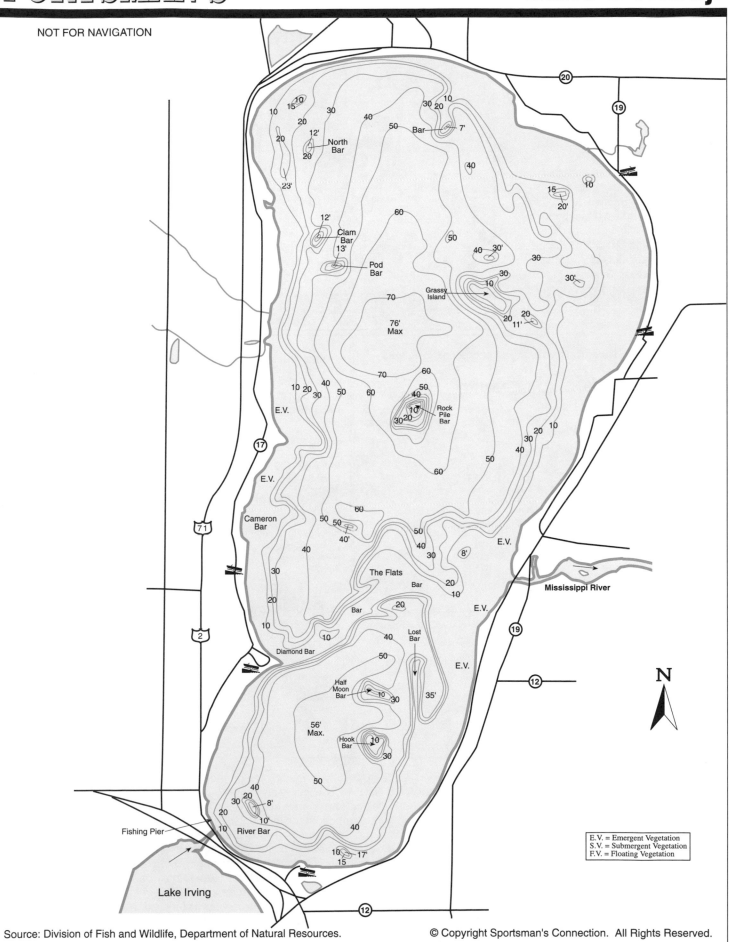

North Bar

12'

20

23'

10 15 10
20
20
30
40
50 Bar 7'
30 10
20

40

15
20'
10

12'
Clam Bar 13'
Pod Bar

60

50

40 30'
30

30

30'

Grassy Island

76' Max

70

20 20
11'

70
60

10 20 40 50 60
30 50 60

E.V.

50
40
10
30 20
Rock Pile Bar

20
30 40

10

20

50

60

E.V.

17

71

60
50 50
40'

Cameron Bar

40

30

20

10

The Flats

Bar

Bar

20

Diamond Bar

10

8'

E.V.

20
10

E.V.

Mississippi River

2

40

Lost Bar

E.V.

19

Half Moon Bar
10 30

35'

E.V.

12

N

56' Max.

50

Hook Bar 10
30

40

50

40 20
30 8'
20 10'

River Bar

10

Fishing Pier

40

10 17'
15

Lake Irving

E.V. = Emergent Vegetation
S.V. = Submergent Vegetation
F.V. = Floating Vegetation

20
19

12

Source: Division of Fish and Wildlife, Department of Natural Resources.

LAKE IRVING

LAKE MARQUETTE

Beltrami County

Location: Township 146 Range 33
Watershed: Mississippi Headwaters
Surface Water Area: 613 acres
Shorelength: 4.8 miles
Secchi disk (water clarity): NA
Water color: NA
Cause of water color: NA
Maximum depth: 16 ft.
Median depth: 8 ft.
Accessibility: City-owned public access on north shore near outlet
Boat Ramp: Concrete
Accommodations: 10 unit parking, dock
Shoreland zoning classif.: Gen. Dev.
Dominant forest/soil type: No Tree/Wet
Management class: Game
Ecological type: Roughfish-Gamefish

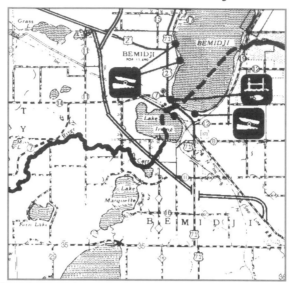

Location: Township 146 Range 33
Watershed: Mississippi Headwaters
Surface Water Area: 504 acres
Shorelength: 4.9 miles
Secchi disk (water clarity): 12.0 ft.
Water color: Greenish
Cause of water color: Algae
Maximum depth: 51 ft.
Median depth: 13 ft.
Accessibility: Access via navigable river channel from Lake Irving
Boat Ramp: Concrete ramp on Lake Irving
Accommodations: NA
Shoreland zoning classif.: Rec. Dev.
Dominant forest/soil type: Decid/Wet
Management class: Centrarchid
Ecological type: Centrarchid

DNR COMMENTS:
Northern Pike and Walleye populations about double local median levels. Yellow Perch population large, with a few catchable Perch available. Bullhead population dominated by the Yellow species; Brown species present; numbers of both may warrant commercial harvest.

FISH STOCKING DATA: NO RECORD OF STOCKING

survey date: 08/07/90

NET CATCH DATA

species	Gill Nets # per net	Gill Nets avg fish wt. (lbs)	Trap Nets # per set	Trap Nets avg fish wt. (lbs)
Tullibee (incl. Cisco)	0.3	0.90	-	-
Northern Pike	7.0	2.75	1.4	2.21
Shorthead Redhorse	3.3	2.40	-	-
Silver Lamprey	0.3	1.30	-	-
White Sucker	6.3	1.74	-	-
Black Bullhead	21.8	0.70	0.3	0.20
Yellow Bullhead	22.5	0.55	2.3	0.92
Brown Bullhead	4.0	1.08	3.5	0.83
Rock Bass	1.5	0.38	0.4	0.39
Pumpkin. Sunfish	3.5	0.21	3.5	0.10
Black Crappie	0.3	0.10	0.9	0.79
Yellow Perch	66.5	0.11	6.8	0.10
Walleye	2.8	1.13	1.1	0.96
Bluegill Sunfish	-	-	0.4	0.07
Largemouth Bass	-	-	0.1	1.80

LENGTH OF SELECTED SPECIES SAMPLED FROM ALL GEAR
Number of fish caught for the following length categories (inches):

species	0-5	6-8	9-11	12-14	15-19	20-24	25-29	>30	Total
Yellow Perch	134	84	2	-	-	-	-	-	220
Yellow Bullhead	-	34	48	8	-	-	-	-	90
Walleye	-	-	2	5	2	2	-	-	11
Tullibee (Cisco)	-	-	-	1	-	-	-	-	1
Rock Bass	-	5	1	-	-	-	-	-	6
Pumpkin. Sunfish	6	8	-	-	-	-	-	-	14
Northern Pike	-	-	-	1	7	15	2	3	28
Brown Bullhead	-	-	4	12	-	-	-	-	16
Black Crappie	1	-	-	-	-	-	-	-	1
Black Bullhead	-	15	66	6	-	-	-	-	87

FISH STOCKING DATA: NO RECORD OF STOCKING

survey date: 06/23/87

NET CATCH DATA

species	Gill Nets # per net	Gill Nets avg fish wt. (lbs)	Trap Nets # per set	Trap Nets avg fish wt. (lbs)
Yellow Perch	25.2	0.21	2.3	0.33
Yellow Bullhead	5.2	0.69	13.4	0.77
White Sucker	5.2	2.34	0.6	2.23
Walleye	6.4	1.28	0.7	2.76
Tullibee (incl. Cisco)	10.6	1.02	-	-
Rock Bass	0.4	0.90	0.7	0.77
Pumpkin. Sunfish	1.2	0.37	3.9	0.34
Northern Pike	18.2	1.81	0.8	2.05
Brown Bullhead	3.0	1.31	3.6	0.68
Black Bullhead	1.4	0.61	1.4	0.69
Bluegill	-	-	0.2	0.55

LENGTH OF SELECTED SPECIES SAMPLED FROM ALL GEAR
Number of fish caught for the following length categories (inches):

species	0-5	6-8	9-11	12-14	15-19	20-24	25-29	>30	Total
Black Bullhead	-	5	12	4	-	-	-	-	21
Bluegill	-	2	-	-	-	-	-	-	2
Brown Bullhead	-	-	31	20	-	-	-	-	51
Northern Pike	-	-	-	8	33	49	5	2	97
Pumpkin. Sunfish	4	40	-	-	-	-	-	-	44
Rock Bass	-	3	3	3	-	-	-	-	9
Tullibee (Cisco)	-	4	15	13	21	-	-	-	53
Walleye	-	-	-	10	20	7	1	-	38
Yellow Bullhead	-	4	36	46	-	-	-	-	86
Yellow Perch	-	95	29	8	-	-	-	-	132

DNR COMMENTS:
Cisco, Northern Pike, White Sucker, and Walleye catch rates all above state and local medians. Black and Brown Bullhead numbers at medians, and Yellow Bullheads more abundant. Pumpkinseed numbers normal for lake class, but Bluegill numbers very low.

FISHING INFORMATION: These two lakes on the south side of the city of Bemidji are connected to each other and to Lake Bemidji by the Schoolcraft River. Both hold decent populations of Northern Pike, Walleyes, and panfish, so it's not surprising that they get a good deal of pressure in summer and winter. Earl Taber of Taber's Bait in Bemidji says spring is the best time to fish **Lake Irving**. You can find Walleyes then at the points on the south and east sides, as well as around a submerged island at mid lake. Many of the Walleyes in Irving have migrated in from Lake Bemidji via the river. Northerns are often found hanging around the north shore, where weeds are heaviest in the spring. You will also do well north and south off the river's inlet and outlet. Fair numbers of Crappies and Largemouth Bass inhabit the small southwest bay. **Lake Marquette** is immediately south of Irving and, while larger and deeper, may be more difficult to fish. There are a lot of Northerns to be found, as well as bunches of Ciscoes and Perch for them to prey on. Find the Northerns cruising the outer edges of weedbeds in the spring. The narrow cinch between the two bays can be a real hotspot for them and a good place to find Walleyes as well. Also, look for Walleyes early in the season at the submerged island toward the north end of the lake, where the bottom rises from 20 feet to about 5 feet. It's the sort of place goggle eyes like in the spring. The submerged island in the northeast corner of the lower bay also is Walleye country.

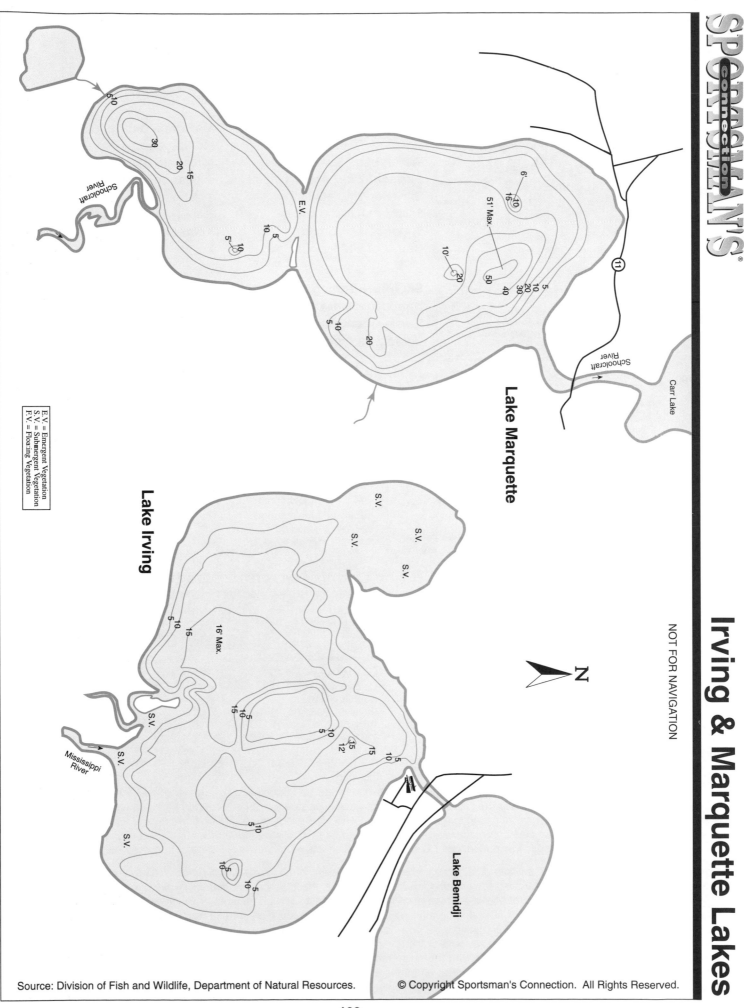

Irving & Marquette Lakes

NOT FOR NAVIGATION

N

Lake Marquette

Lake Irving

Schoolcraft River

Schoolcraft River

Carr Lake

Lake Bemidji

Mississippi River

E.V.
S.V.
F.V.

51' Max.

16' Max.

E.V. = Emergent Vegetation
S.V. = Submergent Vegetation
F.V. = Floaing Vegetation

Source: Division of Fish and Wildlife, Department of Natural Resources.

LAKE PLANTAGANETTE
Hubbard County

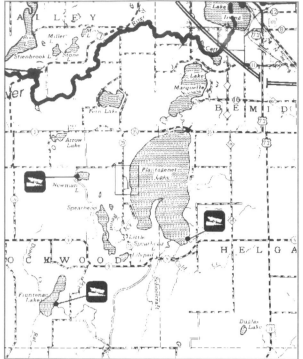

Location: Township 145, 146
Range 33, 34
Watershed: Mississippi Headwaters
Surface Water Area: 2,529 acres
Shorelength: 10.8 miles
Secchi disk (water clarity): 7.1 ft.
Water color: Green
Cause of water color: Algae

Maximum depth: 65 ft.
Median depth: NA
Accessibility: State-owned access on southeast corner; township access on northeast corner
Boat Ramp: Concrete, earth
Accommodations: Resort

Shoreland zoning classification: Recreational Development
Dominant forest/soil type: Conifer/Wet
Management class: Walleye-Centrarchid
Ecological type: Centrarchid-Walleye

FISH STOCKING DATA

year	species	size	# released
90	Muskellunge	Fingerling	3,819
90	Walleye	Fry	750,000
92	Muskellunge	Fingerling	3,797
92	Walleye	Fry	750,000
93	Muskellunge	Fingerling	3,794
94	Muskellunge	Fingerling	3,802
94	Muskellunge	Fry	750,000
95	Muskellunge	Fingerling	3,737
96	Walleye	Fry	740,000
97	Muskellunge	Fingerling	3,794

NET CATCH DATA

survey date: 8/8/94

species	Gill Nets # per net	Gill Nets avg fish wt. (lbs.)	Trap Nets # per set	Trap Nets avg fish wt. (lbs.)
Black Bullhead	-	-	trace	0.35
Black Crappie	trace	0.59	0.3	0.50
Bluegill	-	-	0.3	0.39
Brown Bullhead	0.1	1.46	0.9	1.35
Hybrid Sunfish	-	-	trace	0.61
Lake Whitefish	trace	3.93	-	-
Largemouth Bass	-	-	1.6	0.18
Northern Pike	1.0	2.19	0.4	3.44
Pumpkin. Sunfish	trace	0.04	0.5	0.42
Rock Bass	-	-	1.9	0.67
Shorthead Redhorse	-	-	trace	1.05
Tullibee (Cisco)	3.7	1.07	-	-
Walleye	10.0	1.01	0.9	1.67
White Sucker	8.3	1.47	1.1	2.19
Yellow Bullhead	trace	0.84	0.2	0.47
Yellow Perch	22.5	0.19	8.4	0.13

LENGTH OF SELECTED SPECIES SAMPLED FROM ALL GEAR

Number of fish caught for the following length categories (inches):

species	0-5	6-8	9-11	12-14	15-19	20-24	25-29	>30	Total
Black Crappie	-	1	4	-	-	-	-	-	5
Bluegill	1	3	-	-	-	-	-	-	4
Brown Bullhead	-	-	2	13	-	-	-	-	15
Hybrid Sunfish	-	1	-	-	-	-	-	-	1
Lake Whitefish	-	-	-	-	-	1	-	-	1
Largemouth Bass	21	-	-	-	1	-	-	-	22
Northern Pike	-	-	1	1	5	5	7	1	20
Pumpkin. Sunfish	2	6	-	-	-	-	-	-	8
Rock Bass	2	10	13	1	-	-	-	-	26
Tullibee (Cisco)	-	12	5	5	30	-	-	-	52
Walleye	-	7	52	46	31	13	3	-	152
Yellow Perch	71	333	27	1	-	-	-	-	432

DNR COMMENTS: Walleye numbers down but still above third-quartile range for lake class; average length 13.6 inches, but fish to 26.2 inches captured. Plantaganette is used by the DNR as a source of Muskellunge eggs; lake produces Muskies larger than 50 inches; at this writing (1999), there was a 48-inch minimum length restriction in effect for this species; check current regs before fishing. Northern Pike numbers below normal for lake class; average weight 2.3 lb.; fish to 31 inches sampled; about 50 percent of Pike exceed 21 inches. Yellow Perch numbers about average; average length 7.3 inches; a few fish are grub-infested. Bullhead numbers low.

FISHING INFORMATION: Over 2,500 acres of fairly clear water, a good weedline, and a maximum depth of 65 feet all add up to good fishing. Plantaganette is best known for Walleyes, Northerns, and some Muskies, though there are certainly a fair number of smaller fish, especially Yellow Perch. The Northerns are of above-average size, while the Walleye, though abundant, are on the small side. A 2-pounder is considered a good catch, and 5 pounds is unusual. The most popular (and most productive) area for early Walleyes is the large point coming from the south shore. This has good gravel and sand bars, on which Walleyes feed in the morning; toss them a shiner or minnow on a bottom rig. Other good spots include the two sunken islands near the north shore which are only under 5 feet of water. The lake is connected to the Mississippi by the Schoolcraft River, and the inlet and outlet (on the north and south shores, respectively) are noted Northern Pike hotspots most of the season. Trolling for Northerns over the flats on the east and west shores is also productive. Muskellunge fingerlings have been planted by the DNR, but the majority of those Muskies were still below legal size in 1995. Check current regs for size restrictions.

SPORTSMAN'S CONNECTION

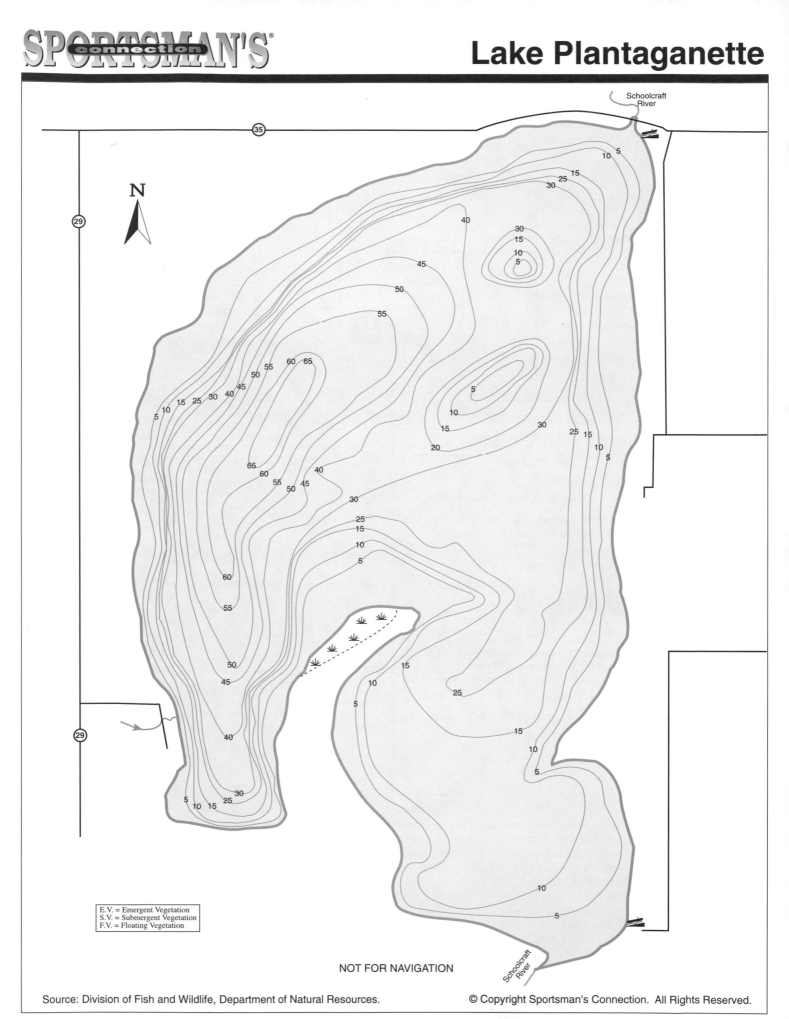

Schoolcraft River

35

N

29

E.V. = Emergent Vegetation
S.V. = Submergent Vegetation
F.V. = Floating Vegetation

29

NOT FOR NAVIGATION

Schoolcraft River

Source: Division of Fish and Wildlife, Department of Natural Resources.

FRONTENAC LAKE

Hubbard County

Location: Township 145 Range 34
Watershed: Mississippi Headwaters
Surface Water Area: 204 acres
Shorelength: 3.2 miles
Secchi disk (water clarity): 8.0 ft.
Water color: Brown
Cause of water color: Bog stain
Maximum depth: 16 ft.
Median depth: NA
Accessibility: Public access on southeast shore
Boat Ramp: Earth
Accommodations: NA
Shoreland zoning classif.: Nat. Envir.
Dominant forest/soil type: Decid/Wet
Management class: Centrarchid
Ecological type: Centrarchid

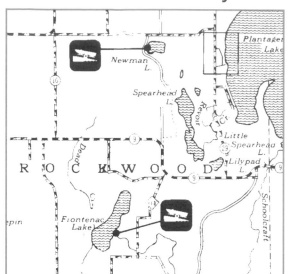

NEWMAN LAKE

Location: Township 145 Range 34
Watershed: Mississippi Headwaters
Surface Water Area: 39 acres
Shorelength: NA
Secchi disk (water clarity): 25.0 ft.
Water color: Clear
Cause of water color: NA
Maximum depth: 63 ft.
Median depth: NA
Accessibility: County-owned public access on west shore
Boat Ramp: Earth
Accommodations: NA
Shoreland zoning classif.: Nat. Envir.
Dominant forest/soil type: NA
Management class: Trout
Ecological type: Unclassified

DNR COMMENTS:
Northern Pike numbers high, but size generally small; mean weight 1.57 lb.; small size structure indicated, with few fish reaching quality length; growth slow. Walleyes fairly numerous at slightly above third-quartile values; mean weight 2.2 lb.; natural reproduction success rate low. Largemouth Bass population up to normal range for lake class. Bluegills scarce. Pumpkinseeds numerous, and population is increasing. Yellow Perch numerous.

FISH STOCKING DATA

No record of stocking since 1987.

NET CATCH DATA
survey date: 07/22/91

species	Gill Nets # per net	Gill Nets avg fish wt. (lbs)	Trap Nets # per set	Trap Nets avg fish wt. (lbs)
Yellow Perch	83.5	0.11	2.2	0.10
Yellow Bullhead	32.5	0.24	9.0	0.28
White Sucker	0.8	2.30	-	-
Walleye	0.5	2.20	0.4	5.55
Pumpkin. Sunfish	14.5	0.27	0.4	0.15
Northern Pike	14.0	1.59	-	-
Largemouth Bass	0.8	1.43	0.1	0.26
Brown Bullhead	1.5	0.62	0.2	1.00
Bluegill	1.3	0.32	0.6	1.00
Black Bullhead	2.8	0.49	-	-
Rock Bass	-	-	0.6	0.27

LENGTH OF SELECTED SPECIES SAMPLED FROM ALL GEAR
Number of fish caught for the following length categories (inches):

species	0-5	6-8	9-11	12-14	15-19	20-24	25-29	>30	Total
Yellow Perch	-	92	8	-	-	-	-	-	100
Yellow Bullhead	-	48	12	-	-	-	-	-	60
Walleye	-	-	-	-	1	1	-	-	2
Pumpkin. Sunfish	-	58	-	-	-	-	-	-	58
Northern Pike	-	-	-	-	29	23	3	1	56
Largemouth Bass	-	-	-	2	1	-	-	-	3
Brown Bullhead	-	-	2	4	-	-	-	-	6
Bluegill	-	5	-	-	-	-	-	-	5
Black Bullhead	-	-	11	-	-	-	-	-	11

FISH STOCKING DATA

year	species	size	# released
90	Rainbow Trout	Fingerling	6,000
91	Rainbow Trout	Fingerling	6,000
92	Rainbow Trout	Fingerling	6,000
93	Rainbow Trout	Fingerling	6,000
94	Rainbow Trout	Fingerling	5,997
95	Rainbow Trout	Fingerling	6,000
96	Rainbow Trout	Fingerling	6,000
97	Rainbow Trout	Fingerling	6,000

NET CATCH DATA
survey date: 7/5/95

species	Gill Nets # per net	Gill Nets avg fish wt. (lbs)	Trap Nets # per set	Trap Nets avg fish wt. (lbs)
Rainbow Trout	11.0	0.48	0.3	0.36

LENGTH OF SELECTED SPECIES SAMPLED FROM ALL GEAR
Number of fish caught for the following length categories (inches):

species	0-5	6-8	9-11	12-14	15-19	20-24	25-29	>30	Total
Rainbow Trout	-	3	20	1	1	-	-	-	25

DNR COMMENTS:
Newman is a designated Trout lake and is stocked with fingerling Rainbow Trout every fall. Lake is open to fishing during the summer Trout season only. No winter angling is allowed. Rainbow Trout numbers stable and moderate with stocking; average length 10.6 inches; length range 8.1 to 16.7 inches; with the exceptions of 13.6- and 16.7-inch "carry-over" fish, all sampled Rainbows were from previous fall stocking.

FISHING INFORMATION: These two lakes are southeast of Bemidji and offer anglers entirely different fishing experiences. Newman is a designated Trout lake, while Frontenac offers a variety of species, including Walleyes, Panfish, and Northern Pike. **Newman Lake** is generally thought of as a good stream Trout lake, according to local anglers. Rainbows are stocked as fingerlings annually, and they survive well, primarily because predators have been removed. Tim Falk of Bluewater Bait & Sports in Bemidji fishes the lake. "Most of the Rainbows are 1 to 1 1/2 pounds, but every once in a while you get a 3-pounder," he says, adding, "The water is very clear and cold, and there are a lot of bulrushes." The access is very sandy and can only handle small boats, but shore fishing is good for a while after the season opens in spring and again in the fall. In the summer, though, the Rainbows go to deeper water near the middle, and you'll need a boat to get down to them. The lake is closed to winter fishing. **Frontenac Lake**, meanwhile, is relatively shallow, heavily weeded, and holds a good population of Northerns and Perch, as well as panfish, Walleyes, and a few Largemouth Bass. The water is fairly clear, and the shoreline has a lot of bulrushes in which you can use jigs tipped with small minnows or worms for panfish. Or try spinnerbaits to attract Bass in the weeds. Northerns roam the lake looking for suckers and Perch that venture out of the weedbeds. Some good spots to look for them include the inlets of Dead Creek on the southwest side and Rat Creek on the south end. The outlet of Frontenac Creek on the east side also is productive.

NOT FOR NAVIGATION

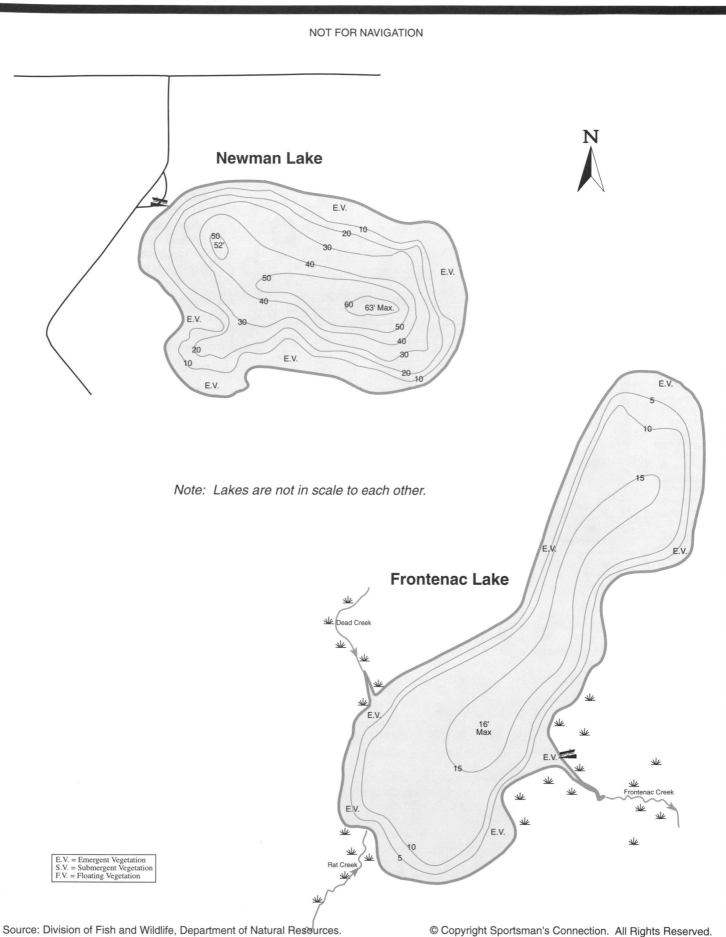

Newman Lake

N

Note: *Lakes are not in scale to each other.*

Frontenac Lake

Dead Creek

Frontenac Creek

Rat Creek

E.V. = Emergent Vegetation
S.V. = Submergent Vegetation
F.V. = Floating Vegetation

HENNEPIN LAKE   EVERGREEN LAKE

Hubbard County

Location: Township 145   Range 34, 35
Watershed: Mississippi Headwaters
Surface Water Area: 407 acres
Shorelength: 4.7 miles
Secchi disk (water clarity): 15.0 ft.
Water color: Clear
Cause of water color: Bog stain
Maximum depth: 14 ft.
Median depth: NA
Accessibility: State-owned public access on west shore
Boat Ramp: Earth
Accommodations: NA
Shoreland zoning classif.: Nat. Envir.
Dominant forest/soil type: Conifer/Loam
Management class: Warm-water Gamefish
Ecological type: Centrarchid

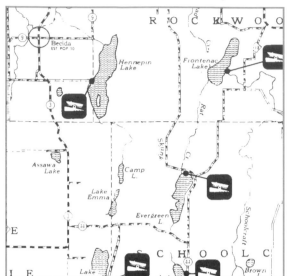

Location: Township 144   Range 34
Watershed: Mississippi Headwaters
Surface Water Area: 200 acres
Shorelength: 3.2 miles
Secchi disk (water clarity): 8.5 ft.
Water color: Brown
Cause of water color: Bog stain
Maximum depth: 38 ft.
Median depth: NA
Accessibility: Township-owned public access on north shore
Boat Ramp: Earth
Accommodations: NA
Shoreland zoning classif.: Nat. Envir.
Dominant forest/soil type: Conifer/Wet
Management class: Centrarchid
Ecological type: Centrarchid

DNR COMMENTS: Lake is subject to low winter oxygen levels and occasional, partial winterkills. Only one Walleye sampled in 1994. Northern Pike numbers much higher; average size 19.3 inches and 2 lb. Only one Largemouth Bass sampled. Black Crappies faring well; mean length 9 inches. Bluegill numbers low. Yellow Perch abundant; 22 percent of individuals are 10 inches or larger; mean weight .4 lb.

FISH STOCKING DATA

year	species	size	# released
90	Walleye	Fry	200,000
91	Walleye	Fry	200,000
92	Walleye	Fry	230,000
93	Walleye	Fry	200,000
94	Walleye	Fry	200,000
96	Walleye	Fry	200,000

survey date: 8/1/94

NET CATCH DATA

	Gill Nets		Trap Nets	
species	# per net	avg fish wt. (lbs)	# per set	avg fish wt. (lbs)
Black Crappie	3.1	0.41	5.7	0.50
Bluegill	-	-	0.3	0.22
Brown Bullhead	11.7	0.19	2.4	0.30
Largemouth Bass	-	-	0.1	2.52
Northern Pike	12.4	2.03	1.6	1.24
Pumpkin. Sunfish	1.3	0.14	0.1	0.20
Walleye	0.1	3.31	-	-
Yellow Perch	31.9	0.37	0.1	0.25

LENGTH OF SELECTED SPECIES SAMPLED FROM ALL GEAR
Number of fish caught for the following length categories (inches):

species	0-5	6-8	9-11	12-14	15-19	20-24	25-29	>30	Total
Black Crappie	-	22	51	-	-	-	-	-	73
Bluegill	-	3	-	-	-	-	-	-	3
Brown Bullhead	-	80	12	-	-	-	-	-	92
Largemouth Bass	-	-	-	-	1	-	-	-	1
Northern Pike	-	1	31	7	11	18	33	-	101
Pumpkin. Sunfish	9	1	-	-	-	-	-	-	10
Walleye	-	-	-	-	1	-	-	-	1
Yellow Perch	2	59	64	-	-	-	-	-	125

FISH STOCKING DATA

year	species	size	# released
90	Walleye	Fingerling	1,040
92	Walleye	Fingerling	4,500
94	Walleye	Fingerling	180
96	Walleye	Fingerling	3,820

survey date: 7/8/92

NET CATCH DATA

	Gill Nets		Trap Nets	
species	# per net	avg fish wt. (lbs)	# per set	avg fish wt. (lbs)
Yellow Perch	63.3	0.09	16.1	0.11
White Sucker	1.3	1.60	-	-
Walleye	3.0	2.67	-	-
Rock Bass	0.3	0.90	1.4	0.22
Northern Pike	2.3	2.72	0.1	4.60
Hybrid Sunfish	0.3	0.40	7.6	0.17
Black Crappie	0.8	0.33	0.4	0.13
Pumpkin. Sunfish	-	-	8.8	0.24
Largemouth Bass	-	-	0.6	0.54
Green Sunfish	-	-	1.3	0.11
Golden Shiner	-	-	0.4	0.07
Brown Bullhead	-	-	0.1	0.70
Bluegill	-	-	33.8	0.25

LENGTH OF SELECTED SPECIES SAMPLED FROM ALL GEAR
Number of fish caught for the following length categories (inches):

species	0-5	6-8	9-11	12-14	15-19	20-24	25-29	>30	Total
Yellow Perch	1	79	-	-	-	-	-	-	80
Walleye	-	-	-	-	3	9	-	-	12
Rock Bass	-	-	1	-	-	-	-	-	1
Northern Pike	-	-	-	1	2	2	4	-	9
Hybrid Sunfish	-	1	-	-	-	-	-	-	1
Black Crappie	-	2	3	-	-	-	-	-	5

DNR COMMENTS: Northern Pike population down significantly to below first-quartile values for lake class; mean weight 2.72 lb., and the weight structure indicates high numbers of quality-length fish; no fish greater than 27 inches sampled, however; growth slow. Walleye numbers normal; however, weight high at 2.64 lb., indicating a large Walleye population; only 1 fish sampled was less than 15 inches. Pumpkinseed, Largemouth Bass, Bluegill populations normal. Black Crappies scarce. No non-game species have reached nuisance population levels in this lake.

FISHING INFORMATION: These two lakes about 12 miles southwest of Bemidji are of the sort which get relatively little pressure, but which offer fairly good fishing much of the time. **Evergreen Lake** is known as a lake you can take the kids to. The reason is that there are plenty of panfish and Northern Pike to latch onto, and the lake isn't difficult to fish. The water is brownish with bog stain, so it offers good daytime fishing, too. The south end is relatively shallow and has weedbeds good for Sunfish. The sunnies are of moderate size, and you can offer nightcrawlers or small minnows on a bare hook right after ice-out or the same bait on a bright jig as the water warms. The lake's weeds also hold decent numbers of Largemouth Bass. Try inside the long point on the west side or the south end. Northerns will be around weedbeds and should respond well to flashy spinnerbaits or bright plugs. Walleyes are stocked and survive well enough. Fish for them around the quick drops off the east and west shores of the north bay. Evergreen is easy to get onto in the winter and provides good fishing then. Meanwhile, the north and south ends of **Hennepin Lake** provide that lake's best fishing opportunities for Northerns and panfish. The south end especially is shallow and has long flats, which can be trolled with shallow-running lures as the weather warms. There is a fairly good population of Walleyes. You'll have to get into the weeds for them, though. Use jigs and minnows or floating Rapalas.

SPORTSMAN'S Connection
Hennepin & Evergreen Lakes

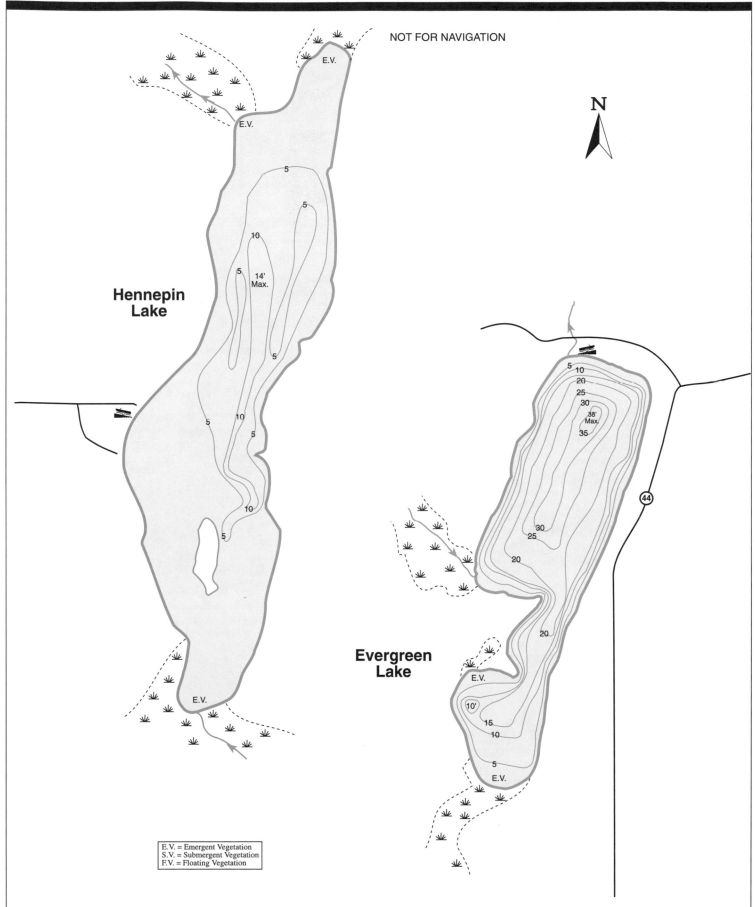

NOT FOR NAVIGATION

N

Hennepin
Lake

5

5

10

5

14'
Max.

5

5

10

5

10

5

E.V.

E.V.

E.V.

E.V.

Evergreen
Lake

5
10
20
25
30
38'
Max.
35

30
25

20

20

E.V.

10'

15

10

5

E.V.

44

E.V. = Emergent Vegetation
S.V. = Submergent Vegetation
F.V. = Floating Vegetation

Source: Division of Fish and Wildlife, Department of Natural Resources.

GRACE LAKE

Location: Township 145, 146 Range 32
Watershed: Mississippi Headwaters
Surface Water Area: 887 acres
Shorelength: 4.4 miles
Secchi disk (water clarity): 14.0 ft.
Water color: Greenish tint
Cause of water color: Algae bloom
Maximum depth: 42 ft.
Median depth: NA
Accessibility: State-owned public access on west shore
Boat Ramp: Concrete
Accommodations: NA
Shoreland zoning classif.: Rec. Dev.
Dominant forest/soil type: Decid/Wet
Management class: Walleye-Centrarchid
Ecological type: Centrarchid-Walleye

Hubbard County

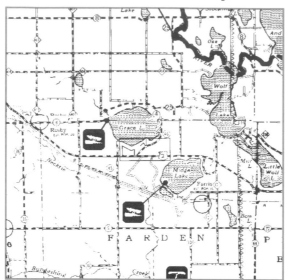

MIDGE LAKE

Location: Township 145 Range 32
Watershed: Mississippi Headwaters
Surface Water Area: 521 acres
Shorelength: 3.5 miles
Secchi disk (water clarity): 7.5 ft.
Water color: Greenish tint
Cause of water color: Algae bloom
Maximum depth: 24 ft.
Median depth: NA
Accessibility: State-owned public access on southwest corner
Boat Ramp: Earth
Accommodations: NA
Shoreland zoning classif.: Rec. Dev.
Dominant forest/soil type: Decid/Wet
Management class: Warm-water Gamefish
Ecological type: Roughfish-Gamefish

DNR COMMENTS:
Walleyes very abundant; numbers double the average for lake class; average size down to about 15 inches and 1.3 lb.; fish to 26 inches present. Northern Pike abundance normal; average size of 21 inches and 2.2 lb. is near lake-class average. Largemouth Bass not sampled, and there is concern that the population may be declining. Black Crappies, once abundant, are rare. Anglers report a few Muskellunge sightings; fish apparently are leftovers from 1984 stocking or a result of natural reproduction. Bluegill numbers very low. Rock Bass common. Yellow Perch numbers up; average length about 7.5 inches.

FISH STOCKING DATA

year	species	size	# released
90	Walleye	Fingerling	43,313
91	Walleye	Fingerling	15,780
91	Walleye	Yearling	12
92	Walleye	Fingerling	18,119
93	Walleye	Fingerling	17,365
93	Walleye	Adult	34
94	Walleye	Fingerling	12,727
96	Walleye	Fingerling	17,690
97	Walleye	Yearling	120

survey date: 7/31/95

NET CATCH DATA

	Gill Nets		Trap Nets	
species	# per net	avg fish wt. (lbs)	# per set	avg fish wt. (lbs)
Bluegill	-	-	trace	0.86
Northern Pike	6.2	2.21	0.9	1.61
Pumpkin. Sunfish	9.0	0.43	0.8	0.36
Rock Bass	2.0	0.37	2.8	0.33
Walleye	13.8	1.28	3.9	1.03
White Sucker	5.1	2.02	0.6	2.49
Yellow Perch	137.6	0.19	21.1	0.13

LENGTH OF SELECTED SPECIES SAMPLED FROM ALL GEAR

Number of fish caught for the following length categories (inches):

species	0-5	6-8	9-11	12-14	15-19	20-24	25-29	>30	Total
Bluegill	-	-	1	-	-	-	-	-	1
Northern Pike	-	-	-	9	31	32	10	3	85
Pumpkin. Sunfish	1	116	-	-	-	-	-	-	117
Rock Bass	8	45	4	-	-	-	-	-	57
Walleye	1	14	20	93	47	36	2	-	213
Yellow Perch	53	380	23	-	-	-	-	-	456

FISH STOCKING DATA

year	species	size	# released
92	Walleye	Fry	300,000
93	Black Crappie	Adult	111
93	Largemouth Bass	Adult	28
93	Walleye	Fry	300,000
94	Walleye	Fry	300,000
96	Walleye	Fry	300,000

survey date: 6/26/90

NET CATCH DATA

	Gill Nets		Trap Nets	
species	# per net	avg fish wt. (lbs)	# per set	avg fish wt. (lbs)
Yellow Perch	2.3	0.23	2.8	0.31
White Sucker	5.0	1.23	0.6	1.62
Walleye	5.3	0.74	-	-
Rock Bass	2.7	0.13	4.8	0.33
Pumpkin. Sunfish	14.7	0.05	53.5	0.09
Northern Pike	32.3	1.87	4.8	0.70
Bluegill	0.3	0.20	174.4	0.20
Black Bullhead	108.7	0.16	56.6	0.22
Largemouth Bass	-	-	0.3	0.40

LENGTH OF SELECTED SPECIES SAMPLED FROM ALL GEAR

Number of fish caught for the following length categories (inches):

species	0-5	6-8	9-11	12-14	15-19	20-24	25-29	>30	Total
Black Bullhead	-	144	20	-	-	-	-	-	164
Bluegill	72	58	1	-	-	-	-	-	131
Largemouth Bass	-	1	1	-	-	-	-	-	2
Northern Pike	-	-	2	-	81	42	6	4	135
Pumpkin. Sunfish	104	16	-	-	-	-	-	-	120
Rock Bass	12	32	2	-	-	-	-	-	46
Walleye	-	-	-	16	-	-	-	-	16
Yellow Perch	1	20	8	-	-	-	-	-	29

DNR COMMENTS:
Northern Pike gill-net catches very high; numbers are 10 times the state median; most fish are 15 to 24 inches, but individuals over 29 inches sampled. Walleye gillnet catch above normal range for lake class; prominent 1986 year class. Many Largemouth Bass observed during survey; anglers report good success for this species. Bluegill numbers above third-quartile range for lake class.

FISHING INFORMATION: Grace is a year-round lake for panfish, and it holds good populations of Northern Pike and Walleyes, as well as some Largemouth Bass. The lake is practically devoid of structure, but there are two rock piles, one at mid lake, the other close to the north shore. These provide good feeding spots for Walleyes and Crappies. Another good Walleye area is the east shore, where there are fairly steep breaks off the weeds. You won't find a lot of Walleyes in Grace, but they've been stocked for many years, and there are some trophies out there. The water is very clear, so you'll do well with live baits. Leeches or shiners fished along the sides of the rocks or breaks should get attention. You'll do best with the sunnies by offering nightcrawlers on a bare hook in the weedbeds. Bass will be in typical haunts near the weedbeds. Northern Pike can be fairly big in Grace and are found in almost all parts of the lake. Your best bet, though, is trolling the outer edges of the weedbeds with spoons and spinnerbaits on a long line. Be aware that there are also some Muskies left over from DNR stocking in the 1980s. These have size restrictions. **Midge Lake**, meanwhile, is also fairly clear and fertile, with good weedbeds. Bullheads are the dominant species, but the lake also holds bundles of hefty Northern Pike. The lake is round and largely without structure, but the weeds hold a lot of forage fish that keep the Northerns big and healthy. There are some decent Bass, too, in the weeds.

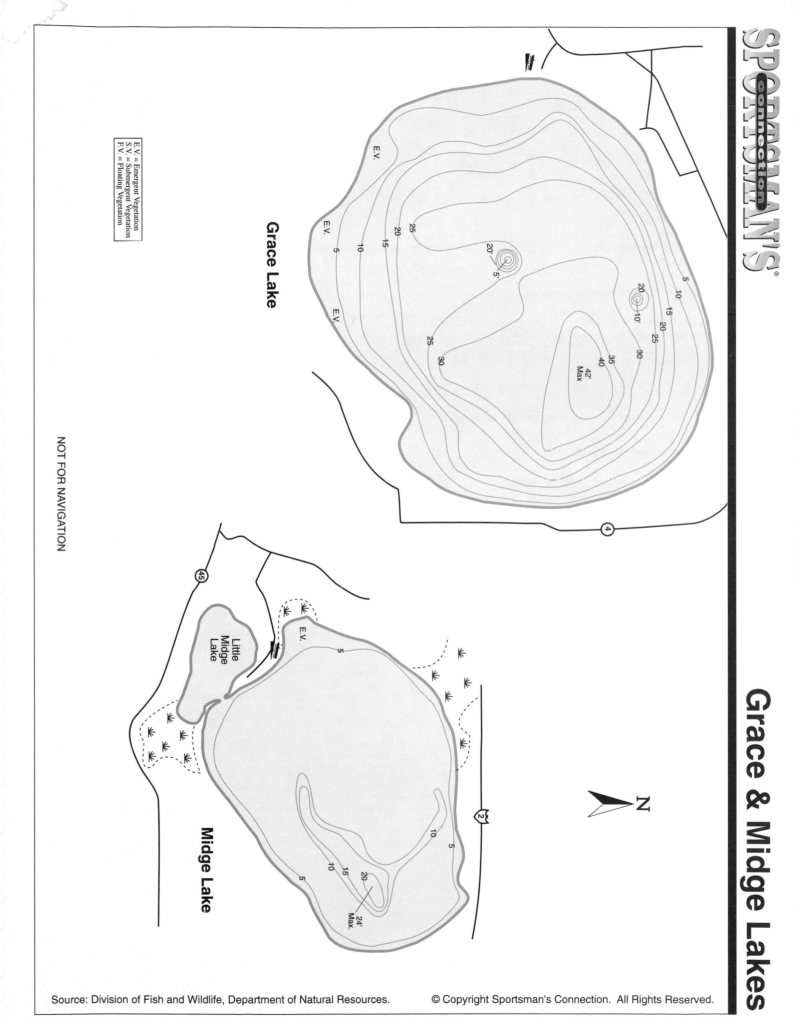

E.V. = Emergent Vegetation
S.V. = Submergent Vegetation
F.V. = Floating Vegetation

Grace Lake

E.V.

E.V.

E.V.

20
25
15
10
5

20
5'

42'
Max

40
35
30
25
30
25
20
15
10
5

NOT FOR NAVIGATION

N

Little
Midge
Lake

Midge Lake

E.V.

5

10

5

5
10
15
20

24'
Max.

WOLF LAKE

LITTLE WOLF LAKE

Beltrami/Cass County

Location: Township 145, 146 Range 32
Watershed: Mississippi Headwaters
Surface Water Area: 1094 acres
Shorelength: 7.6 miles
Secchi disk (water clarity): 7.0 ft.
Water color: Greenish-brown
Cause of water color: Slight algae bloom
Maximum depth: 57 ft.
Median depth: NA
Accessibility: State-owned public access on west shore
Boat Ramp: Concrete
Accommodations: Resorts, camp-ground
Shoreland zoning classif.: Rec. Dev.
Dominant forest/soil type: Decid/Sand
Management class: Walleye
Ecological type: Hard-water Walleye

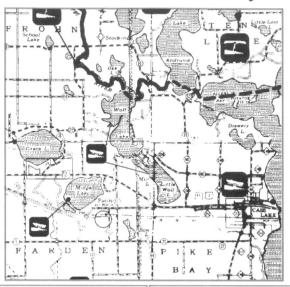

Location: Township 145 Range 31, 32
Watershed: Mississippi Headwaters
Surface Water Area: 490 acres
Shorelength: 4.1 miles
Secchi disk (water clarity): 5.5 ft.
Water color: Green
Cause of water color: Algal bloom and suspended solids
Maximum depth: 24 ft.
Median depth: 17 ft.
Accessibility: Public access at outlet on northwest shore
Boat Ramp: Earth
Accommodations: Resort
Shoreland zoning classif.: Rec. Dev.
Dominant forest/soil type: NA
Management class: Walleye-Centrarchid
Ecological type: Centrarchid-Walleye

DNR COMMENTS:
Since this lake is connected by the Mississippi River to the Cass Lake chain, fish populations are affected by movement among lakes. Walleye numbers average for lake class; mean weight of slightly more than 1 lb. is low; fish to 25.3 inches present. Northern Pike numbers up but below average; average size 22 inches and 2.9 lb.; fish to 38 inches sampled. Black Crappies and Bluegills scarce. Rock Bass abundant; average weight .4 lb. Cisco, Whitefish, and White Sucker common. Yellow Perch numbers average for lake class; average length 7.5 inches.

FISH STOCKING DATA: NO RECORD OF STOCKING

NET CATCH DATA

survey date: 8/26/96

| | Gill Nets | | Trap Nets | |
species	# per net	avg fish wt. (lbs)	# per set	avg fish wt. (lbs)
Black Crappie	trace	0.38	0.3	0.99
Bluegill	-	-	0.2	0.28
Hybrid Sunfish	trace	0.19	-	-
Lake Whitefish	-	-	trace	3.94
Northern Pike	4.3	2.90	0.8	1.18
Pumpkin. Sunfish	-	-	5.3	0.05
Rock Bass	0.8	0.87	4.3	0.36
Tullibee (Cisco)	3.9	1.14	-	-
Walleye	5.7	1.11	0.6	1.08
White Sucker	7.5	1.55	1.6	2.00
Yellow Bullhead	-	-	trace	0.84
Yellow Perch	31.4	0.19	11.1	0.16

LENGTH OF SELECTED SPECIES SAMPLED FROM ALL GEAR
Number of fish caught for the following length categories (inches):

species	0-5	6-8	9-11	12-14	15-19	20-24	25-29	>30	Total
Black Crappie	-	1	2	1	-	-	-	-	4
Bluegill	1	1	-	-	-	-	-	-	2
Hybrid Sunfish	1	-	-	-	-	-	-	-	1
Lake Whitefish	-	-	-	-	1	-	-	-	1
Northern Pike	-	-	1	2	27	16	14	2	62
Pumpkin. Sunfish	61	3	-	-	-	-	-	-	64
Rock Bass	17	27	18	-	-	-	-	-	62
Tullibee (Cisco)	-	3	5	24	15	-	-	-	47
Walleye	-	18	14	10	26	6	1	-	75
Yellow Bullhead	-	-	-	1	-	-	-	-	1
Yellow Perch	124	350	36	-	-	-	-	-	510

FISH STOCKING DATA

year	species	size	# released
90	Muskellunge	Fingerling	225
91	Walleye	Fingerling	8,102
91	Walleye	Yearling	3
92	Muskellunge	Fingerling	245
93	Walleye	Fingerling	6,580
94	Muskellunge	Fingerling	245
95	Walleye	Fingerling	3,980
96	Muskellunge	Fingerling	245
97	Walleye	Fingerling	2,625
97	Walleye	Yearling	100

NET CATCH DATA

survey date: 8/4/97

| | Gill Nets | | Trap Nets | |
species	# per net	avg fish wt. (lbs)	# per set	avg fish wt. (lbs)
Bluegill	-	-	0.8	0.10
Muskellunge	0.2	7.44	0.4	8.62
Northern Pike	0.7	3.34	0.2	1.43
Pumpkin. Sunfish	0.9	0.11	2.1	0.10
Rock Bass	0.8	0.28	1.9	0.19
Walleye	8.1	1.48	0.9	2.66
White Sucker	1.7	1.27	0.1	0.20
Yellow Perch	182.6	0.11	28.0	0.10

LENGTH OF SELECTED SPECIES SAMPLED FROM ALL GEAR
Number of fish caught for the following length categories (inches):

species	0-5	6-8	9-11	12-14	15-19	20-24	25-29	>30	Total
Bluegill	7	-	-	-	-	-	-	-	7
Muskellunge	-	-	-	1	-	1	1	3	6
Northern Pike	-	-	-	-	5	1	1	1	8
Pumpkin. Sunfish	27	-	-	-	-	-	-	-	27
Rock Bass	9	15	-	-	-	-	-	-	24
Walleye	-	-	11	33	11	25	1	-	81
Yellow Perch	154	391	6	-	-	-	-	-	551

DNR COMMENTS:
Little Wolf is managed as a brood stock Muskellunge lake; minimum length limit 48 inches. This species is abundant, with an occasional fish over 50 inches being caught by anglers; one resort recorded 150 released Muskellunge in 1997. Walleye abundant; modal lengths 11 to 14 inches and 20 to 22 inches. Northern Pike numbers low; average weight 2.2 lb.; fish to 33 inches sampled. Bluegill abundance low; average length only 5.6 inches. Yellow Perch numbers four times the lake-class average; 20 percent of Perch exceed 8 inches. Rock Bass numbers high.

FISHING INFORMATION: These two lakes southeast of Bemidji have a great deal to offer anglers and, as a result, get heavy fishing pressure. **Wolf Lake** consists of two bays of nearly equal size holding good structure, fairly clear water, and good weedbeds. The lake also holds good populations of Walleyes, Northern Pike, sunnies, and healthy numbers of forage fish. Walleyes are stocked by the DNR and seem to survive well. Fish the good points and bars for early-season Walleyes. In particular, try those along the west shore of the south bay and on each side of the north bay. In addition, you'll want to check out the great rock piles in the north bay, – one on the north side and the other at the bay's entrance. Fishing these areas with live bait on jigs or bottom rigs early in the season or at night during the summer is going to get plenty of action. The south bay is the weedier of the two and your best bet for finding Largemouth Bass. Try the east side, using minnows or nightcrawlers. Wolf is connected to Lake Andrusia on the northeast by the Mississippi River. **Little Wolf Lake**, meanwhile, is stocked with both Muskellunge and Walleyes, and both species do fairly well. There is a special regulation on Muskies: minimum size limit is 48 inches. Little Wolf is one of the lakes in which the DNR gather Muskie broodstock, so you can bet it's closely watched. Earl Taber of Taber's Baits in Bemidji says Little Wolf, in addition to Muskies, holds good populations of Walleyes, Crappies, and Bluegills, as well as some Largemouths. The lakeshore has a lot of bulrushes which hold the Bass and panfish. In addition, there are bundles of Perch. Find Perch and you'll find Muskies.

Wolf & Little Wolf Lakes

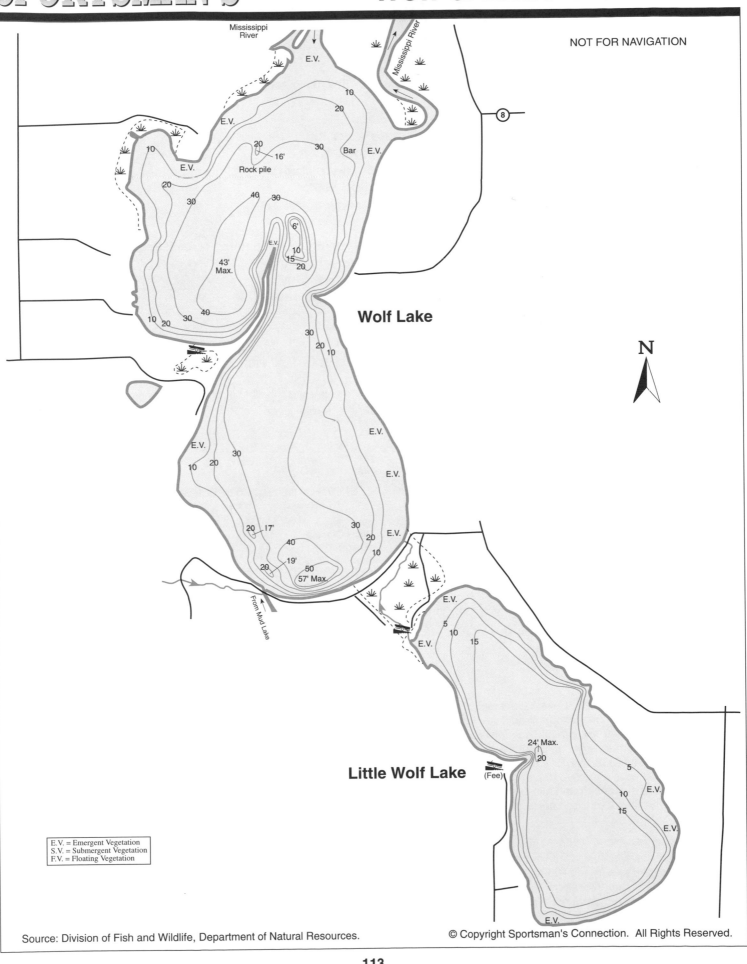

NOT FOR NAVIGATION

Mississippi River

Mississippi River

8

E.V.

10

20

20   16'   30   Bar   E.V.

Rock pile

10

E.V.

20

30   40   30

6'

E.V.   10   15   20

43' Max.

10   20   30   40

Wolf Lake

N

30   20   10

E.V.

E.V.

E.V.

30

E.V.   10   20   30

E.V.

20   17'

40   30

20   19'   50   20   10

57' Max.

From Mud Lake

E.V.

5   10   15

E.V.

E.V.

Little Wolf Lake   (Fee)

24' Max.   20

5   10   E.V.

15

E.V.

E.V.

E.V. = Emergent Vegetation
S.V. = Submergent Vegetation
F.V. = Floating Vegetation

Source: Division of Fish and Wildlife, Department of Natural Resources.

STUMP LAKE
Beltrami County

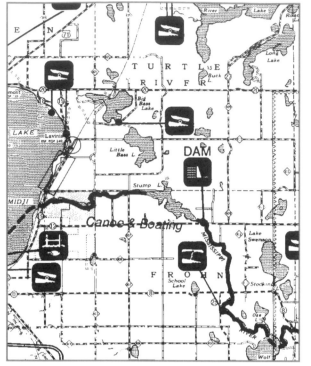

Location: Township 146, 147 Range 32, 33

Watershed: NA

Surface Water Area: 290 acres

Shorelength: NA

Secchi disk (water clarity): 9.6 ft.

Water color: NA

Cause of water color: NA

Maximum depth: 24 ft.

Median depth: NA

Accessibility: From Lake Bemidji

Boat Ramp: See Lake Bemidji

Accommodations: NA

Shoreland zoning classification: Natural Environment

Dominant forest/soil type: NA

Management class: NA

Ecological type: NA

FISH STOCKING DATA

year	species	size	# released
90	Muskellunge	Fingerling	1,820
92	Muskellunge	Fingerling	1,986

NET CATCH DATA

survey date: 8/12/96

	Gill Nets		Trap Nets	
species	# per net	avg fish wt. (lbs.)	# per set	avg fish wt. (lbs.)
Black Crappie	0.7	0.73	0.7	0.47
Bluegill	0.3	0.23	3.2	0.42
Brown Bullhead	0.5	0.66	0.2	1.43
Hybrid Sunfish	7.7	0.24	2.4	0.26
Largemouth Bass	1.3	1.42	-	-
Northern Pike	13.5	2.12	1.2	1.97
Pumpkin. Sunfish	2.3	0.11	3.8	0.22
Rock Bass	2.3	0.29	0.6	0.64
Walleye	0.7	1.15	0.1	2.65
Yellow Bullhead	8.0	0.69	5.1	0.85
Yellow Perch	32.8	0.18	4.8	0.17

LENGTH OF SELECTED SPECIES SAMPLED FROM ALL GEAR

Number of fish caught for the following length categories (inches):

species	0-5	6-8	9-11	12-14	15-19	20-24	25-29	>30	Total
Black Crappie	-	5	4	1	-	-	-	-	10
Bluegill	4	26	1	-	-	-	-	-	31
Brown Bullhead	-	1	2	2	-	-	-	-	5
Hybrid Sunfish	29	39	-	-	-	-	-	-	68
Largemouth Bass	-	1	2	3	2	-	-	-	8
Northern Pike	-	-	-	6	41	32	9	4	92
Pumpkin. Sunfish	29	19	-	-	-	-	-	-	48
Rock Bass	8	4	7	-	-	-	-	-	19
Walleye	-	-	-	3	1	1	-	-	5
Yellow Bullhead	-	17	48	29	-	-	-	-	94
Yellow Perch	70	156	14	-	-	-	-	-	240

DNR COMMENTS: Lake is a riverine system, so the fish community can be influenced by river flows. Walleye numbers low for lake class; fish are probably migrants from adjacent Lake Bemidji. Northern Pike population up; average weight of 2.1 lb. is attractive to some anglers; more than half the sample was infected with black spot. Largemouth Bass sample not as large as expected, possibly due to weather conditions at time of sampling; average length 13 inches; fish to 19 inches captured. Black Crappie abundance down considerably, although a few Crappies near 1/2 lb. are still available; anglers report modest success for this species. Bluegills scarce, but average length of 7.5 inches is attractive to anglers. Yellow Perch abundant; average length about 7 inches; most fish infected with black spot. A few Muskellunge migrants from Lake Bemidji present. Pumpkinseed, Rock Bass, hybrid Sunfish present but not abundant. White Sucker, Redhorse, Burbot, and Cisco present.

FISHING INFORMATION: Stump Lake is connected to Lake Bemidji via the Mississippi River chain. It is quite shallow, but is saved from winterkill by the river's flow. Carl Knowlton at Kobilka's Sporting Goods in Bemidji says Stump holds good populations of Northern Pike and Largemouth Bass, in addition to a modest number of Crappies. There also are some Perch, but they're mostly small and infected with black spot. Luxuriant weedbeds dominate the lake, so you'll have to fish for the Crappies and Bass with small jigs and minnows or spinnerbaits. Topwater gear, too, works well in summer for the bigmouth. Knowlton says the Crappies in Stump are big, and Bass can run as large as 6 pounds. Muskies also roam this section of the river system. Stump Lake is accessible by the river's inlet on its west side.

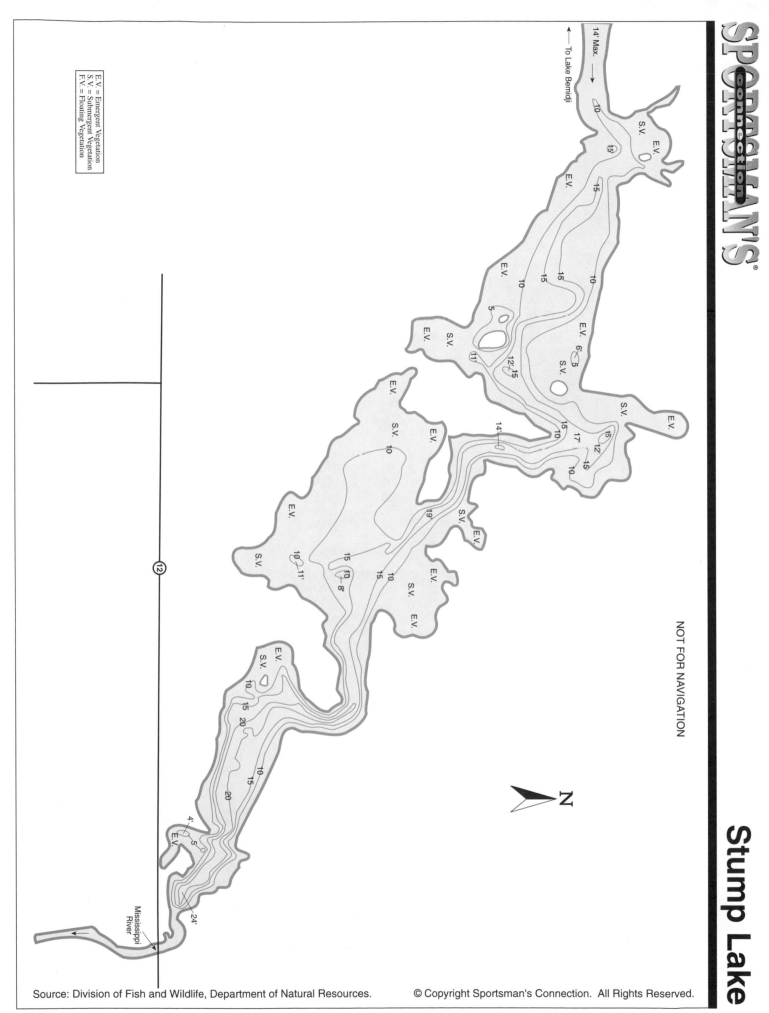

Stump Lake

NOT FOR NAVIGATION

N

14' Max.

← To Lake Bemidji

E.V. = Emergent Vegetation
S.V. = Submergent Vegetation
F.V. = Floating Vegetation

S.V.
E.V.
E.V.
15
15
E.V.
10
15
15
10
E.V.
10
5
E.V.
S.V.
6'
11'
5
S.V.
12'
15
E.V.
S.V.
E.V.
15
10
17'
15
12'
15
14'
10
15
E.V.
S.V.
E.V.
10
19'
S.V.
E.V.
E.V.
15
10
8'
15
10
S.V.
E.V.
S.V.
10
11'
10
E.V.
E.V.
E.V.
S.V.
10
15
20
10
15
20
4'
5
E.V.
24'
Mississippi River

12

Source: Division of Fish and Wildlife, Department of Natural Resources.

LAKE ANDRUSIA
Beltrami County

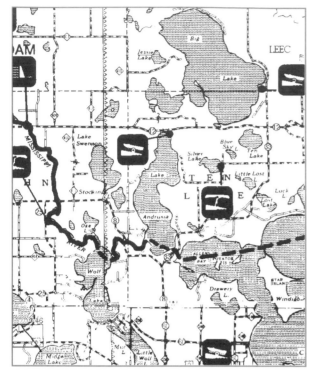

Location: Township 146 Range 31

Watershed: Mississippi Headwaters

Surface Water Area: 1,510 acres

Shorelength: 10.0 miles

Secchi disk (water clarity): 6.3 ft.

Water color: Light green

Cause of water color: Algae

Maximum depth: 60 ft.

Median depth: 26 ft.

Accessibility: Public access on north shore

Boat Ramp: Concrete

Accommodations: Campground, resort

Shoreland zoning classification: Recreational Development
Dominant forest/soil type: Decid/Sand
Management class: Walleye
Ecological type: Hard-water Walleye

FISH STOCKING DATA

year	species	size	# released
90	Walleye	Fry	1,710,000
91	Walleye	Fry	1,300,000
92	Walleye	Fry	4,700,000
93	Walleye	Fry	1,940,000
94	Walleye	Fry	4,590,000
95	Walleye	Fry	700,000
96	Walleye	Fry	4,880,000

NET CATCH DATA

survey date: 07/06/92

species	Gill Nets # per net	Gill Nets avg fish wt. (lbs.)	Trap Nets # per set	Trap Nets avg fish wt. (lbs.)
Yellow Perch	107.0	0.15	16.3	0.13
White Sucker	5.3	1.74	2.6	2.20
Walleye	10.4	1.18	0.7	1.06
Tullibee (Cisco)	6.7	1.31	-	-
Shorthead Redhorse	0.1	2.30	-	-
Rock Bass	2.3	0.40	6.0	0.40
Pumpkinseed Sunfish	0.1	0.30	14.0	0.21
Northern Pike	5.9	1.90	0.7	0.80
Burbot	0.3	2.20	-	-
Black Crappie	0.1	0.80	0.1	0.50

LENGTH OF SELECTED SPECIES SAMPLED FROM ALL GEAR

Number of fish caught for the following length categories (inches):

species	0-5	6-8	9-11	12-14	15-19	20-24	25-29	>30	Total
Yellow Perch	-	80	21	-	-	-	-	-	101
Walleye	-	1	3	27	36	6	-	-	73
Tullibee	-	-	2	19	27	-	-	-	48
Rock Bass	2	7	8	1	-	-	-	-	18
Pumpkin. Sunfish	-	1	-	-	-	-	-	-	1
Northern Pike	-	-	-	1	12	23	5	-	41
Black Crappie	-	-	-	1	-	-	-	-	1

DNR COMMENTS: Northern Pike population unusually high for this lake, but between first- and third-quartile values for lake class; weight also within these limits; five year classes sampled; recruitment generally good; growth above average. Walleye population above third- quartile values for lake class; growth rate slower than statewide average, but weight per gillnet lift was between first- and third-quartile values; recruitment generally good. Largemouth Bass and Bluegills sampled at between first- and third-quartile values. A few Black Crappies caught; size generally large. Cisco population generally fluctuates between first and third quartiles, but is up this year (1999); size has likewise fluctuated, but is between first and third quartiles. Some large Redhorse caught.

FISHING INFORMATION: One of the better spots for early-season Walleye in Beltrami County is Lake Andrusia, which is located roughly six miles east of Bemidji. The lake is one link in the chain of the Mississippi River which gives the water a good early flow. The Walleye population is good, and there are fair numbers of Northern Pike and some good Rock Bass. Andrusia is also full of Yellow Perch. Walleye fry have been stocked by the DNR for many years, and there has been good natural reproduction for several years as well. There are three obviously good fishing areas in Andrusia: the inlet of the river from Wolf Lake in the southwest corner; the river's outlet into big Cass Lake in the southeast corner; and the inlet from Big Lake at the upper north end. Another good spot, especially for early Walleyes, is at the narrows about one-third of the way down from the north end. In addition, you'll find good sand bars coming off both the east and west shores. There's heavy Walleye feeding there at roughly 8 to15 feet down. You will also find goggle eyes at shallow shelves along the east and west shorelines. Andrusia's shoreline measures 10 miles, so if the "hotspots" are crowded, don't hesitate to go off on your own to fish shoreline shelves. The connections of Big Lake and the river are good places for Northerns, and you can pick up some nice Rock Bass there, as well. You may run across a Muskie too, but you'll want to check current regs before taking one. Your best bet for boat launching is the concrete ramp at the lake's north end on County Road 12.

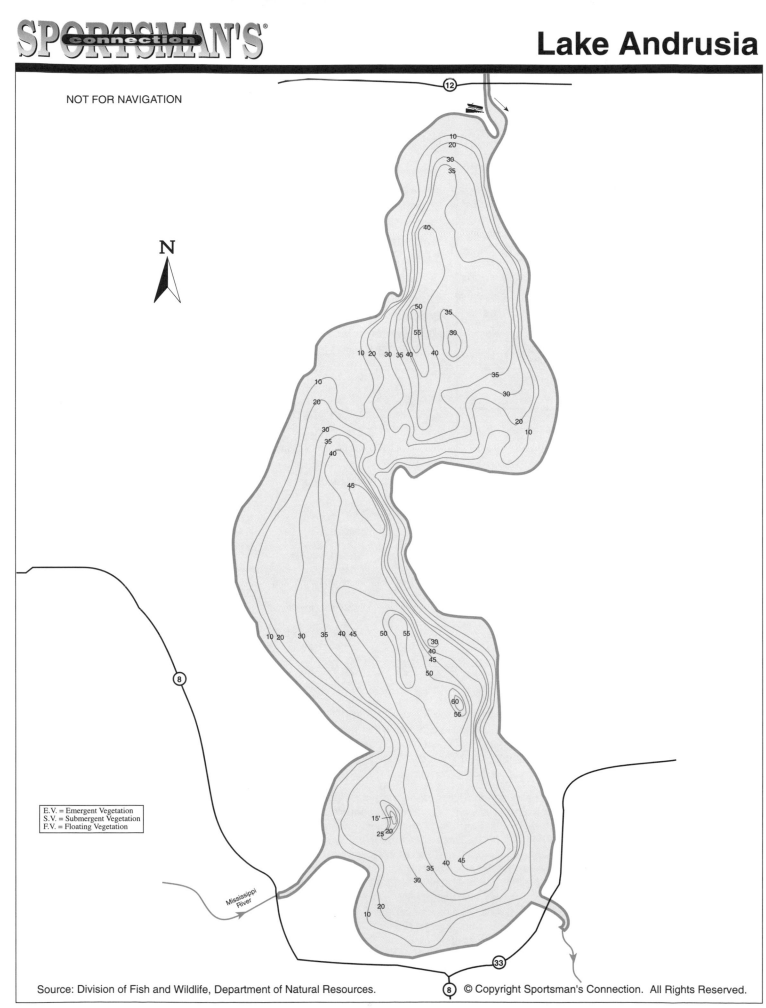

SPORTSMAN'S Connection®

NOT FOR NAVIGATION

N

E.V. = Emergent Vegetation
S.V. = Submergent Vegetation
F.V. = Floating Vegetation

Mississippi River

Source: Division of Fish and Wildlife, Department of Natural Resources.

CASS LAKE
Beltrami County

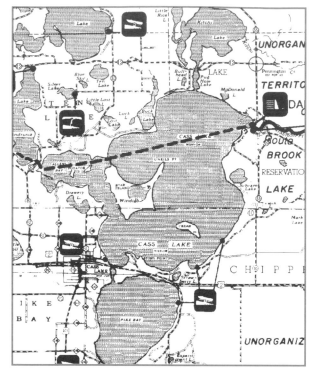

Location: Township 145, 146
Range 30, 31
Watershed: Mississippi Headwaters
Surface Water Area: 15,596 acres
Shorelength: 26.9 miles
Secchi disk (water clarity): NA
Water color: NA
Cause of water color: NA

Maximum depth: 120 ft.
Median depth: 47 ft.
Accessibility: Accesses on the east shore at Knutson Dam; Wanaki & Norway Beach campgrounds; west shore off Hwy. 2
Boat Ramp: Concrete, metal
Accommodations: Campgrounds, resort, fishing pier

Shoreland zoning classification: General Development
Dominant forest/soil type: NA
Management class: Walleye
Ecological type: Hard-water Walleye

FISH STOCKING DATA: NO RECORD OF STOCKING

LENGTH OF SELECTED SPECIES SAMPLED FROM ALL GEAR

Number of fish caught for the following length categories (inches):

species	0-5	6-8	9-11	12-14	15-19	20-24	25-29	>30	Total
Yellow Perch	330	470	106	4	-	-	-	-	910
Yellow Bullhead	-	-	2	1	-	-	-	-	3
Walleye	-	4	34	139	77	19	2	-	275
Tullibee (Cisco)	-	40	37	81	2	-	-	-	160
Rock Bass	13	12	20	-	-	-	-	-	45
Pumpkin. Sunfish	20	-	-	-	-	-	-	-	20
Northern Pike	-	-	1	-	20	28	7	2	58
Lake Whitefish	-	-	-	2	5	2	-	-	9
Black Crappie	-	1	-	-	-	-	-	-	1
Black Bullhead	-	-	1	-	-	-	-	-	1

NET CATCH DATA

survey date: 9/15/97

	Gill Nets		Trap Nets	
species	# per net	avg fish wt. (lbs.)	# per set	avg fish wt. (lbs.)
Yellow Perch	45.5	0.18	-	-
Yellow Bullhead	0.2	0.90	-	-
White Sucker	4.3	1.31	-	-
Walleye	13.8	1.10	-	-
Tullibee (Cisco)	8.0	0.53	-	-
Shorthead Redhorse	0.2	2.93	-	-
Rock Bass	2.3	0.48	-	-
Pumpkin. Sunfish	1.0	0.05	-	-
Northern Pike	2.9	2.39	-	-
Lake Whitefish	0.5	1.90	-	-
Black Crappie	trace	0.30	-	-
Black Bullhead	trace	0.60	-	-

DNR COMMENTS: Walleye population appears abundant; average weight 1.1 lb., which is at the low end of the normal range; consistent recruitment for this species. Northern Pike population stable and within normal range for lake class; good numbers of fish in the 15- to 24-inch length range; fish over 29 inches present. Black Crappie numbers very low. Rock Bass population near low end of normal range for lake class; average weight .48 lb. Pumpkinseed scarce. Yellow Perch abundant and small. Black and Yellow Bullheads scarce. Good numbers of Ciscoes sampled; fish over 15 inches captured.

FISHING INFORMATION: Huge Cass Lake is in the southeast corner of Beltrami County, with a sizeable portion of it extending into Cass County. It's one of those Minnesota lakes that always end up on someone's list of great fishing places. And with good reason. For it offers fine populations of Walleyes, Northern Pike, and Perch and is also popular with Muskie anglers. What's more, Cass is full of structure, with good holes and weedlines that hold almost limitless numbers of forage fish to provide food for the gamefish. Action starts in the spring with Walleyes and Crappies. Allens Bay at the west end of the lower arm is an early favorite. Good rocky points, holes as deep as 50 feet, and a shallow, weedy shoreline pretty well assure Walleyes in the morning. The Walleye in Cass are not especially large, and 2-pounders are considered good-size. Use Shiners or leeches along the dropoffs to get their attention. There are a very few Crappies in Cass, but those you take will often be well above average in size. Northern Pike are abundant early at the Mississippi River inlet on the west side and around both Star and Cedar Islands, as well as near the river's outlet in the northeast. Because the lake has plenty of deep spots – up to 120 feet – Walleye and Northern fishing is better during the hot summer months than it is in most other regional lakes. Yellow Perch-fishing is another good summer and winter sport on Cass. The lake is full of Perch, and it's not unusual to pull out a lot of them ranging from 8 to 12 inches. A 1/4- or 1/8-ounce jig tipped with a minnow is productive. Meanwhile, there are some big Leech Lake-strain Muskellunge in Cass, and Cedar Island at the south part of the lake is a good spot to fish for them. Of course, you wouldn't want to hold your breath waiting for one to strike. But don't despair, either. Anglers DO take them in Cass; maybe you'll be one of the lucky ones.

SPORTSMAN'S Connection®

Cass Lake

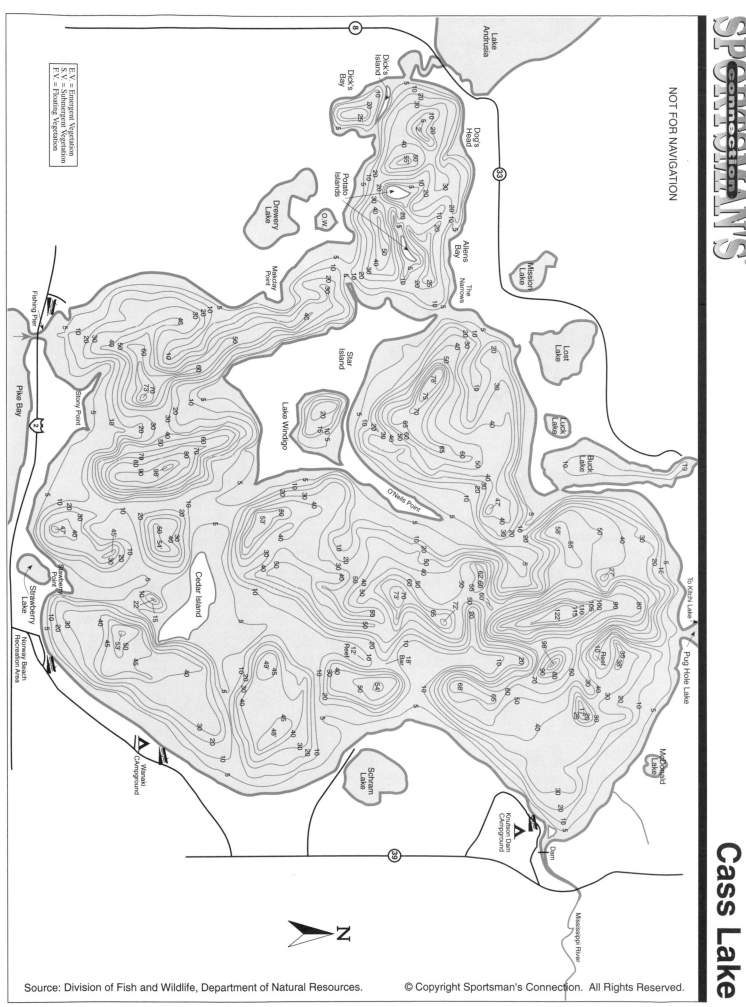

E.V. = Emergent Vegetation
S.V. = Submergent Vegetation
F.V. = Floating Vegetation

N

PIKE BAY
Cass County

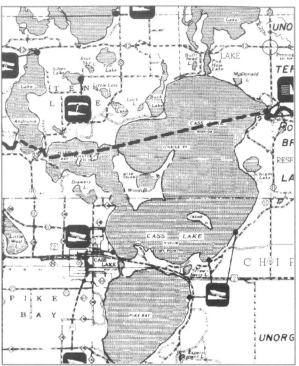

Location: Township 145
Range 30, 31
Watershed: Mississippi Headwaters
Surface Water Area: 4,760 acres
Shorelength: 10.5 miles
Secchi disk (water clarity): 10.0 ft.
Water color: Light green
Cause of water color: Algae

Maximum depth: 100 ft.
Median depth: 24 ft.
Accessibility: Public accesses
on east shore (Ojibway Beach)
and south shore campground
Boat Ramp: Metal (both)
Accommodations: Campground

Shoreland zoning classification: General Development
Dominant forest/soil type: NA
Management class: Walleye
Ecological type: Hard-water Walleye

FISH STOCKING DATA

year	species	size	# released
90	Walleye	Fingerling	47,085
96	Walleye	Fingerling	42,220

NET CATCH DATA

survey date: 7/19/94

	Gill Nets		Trap Nets	
species	# per net	avg fish wt. (lbs.)	# per set	avg fish wt. (lbs.)
Black Bullhead	0.1	0.95	trace	0.60
Black Crappie	-	-	trace	0.61
Bluegill	-	-	0.3	0.32
Bowfin (Dogfish)	-	-	0.1	5.51
Brown Bullhead	0.1	0.93	0.5	0.95
Largemouth Bass	-	-	0.3	3.20
Northern Pike	3.1	3.60	0.1	1.45
Pumpkin. Sunfish	1.3	0.17	2.3	0.29
Rock Bass	8.5	0.49	4.7	0.25
Tullibee (Cisco)	3.0	0.38	-	-
Walleye	5.3	1.84	0.3	0.87
White Sucker	5.9	1.64	0.3	0.14
Yellow Bullhead	0.1	1.54	0.1	0.50
Yellow Perch	133.4	0.14	31.8	0.13

LENGTH OF SELECTED SPECIES SAMPLED FROM ALL GEAR

Number of fish caught for the following length categories (inches):

species	0-5	6-8	9-11	12-14	15-19	20-24	25-29	>30	Total
Black Bullhead	-	-	3	-	-	-	-	-	3
Black Crappie	-	-	1	-	-	-	-	-	1
Bluegill	-	4	-	-	-	-	-	-	4
Brown Bullhead	-	-	5	4	-	-	-	-	9
Largemouth Bass	-	-	-	-	4	-	-	-	4
Northern Pike	-	-	-	1	8	21	14	5	49
Pumpkin. Sunfish	18	36	-	-	-	-	-	-	54
Rock Bass	34	123	40	-	-	-	-	-	197
Tullibee (Cisco)	-	6	36	3	-	-	-	-	45
Walleye	-	-	16	10	40	17	1	-	84
Yellow Bullhead	-	1	1	2	-	-	-	-	4
Yellow Perch	117	453	32	-	-	-	-	-	602

DNR COMMENTS: Walleye abundance about average for lake class; 70 percent of population exceeds 15 inches; fish over 25 inches present; most are cohorts of stocked year classes. Northern Pike numbers low; average length well above average at roughly 24 inches; fish to 36 inches captured; recruitment constant. Lake contains a good, fishable population of Muskellunge. Yellow Perch abundant and offer a good winter fishery; average length 7.1 inches; 25 percent of population exceeds 8 inches. Largemouth Bass, Bluegill, Black Crappie, and Pumpkinseed populations low. Whitefish and Cisco are netted by Native Americans and may offer limited angling opportunities. About half the Ciscoes are infested with the parasite Triaenophorus.

FISHING INFORMATION: Pike Bay is a big, clear lake holding lots of Walleyes and Perch. There are also decent numbers of Northern Pike and a few nice Largemouth Bass. Pike Bay is very clear and full of food. But it can be tough to fish for an inexperienced angler. The reason it can be so tough is that it is deep — maximum depth is 100 feet — with lots of places where fish feed, but which are hard for anglers to reach. Forage fish are plentiful in deep areas, which means that gamefish don't have to go to the easily-fished shallows in search of food. They can stay deep and relatively safe. Even spring Walleye anglers know they have to get up early and go deep. Sunrise is considered by local anglers to be the best Walleye time, and 15 feet is considered the minimum fishing depth. The best thing to do is look for shiners and Yellow Perch off a shelf, such as those you'll find at the north-center of the lake. As the water warms, fish will go even deeper. Be advised: there's oxygen as deep as 50 feet, so you'll want to get your gear right down there. Largemouth Bass fishing is generally fairly good, and 3-pounders are not all that unusual. Early morning, evening, and night fishing are the most productive, and shallow weeded areas are your best opportunity in the spring. There are some Northern Pike and, on occasion, a good-sized Muskellunge is caught. These fish, too, spend more time in deep water in Pike Bay than they do in other lakes. But take the time to learn the lake and the deeper water fishing techniques required, and you will be rewarded with excellent catches of quality fish.

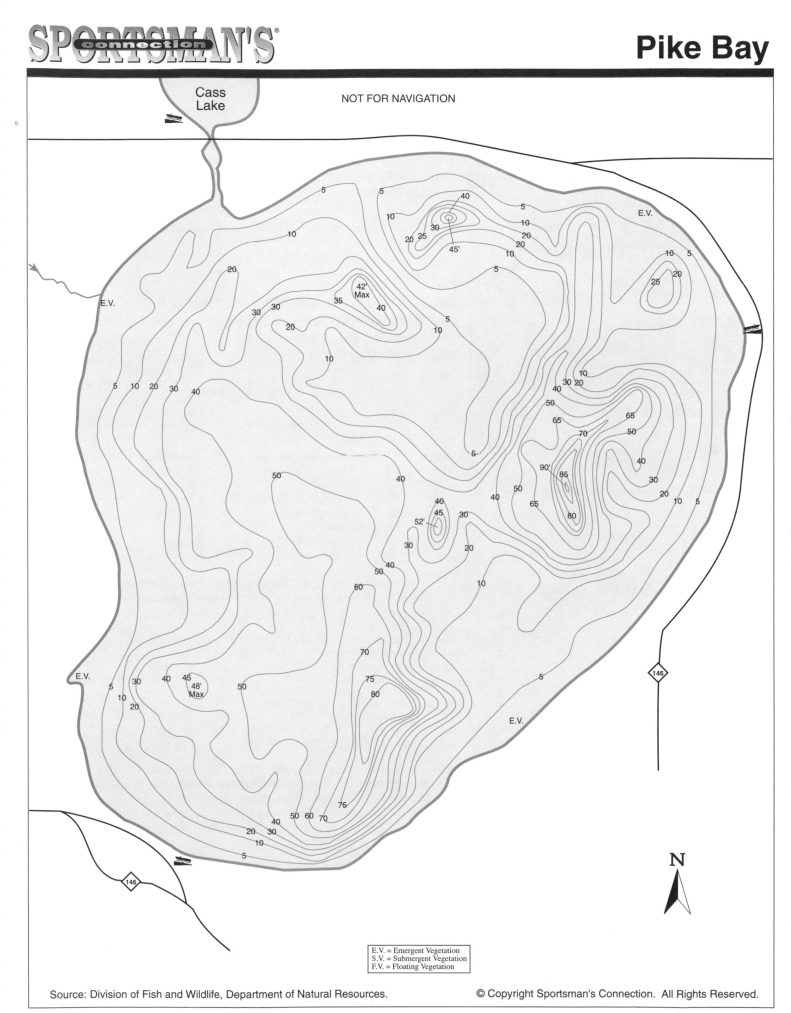

SPORTSMAN'S
Connection

Cass Lake

NOT FOR NAVIGATION

E.V. = Emergent Vegetation
S.V. = Submergent Vegetation
F.V. = Floating Vegetation

N

Source: Division of Fish and Wildlife, Department of Natural Resources.

BIG LAKE
Beltrami County

Location: Township 146, 147 Range 31
Watershed: Mississippi Headwaters
Surface Water Area: 3533 acres
Shorelength: 14.3 miles
Secchi disk (water clarity): 12.0 ft.
Water color: Greenish tint
Cause of water color: Slight algae bloom

Maximum depth: 35 ft.
Median depth: 14 ft.
Accessibility: Public access on east shore
Boat Ramp: Concrete
Accommodations: Resort

Shoreland zoning classification: Recreational Development
Dominant forest/soil type: No Tree/Wet
Management class: Walleye
Ecological type: Hard-water Walleye

FISH STOCKING DATA

year	species	size	# released
90	Muskellunge	Fingerling	3,449
90	Muskellunge	Yearling	162
91	Muskellunge	Fingerling	3,093
91	Muskellunge	Adult	13
92	Walleye	Fingerling	56,748
92	Walleye	Adult	421
93	Muskellunge	Fingerling	2,069
93	Muskellunge	Yearling	126
94	Muskellunge	Fingerling	3,647
96	Muskellunge	Fingerling	3,602

NET CATCH DATA

survey date: 6/26/95

species	Gill Nets # per net	Gill Nets avg fish wt. (lbs.)	Trap Nets # per set	Trap Nets avg fish wt. (lbs.)
Black Crappie	0.3	0.62	1.5	0.51
Bluegill	2.3	0.30	16.0	0.34
Bowfin (Dogfish)	0.1	6.02	0.5	4.89
Brown Bullhead	2.7	1.05	0.9	1.05
Largemouth Bass	0.3	1.20	0.3	0.83
Muskellunge	0.1	5.61	-	-
Northern Pike	19.1	1.59	1.3	1.37
Pumpkin. Sunfish	3.8	0.21	5.1	0.29
Rock Bass	10.9	0.50	4.7	0.40
Tullibee (Cisco)	5.9	0.69	-	-
Walleye	13.5	1.10	trace	4.63
Yellow Perch	40.7	0.16	1.8	0.24

LENGTH OF SELECTED SPECIES SAMPLED FROM ALL GEAR
Number of fish caught for the following length categories (inches):

species	0-5	6-8	9-11	12-14	15-19	20-24	25-29	>30	Total
Black Crappie	1	1	20	1	-	-	-	-	23
Bluegill	37	181	2	-	-	-	-	-	220
Largemouth Bass	1	-	3	4	1	-	-	-	9
Muskellunge	-	-	-	1	-	-	-	1	2
Northern Pike	-	1	8	20	157	91	18	6	301
Pumpkin. Sunfish	43	75	-	-	-	-	-	-	118
Rock Bass	6	146	52	-	-	-	-	-	204
Tullibee (Cisco)	-	19	42	19	8	-	-	-	88
Walleye	-	2	52	76	62	12	-	-	204
Yellow Perch	114	210	35	-	-	-	-	-	359

DNR COMMENTS: Walleye population above third-quartile level for lake class; one-third of population exceeds 15 inches; fish to 25 inches sampled; strong 1992 year class; some natural reproduction. Northern Pike numbers above third-quartile range; more than 50 percent of the population was between 15 and 20 inches; fish to 35 inches captured. Muskellunge size range 10.8 to 40.3 inches; all fish from stocked year classes, but natural reproduction may be occurring. Largemouth Bass abundance below average for lake class; fish to 15.8 inches sampled. Black Crappie numbers above average; most fish were 9 to 10.5 inches. Bluegill population average; size good.

FISHING INFORMATION: This lake is several miles north of the city of Cass Lake and not too far from U.S. Highway 2. Tim Falk, owner of Bluewater Bait & Sport, says, "It's an excellent Walleye lake with really good structure and good points." Angler Chuck Cole adds there are a lot of Northerns. Where are some good spots to look for Walleyes? "I've fished for them early in the season off the rocky point near the Maple Beach Resort at the northeast side of the lake. We got some 5-pounders there," says Falk. "Then there's a trough near the middle that we fish with jigs, going back and forth in the summer, and there are some rock piles just south of the public access area at the southeast corner of the lake." In addition, you'll want to try the long, needle-like point on the southwest side that has steep breaks on its east side. Because the water is quite clear, you'll want to fish deeper water during bright summer days. Lots of average-size Northern Pike can be found off the weedbeds in any part of the lake. Take along a bunch of lures and leaders, because you could tangle with a 20-pound Muskie. Both the Walleyes and Muskellunge have been stocked and seem to survive well. There's definitely natural reproduction among Walleyes, and there may even be some among the Muskies. While you're here, don't overlook the nice panfish and Largemouth Bass in the weedbeds. The small arm off the southwest corner of the main lake is a good Bass spot.

NOT FOR NAVIGATION

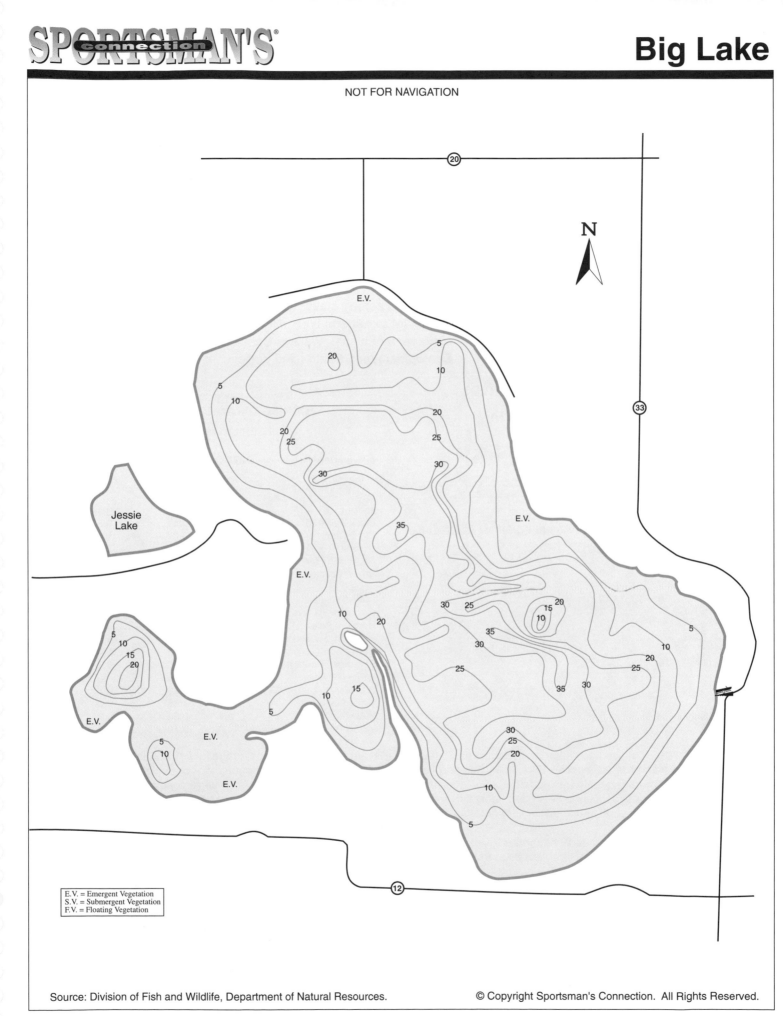

E.V. = Emergent Vegetation
S.V. = Submergent Vegetation
F.V. = Floating Vegetation

KITCHI LAKE
Beltrami County

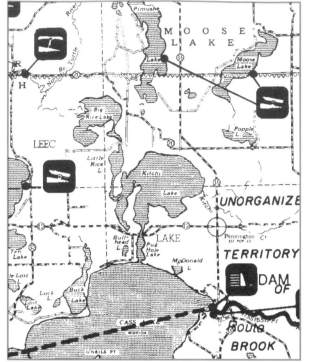

Location: Township 146, 147 Range 30
Watershed: Mississippi Headwaters
Surface Water Area: 1,758 acres
Shorelength: 12.0 miles
Secchi disk (water clarity): 3.8 ft.
Water color: Green
Cause of water color: Algae

Maximum depth: 50 ft.
Median depth: NA
Accessibility: Access via navigable channel from Cass Lake
Boat Ramp: Ramps on Cass Lake
Accommodations: Resort, campground

Shoreland zoning classification: Recreational Development
Dominant forest/soil type: No Tree/Wet
Management class: Walleye-Centrarchid
Ecological type: Centrarchid-Walleye

FISH STOCKING DATA: NO RECORD OF STOCKING

LENGTH OF SELECTED SPECIES SAMPLED FROM ALL GEAR
Number of fish caught for the following length categories (inches):

species	0-5	6-8	9-11	12-14	15-19	20-24	25-29	>30	Total
Black Bullhead	-	-	3	3	1	-	-	-	7
Black Crappie	-	35	8	3	-	-	-	-	46
Bluegill	8	27	40	-	-	-	-	-	75
Brown Bullhead	-	-	7	37	1	-	-	-	45
Hybrid Sunfish	-	1	-	-	-	-	-	-	1
Largemouth Bass	-	-	-	4	1	-	-	-	5
Northern Pike	-	-	-	2	15	71	11	2	101
Pumpkin. Sunfish	29	55	1	-	-	-	-	-	88
Rock Bass	2	5	20	-	-	-	-	-	27
Tullibee	-	-	9	12	39	-	-	-	60
Walleye	-	4	9	26	31	13	5	-	85
Yellow Bullhead	-	-	5	9	-	-	-	-	14
Yellow Perch	17	441	16	-	-	-	-	-	474

NET CATCH DATA
survey date: 08/23/93

species	Gill Nets # per net	Gill Nets avg fish wt. (lbs.)	Trap Nets # per set	Trap Nets avg fish wt. (lbs.)
Black Bullhead	0.3	0.67	0.2	1.04
Black Crappie	1.5	0.17	1.4	0.40
Bluegill	0.4	0.52	4.3	0.44
Bowfin (Dogfish)	-	-	1.2	4.96
Brown Bullhead	0.1	1.14	2.8	1.07
Burbot	-	-	0.1	0.13
Hybrid Sunfish	-	-	0.1	0.46
Largemouth Bass	0.1	1.37	0.3	1.66
Northern Pike	6.3	2.12	0.4	2.33
Pumpkin. Sunfish	0.7	0.13	4.6	0.26
Rock Bass	0.3	0.78	1.4	0.52
Shorthead Redhorse	0.1	2.76	0.1	2.98
Tullibee (Cisco)	4.0	1.15	-	-
Walleye	4.9	1.16	0.7	1.93
White Sucker	3.1	1.88	2.7	2.61
Yellow Bullhead	0.4	0.80	0.5	0.67
Yellow Perch	46.0	0.10	11.7	0.09

DNR COMMENTS: Walleye population down somewhat, but still near average for lake class; average length 14.5 inches. Northern Pike numerous; most fish 19 to 22 inches; Pike 30 inches and larger sampled. No Muskellunge captured, but anglers report catching this species. Quality-size Largemouth Bass present; population may be greater than survey suggests. Bluegill population low, but fish over 9 inches captured. Black Crappie numbers good; most fish small. Yellow Perch abundant, but most are between 5 and 7 inches; about half the population has black spot, and a few fish are grub-infested.

FISHING INFORMATION: Located just north of – and connected to – Cass Lake, Kitchi has produced good Walleyes for many years. In addition it has good populations of Northern Pike, Bluegills, and Black Crappies, as well as decent numbers of Largemouth Bass. "This is a good Walleye lake," says Carl Knowlton of Kobilka's Sporting Goods in Bemidji. "It's especially good for trolling at night in shallow water with a Rapala." Structure includes the long peninsula separating the bays on the southeast, a sunken island about 8 feet underwater off the point of the peninsula, and the steep offshore breaks in the southwest bay, where you can do well jigging. Many of the fish in Kitchi have come up from Cass Lake, so there's usually a fresh supply during the summer. Northerns can be fished in most of the lake, but early in the season you'll want to troll the flats off the weedbeds on the lake's east side. Other Northern hotspots are the inlet of the Turtle River on the west side, the outlet on the south side to Cass Lake, and the outlet to Sucker and Kitchi Creeks on the east side. Excellent weedbeds on the east side hold panfish and Bass. The water gets murky green from suspended algae, so you may want to use a bright jig tipped with a minnow or worm to get the attention of Crappies and Bluegills. Spinnerbaits and topwater lures work well for Largemouths in the summer. Pike Hole, at the south end of the lake past Walker Bay, is a favorite winter fishing spot. Public access to Kitchi is from Cass Lake's northeast side off Highway 39. The site has a concrete ramp.

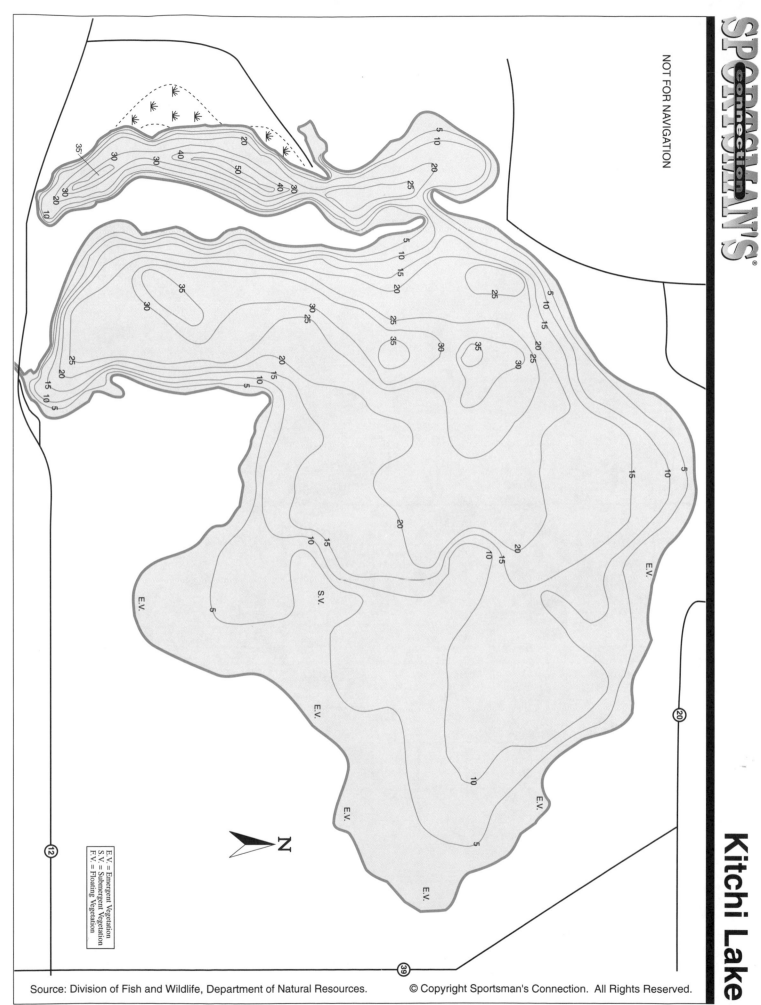

Kitchi Lake

E.V. = Emergent Vegetation
S.V. = Submergent Vegetation
F.V. = Floating Vegetation

N

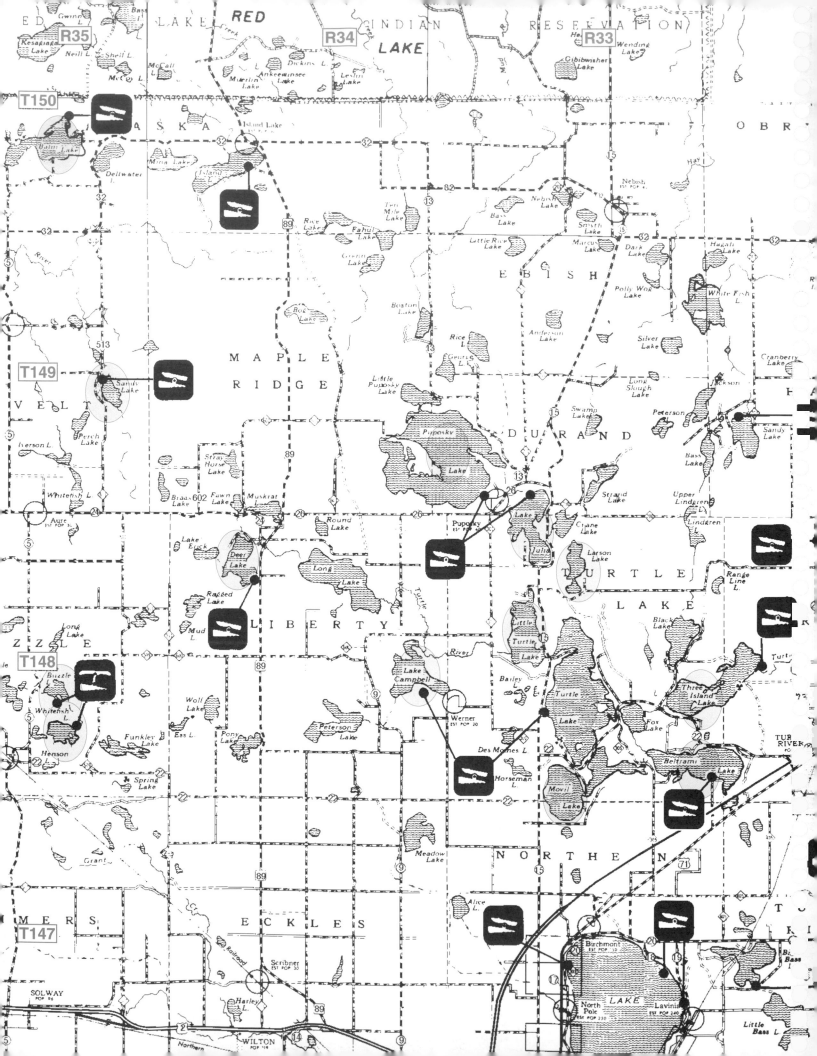

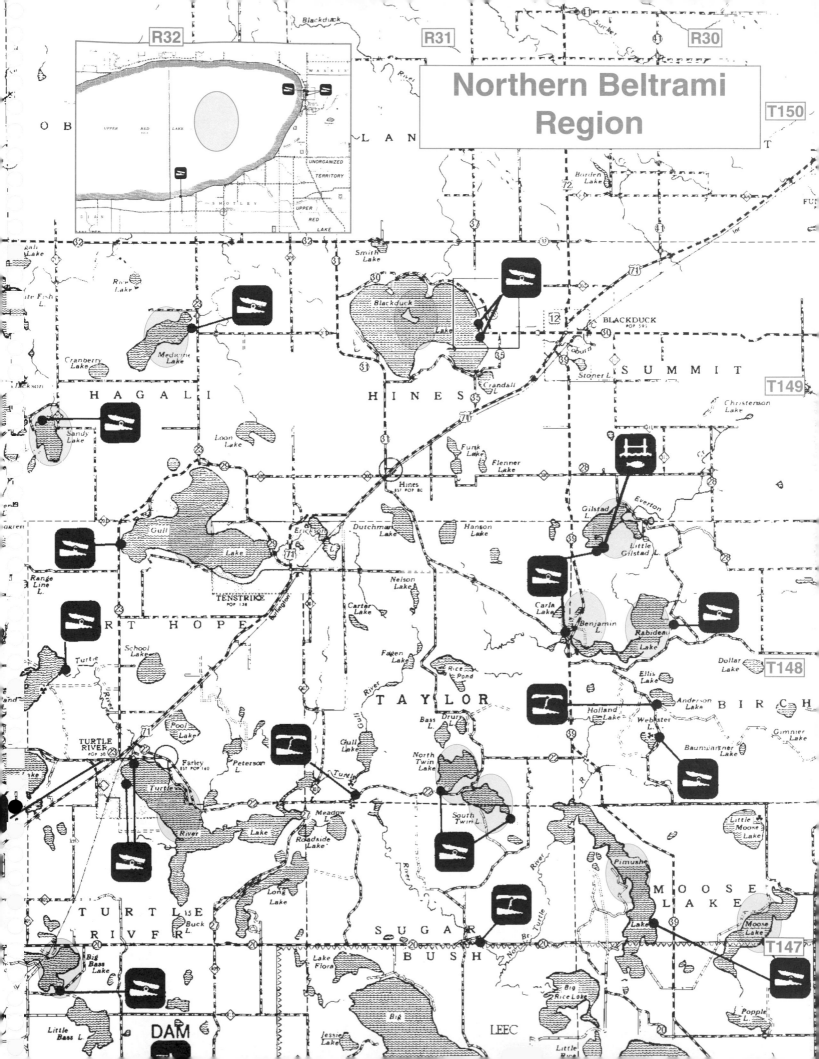

Northern Beltrami Region

MOOSE LAKE
Beltrami County

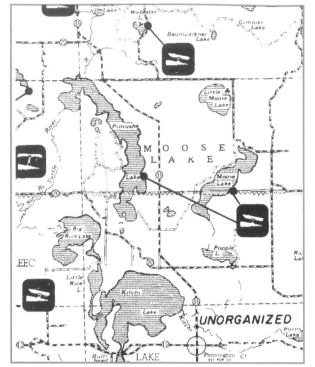

Location: Township 147 Range 30
Watershed: Mississippi Headwaters
Surface Water Area: 568 acres
Shorelength: 6.9 miles
Secchi disk (water clarity): 13.0 ft.
Water color: Gray
Cause of water color: Algae

Maximum depth: 71 ft.
Median depth: 15 ft.
Accessibility: State-owned public access on east shore
Boat Ramp: Concrete
Accommodations: Resort

Shoreland zoning classification: Recreational Development
Dominant forest/soil type: Decid/Loam
Management class: Walleye-Centrarchid
Ecological type: Centrarchid-Walleye

FISH STOCKING DATA

year	species	size	# released
91	Walleye	Fry	240,000
93	Walleye	Fry	240,000
95	Walleye	Fry	240,000
97	Walleye	Fry	240,000

NET CATCH DATA

survey date: 7/15/96

	Gill Nets		Trap Nets	
		avg fish		avg fish
species	# per net	wt. (lbs.)	# per set	wt. (lbs.)
Black Bullhead	0.1	0.52	-	-
Black Crappie	-	-	0.7	0.79
Bluegill	8.3	0.32	79.0	0.27
Brown Bullhead	0.4	0.98	1.6	0.70
Largemouth Bass	0.2	1.10	0.3	0.65
Northern Pike	12.8	2.33	0.4	1.99
Pumpkin. Sunfish	1.0	0.20	1.8	0.20
Rock Bass	0.6	0.39	1.1	0.27
Walleye	10.0	1.08	0.5	3.76
White Sucker	0.1	4.01	-	-
Yellow Perch	36.9	0.17	0.4	0.16

LENGTH OF SELECTED SPECIES SAMPLED FROM ALL GEAR

Number of fish caught for the following length categories (inches):

species	0-5	6-8	9-11	12-14	15-19	20-24	25-29	>30	Total
Black Bullhead	-	-	1	-	-	-	-	-	1
Black Crappie	-	2	4	2	-	-	-	-	8
Bluegill	84	574	5	-	-	-	-	-	663
Brown Bullhead	-	1	16	6	-	-	-	-	23
Largemouth Bass	-	3	1	1	1	-	-	-	6
Northern Pike	-	-	1	7	53	36	15	8	120
Pumpkin. Sunfish	10	20	-	-	-	-	-	-	30
Rock Bass	5	13	-	-	-	-	-	-	18
Walleye	-	15	21	32	13	11	4	-	96
Yellow Perch	81	248	8	-	-	-	-	-	337

DNR COMMENTS: Walleye population about double the lake-class average; average size low at 14 inches and 1.1 lb., this a result of strong 1993-95 year classes; fish to 29.5 inches sampled. Northern Pike abundance above average; average weight 2.3 lb.; Neascus present on some Pike. Largemouth Bass common; fish over 20 inches sampled; average size of net sample .75 lb. and 9.7 inches. Rock Bass numbers average. Black Crappie population may be good; average size large at 11.4 inches; fish over 14 inches sampled. Bluegill numbers very high at double the normal; 40 percent of population exceeds 7 inches. Pumpkinseed present. Brown Bullhead numbers about average for lake class; average weight .7 lb. Black Bullheads scarce.

FISHING INFORMATION: Located north of Cass Lake, Moose is known for a variety of species including Northern Pike, Walleyes, Bluegills, and Largemouth Bass. It's a nice lake to fish, with good shoreline vegetation, some deep holes, and several good points with bars. The lake is stocked with Walleye fry every other year, and the little guys seem to survive well in spite of heavy Northern Pike predation. Fish for Walleyes in early season off the points along the north and south sides. The water is clear, and you can do well jigging with live bait or with a bottom rig tossed where Walleyes could be looking for crawdads and minnows. The north and south ends of the lake are both shallow and more heavily weeded than other areas and are good spots to start fishing for panfish and Bass. The Crappies are spectacular, and the Bass are no slouches, either. Ice goes out early at the ends, and you'll do well then with minnows or nightcrawlers on a hook or small jig. In late spring after the season opens, fish for Largemouths in the same places, using spinnerbaits or a pig-and-jig combination. You probably won't find a lot of Bass, but there are some hefty ones available to the good angler. The Northerns here are of average size and may be a little difficult to catch because of the clear water and an abundance of forage fish. Your best bet is to troll the weedbeds slowly with a long line so that you don't spook the Pike. Or still-fish outside the north and south weedbeds with live bait.

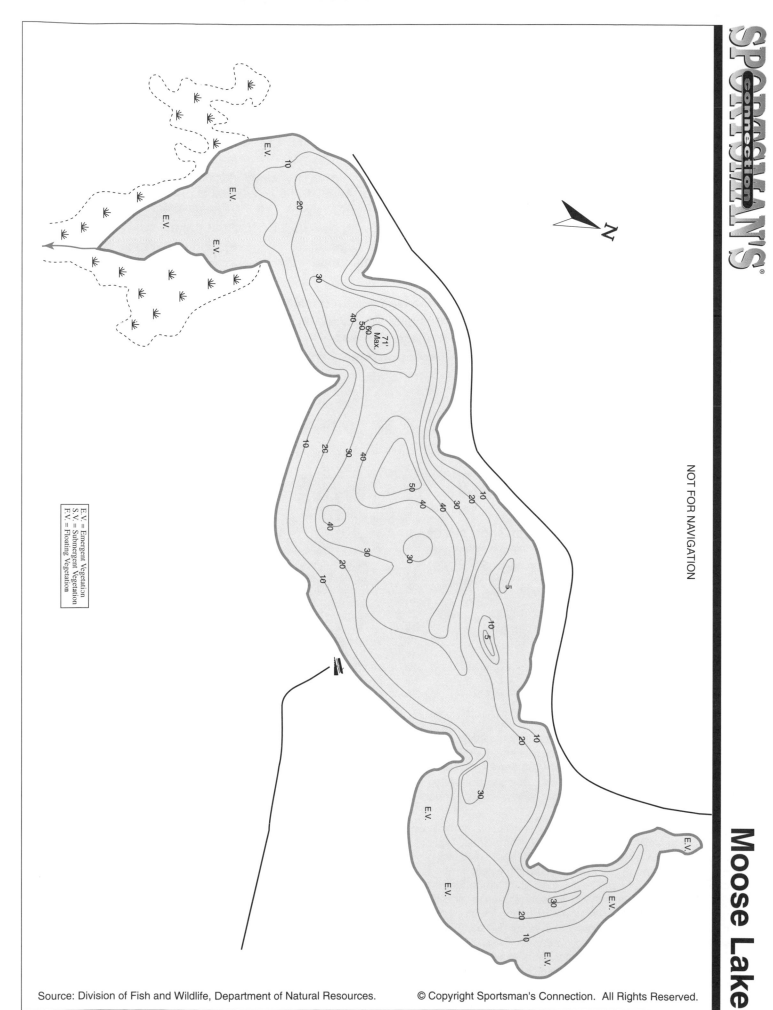

NOT FOR NAVIGATION

E.V. = Emergent Vegetation
S.V. = Submergent Vegetation
F.V. = Floating Vegetation

71'
Max.

E.V.
E.V.
E.V.
E.V.

PIMUSHE LAKE
Beltrami County

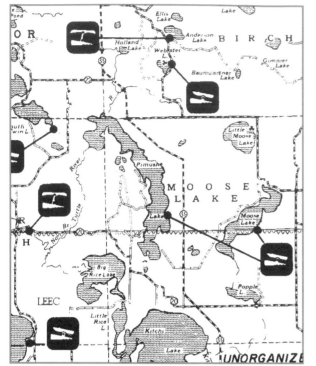

Location: Township 147, 148 Range 30, 31

Watershed: Mississippi Headwaters
Surface Water Area: 1,268 acres
Shorelength: 15.7 miles
Secchi disk (water clarity): 5.6 ft.
Water color: Greenish-brown
Cause of water color: Algae and bog stain

Maximum depth: 40 ft.
Median depth: NA
Accessibility: Public access on east shore (Chippewa National Forest)
Boat Ramp: Gravel
Accommodations: Resort

Shoreland zoning classification: Recreational Development
Dominant forest/soil type: Decid/Loam
Management class: Walleye-Centrarchid
Ecological type: Centrarchid-Walleye

FISH STOCKING DATA: NO RECORD OF STOCKING

LENGTH OF SELECTED SPECIES SAMPLED FROM ALL GEAR

Number of fish caught for the following length categories (inches):

species	0-5	6-8	9-11	12-14	15-19	20-24	25-29	>30	Total
Black Crappie	-	12	5	-	-	-	-	-	17
Bluegill	19	77	29	-	-	-	-	-	125
Brown Bullhead	-	2	22	35	-	-	-	-	59
Largemouth Bass	-	-	-	2	1	-	-	-	3
Northern Pike	-	-	1	4	71	42	1	-	119
Pumpkin. Sunfish	3	16	1	-	-	-	-	-	20
Rock Bass	3	3	6	-	-	-	-	-	12
Tullibee (Cisco)	-	-	8	1	14	-	-	-	23
Walleye	-	2	3	5	36	6	1	-	53
Yellow Bullhead	-	1	40	4	-	-	-	-	45
Yellow Perch	3	209	35	1	-	-	-	-	248

NET CATCH DATA

survey date: 08/16/93

species	Gill Nets # per net	Gill Nets avg fish wt. (lbs.)	Trap Nets # per set	Trap Nets avg fish wt. (lbs.)
Black Crappie	0.3	0.12	1.1	0.22
Bluegill	0.8	0.39	9.6	0.32
Bowfin (Dogfish)	0.1	3.42	0.7	4.51
Brown Bullhead	1.1	0.80	3.8	0.78
Largemouth Bass	0.3	1.11	-	-
Northern Pike	8.3	1.33	1.6	1.10
Pumpkin. Sunfish	0.1	0.43	1.6	0.27
Rock Bass	0.3	0.52	0.7	0.31
Tullibee (incl. Cisco)	1.9	1.47	-	-
Walleye	4.2	1.74	0.3	1.32
White Sucker	1.7	2.33	0.4	2.98
Yellow Bullhead	1.3	0.63	2.5	0.57
Yellow Perch	21.3	0.13	2.3	0.18

DNR COMMENTS: Northern Pike population slightly above average; about 75% of Pike were between 16 and 22 inches; a few had Neascus (black spot). Walleye numbers about average for comparable lakes; average length 16.8 inches; fish to 28.1 inches captured; natural reproduction consistent; good 1988 and 1989 year classes. Largemouth Bass numbers low; some fish as large as 18 inches were captured. Black Crappie numbers low. Bluegill captured in fair numbers; 23% of population exceeds 8 inches. Pumpkinseed numbers low, but size good. Rock Bass scarce. Yellow Perch numbers up, but most fish are too small to interest adult anglers.

FISHING INFORMATION: Located about 10 miles north of Cass Lake in the Chippewa National Forest, this lake has a good reputation among local anglers for big Bluegills, Northern Pike, Walleyes and Largemouth Bass. The lake also has good structure: weedbeds, points, rocky reefs, and some fairly deep holes. Anglers do well here, beginning at ice-out, when some nifty Bluegills (as heavy as a pound) can be taken in the deep weeds, especially in the shallower areas at the lake's south end. Early-season Walleyes are usually found at the rocky reefs and bars, where they like to feed after spawning. Some of the "hotspots" include the bar crossing the south end of the lake, the steep breaks off the east shoreline, and the sandy points along the west shoreline. Using shiners or leeches on a rig along the bottom in these places will usually get some action. As the water warms and days become brighter, the Walleyes will head for deep water, but the same points and bars remain good spots to fish at night or early in the morning. The bays at both the south and north ends of the lake have been good areas for Bass over the years, for their weedbeds provide the sort of cover Bass like best. After the opening, use a pig-and-jig combination; later you'll want to consider spinnerbaits or topwater lures. Northerns are not to be overlooked here. There are, in fact, plenty of them. Most are in the 2- to 3-pound range, but lunkers are frequently caught. Generally, the south end is most Pike-productive, but you also will want to try around the creek inlets and outlets on the north end.

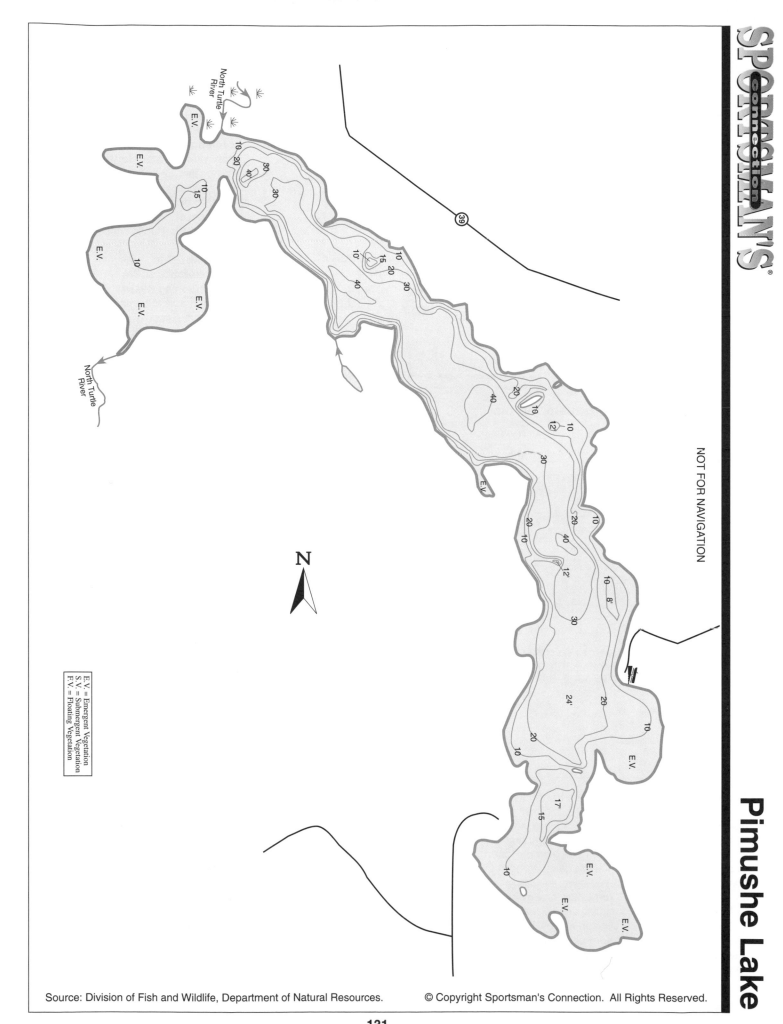

NOT FOR NAVIGATION

E.V. = Emergent Vegetation
S.V. = Submergent Vegetation
F.V. = Floating Vegetation

North Turtle River

North Turtle River

NORTH TWIN LAKE   SOUTH TWIN LAKE
Beltrami County

Location: Township 148   Range 31
Watershed: Mississippi Headwaters
Surface Water Area: 313 acres
Shorelength: 3.5 miles
Secchi disk (water clarity): 17.0 ft.
Water color: Blue-green
Cause of water color: Suspended solids and light algae bloom
Maximum depth: 65 ft.
Median depth: 18 ft.
Accessibility: Public access on southwest corner, off County Road 22
Boat Ramp: Concrete
Accommodations: Campground, Picnic area
Shoreland zoning classif.: Rec. Dev.
Dominant forest/soil type: NA
Management class: Walleye-Centrarchid
Ecological type: Centrarchid-Walleye

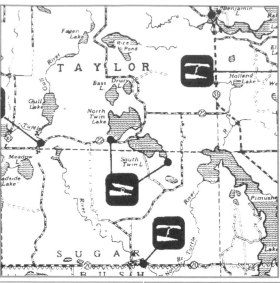

Location: Township 147, 148   Range 31
Watershed: Mississippi Headwaters
Surface Water Area: 205 acres
Shorelength: 2.8 miles
Secchi disk (water clarity): 21.0 ft.
Water color: Blue-green
Cause of water color: Algae
Maximum depth: 48 ft.
Median depth: 20 ft.
Accessibility: Public access on southeast corner
Boat Ramp: Concrete
Accommodations: NA
Shoreland zoning classif.: Rec. Dev.
Dominant forest/soil type: Decid/Loam
Management class: Walleye-Centrarchid
Ecological type: Centrarchid

NORTH TWIN LAKE

DNR COMMENTS:
Walleye and Northern Pike populations stable. Largemouth Bass numbers have been consistent since 1956. Smallmouth Bass captures have decreased, and only one fish was collected in 1985. Bluegill and Pumpkinseed populations have remained stable since 1978. Black Crappie numbers tend to be low in this lake's history.

FISH STOCKING DATA

year	species	size	# released
92	Walleye	Fingerling	16,576
95	Walleye	Fingerling	3,750

NET CATCH DATA
survey date: 07/01/85

	Gill Nets		Trap Nets	
species	# per net	avg fish wt. (lbs)	# per set	avg fish wt. (lbs)
Yellow Perch	7.5	0.18	0.1	3.80
White Sucker	0.5	2.40	-	-
Walleye	6.3	1.36	-	-
Rock Bass	5.8	0.28	3.0	0.34
Pumpkin. Sunfish	0.5	0.10	1.8	0.20
Northern Pike	10.0	1.97	0.8	1.49
Largemouth Bass	1.5	1.23	1.1	0.50
Bluegill	6.0	0.24	32.1	0.24
Smallmouth Bass	-	-	32.1	0.24
Black Crappie	-	-	0.3	0.75

LENGTH OF SELECTED SPECIES SAMPLED FROM ALL GEAR
Number of fish caught for the following length categories (inches):

species	0-5	6-8	9-11	12-14	15-19	20-24	25-29	>30	Total
Black Crappie	-	-	2	-	-	-	-	-	2
Bluegill	24	155	11	-	-	-	-	-	190
Largemouth Bass	-	5	2	4	4	-	-	-	15
Northern Pike	-	-	1	1	23	15	4	2	46
Rock Bass	7	31	8	-	-	-	-	-	46
Smallmouth Bass	-	-	-	-	1	-	-	-	1
Walleye	-	2	-	11	6	7	-	-	26
Yellow Perch	-	23	6	1	-	-	-	-	30

SOUTH TWIN LAKE

FISH STOCKING DATA

year	species	size	# released
90	Walleye	Fingerling	5,325
93	Walleye	Fingerling	4,100
93	Walleye	Adult	10
96	Walleye	Fingerling	4,500

NET CATCH DATA
survey date: 6/19/95

	Gill Nets		Trap Nets	
species	# per net	avg fish wt. (lbs)	# per set	avg fish wt. (lbs)
Black Crappie	-	-	0.4	0.43
Bluegill	14.7	0.15	88.4	0.18
Brown Bullhead	-	-	0.3	0.90
Largemouth Bass	0.8	0.55	0.6	0.56
Northern Pike	27.0	2.49	1.8	1.50
Pumpkin. Sunfish	-	-	2.5	0.16
Rock Bass	1.5	0.27	6.8	0.27
Walleye	3.7	1.13	0.4	1.73
White Sucker	2.3	3.31	-	-
Yellow Perch	23.2	0.21	1.6	0.27

LENGTH OF SELECTED SPECIES SAMPLED FROM ALL GEAR
Number of fish caught for the following length categories (inches):

species	0-5	6-8	9-11	12-14	15-19	20-24	25-29	>30	Total
Black Crappie	-	-	3	-	-	-	-	-	3
Bluegill	121	193	-	-	-	-	-	-	314
Brown Bullhead	-	-	2	-	-	-	-	-	2
Largemouth Bass	2	3	2	3	-	-	-	-	10
Northern Pike	-	-	8	20	53	54	33	8	176
Pumpkin. Sunfish	12	8	-	-	-	-	-	-	20
Rock Bass	13	50	-	-	-	-	-	-	63
Walleye	-	2	10	-	10	3	-	-	25
Yellow Perch	12	95	21	-	-	-	-	-	128

DNR COMMENTS:
Walleye population about average for lake class; average size 14.5 inches and 1.2 lb; fish to 22 inches sampled. Northern Pike numbers up and triple the lake-class average; average size 21 inches and 2.5 lb.; fish to 34 inches present. Anglers report a few Muskellunge sightings; last stocking of this species in 1977. Largemouth Bass numbers average; average length 9.5 inches. Black Crappie numbers down; average length 9 inches. Bluegills abundant; average length 6.2 inches. Yellow Perch numbers down; average length 8 inches.

FISHING INFORMATION: Located north of the city of Cass Lake, these two lakes are well known for their Northern Pike, Largemouth Bass, and panfish, as well as Walleye. They get heavy fishing pressure in summer. **South Twin** holds fair numbers of Largemouth Bass and an abundance of Northerns, in addition to the Walleyes. The north shore has particularly nice reeds and lily pads where you can fish for Bass with spinnerbaits or a pig-and-jig combination. The Bass are not as big as those in the neighboring lake, but there are more of them. Crappie and Bluegill numbers also are good; try the north and east sides close to shore, where the lily pads are heaviest. Northerns can be just about anyplace; trolling along the outer edges of the weedbeds is a good way to start looking for them. There's some decent structure to fish for Walleyes, including a sunken island near mid lake, a point off the southeast side, and another point in the southwest corner. **North Twin Lake**, meanwhile, has (at this 1999 writing) a 22- to 30-inch slot limit on Northern Pike, and only one fish over 30 inches may be kept. The DNR wants you to take the small ones and let the big ones get bigger (check current fishing regs under "experimental lakes"). Jo Clayton at Kobilka's Sporting Goods in Bemidji says: "There are more Bass in South Twin, but North Twin has the big ones. You can find some 4- or 5-pounders there. And there are a few Muskies in the lake, too." The lake's west side has lots of cabbage beds, where anglers take nice Bluegills and Crappies. Both Walleye and Northern Pike numbers are good, and there's some natural reproduction of both species. The sharp point off the north side can be productive for Walleyes.

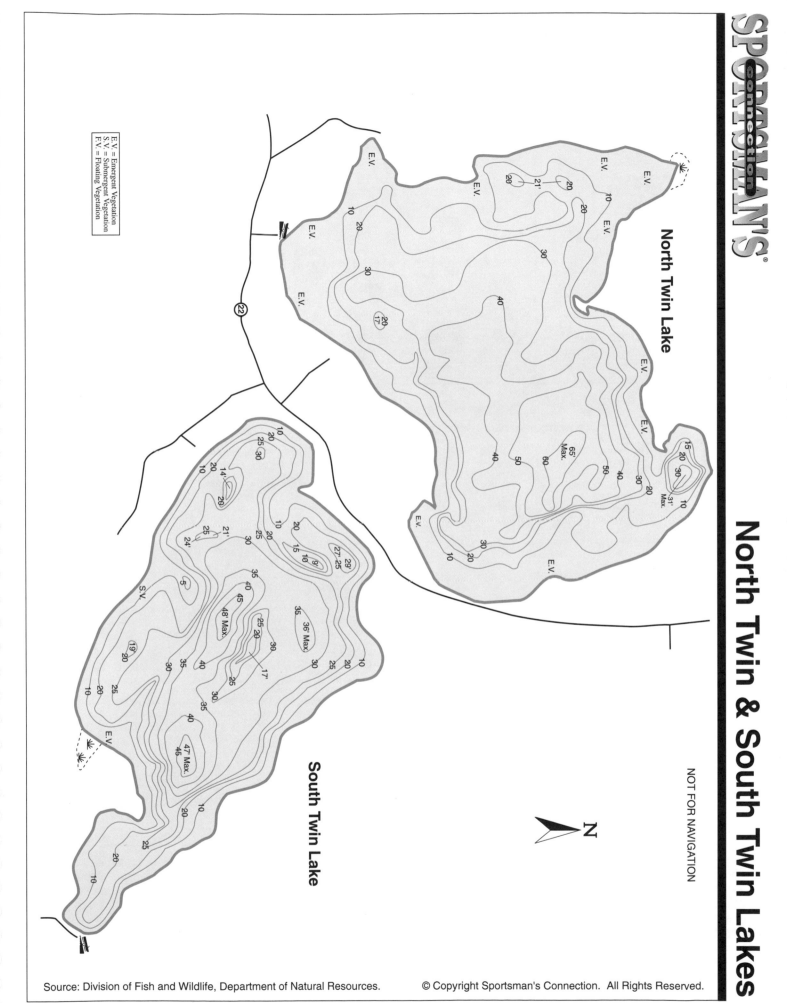

North Twin Lake

South Twin Lake

North Twin & South Twin Lakes

NOT FOR NAVIGATION

N

E.V. = Emergent Vegetation
S.V. = Submergent Vegetation
F.V. = Floating Vegetation

BENJAMIN LAKE   GILSTAD LAKE

Beltrami County

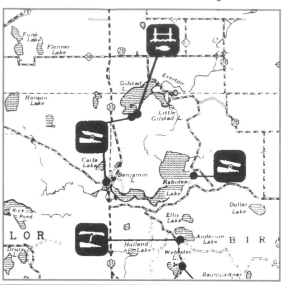

Location: Township 148 Range 30, 31
Watershed: Mississippi Headwaters
Surface Water Area: 30 acres
Shorelength: NA
Secchi disk (water clarity): 28.0 ft.
Water color: Green-brown
Cause of water color: Suspended algae and bog stain
Maximum depth: 128 ft.
Median depth: NA
Accessibility: Public access on south shore
Boat Ramp: Gravel
Accommodations: NA
Shoreland zoning classif.: Nat. Envir.
Dominant forest/soil type: NA
Management class: Stream Trout
Ecological type: Centrarchid

Location: Township 148, 149 Range 30
Watershed: Mississippi Headwaters
Surface Water Area: 294 acres
Shorelength: 3.3 miles
Secchi disk (water clarity): 8.0 ft.
Water color: Green
Cause of water color: Phytoplankton bloom
Maximum depth: 55 ft.
Median depth: 15 ft.
Accessibility: Public access located on south shore
Boat Ramp: Concrete
Accommodations: NA
Shoreland zoning classif.: Rec. Dev.
Dominant forest/soil type: Decid/Loam
Management class: Walleye-Centrarchid
Ecological type: Centrarchid

DNR COMMENTS:
Lake is managed for stream Trout and stocked each October with Rainbow fingerlings. Rainbow numbers down; mean size 10.2 inches and .45 lb.; fish from the 1994 year class averaged 13.1 inches; anglers report a few large Trout in the lake. A single White Sucker and a lone Bluegill sampled in test nets.

FISH STOCKING DATA

year	species	size	# released
90	Rainbow Trout	Fingerling	4,500
91	Rainbow Trout	Fingerling	4,500
92	Rainbow Trout	Fingerling	4,500
93	Rainbow Trout	Fingerling	4,500
94	Rainbow Trout	Fingerling	4,500
95	Rainbow Trout	Fingerling	4,500
96	Rainbow Trout	Fingerling	4,500
97	Rainbow Trout	Fingerling	4,500

NET CATCH DATA
survey date: 6/17/96

	Gill Nets		Trap Nets	
species	# per net	avg fish wt. (lbs)	# per set	avg fish wt. (lbs)
Bluegill	-	-	0.1	1.19
Rainbow Trout	15.0	0.45	0.5	0.29
White Sucker	0.3	2.18	-	-

LENGTH OF SELECTED SPECIES SAMPLED FROM ALL GEAR
Number of fish caught for the following length categories (inches):

species	0-5	6-8	9-11	12-14	15-19	20-24	25-29	>30	Total
Bluegill	-	-	1	-	-	-	-	-	1
Rainbow Trout	-	13	25	11	-	-	-	-	49

FISH STOCKING DATA

year	species	size	# released
93	Walleye	Fingerling	2,000
96	Walleye	Fingerling	1,300

NET CATCH DATA
survey date: 07/31/90

	Gill Nets		Trap Nets	
species	# per net	avg fish wt. (lbs)	# per set	avg fish wt. (lbs)
Yellow Perch	19.3	0.08	5.5	0.11
Yellow Bullhead	0.5	0.67	4.9	0.48
White Sucker	0.5	2.50	0.1	3.90
Walleye	1.2	2.46	-	-
Tullibee (Cisco)	4.7	1.09	-	-
Pumpkin. Sunfish	0.3	0.10	3.4	0.13
Northern Pike	9.0	2.79	0.3	1.70
Largemouth Bass	0.2	1.40	0.3	0.10
Brown Bullhead	0.5	0.70	0.9	0.75
Bluegill	1.2	0.10	24.2	0.10
Black Crappie	2.5	0.25	4.5	0.34
Black Bullhead	0.8	0.50	0.1	0.70
Rock Bass	-	-	0.3	0.80

LENGTH OF SELECTED SPECIES SAMPLED FROM ALL GEAR
Number of fish caught for the following length categories (inches):

species	0-5	6-8	9-11	12-14	15-19	20-24	25-29	>30	Total
Black Bullhead	-	1	5	-	-	-	-	-	6
Bluegill	73	74	1	-	-	-	-	-	148
Brown Bullhead	-	2	3	9	-	-	-	-	14
Largemouth Bass	2	1	-	-	-	-	-	-	3
Northern Pike	-	-	-	-	11	34	12	-	57
Pumpkin. Sunfish	24	14	1	-	-	-	-	-	39
Rock Bass	-	-	2	1	-	-	-	-	3
Tullibee(Cisco)	-	-	13	3	12	-	-	-	28
Yellow Bullhead	-	11	37	14	-	-	-	-	62

DNR COMMENTS:
Northern Pike numbers slightly above the third-quartile range. Black Crappie numbers about twice the state median level and at an all-time high for this lake. Walleye catch rate low, with all fish captured representing one year class (1982 stocking). Largemouth Bass catch low; however, quality-size fish of 3 to 4 lb. captured.

FISHING INFORMATION: We spoke with Earl Taber of Taber's Baits and Jo Clayton of Kobilka's in Bemidji about these lakes southwest of Hines on U.S. Highway 71. **Benjamin** is a designated stream Trout lake and is stocked annually with approximately 4,500 Rainbows. "Most of the Trout are in the 1- to 1 1/2-pound range," Taber told us, "but every now and then you'll catch a nice one. A few years ago a fellow caught a 7-pounder there." You would have to be very lucky to duplicate that feat, but the Trout fishing is good much of the time. The water is extremely clear and cold, reaching a depth of 128 feet. In mid May, following the opening of the season, Trout will still be in relatively shallow water and can be fished successfully from shore. It doesn't take long for the water to warm, however, and then the Rainbows will head to deep water. Then you'll not only need a boat, but you'll want plenty of lead to get your bait down near the thermocline, where the Trout while away the dog days. Nearby **Lake Gilstad** is a "beautiful Largemouth Bass lake," according to Jo Clayton, who fishes many of the lakes in the area. "It also has good Northerns," she added. There are fairly good numbers of Panfish around, too, and bazillions of Yellow Perch. Taber told us that the Bluegills and Crappies are typically three to a pound.

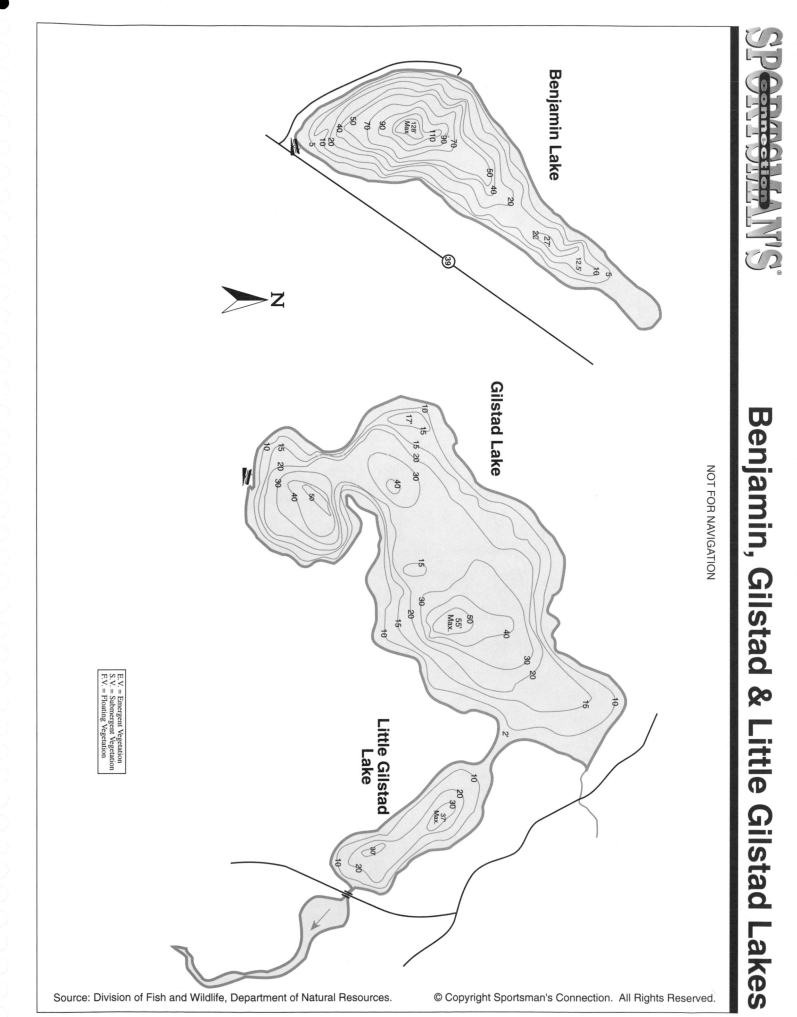

Benjamin Lake

Gilstad Lake

Little Gilstad Lake

NOT FOR NAVIGATION

N

E.V. = Emergent Vegetation
S.V. = Submergent Vegetation
F.V. = Floating Vegetation

RABIDEAU LAKE
Beltrami County

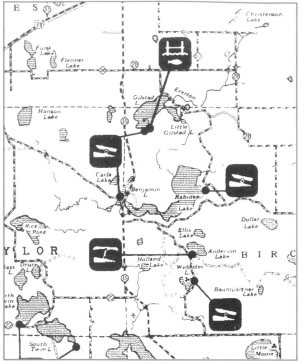

Location: Township 147, 148 Range 30

Watershed: Mississippi Headwaters

Surface Water Area: 577 acres

Shorelength: 7.0 miles

Secchi disk (water clarity): 9.0 ft.

Water color: Reddish tint

Cause of water color: Bog stain

Maximum depth: 60 ft.

Median depth: 6 ft.

Accessibility: State-owned public access on northeast corner

Boat Ramp: Concrete

Accommodations: NA

Shoreland zoning classification: Recreational Development

Dominant forest/soil type: Decid/Loam

Management class: Centrarchid

Ecological type: Centrarchid

FISH STOCKING DATA

year	species	size	# released
92	Walleye	Fingerling	16,576
94	Walleye	Fingerling	9,557
94	Walleye	Adult	1
96	Bluegill	Adult	240
96	Largemouth Bass	Adult	36
96	Walleye	Fry	200,000

NET CATCH DATA

survey date: 08/06/90

	Gill Nets		Trap Nets	
species	# per net	avg fish wt. (lbs.)	# per set	avg fish wt. (lbs.)
Yellow Perch	51.7	0.23	9.8	0.18
Walleye	2.7	2.73	0.4	2.95
Tullibee (incl. Cisco)	0.1	1.90	-	-
Pumpkin. Sunfish	0.9	0.20	2.7	0.12
Northern Pike	5.0	1.54	1.2	1.78
Largemouth Bass	0.1	1.40	0.4	0.15
Bluegill	0.6	0.58	8.0	0.19
Black Crappie	1.9	0.70	-	-
Black Bullhead	59.4	0.49	0.8	0.24

LENGTH OF SELECTED SPECIES SAMPLED FROM ALL GEAR

Number of fish caught for the following length categories (inches):

species	0-5	6-8	9-11	12-14	15-19	20-24	25-29	>30	Total
Yellow Perch	-	42	55	8	-	-	-	-	105
Walleye	-	-	1	2	8	5	3	-	19
Tullibee (Cisco)	-	-	-	-	1	-	-	-	1
Pumpkin. Sunfish	2	3	1	-	-	-	-	-	6
Northern Pike	-	-	1	3	13	15	2	1	35
Largemouth Bass	-	-	-	1	-	-	-	-	1
Brown Bullhead	-	-	28	14	-	-	-	-	42
Bluegill	-	2	2	-	-	-	-	-	4
Black Crappie	1	3	3	7	-	-	-	-	14
Black Bullhead	-	6	102	6	-	-	-	-	114

DNR COMMENTS: Northern Pike gillnet catch about equal to the local median but lower than the lake-class median; most fish sampled were smaller than 20 inches. Gillnet indices for Black Bullhead and Yellow Perch considerably above both class and local medians. Walleye numbers slightly above class median but only about one-third of the local median; some natural reproduction occurring; six year classes sampled. Trapnet catches of Bluegill and Largemouth Bass generally below class and local medians. Size distribution of Bluegill showed few fish over 8 inches, although some anglers report doing well for larger Bluegills.

FISHING INFORMATION: There are mixed opinions about this lake on State Highway 39 in Blackduck State Forest. None of them is bad, but some people say the lake's good only for Walleyes, while others say it's best for Crappies and Northerns. We talked with a Bemidji fisherman named Chuck Cole at the Bluewater Bait & Sports store. "It's a good lake; the Walleyes really hit there," he said. "I've caught nice Crappies and Northerns there, too, and some nice Largemouth Bass." Walleyes are stocked and have a good forage base to grow on. Cole told us they don't come easily, however; you have to work for them. He said he likes to go out early for them and fish with crankbaits until about 11 a.m. "There are some good humps in the north end where they hold well," he noted. The deep, southeast end of the lake has very steep drops from the shoreline – the sort of area where Walleyes like to feed in the spring. The north end, on the other hand, is best for Northerns early in the season. It is heavily weeded, and the water is bog-stained, so you'll want to use flashy spinnerbaits or vibrating crankbaits to get attention. Fishing with live bait under a bobber in the narrows between the two lakes can be productive, too. Bluegills and Crappies are chiefly found in the weedy north bay as soon as the ice goes out. Use bright jigs tipped with worms or minnows. You'll also find Largemouth Bass in the same weeds; toss them a pig-and-jig combination. Many anglers like the lake for winter fishing; they get nice Northerns and Perch. But Cole warned that there are springs out there, and the ice can be dangerous. Check with locals before you head out onto it.

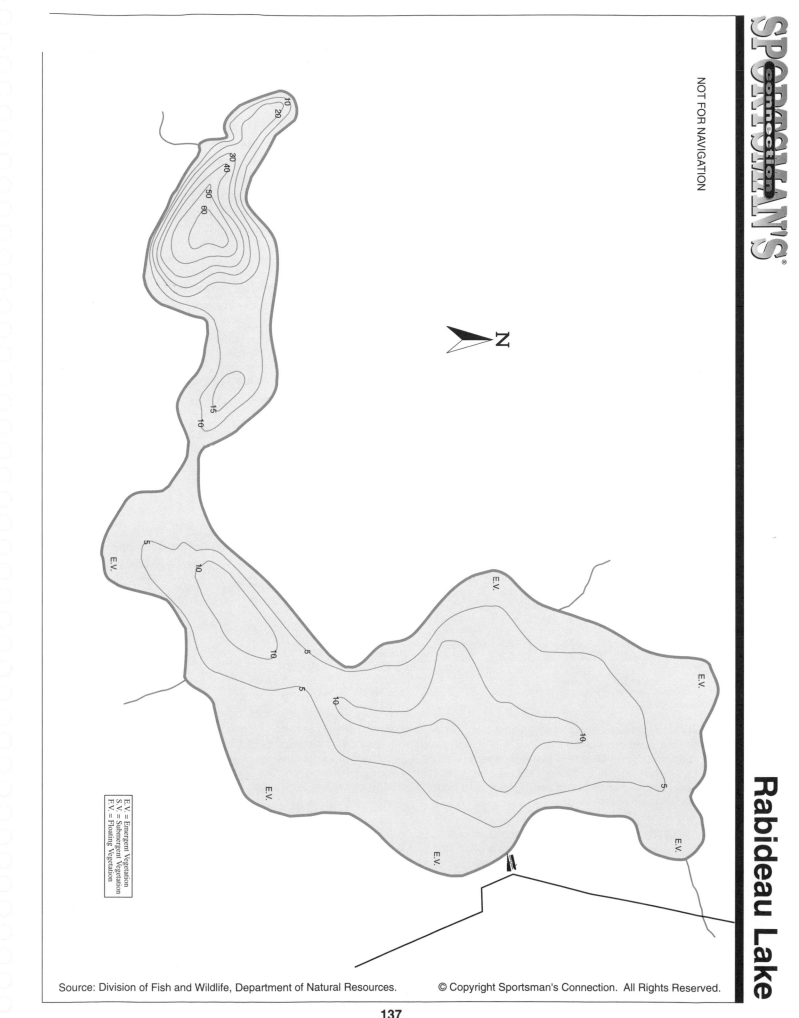

NOT FOR NAVIGATION

N

E.V. = Emergent Vegetation
S.V. = Submergent Vegetation
F.V. = Floating Vegetation

10
20
30
40
50
60
15
10
5
10
10
5
5
10
10
5
E.V.
E.V.
E.V.
E.V.
E.V.
E.V.

Rabideau Lake

Source: Division of Fish and Wildlife, Department of Natural Resources.

BLACKDUCK LAKE
Beltrami County

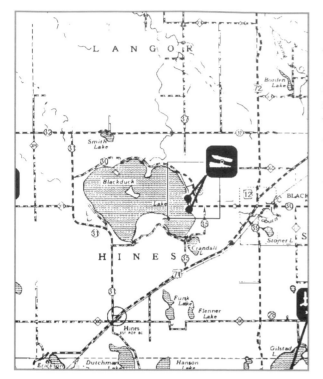

Location: Township 149 Range 31
Watershed: Red Lakes
Surface Water Area: 2596 acres
Shorelength: 8.5 miles
Secchi disk (water clarity): 6.5 ft.
Water color: Green
Cause of water color: Algae

Maximum depth: 28 ft.
Median depth: 15 ft.
Accessibility: Two county accesses on east shore
Boat Ramp: Concrete (both)
Accommodations: Park, resort

Shoreland zoning classification: Recreational development
Dominant forest/soil type: Deciduous/Loam
Management class: Walleye-Centrarchid
Ecological type: Centrarchid-Walleye

FISH STOCKING DATA

year	species	size	# released
90	Walleye	Fry	1,300,000
91	Walleye	Fry	1,375,000
93	Walleye	Fry	1,375,000
94	Walleye	Fry	1,375,000
96	Walleye	Fry	2,075,000
97	Walleye	Fry	2,500,000

NET CATCH DATA

survey date: 7/8/96

species	Gill Nets # per net	Gill Nets avg fish wt. (lbs.)	Trap Nets # per set	Trap Nets avg fish wt. (lbs.)
Black Crappie	0.1	1.16	0.7	1.11
Bluegill	trace	1.22	1.5	0.42
Brown Bullhead	2.0	1.47	1.0	1.16
Freshwater Drum	2.7	5.90	0.6	6.31
Lake Whitefish	0.6	2.19	-	-
Northern Pike	5.4	2.07	0.5	1.48
Pumpkin. Sunfish	0.8	0.18	5.2	0.16
Rock Bass	1.7	0.39	0.7	0.36
Walleye	17.4	1.34	0.3	1.57
Yellow Perch	50.7	0.14	9.3	0.10

LENGTH OF SELECTED SPECIES SAMPLED FROM ALL GEAR

Number of fish caught for the following length categories (inches):

species	0-5	6-8	9-11	12-14	15-19	20-24	25-29	>30	Total
Black Bullhead	-	-	2	-	-	-	-	-	2
Black Crappie	1	-	-	11	-	-	-	-	12
Bluegill	13	2	9	-	-	-	-	-	24
Brown Bullhead	-	1	-	42	2	-	-	-	45
Lake Whitefish	-	-	1	1	7	-	-	-	9
Northern Pike	-	-	-	-	32	48	7	2	89
Pumpkin. Sunfish	63	27	-	-	-	-	-	-	90
Rock Bass	11	15	11	-	-	-	-	-	37
Walleye	-	3	95	31	124	12	1	-	266
Yellow Perch	586	226	87	1	-	-	-	-	900

DNR COMMENTS: Walleye numbers at an all-time high; 44 percent of population is between 16 and 20 inches; fish to 25.4 inches captured. Northern Pike numbers highest since 1978 and near average for lake class; average weight 2.1 lb.; Pike to 35.4 inches sampled. Yellow Perch numbers above lake-class average; average length 6.5 inches. Black Crappie numbers up but below lake-class average; average size 11.8 inches and .6 lb. Bluegill abundance up but below average; average length 6.5 inches. Rock Bass common; average length 7.3 inches. Whitefish population average for lake class. Commercial harvest appears to have been successful in reducing the Brown and Black Bullhead populations.

FISHING INFORMATION: Located just two miles west of U.S. Highway 71 and the town of Blackduck, this 2,600-acre lake has been a good Walleye producer for many years. It also has a good Northern Pike population and a lot of Yellow Perch and other forage fish. One of the reasons for the big Walleye numbers is the connection to giant Red Lake through the Blackduck River. The river flows north (eventually connected to Hudson's Bay), and Walleyes in the big lake frequently take the upstream run to Blackduck after the spawn. Moose Point on the south shore is a good place to start for spring Walleye, and local anglers like to use leeches or shiners fished along the bottom and the slopes of sand or gravel bars. Another nice spot is off Big Island at the middle of the lake. Too, the sloping bars off the island's points are typically good producers. And, the good weedbeds along most of the shorelines are home to Perch and suckers. Troll the flats off these weeds for nice-size Northerns. Use live bait in 8 to 15 feet of water, moving slowly and following any schools of forage fish you spot. In summer you will want to troll or drift deeper waters during the day, or bounce a jig up the drop-offs, like those around the steep bank on the south shore. At night – or just after sunset or at sunrise – go back to the points off the shores and the island for feeding Walleyes. You'll find good public access at Pine Tree State Park, near the city of Blackduck and east of the lake.

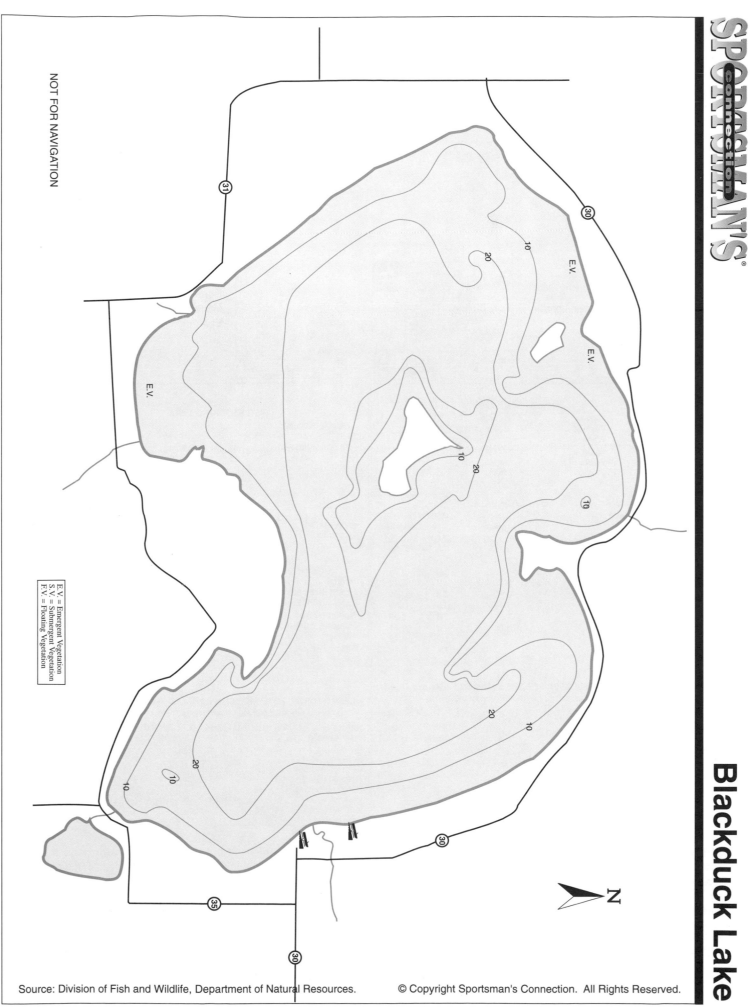

NOT FOR NAVIGATION

E.V. = Emergent Vegetation
S.V. = Submergent Vegetation
F.V. = Floating Vegetation

E.V.

E.V.

E.V.

E.V.

10

20

10

10

20

10

20

10

20

10

10

20

31

30

30

30

35

30

N

Blackduck Lake

MEDICINE LAKE
SANDY LAKE

Beltrami County

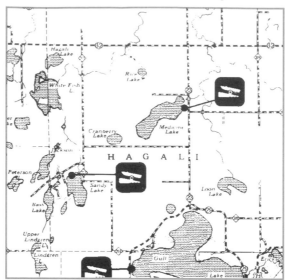

Location: Township 149 Range 32
Watershed: Red Lakes
Surface Water Area: 446 acres
Shorelength: 4.2 miles
Secchi disk (water clarity): 6.5 ft.
Water color: Green-brown
Cause of water color: Bog stain and suspended phytoplankton
Maximum depth: 44 ft.
Median depth: 12 ft.
Accessibility: State-owned public access on northeast shore
Boat Ramp: Earth
Accommodations: Resort
Shoreland zoning classif.: NA
Dominant forest/soil type: Decid/Loam
Management class: Walleye
Ecological type: Centrarchid

Location: Township 149 Range 32
Watershed: Red Lakes
Surface Water Area: 260 acres
Shorelength: 2.8 miles
Secchi disk (water clarity): 6.7 ft.
Water color: Blue-brown
Cause of water color: Bog stain
Maximum depth: 30 ft.
Median depth: NA
Accessibility: County-owned access on north shore
Boat Ramp: Earth
Accommodations: NA
Shoreland zoning classif.: Nat. Envir.
Dominant forest/soil type: Decid/Loam
Management class: Walleye-Centrarchid
Ecological type: Centrarchid

DNR COMMENTS:
Northern Pike numbers at an all-time high at six times the local median value; most fish are 15 to 19 inches and in poor condition. Walleye population down slightly but still above state and local medians; population maintained by stocking.

FISH STOCKING DATA

year	species	size	# released
90	Walleye	Fingerling	28,300
92	Walleye	Fingerling	26,960
94	Walleye	Fingerling	14,656
96	Walleye	Fingerling	11,800

NET CATCH DATA
survey date: 06/18/86

| | Gill Nets | | Trap Nets | |
| | | avg fish | | avg fish |
species	# per net	wt. (lbs)	# per set	wt. (lbs)
Yellow Perch	10.0	0.15	0.3	0.35
White Sucker	3.0	2.34	-	-
Walleye	5.3	1.55	0.2	0.75
Rock Bass	0.3	0.35	2.2	0.42
Pumpkin. Sunfish	0.1	0.33	12.0	0.35
Northern Pike	19.2	1.12	0.3	0.80
Brown Bullhead	0.2	1.00	3.8	0.98
Black Crappie	1.3	0.30	2.0	0.71
Largemouth Bass	-	-	1.2	2.26
Bluegill	-	-	7.5	0.55

LENGTH OF SELECTED SPECIES SAMPLED FROM ALL GEAR
Number of fish caught for the following length categories (inches):

species	0-5	6-8	9-11	12-14	15-19	20-24	25-29	>30	Total
Black Crappie	1	3	7	8	-	-	-	-	19
Bluegill	3	10	32	-	-	-	-	-	45
Brown Bullhead	-	-	-	24	-	-	-	-	24
Largemouth Bass	-	-	-	1	6	-	-	-	7
Northern Pike	-	-	-	6	79	30	-	2	117
Pumpkin. Sunfish	4	72	-	-	-	-	-	-	76
Rock Bass	1	9	5	-	-	-	-	-	15
Walleye	-	-	7	2	19	5	-	-	33
Yellow Perch	3	48	6	2	-	-	-	-	59

FISH STOCKING DATA

year	species	size	# released
90	Walleye	Fingerling	15,000
93	Walleye	Fingerling	4,000
96	Walleye	Fingerling	2,866

NET CATCH DATA
survey date: 7/22/96

| | Gill Nets | | Trap Nets | |
| | | avg fish | | avg fish |
species	# per net	wt. (lbs)	# per set	wt. (lbs)
Black Crappie	4.7	0.24	5.0	0.31
Bluegill	2.8	0.22	10.3	0.19
Brown Bullhead	2.2	1.20	0.2	1.76
Largemouth Bass	-	-	0.9	2.46
Northern Pike	5.7	1.59	2.4	1.60
Pumpkin. Sunfish	1.3	0.15	3.4	0.24
Walleye	4.7	0.78	0.2	2.00
Yellow Perch	11.0	0.14	0.7	0.16

LENGTH OF SELECTED SPECIES SAMPLED FROM ALL GEAR
Number of fish caught for the following length categories (inches):

species	0-5	6-8	9-11	12-14	15-19	20-24	25-29	>30	Total
Black Crappie	22	30	21	-	-	-	-	-	73
Bluegill	45	65	-	-	-	-	-	-	110
Brown Bullhead	-	-	3	11	1	-	-	-	15
Largemouth Bass	-	-	-	2	6	-	-	-	8
Northern Pike	-	-	3	13	21	12	4	3	56
Pumpkin. Sunfish	17	22	-	-	-	-	-	-	39
Walleye	-	-	4	19	6	1	-	-	30
Yellow Perch	14	58	-	-	-	-	-	-	72

DNR COMMENTS:
Walleye numbers well above normal range for lake class; average size 13 inches and .8 lb.; fish to 22.3 inches sampled. Northern Pike population down but in normal range; most Pike sampled were 13 to 18 inches; mean weight 1.6 lb.; fish to 32.8 inches captured. Black Crappie abundance above average; average length 7.9 inches; mean weight .3 lb. Bluegill numbers slightly below average; most fish are between 5.5 and 6.5 inches. Pumpkinseed common. Largemouth Bass abundance appears near-average; mean weight 2.5 lb., which is well above lake-class average. Yellow Perch numbers average; typical length 7 inches.

FISHING INFORMATION: These two lakes west of Blackduck hold a variety of game fish but are best known for good panfishing. Speaking of **Medicine Lake**, Earl Taber of Bemidji says he's seen "1 1/2- to 2-pound crappies come out of there." You'll understand why when you see the weedline, for the lake's bulrushes and lily pads offer about everything panfish need. The lake is also full of Northern Pike, most of them small. Which is why there's a 22- to 30-inch protected slot limit for this species and why you can only keep one Pike larger than 30 inches. The DNR wants you to keep the small ones and let the bigger ones grow. Along with the Pike and panfish, you'll find a fair number of Walleyes in the 2-pound range. Fish them at the deep weedlines, where you'll also encounter some nice Largemouth Bass. Nearby **Sandy Lake** is also popular for its panfish. It has a fine weedline offering excellent spawning and protective cover for Bluegills, Black Crappie, and Perch. There are a few Largemouth Bass in the weeds, as well, especially along the northeast corner and on the west side where bulrushes show. The DNR stocks Walleyes that seem to survive well and attain good size. Northerns are not nearly as abundant here as in Medicine Lake, but their average size is nearly double that of Medicine's snakes.

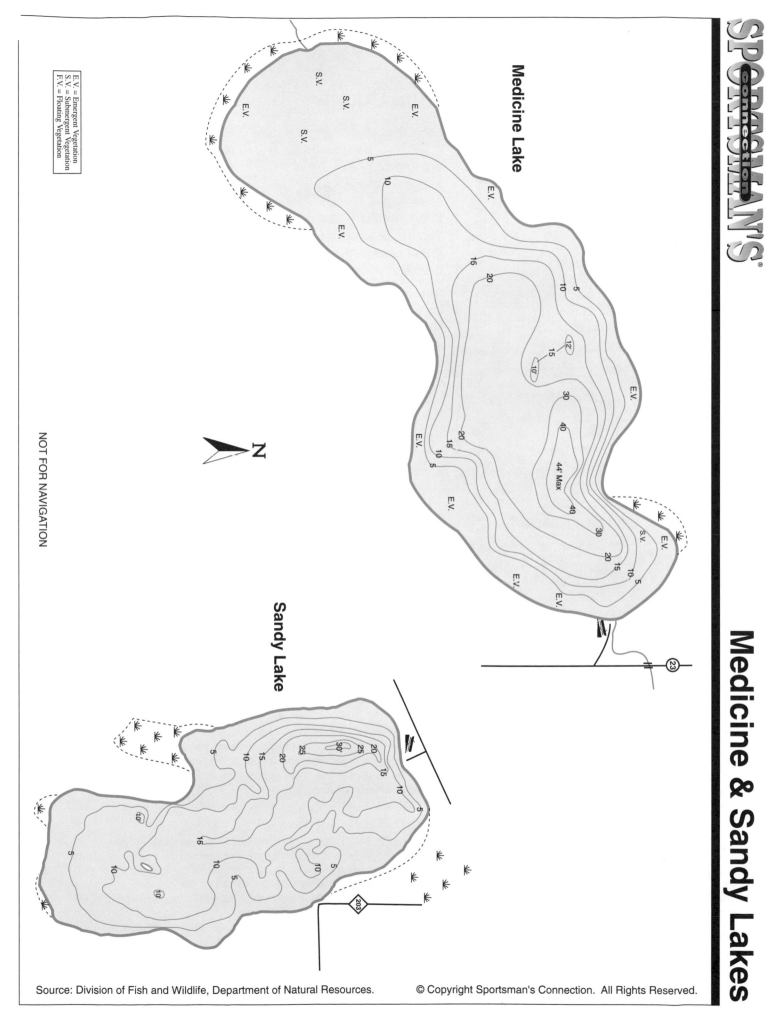

Medicine Lake

Sandy Lake

E.V. = Emergent Vegetation
S.V. = Submergent Vegetation
F.V. = Floating Vegetation

N

NOT FOR NAVIGATION

UPPER RED LAKE
Beltrami County

Location: Township 151-155
Range 30-35
Watershed: Red Lakes
Surface Water Area: 107,832 acres
Shorelength: 69.0 miles
Secchi disk (water clarity): NA
Water color: NA
Cause of water color: NA

Maximum depth: 35 ft.
Median depth: 18 ft.
Accessibility: Three accesses on the Tamarack River; one on the south shore
Boat Ramp: Concrete
Accommodations: Resort, campground

Shoreland zoning classification: General Development
Dominant forest/soil type: NA
Management class: Walleye
Ecological type: Hard-water Walleye

FISH STOCKING DATA: NO RECORD OF STOCKING

NET CATCH DATA

survey date: 9/30/97

species	Gill Nets # per net	avg fish wt. (lbs.)	Trap Nets # per set	avg fish wt. (lbs.)
Yellow Perch	20.1	0.10	-	-
White Sucker	2.0	0.94	-	-
Walleye	3.4	1.22	-	-
Shorthead Redhorse	0.1	0.90	-	-
Quillback	0.3	2.50	-	-
Northern Pike	2.3	1.89	-	-
Lake Whitefish	0.4	0.20	-	-
Freshwater Drum	0.9	0.67	-	-
Black Crappie	6.9	0.17	-	-

LENGTH OF SELECTED SPECIES SAMPLED FROM ALL GEAR
Number of fish caught for the following length categories (inches):

species	0-5	6-8	9-11	12-14	15-19	20-24	25-29	>30	Total
Yellow Perch	109	41	11	-	-	-	-	-	161
Walleye	-	1	8	6	9	3	-	-	27
Northern Pike	-	-	-	1	6	9	2	-	18
Lake Whitefish	-	2	1	-	-	-	-	-	3
Black Crappie	1	53	-	1	-	-	-	-	55

DNR COMMENTS: The Red Lake walleye population has been intensively commercially harvested for over 80 years. Classic symptoms of over-exploitation have been noted for many years. Gillnet catches in 1997 represented the lowest abundance of this species ever documented in Red Lake. Estimates of mature female Walleye biomass suggest that the reproductive potential of fish in the system may have fallen well below the level necessary to produce 1,000 fry per acre – the minimum number believed necessary to establish a moderate year class. Angling is prohibited for this species until the fishery has recovered. Both Yellow Perch and Black Crappie had moderate year classes likely to recruit to the sport fishery in 1998 and beyond.

FISHING INFORMATION: Located high in the northwest corner of Beltrami County, Upper Red Lake has been famous for its Walleyes. But no longer. By 1997, both commercial and angler overharvest had reduced the numbers of this species to a pittance. From there, the population simply crashed. The Red Lake Band of Chippewa Indians was forced to close its commercial fishing operation in 1997, and in 1998, it banned angling altogether in waters under its control. In 1999, the Minnesota DNR climbed on the bandwagon, imposing a zero-bag limit on Red Lake Walleyes in the 50,000 acres under state control. So Walleye fishing on Upper Red is *verboten* and will remain so until the fishery has recovered. Progress is being monitored by a technical committee composed of Reservation, DNR, University of Minnesota, and federal representatives. Stay tuned, and check fishing regs anew each year to see when angling will resume. Meanwhile, a veteran angler on the lake tells us that the lake's north shoreline offers good angling for Northern Pike, and there are some decent-size ones to be had. The lake's Perch and Crappies also are worth a look, and the Whitefish are great for smoking; take them in the winter. Three launching areas await in the town of Waskish in the lake's northeast corner, off County Road 72. The folks at both the Sunset Resort and the Minnow Station in Waskish happily share current fishing information with visitors.

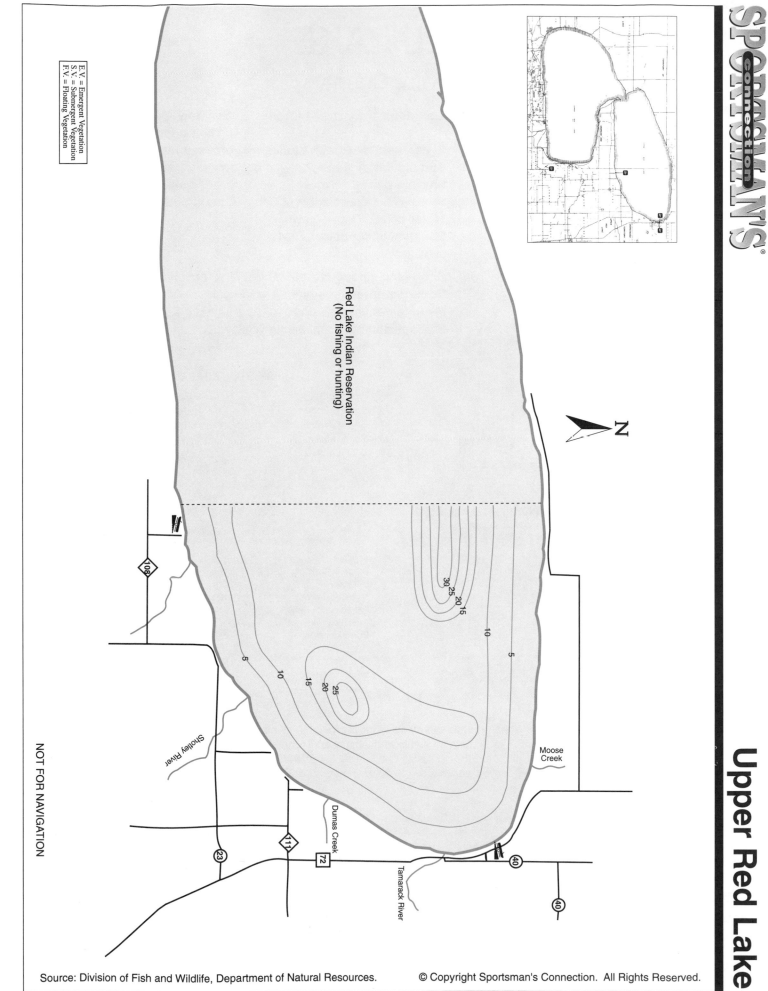

SPORTSMAN'S Connection®

E.V. = Emergent Vegetation
S.V. = Submergent Vegetation
F.V. = Floating Vegetation

Red Lake Indian Reservation
(No fishing or hunting)

N

30 25 20 15
10
5

5
10
15
20
25

Moose
Creek

Snoley River

Dumas Creek

Tamarack River

108
23
11
72
40
40

NOT FOR NAVIGATION

Source: Division of Fish and Wildlife, Department of Natural Resources.

GULL LAKE
Beltrami County

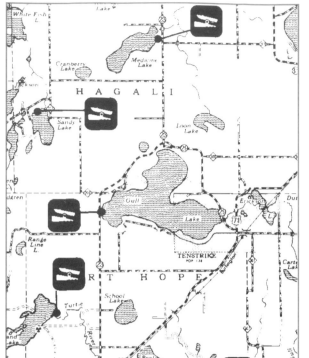

Location: Township 148, 149 Range 32

Watershed: Mississippi Headwaters

Surface Water Area: 2243 acres

Shorelength: 11.6 miles

Secchi disk (water clarity): 6.2 ft.

Water color: Green-brown

Cause of water color: Phyto-plankton

Maximum depth: 23 ft.

Median depth: 9 ft.

Accessibility: State-owned access on southwest shore

Boat Ramp: Concrete

Accommodations: Resort

Shoreland zoning classification: Recreational Development

Dominant forest/soil type: Decid/Loam

Management class: Walleye-Centrarchid

Ecological type: Centrarchid-Walleye

FISH STOCKING DATA

year	species	size	# released
90	Walleye	Fingerling	29,047
91	Walleye	Fingerling	11,220
93	Walleye	Fry	1,900,000
95	Walleye	Fry	1,900,000

LENGTH OF SELECTED SPECIES SAMPLED FROM ALL GEAR

Number of fish caught for the following length categories (inches):

species	0-5	6-8	9-11	12-14	15-19	20-24	25-29	>30	Total
Black Bullhead	-	-	1	5	-	-	-	-	6
Black Crappie	-	7	7	1	-	-	-	-	15
Bluegill	42	209	2	-	-	-	-	-	253
Brown Bullhead	-	1	15	16	-	-	-	-	32
Hybrid Sunfish	-	1	-	-	-	-	-	-	1
Largemouth Bass	-	-	2	-	2	-	-	-	4
Northern Pike	-	1	3	14	90	53	12	5	178
Pumpkin. Sunfish	51	71	1	-	-	-	-	-	123
Rock Bass	10	36	9	-	-	-	-	-	55
Walleye	-	1	4	40	53	6	2	-	106
Yellow Bullhead	-	3	45	2	-	-	-	-	50
Yellow Perch	345	147	1	-	-	-	-	-	493

NET CATCH DATA

survey date: 7/5/94

	Gill Nets		Trap Nets	
		avg fish		avg fish
species	# per net	wt. (lbs.)	# per set	wt. (lbs.)
Black Crappie	0.7	0.49	0.3	0.77
Bluegill	1.9	0.38	15.0	0.34
Hybrid Sunfish	trace	0.20	-	-
Largemouth Bass	-	-	0.3	1.83
Northern Pike	11.1	1.74	0.7	1.40
Pumpkin. Sunfish	5.2	0.20	3.0	0.25
Rock Bass	3.2	0.36	0.5	0.52
Walleye	6.8	1.28	0.3	4.30
White Sucker	2.1	1.69	trace	3.42
Yellow Bullhead	1.9	0.69	1.5	0.82
Yellow Perch	35.0	0.10	3.6	0.10

DNR COMMENTS: Walleye numbers more than double the average for comparable lakes; 70 percent of population measures 13 to 18 inches; fish to 26 inches present. Northern Pike population stable and slightly above normal. Largemouth Bass numbers low; a few fish 16 to 18 inches captured. Black Crappie numbers low, but size good. Bluegill abundance about average; fish to 10 inches captured; average length 7 inches. Yellow Perch abundant and small. Yellow, Brown, and Black Bullheads found throughout the lake; these species are being harvested commercially.

FISHING INFORMATION: This 2,200-acre lake west of Tenstrike on U.S. Highway 71 is surprisingly shallow for the region. Its maximum depth is 23 feet, and the average is just 9 feet. But even so, it's never been known to winterkill. In fact, it has a good reputation for Northern Pike, Bluegills and Walleyes. A well-weeded shoreline with plenty of bulrushes and lily pads provides excellent habitat for spawning and feeding. Northerns spend the spring cruising off the weedlines, especially near heavy bulrush growth. You'll find such rushes on the west and north shores of the lake's big west bay and along the north shore of the eastern bay. Backtrolling or just drifting a Shiner or Fathead minnow there is a favorite technique. Fishing the weeds for Bluegills gets tricky as the summer progresses and the weeds thicken, but in the spring you can do well with worms on a plain hook or a tiny jig. Fly fishing with small poppers is great, too, when conditions are right. There are some Largemouth Bass and Crappie in the weeds, though Bluegills are much more abundant. The lake is actually managed for Walleyes, and the DNR has stocked fry and fingerlings for a number of years. While Gull isn't among the best Walleye lakes in the area, it does have a fair number of good-sized goggle eyes. The best place to catch them in the spring is the long rock-and-bulrush bar dividing the two big bays. The bar, called "the Dike" by local anglers, is navigable at its south end. Walleyes feed there in the spring and are often caught there after dark during the summer, as well. Gull is definitely worth a good, long look.

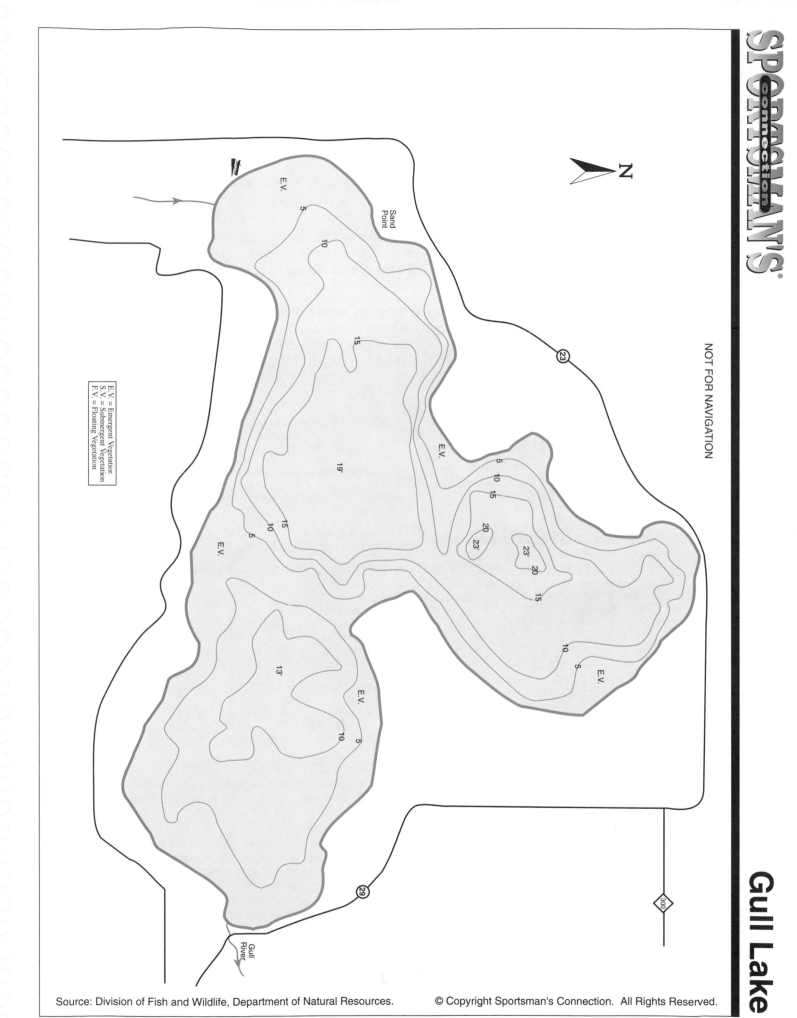

Gull Lake

NOT FOR NAVIGATION

N

Sand Point

E.V. = Emergent Vegetation
S.V. = Submergent Vegetation
F.V. = Floating Vegetation

E.V.

E.V.

E.V.

E.V.

E.V.

5

10

15

19'

10

15

5

23'

23'

20

20

15

10

15

5

10

5

13'

10

5

23

29

Gull River

300'

Source: Division of Fish and Wildlife, Department of Natural Resources.

© Copyright Sportsman's Connection. All Rights Reserved.

TURTLE RIVER LAKE

Beltrami County

Location: Township 147, 148 Range 32
Watershed: Mississippi Headwaters
Surface Water Area: 1737 acres
Shorelength: 15.1 miles
Secchi disk (water clarity): 11.0 ft.
Water color: Green
Cause of water color: Algae

Maximum depth: 55 ft.
Median depth: 19 ft.
Accessibility: Access on northwest shore at inlet
Boat Ramp: Concrete
Accommodations: Resort

Shoreland zoning classification: Recreational Development
Dominant forest/soil type: Decid/Loam
Management class: Walleye-Centrarchid
Ecological type: Centrarchid-Walleye

FISH STOCKING DATA: NO RECORD OF STOCKING

LENGTH OF SELECTED SPECIES SAMPLED FROM ALL GEAR

Number of fish caught for the following length categories (inches):

species	0-5	6-8	9-11	12-14	15-19	20-24	25-29	>30	Total
Black Bullhead	-	-	2	-	-	-	-	-	2
Black Crappie	-	-	4	2	-	-	-	-	6
Bluegill	67	125	4	-	-	-	-	-	196
Brown Bullhead	-	-	3	13	-	-	-	-	16
Hybrid Sunfish	-	4	-	-	-	-	-	-	4
Largemouth Bass	-	-	-	1	-	-	-	-	1
Northern Pike	-	-	-	-	23	49	16	1	89
Pumpkin. Sunfish	16	74	-	-	-	-	-	-	90
Rock Bass	16	40	34	2	-	-	-	-	92
Tullibee	-	16	74	12	9	-	-	-	111
Walleye	-	1	54	41	47	28	-	-	171
Yellow Bullhead	-	1	15	8	-	-	-	-	24
Yellow Perch	7	367	50	-	-	-	-	-	424

NET CATCH DATA

survey date: 07/12/93

	Gill Nets		Trap Nets	
		avg fish		avg fish
species	# per net	wt. (lbs.)	# per set	wt. (lbs.)
Black Bullhead	0.1	0.52	-	0.57
Black Crappie	0.3	0.61	0.1	0.71
Bluegill	0.7	0.25	9.5	0.17
Bowfin (Dogfish)	0.2	5.11	0.7	4.92
Brown Bullhead	0.1	1.12	0.7	0.98
Burbot	0.1	2.76	-	-
Hybrid Sunfish	-	-	0.2	0.33
Largemouth Bass	-	-	-	1.23
Northern Pike	5.6	2.25	0.6	3.20
Pumpkin. Sunfish	0.3	0.17	4.1	0.20
Rock Bass	2.9	0.44	2.5	0.34
Silver Redhorse	0.1	1.82	-	-
Tullibee (Cisco)	9.4	0.45	-	-
Walleye	11.6	1.09	0.4	1.75
White Sucker	4.4	1.61	0.9	0.66
Yellow Bullhead	0.4	0.67	0.9	0.66
Yellow Perch	40.9	0.12	6.3	0.16

DNR COMMENTS: Walleye population very healthy, with most year classes present; length range 8 to 23.6 inches; average length 13.9 inches; natural reproduction maintains population. Northern Pike numbers normal for lake class; length range 15 to 29 inches; average length 21 inches. Black Crappie and Largemouth Bass populations low; all Crappies were 9 inches or larger. Bluegill numbers fairly good, but fish are generally small; only four sampled fish exceeded 9 inches in length.

FISHING INFORMATION: Located immediately east of U.S. Highway 71 at the town of the same name, Turtle River Lake offers a nice variety of game fish, including Northern Pike, Black Crappie and Bluegills. Too, there are fairly good numbers of Walleyes and Largemouth Bass. Made up of three narrow bays, the lake offers interesting structure, a good weedline with bulrushes, and interesting challenges to the experienced angler. Shoreline vegetation offers excellent habitat for panfish following the spawn and can be fished effectively with nightcrawlers or small minnows on a small jig or a plain hook. There aren't a lot of Bass in those weeds, but some big bucketmouths have been taken by anglers over the years. You'll have to go right into the weeds after them early in the year. Using bright jigs and minnows or topwater lures, cast carefully into the bulrushes. Hungry Northerns will be cruising the flats outside weedlines in the spring. You'll have to compete for attention, and live bait on a flashy lure can work well. Although the Northerns are well distributed, they do like some places better than others. Early hotspots include the inlet and outlet of the Turtle River in the northwest bay and the east bay, respectively. The southern bay and the narrows leading to the east bay are also productive. Walleyes reproduce naturally and move in, as well, from other lakes on the Turtle River chain. Stevens Point on the west shore is a popular spot for Walleye anglers; so is the point southwest of the river inlet. And if you get tired of fishing there, there are also plenty of good breaks and sandy points to try.

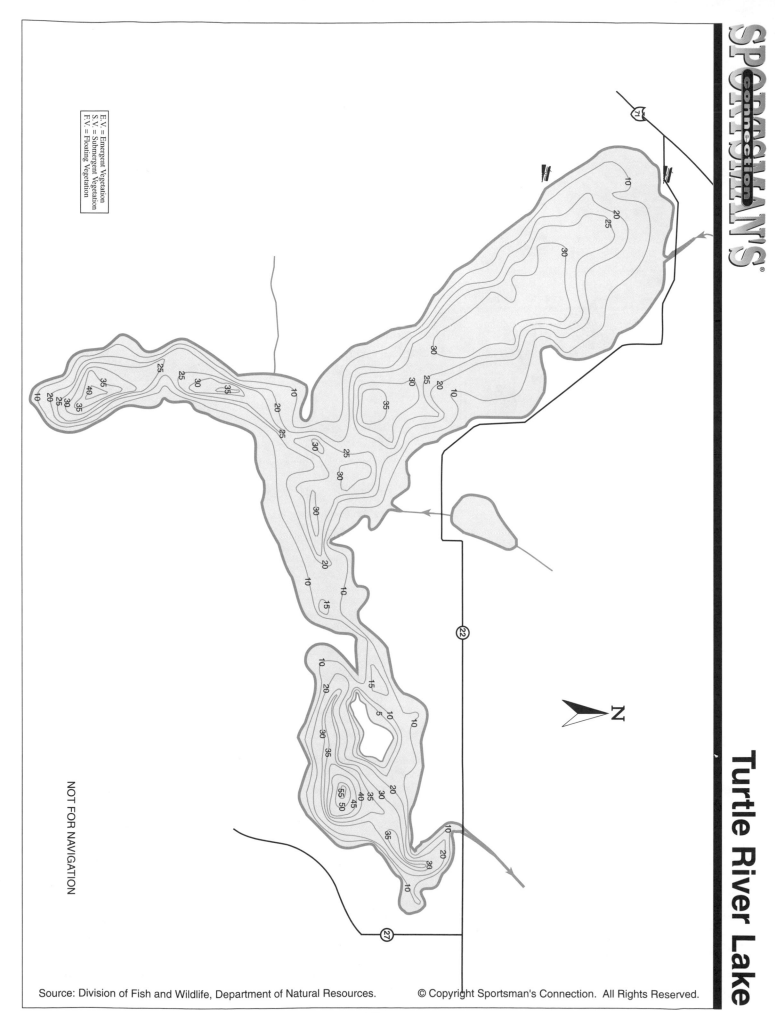

E.V. = Emergent Vegetation
S.V. = Submergent Vegetation
F.V. = Floating Vegetation

N

NOT FOR NAVIGATION

BIG BASS LAKE
Beltrami County

Location: Township 147 Range 32, 33
Watershed: Mississippi Headwaters
Surface Water Area: 380 acres
Shorelength: NA
Secchi disk (water clarity): 13.0 ft.
Water color: Gray-green
Cause of water color: Algae

Maximum depth: 17 ft.
Median depth: NA
Accessibility: State-owned public access on south shore
Boat Ramp: Concrete
Accommodations: NA

Shoreland zoning classification: Recreational Development
Dominant forest/soil type: NA
Management class: Walleye-Centrarchid
Ecological type: Centrarchid-Walleye

FISH STOCKING DATA

year	species	size	# released
92	Walleye	Fingerling	25,354
95	Walleye	Fingerling	11,478

NET CATCH DATA

survey date: 6/16/97

	Gill Nets		Trap Nets	
species	# per net	avg fish wt. (lbs.)	# per set	avg fish wt. (lbs.)
Black Crappie	1.9	0.29	1.9	0.33
Bluegill	18.2	0.23	28.9	0.35
Brown Bullhead	0.2	1.13	-	-
Hybrid Sunfish	0.8	0.41	0.6	0.37
Largemouth Bass	0.2	3.53	-	-
Northern Pike	11.1	2.49	0.6	1.66
Pumpkin. Sunfish	3.6	0.20	3.7	0.27
Walleye	4.8	2.08	0.6	5.28
White Sucker	4.1	2.66	0.1	4.52
Yellow Perch	12.9	0.16	0.4	0.09

LENGTH OF SELECTED SPECIES SAMPLED FROM ALL GEAR

Number of fish caught for the following length categories (inches):

species	0-5	6-8	9-11	12-14	15-19	20-24	25-29	>30	Total
Black Crappie	-	30	-	-	-	-	-	-	30
Bluegill	126	231	9	-	-	-	-	-	366
Brown Bullhead	-	-	1	1	-	-	-	-	2
Hybrid Sunfish	-	11	-	-	-	-	-	-	11
Largemouth Bass	-	-	-	-	2	-	-	-	2
Northern Pike	-	-	1	5	38	31	26	3	104
Pumpkin. Sunfish	26	32	-	-	-	-	-	-	58
Walleye	-	-	-	17	11	13	6	-	47
Yellow Perch	24	91	4	-	-	-	-	-	119

DNR COMMENTS: Walleye population excellent for lake class; length range 12.8 to 29.3 inches; most fish are 13 to 16 inches and average about 1 lb. Northern Pike numbers down but still above the lake-class average; fish to 31.2 inches sampled; average size 22 inches and 2.5 lb.; about one-fourth of Pike were infected with Neascus. Largemouth Bass sampled by electrofishing; fish to 18.4 inches captured; about half the population was age 3 and averaged 10 inches in length. Bluegill numbers good; average length 7 inches; fish to 9.7 inches sampled. Black Crappie abundance near lake-class average; all sampled fish measured 7 to 9 inches. Yellow Perch numbers average; length about 7 inches. Pumpkinseed and hybrid Sunfish numbers fairly low; average length 6.5 inches. Brown Bullheads scarce. White Suckers common.

FISHING INFORMATION: Big Bass Lake, just a short distance northeast of Bemidji, offers good fishing for Northern Pike, Walleyes, Bass, and panfish. But it is best known by local anglers for the many Bluegills it produces. Fairly shallow and weedy, Big Bass offers good spawning and protective cover. Jigging with worms or crawlers in shallow water is a good way to get attention from the panfish early in the year; many anglers like to throw spinnerbaits at the Largemouth Bass later in the season. Tim Falk, of Bluewater Bait in Bemidji, says he finds the extensive weeds in the northeast corner a good spot for Bass. The Northerns prowl the band of submerged vegetation around the fringes of the lake and are relatively abundant. Average size is relatively small, but there are some big ones among the many present. Casting or trolling just outside the weedbeds is the best way to catch these alligators early in the season. As the weather warms, though, live suckers or shiners fished in the deeper parts of the lake are more productive. Walleyes are stocked by the DNR as fingerlings and survive well. The average Walleye runs around 2 pounds – great table fare. Until recently, the Northerns, Bass, and Walleye populations were kept in check by a shortage of forage fish. That situation appears to have cured itself, however, and the gamefish are once again free to eat and grow. All the better for you.

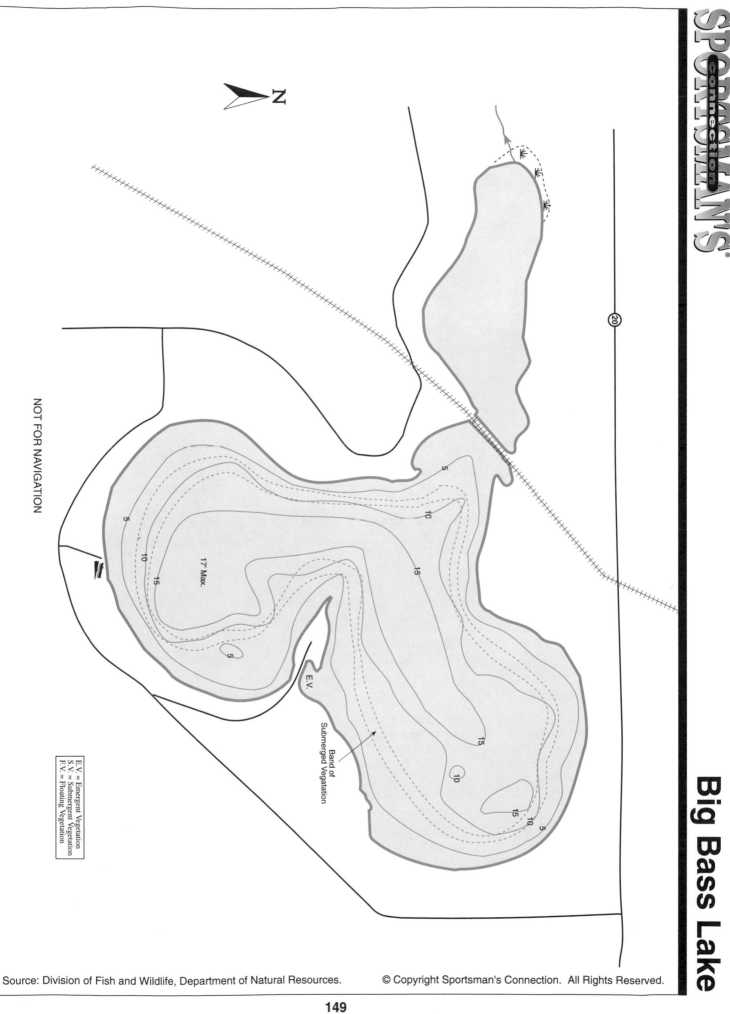

NOT FOR NAVIGATION

N

17' Max.

5

10

15

5

10

15

E.V.

Band of
Submerged Vegatation

5

10

15

5

10

15

20

E.V. = Emergent Vegetation
S.V. = Submergent Vegetation
F.V. = Floating Vegetation

BELTRAMI LAKE
Beltrami County

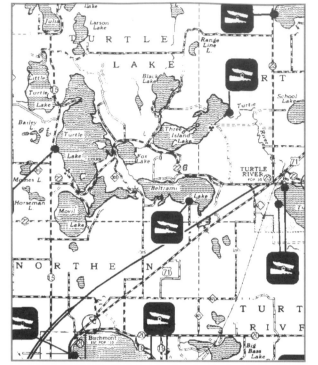

Location: Township 148 Range 32,33

Watershed: Mississippi Headwaters

Surface Water Area: 543 acres

Shorelength: 6.7 miles

Secchi disk (water clarity): 12.0 ft.

Water color: Light green

Cause of water color: Algae

Maximum depth: 50 ft.

Median depth: 13 ft.

Accessibility: State-owned access on southeast shore

Boat Ramp: Earth

Accommodations: NA

Shoreland zoning classification: Recreational Development

Dominant forest/soil type: Decid/Sand

Management class: Walleye-Centrarchid

Ecological type: Centrarchid-Walleye

FISH STOCKING DATA

year	species	size	# released
92	Walleye	Fry	300,000
94	Walleye	Fry	300,000
95	Walleye	Fry	300,000
97	Walleye	Fry	300,000

NET CATCH DATA

survey date: 07/26/93

	Gill Nets		Trap Nets	
species	# per net	avg fish wt. (lbs.)	# per set	avg fish wt. (lbs.)
Black Crappie	0.9	0.35	0.3	0.41
Bluegill	6.6	0.17	16.4	0.16
Hybrid Sunfish	-	-	0.1	0.17
Largemouth Bass	2.2	0.195	0.1	0.44
Northern Pike	7.1	2.60	0.4	2.72
Pumpkin. Sunfish	2.6	0.15	1.3	0.19
Rock Bass	11.9	0.50	2.8	0.12
Tullibee (Cisco)	0.3	0.91	-	-
Walleye	2.9	1.05	0.8	1.16
White Sucker	1.0	2.20	0.1	3.53
Yellow Perch	4.4	0.12	0.8	0.09

LENGTH OF SELECTED SPECIES SAMPLED FROM ALL GEAR

Number of fish caught for the following length categories (inches):

species	0-5	6-8	9-11	12-14	15-19	20-24	25-29	>30	Total
Black Crappie	-	3	8	-	-	-	-	-	11
Bluegill	69	133	5	-	-	-	-	-	207
Brown Bullhead	-	-	-	2	-	-	-	-	2
Hybrid Sunfish	-	1	-	-	-	-	-	-	1
Largemouth Bass	-	1	7	11	2	-	-	-	21
Northern Pike	-	-	-	4	10	31	20	3	68
Pumpkin. Sunfish	12	23	-	-	-	-	-	-	35
Rock Bass	23	51	56	2	-	-	-	-	132
Tullibee(Cisco)	-	-	-	3	-	-	-	-	3
Walleye	-	2	3	11	15	2	-	-	33
Yellow Perch	2	41	4	-	-	-	-	-	47

DNR COMMENTS: Northern Pike population high; size range good, with about half the sample being between 17 and 21 inches; Pike to 34 inches sampled; good reproduction. Walleyes reproducing naturally; largest fish sampled 20.4 inches, with most fish in 13- 19-inch range; population below average. Largemouth Bass numbers up; size good, with largest fish captured measuring 15.5 inches; average length 11.7 inches. Black Crappie numbers stable and low; size good at 8.5 inches. Bluegill present in below-average numbers; length average at 5.8 inches. Pumpkinseed population low, but average size good at 5.8 inches. Rock Bass abundant, though small at 5 inches on average. Yellow Perch numbers low; weight generally below average, as well; fish up to 10.9" captured. Cisco numbers down sharply.

FISHING INFORMATION: Beltrami Lake is north and east of Bemidji, close to the smaller community of Turtle River on U.S. Highway 71. At 700 acres, the lake is relatively small, but it has a good weedline, clear water, and a sand and rubble bottom. What's more it has some good structure, the kind that attracts Walleyes. The lake has an excellent Northern Pike population, good Crappies and Bass, and a decent number of Walleye, thanks to fry stocking by the DNR. A large number of Ciscoes give the Northerns plenty of food and are responsible for their being above average in size. Northerns spawn around the connections to the Turtle River and in the flats along the east shore. There are also some nice Rock Bass in those areas. While there isn't a lot of weedline (about 50%), there is wild rice in the lily pads – which means some good Largemouth Bass fishing. Use spinnerbaits or a pig-and-jig combo in the weeds. Some of the better fishing is at night during the summer. Walleyes don't seem to reproduce well in Beltrami, but they have plenty of Yellow Perch to feed on. Some of the best places for early-season angling are the large point about mid lake on the south shore, the sunken island in the west bay, the prominent bar in the center of the east bay, and the two sunken islands in the east bay. Shiners and leeches fished on a bottom rig work very well in these spots early in the day. Retrieve them gradually up the slopes where the fish may be feeding.

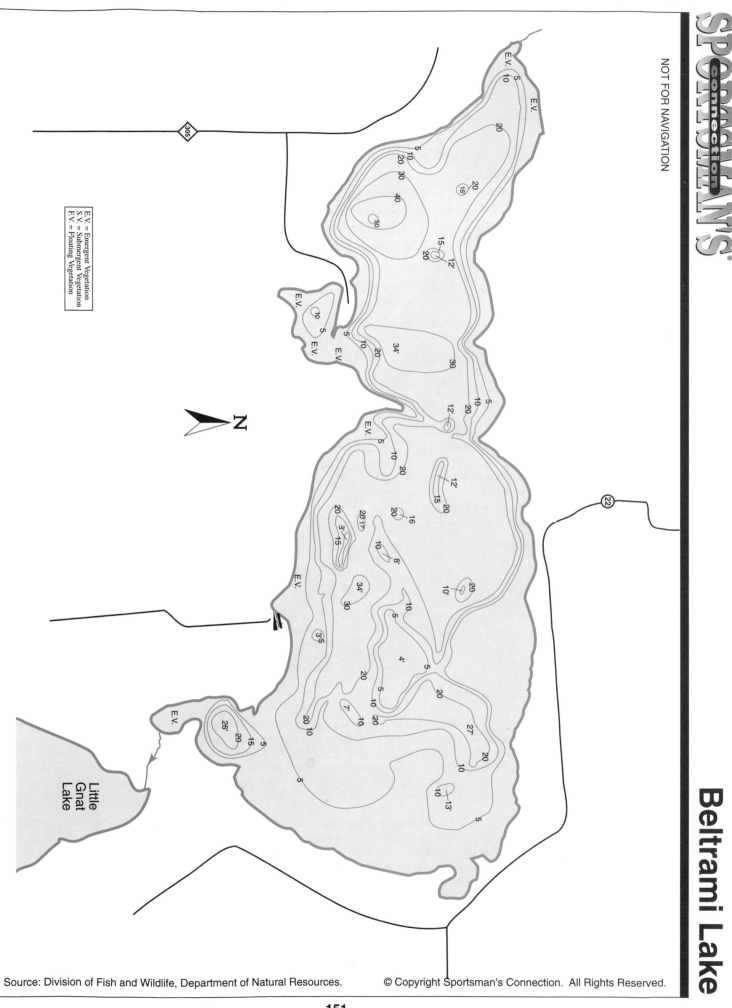

E.V. = Emergent Vegetation
S.V. = Submergent Vegetation
F.V. = Floating Vegetation

N

Little
Gnat
Lake

Beltrami Lake

THREE ISLAND LAKE
Beltrami County

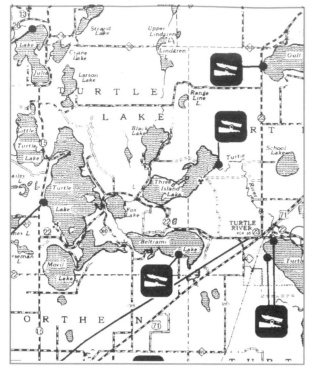

Location: Township 148, Range 32, 33
Watershed: Mississippi Headwaters
Surface Water Area: 678 acres
Shorelength: 7.3 miles
Secchi disk (water clarity): NA
Water color: Grey-green
Cause of water color: Algae

Maximum depth: 25 ft.
Median depth: 6 ft.
Accessibility: State-owned public access on northeast corner
Boat Ramp: Earth
Accommodations: Resort, county park, campground

Shoreland zoning classification: Natural Environment
Dominant forest/soil type: No Tree/Wet
Management class: Walleye-Centrarchid
Ecological type: Centrarchid-Walleye

FISH STOCKING DATA: NO RECORD OF STOCKING

NET CATCH DATA

survey date: 7/29/96

species	Gill Nets # per net	Gill Nets avg fish wt. (lbs.)	Trap Nets # per set	Trap Nets avg fish wt. (lbs.)
Black Crappie	0.5	0.29	0.6	0.76
Bluegill	0.3	0.72	1.1	0.69
Bowfin (Dogfish)	5.1	1.08	2.4	0.78
Hybrid Sunfish	-	-	trace	0.18
Largemouth Bass	-	-	0.3	2.46
Northern Pike	11.5	2.04	1.3	1.38
Pumpkin. Sunfish	4.1	0.14	4.9	0.18
Rock Bass	3.1	0.45	2.2	0.47
Shorthead Redhorse	0.1	4.86	-	-
Walleye	8.1	1.40	0.8	2.47
White Sucker	4.4	2.50	-	-
Yellow Bullhead	-	-	0.6	0.90
Yellow Perch	49.0	0.16	5.7	0.18

LENGTH OF SELECTED SPECIES SAMPLED FROM ALL GEAR

Number of fish caught for the following length categories (inches):

species	0-5	6-8	9-11	12-14	15-19	20-24	25-29	>30	Total
Black Crappie	-	7	1	3	-	-	-	-	11
Bluegill	-	8	7	-	-	-	-	-	15
Brown Bullhead	1	1	26	42	-	-	-	-	70
Hybrid Sunfish	1	-	-	-	-	-	-	-	1
Largemouth Bass	-	-	-	2	1	-	-	-	3
Northern Pike	-	-	12	5	21	55	14	1	108
Pumpkin. Sunfish	59	33	-	-	-	-	-	-	92
Rock Bass	9	29	13	-	-	-	-	-	51
Walleye	-	-	5	11	52	5	2	-	75
Yellow Bullhead	-	-	5	2	-	-	-	-	7
Yellow Perch	142	292	26	-	-	-	-	-	460

DNR COMMENTS: Walleye population above third-quartile values for lake class; modal length 15 to 18 inches; fish to 27 inches captured; average weight 1.4 lb. Northern Pike numbers above average; average size 21 inches and 2 lb.; fish to 32 inches captured. Largemouth Bass sample inadequate for accurate population assessment. Black Crappie abundance below normal range; average weight of .8 lb. is above normal. Bluegill numbers low for lake class; average weight .75 lb. Rock Bass numbers average. Yellow Perch abundance near the high end of the normal range; average length 6.9 inches; fish to 11.3 inches sampled; some Perch parasite-infested.

FISHING INFORMATION: Most anglers would start looking elsewhere after seeing this relatively small lake. It is stained with bog runoff, has an average depth of only 6 feet, is surrounded by a heavy weedline, and has a huge Bullhead population. Despite those negatives, though, it's worth a second look. For both Northern Pike and Walleye are found here in numbers well above the regional average. One of the reasons for this is that Three Island connects to Turtle and Turtle River Lakes via the Turtle River, and fish freely move in and out. Three Island also has a great deal of vegetation – including wild rice beds – that provide the basis for an excellent food chain. Fishing off the beds of emergent vegetation is the best way to find Northerns here. Pay particular attention to the river's inlet on the southwest corner and to the outlet in the northeast near the public access area. The flats just off the weedlines are the best places to slow-troll or drift-fish for Northerns. Offer shiners or suckers with a bright lure to get attention in the dark water. Most of the Walleyes are on the small side, though every once in a while a 5-plus-pounder is caught. There are at least three visible islands which provide good spots to look for Walleyes, as well as several sunken islands on the east side (which actually emerge in low water years). Anglers do well at these spots with live baits and jigs or bottom rigs. There is an earth ramp at the lake's northeast corner, not far northwest of the town of Turtle River.

Three Island Lake

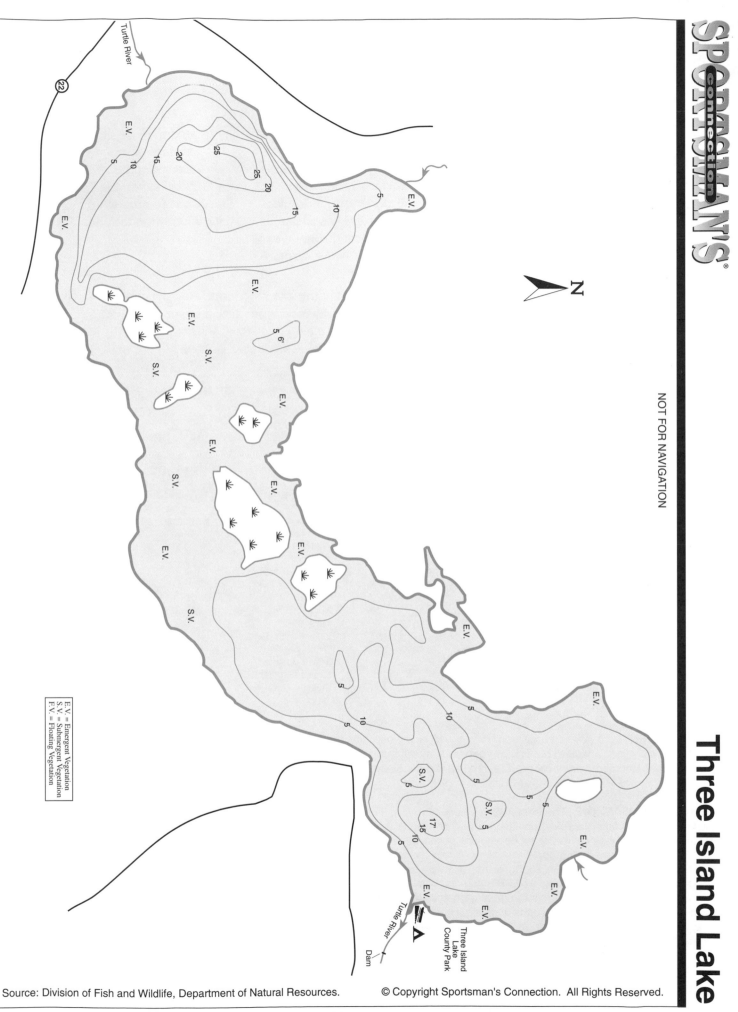

Turtle River

22

E.V.
E.V.
5
10
15
20
25
25
20
20
15
10
5
E.V.
E.V.

N

NOT FOR NAVIGATION

E.V.
E.V.
S.V.
S.V.
5 6'
E.V.
E.V.
S.V.
E.V.
E.V.
E.V.
S.V.
E.V.
E.V.
5
5
10
5
10
5
E.V.
E.V.
E.V.
S.V.
5
5
S.V.
5
5
17'
15
10
5
E.V.
E.V.
E.V.

E.V. = Emergent Vegetation
S.V. = Submergent Vegetation
F.V. = Floating Vegetation

Turtle River
Dam

Three Island
Lake
County Park

MOVIL LAKE
Beltrami County

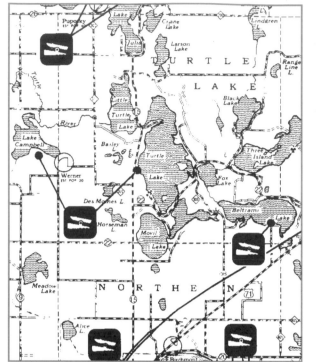

Location: Township 147, 148 Range 33
Watershed: Mississippi Headwaters
Surface Water Area: 923 acres
Shorelength: 8.2 miles
Secchi disk (water clarity): 13.0 ft.
Water color: Gray-green
Cause of water color: Algae

Maximum depth: 51 ft.
Median depth: 15 ft.
Accessibility: Through the channel from Big Turtle Lake
Boat Ramp: NA
Accommodations: Resort

Shoreland zoning classification: Recreational Development
Dominant forest/soil type: Decid/Loam
Management class: Walleye-Centrarchid
Ecological type: Centrarchid-Walleye

FISH STOCKING DATA

year	species	size	# released
90	Walleye	Fry	400,000

NET CATCH DATA

survey date: 6/20/89

	Gill Nets		Trap Nets	
species	# per net	avg fish wt. (lbs.)	# per set	avg fish wt. (lbs.)
Yellow Perch	14.2	0.15	3.8	0.22
White Sucker	4.2	1.71	0.7	2.34
Walleye	1.5	1.59	0.7	0.50
Tullibee (Cisco)	2.3	1.44	-	-
Rock Bass	1.5	0.50	10.3	0.28
Pumpkin. Sunfish	0.3	0.15	8.0	0.15
Northern Pike	12.2	2.30	1.1	1.26
Burbot	0.2	1.60	-	-
Largemouth Bass	-	-	1.2	0.28
Hybrid Sunfish	-	-	0.2	0.15
Brown Bullhead	-	-	0.8	1.10
Bowfin (Dogfish)	-	-	1.5	4.78
Bluegill	-	-	13.7	0.15

LENGTH OF SELECTED SPECIES SAMPLED FROM ALL GEAR

Number of fish caught for the following length categories (inches):

species	0-5	6-8	9-11	12-14	15-19	20-24	25-29	>30	Total
Bluegill	40	69	1	-	-	-	-	-	110
Brown Bullhead	-	-	2	4	2	-	-	-	8
Hybrid Sunfish	1	-	1	-	-	-	-	-	2
Largemouth Bass	-	6	7	1	-	-	-	-	14
Northern Pike	-	-	4	3	38	29	7	5	86
Pumpkin. Sunfish	18	79	1	-	-	-	-	-	98
Rock Bass	40	61	30	1	-	-	-	-	132
Tullibee	-	-	-	1	12	-	-	-	13
Walleye	-	1	4	6	2	4	-	-	17
Yellow Perch	1	99	29	2	-	-	-	-	131

DNR COMMENTS: Walleye population up but well below the local median. Northern Pike numbers well above local median. Yellow Perch numbers near average, but fish are generally small and grub-infested. Black Crappie were not captured but are known to be present. Sunfish numbers near local median, but fish are generally small.

FISHING INFORMATION: The best fishing in this 800-acre lake, which is several miles west of U.S. Highway 71, near Tenstrike, is for Northern Pike. In fact, the Pike population is well above the regional average. There are also good numbers of Yellow Perch, panfish and Walleyes. A few monster Northerns have been pulled out of Movil, but most are in the 2- to 5-pound range. The heavily-weeded areas such as the small bay on the north side of the lake's east arm, hold plenty of suckers and smaller fish that attract the Northerns to them. Drifting off the weedbeds in the spring is the best way to get attention; the Pike are often in 5- to 15-foot depths. Live bait, such as fathead minnows or leeches, works well. Panfish, especially Bluegills, are plentiful in the abundant weeds, too. Using spinning gear to toss earthworms near the vegetation is the best approach. Getting into the weeds is fairly easy in the spring, but it gets tougher as the water warms and the cabbage and lily pads thicken. The lake is actually managed for Walleye and is stocked regularly with fry. It's not all that easy to catch Walleyes here, though. For the water is crystal-clear, and the fish are easily spooked by sounds or movement on the surface. Best to fish in low-light conditions. There are some bars to fish, especially the ones at mid lake, off the north and south shorelines. There are also some nice sunken islands in the big bay on the west shore. The best access to Movil is from Turtle Lake via the Turtle River.

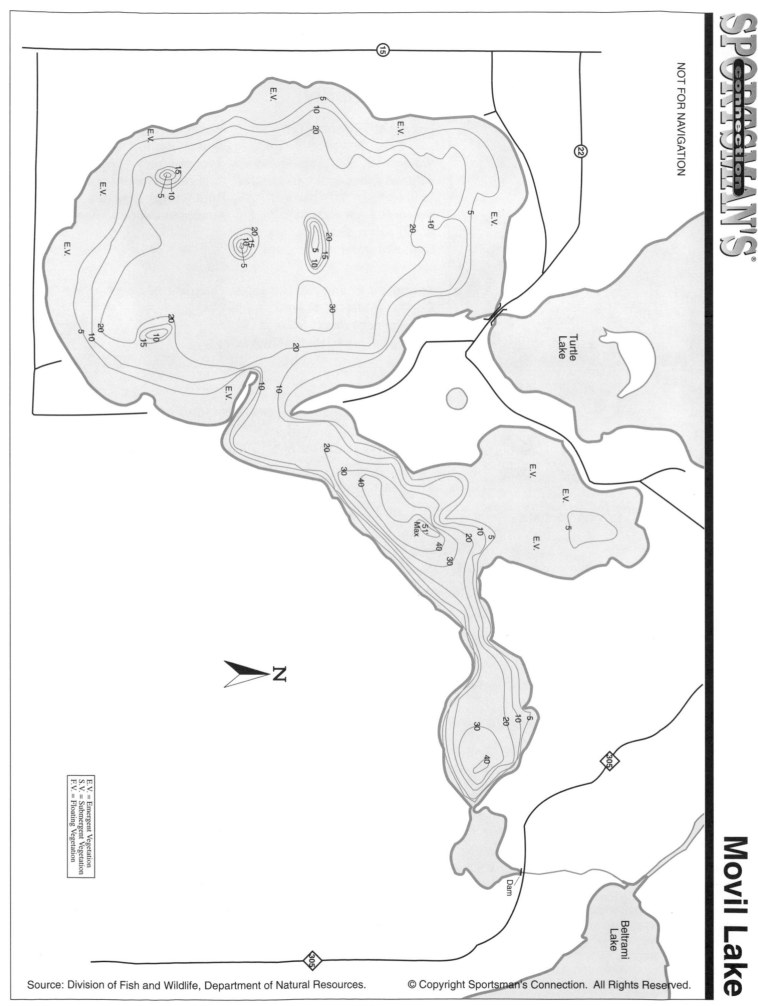

N

E.V. = Emergent Vegetation
S.V. = Submergent Vegetation
F.V. = Floating Vegetation

Turtle
Lake

Beltrami
Lake

Dam

51'
Max

Movil Lake

TURTLE LAKE
Beltrami County

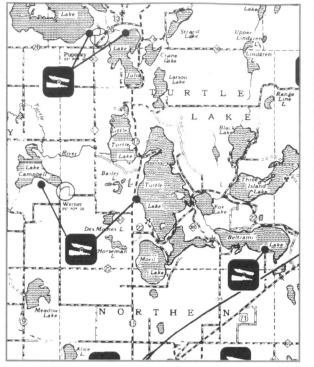

Location: Township 148 Range 33

Watershed: Mississippi Headwaters

Surface Water Area: 1436 acres

Shorelength: 11.4 miles

Secchi disk (water clarity): 7.0 ft.

Water color: Green

Cause of water color: Light algae bloom

Maximum depth: 45 ft.

Median depth: 14 ft.

Accessibility: State-owned public access on west shore

Boat Ramp: Concrete

Accommodations: Resort

Shoreland zoning classification: Recreational Development

Dominant forest/soil type: Decid/Loam

Management class: Walleye

Ecological type: Hard-water Walleye

FISH STOCKING DATA

year	species	size	# released
91	Walleye	Fry	700,000
95	Walleye	Fry	700,000
97	Walleye	Fry	700,000

NET CATCH DATA

survey date: 8/9/93

	Gill Nets		Trap Nets	
species	# per net	avg fish wt. (lbs.)	# per set	avg fish wt. (lbs.)
Black Crappie	-	-	0.9	0.68
Bluegill	-	-	11.8	0.29
Bowfin (Dogfish)	-	-	1.4	5.29
Brown Bullhead	0.1	1.17	1.3	1.23
Hybrid Sunfish	-	-	0.3	0.33
Largemouth Bass	-	-	1.3	1.00
Northern Pike	4.1	2.65	0.7	1.17
Pumpkin. Sunfish	0.1	0.04	3.3	0.25
Rock Bass	3.2	0.68	4.8	0.29
Tullibee (Cisco)	4.0	0.81	-	-
Walleye	5.8	1.21	0.8	1.74
White Sucker	2.7	1.85	0.4	2.93
Yellow Perch	31.8	0.13	4.6	0.13

LENGTH OF SELECTED SPECIES SAMPLED FROM ALL GEAR

Number of fish caught for the following length categories (inches):

species	0-5	6-8	9-11	12-14	15-19	20-24	25-29	>30	Total
Black Crappie	-	-	6	4	1	-	-	-	11
Bluegill	19	99	24	-	-	-	-	-	142
Brown Bullhead	-	-	-	14	2	-	-	-	16
Hybrid Sunfish	-	3	1	-	-	-	-	-	4
Largemouth Bass	-	-	8	6	1	-	-	-	15
Northern Pike	-	-	-	3	15	26	8	5	57
Pumpkin. Sunfish	10	29	1	-	-	-	-	-	40
Tullibee (Cisco)	-	-	32	5	10	1	-	-	48
Walleye	-	1	21	12	33	12	-	-	79
Yellow Perch	1	313	27	-	-	-	-	-	341
Rock Bass	21	25	45	4	-	-	-	-	95

DNR COMMENTS: Walleye population down slightly but still near average for lake class.; average length 14.6 inches; many small fish sampled, indicating good prospects for the future. Northern Pike numbers near average; size better than average, probably due to the Cisco forage base. Largemouth Bass present in better-than-average numbers; most fish fairly small; extensive vegetation beds make fishing difficult. Bluegill size structure fair, with a few 9- to 10-inch fish sampled; average size 6.6 inches. Black Crappie numbers near average; a few good-size fish available. Yellow Perch are generally too small to interest adult anglers, though a few nice-size fish are available.

FISHING INFORMATION: Turtle Lake, located just west of the town of Turtle River on U.S. Highway 71, offers anglers as good a fishing experience as they are likely to find in the region. Part of the Turtle River chain, this lake has big populations of Northern Pike and Walleyes, as well as good numbers of Largemouth Bass and panfish. Big, old Turtle is fairly clear and has an abundance of structure to fish. Anglers specifically targeting Northerns have found that long-lining is their best bet, especially on sunny days, because fish here are easily spooked. The size of the Pike, meanwhile, makes it smart to use heavier-than-normal line. There are, indeed, some big ones out there, and they can really tear up the light equipment. The points you see on the map are all good Walleye feeding areas in the spring or very early mornings in the summer. Live bait drawn over the sandy bottoms will get attention. The three islands that give the lake its name are also good Walleye-holding areas. On bright spring and fall days and especially in the summer, you'll have to fish fairly deep for your Walleyes.

NOT FOR NAVIGATION

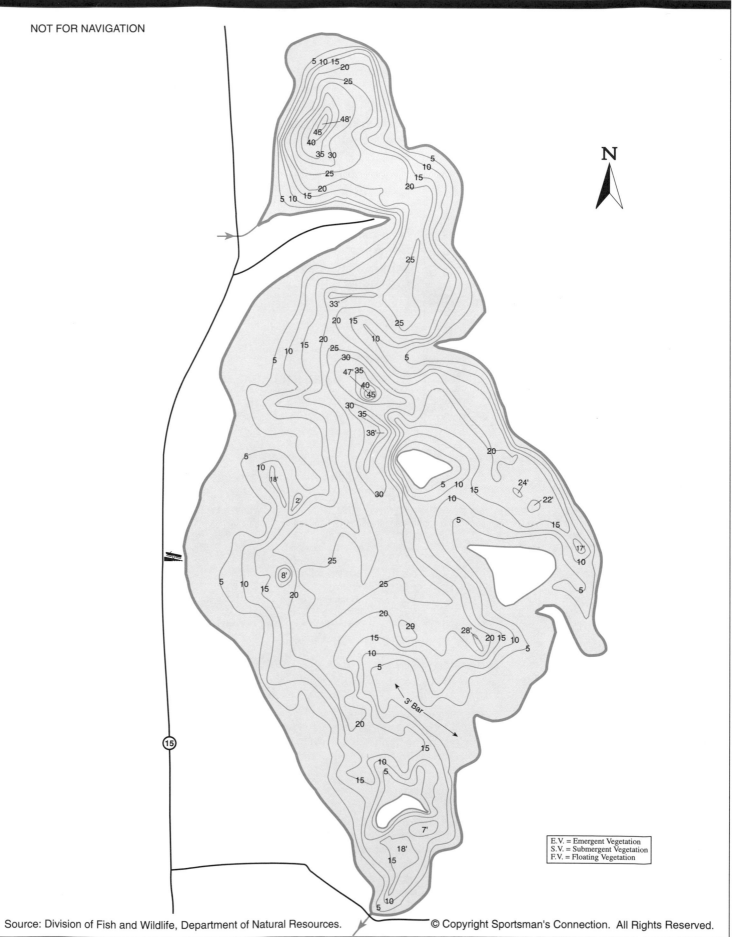

N

E.V. = Emergent Vegetation
S.V. = Submergent Vegetation
F.V. = Floating Vegetation

LITTLE TURTLE LAKE
Beltrami County

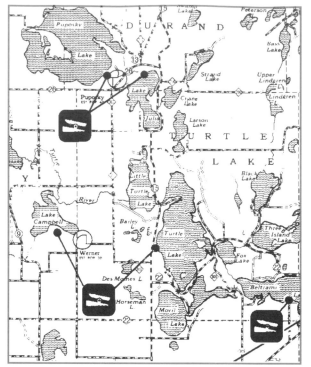

Location: Township 148
Range 33
Watershed: Mississippi Headwaters
Surface Water Area: 464 acres
Shorelength: 5.5 miles
Secchi disk (water clarity): 4.8 ft.
Water color: Green
Cause of water color: Algae

Maximum depth: 25 ft.
Median depth: NA
Accessibility: Via navigable
channel from Turtle Lake
Boat Ramp: Concrete ramp on
Turtle Lake
Accommodations: NA

Shoreland zoning classification: Natural Environment
Dominant forest/soil type: Decid/Loam
Management class: Walleye-Centrarchid
Ecological type: Centrarchid-Walleye

FISH STOCKING DATA: NO RECORD OF STOCKING

NET CATCH DATA

survey date: 7/25/88

species	Gill Nets # per net	Gill Nets avg fish wt. (lbs.)	Trap Nets # per set	Trap Nets avg fish wt. (lbs.)
Yellow Perch	6.4	0.09	57.2	trace
White Sucker	3.6	1.75	0.3	2.42
Walleye	7.2	1.11	0.7	2.45
Tullibee (Cisco)	4.1	1.50	-	-
Rock Bass	0.2	0.94	1.0	0.61
Pumpkin. Sunfish	1.0	0.51	3.6	0.25
Northern Pike	8.3	1.54	2.8	1.42
Largemouth Bass	0.2	1.28	0.2	2.32
Brown Bullhead	1.9	1.02	2.4	0.82
Black Crappie	0.3	0.66	1.1	0.59
Bowfin (Dogfish)	-	-	0.1	6.38
Bluegill	-	-	4.1	0.43

LENGTH OF SELECTED SPECIES SAMPLED FROM ALL GEAR
Number of fish caught for the following length categories (inches):

species	0-5	6-8	9-11	12-14	15-19	20-24	25-29	>30	Total
Black Crappie	-	-	8	5	-	-	-	-	13
Bluegill	7	9	19	1	-	-	-	-	36
Brown Bullhead	-	-	11	26	2	-	-	-	39
Largemouth Bass	-	-	-	3	1	-	-	-	4
Northern Pike	-	-	-	-	55	38	7	-	100
Pumpkin. Sunfish	17	14	10	-	-	-	-	-	41
Rock Bass	-	1	9	1	-	-	-	-	11
Tullibee (Cisco)	-	2	7	1	27	-	-	-	37
Walleye	-	4	11	17	26	12	1	-	71
Yellow Perch	1	70	2	-	-	-	-	-	73

DNR COMMENTS: Walleye catch rates up from those of earlier surveys and twice the local average. Northern Pike, Bluegill, Pumpkin-seed, and Brown Bullhead catch rates stable. Yellow Perch numbers down to 6.3/gillnet lift, compared to 41.6 in 1983 and 22.1 in 1971. Over all, fishery quality is excellent, with numerous panfish, Northern Pike, and Walleye present.

FISHING INFORMATION: Little Turtle Lake is just northwest of its larger namesake and also offers excellent Walleye and Northern fishing as well as good Bass and Panfish. Shallower and somewhat more cloudy than Big Turtle, Little Turtle is probably the easier lake to fish. Three sunken islands – two at the north end, one near the south shore – are good Walleye areas. The nice points are just as good, though, so you have plenty of choices. The lake's weedlines support fine populations of bucketmouth Bass, Bluegills, and Crappies. Try your luck with crawlers or minnows for the panfish and spinnerbaits or pig-and-jig for the bigmouths. Access to both lakes is from Big Turtle's west shoreline on Highway 15. The channel between the lakes is easily navigable to anything smaller than the presidential yacht. Drop in. Catch fish. Have fun.

SPORTSMAN'S connection

NOT FOR NAVIGATION

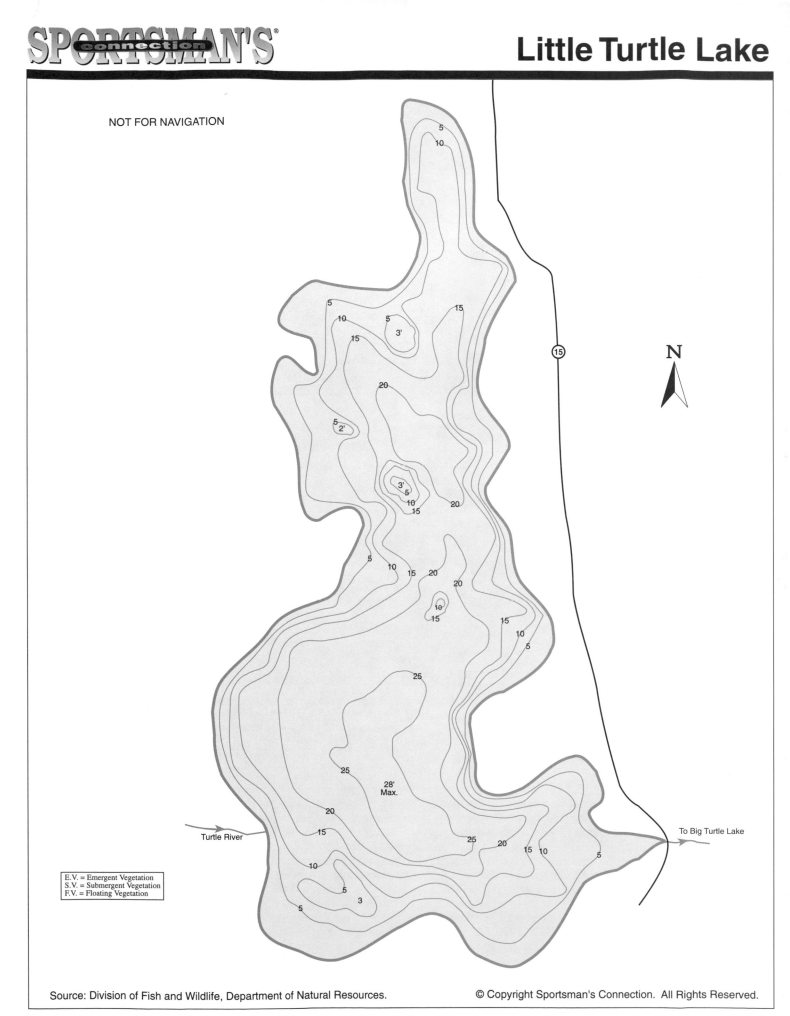

5
10
5
10
15
5
10
15
3'
20
5 2'
3' 5
10
15
20
5
10 15 20
20
10
15
15
10
5
25
25
28' Max.
20
15
25 20
15 10
5
10
5 3
5

N

⑮

To Big Turtle Lake

Turtle River

E.V. = Emergent Vegetation
S.V. = Submergent Vegetation
F.V. = Floating Vegetation

Source: Division of Fish and Wildlife, Department of Natural Resources.

LAKE JULIA

Beltrami County

LARSON LAKE

Location: Township 148,149 Range 33
Watershed: Mississippi Headwaters
Surface Water Area: 450 acres
Shorelength: 5.4 miles
Secchi disk (water clarity): 10 ft.
Water color: Green
Cause of water color: Phytoplankton bloom
Maximum depth: 43 ft.
Median depth: NA
Accessibility: State-owned public access on north shore
Boat Ramp: Concrete
Accommodations: NA
Shoreland zoning classlf.: Rec. Dev.
Dominant forest/soil type: Decid/Loam
Management class: Walleye
Ecological type: Hard-water Walleye

Location: Township 148 Range 33
Watershed: Mississippi Headwaters
Surface Water Area: 178 acres
Shorelength: 3.3 miles
Secchi disk (water clarity): 8.4 ft.
Water color: Brown
Cause of water color: Bog stain
Maximum depth: 48 ft.
Median depth: NA
Accessibility: Public access off fire road on west shore
Boat Ramp: NA
Accommodations: NA
Shoreland zoning classif.: Nat. Envir.
Dominant forest/soil type: Decid/Loam
Management class: Warm-water gamefish
Ecological type: Roughfish-Gamefish

DNR COMMENTS:
Walleye abundance at an all-time high and far above lake-class average; average size 14.7 inches and 1.3 lb.; fish to 25.6 inches sampled; nearly half the population is infected with Neascus. Northern Pike numbers near average; mean weight 2.4 lb; fish to 36.7 inches captured. Yellow Perch numbers down slightly but still high; average size 9 inches and .4 lb.; parasites common. Rock Bass abundance high; average weight .3 lb. Pumpkinseed numbers near low end of the normal range for lake class. Brown Bullhead numbers average.

FISH STOCKING DATA

year	species	size	# released
90	Walleye	Fry	250,000
91	Walleye	Fry	250,000
93	Walleye	Fry	167,000
94	Walleye	Fry	167,000
96	Walleye	Fry	250,000
97	Walleye	Fry	400,000

NET CATCH DATA

survey date: 8/20/96

	Gill Nets		Trap Nets	
species	# per net	avg fish wt. (lbs)	# per set	avg fish wt. (lbs)
Brown Bullhead	0.8	1.18	0.2	1.33
Northern Pike	6.4	2.44	2.0	2.09
Pumpkin. Sunfish	-	-	3.8	0.06
Rock Bass	2.4	0.35	2.1	0.26
Walleye	16.9	1.31	2.1	1.93
Yellow Perch	67.1	0.45	5.6	0.14

LENGTH OF SELECTED SPECIES SAMPLED FROM ALL GEAR
Number of fish caught for the following length categories (inches):

species	0-5	6-8	9-11	12-14	15-19	20-24	25-29	>30	Total
Brown Bullhead	1	2	-	5	1	-	-	-	9
Northern Pike	-	-	10	-	19	33	10	4	76
Pumpkin. Sunfish	34	-	-	-	-	-	-	-	34
Rock Bass	10	28	3	-	-	-	-	-	41
Walleye	2	10	19	99	16	20	5	-	171
Yellow Perch	61	277	304	12	-	-	-	-	654

FISH STOCKING DATA: NO RECORD OF STOCKING

NET CATCH DATA

survey date: 08/19/86

	Gill Nets		Trap Nets	
species	# per net	avg fish wt. (lbs)	# per set	avg fish wt. (lbs)
Northern Pike	18.5	1.67	2.0	2.27
Brown Bullhead	3.0	0.23	29.0	0.20

LENGTH OF SELECTED SPECIES SAMPLED FROM ALL GEAR
Number of fish caught for the following length categories (inches):

species	0-5	6-8	9-11	12-14	15-19	20-24	25-29	>30	Total
Brown Bullhead	-	87	4	3	-	-	-	-	94
Northern Pike	-	1	1	2	23	14	-	2	43

DNR COMMENTS:
Northern Pike abundance well above lake-class average; average weight 1.67 lb.; most pike measure 15 to 19 inches. Brown Bullhead numbers average; some 12-inch-plus fish present.

FISHING INFORMATION: Lake Julia, located directly north of Bemidji on State Highway 15, is one of nearly a dozen good fishing lakes in the area. Earl Taber of Taber's Bait in Bemidji describes Julia as a "good Walleye lake that holds some big ones." Many Walleyes taken in test nets exceed 3 pounds, and some are even larger – much larger. The water is somewhat stained, and there are lots of weeds and a mucky bottom, so you'll have to do a good deal of weed-fishing for your Walleyes. Simply casting into the weedbeds and bringing your lure back to the boat is a fairly good approach. You may also find some sandy bottoms off points along the east side that have been swept by westerly winds. If so, try a Shiner or Fathead minnow on a bottom rig or a jig. That usually produces well. Northern Pike anglers like to backtroll along the outer edges of Julia's weedbeds, using spinnerbaits or a lip-hooked shiner. The Northerns aren't particularly large, but there are plenty of them. There are also a lot of Yellow Perch in the weedbeds and they, along with Pike, provide good winter fishing for area anglers. **Larson Lake**, meanwhile, is about 10 miles north of Bemidji. It is heavily weeded, fairly clear, and has large numbers of Northern Pike, quite a few Bullheads, and a decent number of Crappies. Tim Falk at Bluewater Baits in Bemidji says there are plenty of 1/2-pound Crappies. He says Larson's a beautiful lake with no pressure, and it's reachable only by a fire road on its west side.

NOT FOR NAVIGATION

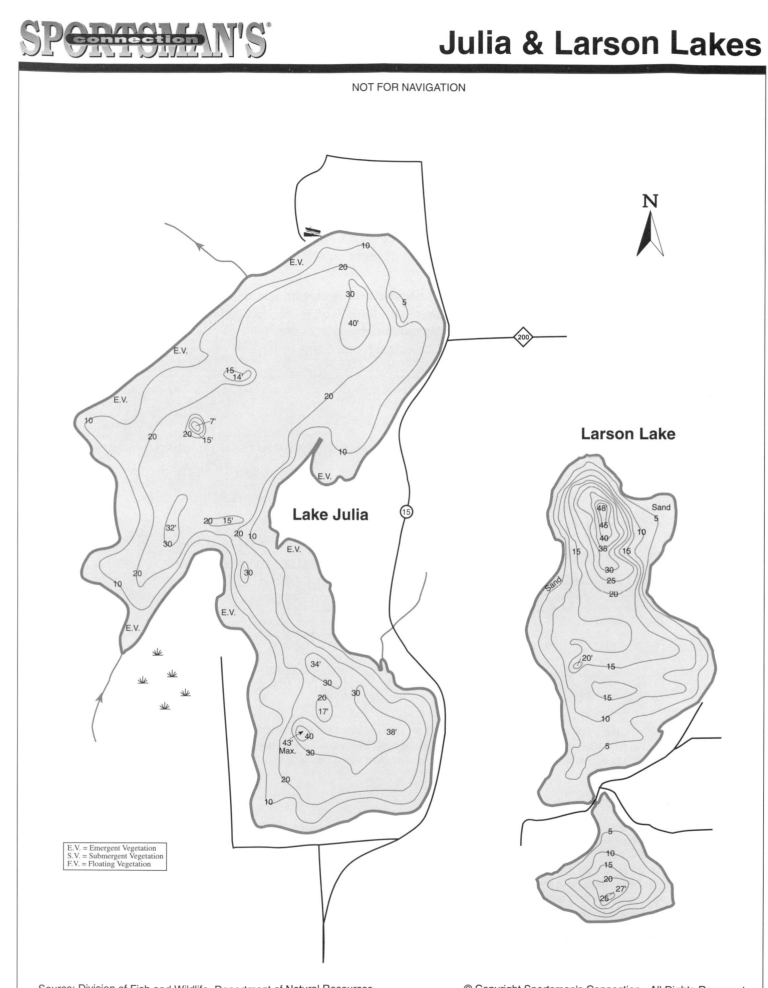

Larson Lake

Lake Julia

E.V. = Emergent Vegetation
S.V. = Submergent Vegetation
F.V. = Floating Vegetation

LAKE PUPOSKY
Beltrami County

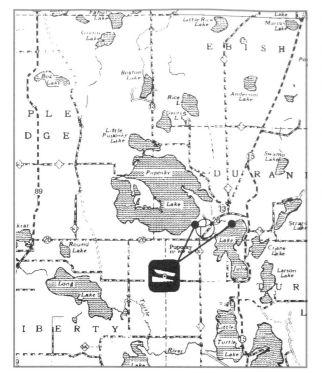

Location: Township 149
Range 33, 34
Watershed: Red Lakes
Surface Water Area: 2142 acres
Shorelength: 10.2 miles
Secchi disk (water clarity): NA
Water color: NA
Cause of water color: NA

Maximum depth: 14 ft.
Median depth: NA
Accessibility: State-owned access on southeast shore
Boat Ramp: Earth
Accommodations: NA

Shoreland zoning classification: Natural Environment
Dominant forest/soil type: No tree/Wet
Management class: Game
Ecological type: Game

FISH STOCKING DATA: NO RECORD OF STOCKING

NET CATCH DATA

survey date: 7/23/86

species	Gill Nets # per net	Gill Nets avg fish wt. (lbs.)	Trap Nets # per set	Trap Nets avg fish wt. (lbs.)
Yellow Perch	24.0	0.15	9.0	0.24
Northern Pike	7.0	3.50	1.0	1.70
Black Bullhead	82.0	0.29	25.0	0.20

LENGTH OF SELECTED SPECIES SAMPLED FROM ALL GEAR

Number of fish caught for the following length categories (inches):

species	0-5	6-8	9-11	12-14	15-19	20-24	25-29	>30	Total
Black Bullhead	-	12	13	-	-	-	-	-	25
Northern Pike	-	-	-	-	2	4	2	-	8
Yellow Perch	-	21	3	-	-	-	-	-	24

DNR COMMENTS: Lake Puposky is a winterkill lake that provides a Northern Pike and Yellow Perch sport fishery. During periods of several years with no winterkill there is a good potential for excellent Northern Pike angling and spearing. The population of Northern Pike is above local and state medians, with fish 7 years of age and over being present.

FISHING INFORMATION: This lake is roughly 18 miles north of Bemidji, near Highway 15. It is so shallow (maximum depth of 14 feet) that we wondered whether it was just a waterfowl hangout or had fish in it. We talked with Earl Taber of Taber's Baits in Bemidji who eased our minds. "Puposky is subject to occasional winterkill," Taber said, "but it doesn't happen often. The rest of the time it has a lot of Northern. Most of them are on the small side, but there's good fishing." The fact is that the Northern population is well above the local and state average. And not only is the summer fishing good but the lake offers good spearing opportunities in winter. In sum, this is a good place to take young anglers who are tired of hooking sunnies and want to move up to bigger fish. Local anglers agree it's difficult to say which part of the lake provides the best fishing. Almost all of the bottom is in the 4- to 6-foot depth range, and roughly 95 percent of the lake is weeded. You may want to consider the shores off the island on the northwest side. Take some topwater lures with you in warm weather. Yellow Perch reach jumbo size in good years. And, as in many other shallow, fertile lakes, the Bullhead are plentiful. Public access is in the lake's southeast corner. It offers an earth ramp and eight parking spots.

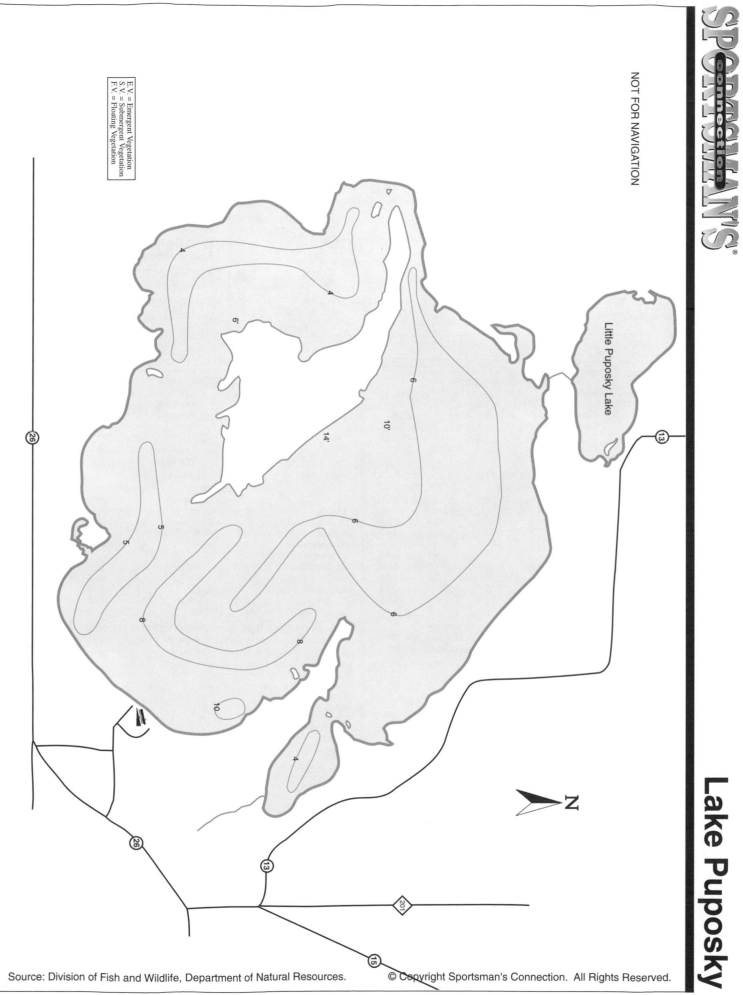

E.V. = Emergent Vegetation
S.V. = Submergent Vegetation
F.V. = Floating Vegetation

Little Puposky Lake

N

Lake Puposky

CAMPBELL LAKE   DEER LAKE

Beltrami County

Location: Township 148   Range 33, 34
Watershed: Mississippi Headwaters
Surface Water Area: 475 acres
Shorelength: 5.6 miles
Secchi disk (water clarity): 7.3 ft.
Water color: Gray-brown
Cause of water color: Algae
Maximum depth: 25 ft.
Median depth: 12 ft.
Accessibility: Public access on south-southwest shore
Boat Ramp: Concrete
Accommodations: Resort
Shoreland zoning classif.: Nat. Envir.
Dominant forest/soil type: No Tree/Wet
Management class: Walleye-Centrarchid
Ecological type: Centrarchid

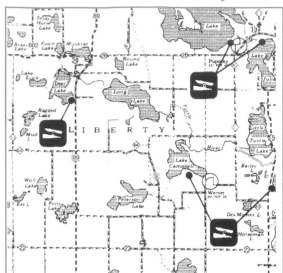

Location: Township 148   Range 34
Watershed: Mississippi Headwaters
Surface Water Area: 262 acres
Shorelength: 4.6 miles
Secchi disk (water clarity): 13.0 ft.
Water color: Greenish tint
Cause of water color: Algae
Maximum depth: 42 ft.
Median depth: 20 ft.
Accessibility: State-owned access on east-southeast corner
Boat Ramp: Asphalt
Accommodations: NA
Shoreland zoning classif.: Rec. Dev.
Dominant forest/soil type: Decid/Loam
Management class: Walleye-Centrarchid
Ecological type: Centrarchid-Walleye

DNR COMMENTS:
Northern Pike remain abundant with some nice fish available. Walleye numbers stable; ageing data corresponds with stocked year classes. Largemouth Bass numbers low, but nice-size fish present. Bluegill numbers well above state and local medians though size is generally small. Yellow Perch numbers high, with nearly all fish sampled being less than 7 inches.

FISH STOCKING DATA

year	species	size	# released
90	Walleye	Fingerling	18,825
92	Walleye	Fingerling	14,795
94	Walleye	Fingerling	11,980
94	Walleye	Adult	8
96	Walleye	Fingerling	12,600

NET CATCH DATA

survey date: 7/9/90

	Gill Nets		Trap Nets	
species	# per net	avg fish wt. (lbs)	# per set	avg fish wt. (lbs)
Yellow Perch	42.2	0.10	3.4	0.09
Walleye	3.8	0.93	0.5	0.95
Tullibee (Cisco)	1.2	1.30	-	-
Rock Bass	1.0	0.23	1.8	0.16
Pumpkin. Sunfish	32.7	0.12	19.0	0.09
Northern Pike	9.8	2.70	0.4	1.60
Bluegill	5.5	0.26	29.0	0.13
Black Crappie	1.0	0.18	0.3	0.45
Largemouth Bass	-	-	0.1	3.00

LENGTH OF SELECTED SPECIES SAMPLED FROM ALL GEAR

Number of fish caught for the following length categories (inches):

species	0-5	6-8	9-11	12-14	15-19	20-24	25-29	>30	Total
Yellow Perch	-	103	-	-	-	-	-	-	103
Walleye	-	-	3	10	9	1	-	-	23
Tullibee (Cisco)	-	-	2	1	4	-	-	-	7
Rock Bass	2	4	-	-	-	-	-	-	6
Pumpkin. Sunfish	40	53	-	-	-	-	-	-	93
Northern Pike	-	-	-	-	5	40	12	2	59
Brown Bullhead	-	1	5	6	-	-	-	-	12
Bluegill	3	25	1	-	-	-	-	-	29
Black Crappie	-	6	-	-	-	-	-	-	6
Black Bullhead	-	-	2	-	-	-	-	-	2

FISH STOCKING DATA

year	species	size	# released
91	Walleye	Fingerling	5,115
93	Walleye	Fingerling	3,224
93	Walleye	Adult	2
95	Walleye	Fingerling	1,367
97	Walleye	Fingerling	4,450
97	Walleye	Yearling	70

NET CATCH DATA

survey date: 7/14/97

	Gill Nets		Trap Nets	
species	# per net	avg fish wt. (lbs)	# per set	avg fish wt. (lbs)
Black Crappie	-	-	5.4	0.15
Bluegill	0.2	0.38	28.9	0.30
Hybrid Sunfish	0.8	0.31	4.1	0.31
Largemouth Bass	0.5	1.55	-	-
Northern Pike	4.7	2.85	0.8	2.66
Pumpkin. Sunfish	0.7	0.28	5.5	0.15
Rock Bass	3.0	0.47	1.9	0.29
Walleye	6.5	1.50	0.3	4.22
Yellow Perch	55.3	0.12	1.5	0.12

LENGTH OF SELECTED SPECIES SAMPLED FROM ALL GEAR

Number of fish caught for the following length categories (inches):

species	0-5	6-8	9-11	12-14	15-19	20-24	25-29	>30	Total
Black Crappie	25	16	2	-	-	-	-	-	43
Bluegill	13	176	-	-	-	-	-	-	189
Brown Bullhead	-	-	2	-	-	-	-	-	2
Hybrid Sunfish	13	25	-	-	-	-	-	-	38
Largemouth Bass	-	-	-	2	1	-	-	-	3
Northern Pike	-	-	-	1	9	16	5	3	34
Pumpkin. Sunfish	27	21	-	-	-	-	-	-	48
Rock Bass	15	9	9	-	-	-	-	-	33
Tullibee (Cisco)	-	3	5	30	7	-	-	-	45
Walleye	-	-	10	11	10	9	1	-	41
Yellow Perch	68	162	-	-	-	-	-	-	230

DNR COMMENTS:
Walleye numbers have been increasing and are now above the normal range for lake class; modal lengths 11 to 13 inches and 18 to 22 inches. Northern Pike abundance average for lake class; modal length range 18 to 22 inches; fish to 36 inches sampled; average weight 2.9 lb. Black Crappie numbers at all-time high and above lake-class average; strong 1996 year class; average length about 8 inches. Bluegill abundance average; modal length 6.5 to 8.5 inches; fish to 9 inches sampled. Largemouth Bass sample inadequate for accurate population assessment.

FISHING INFORMATION: Located 10 miles north of Bemidji, these two smallish lakes are regularly stocked with Walleyes, usually fingerlings. Earl Taber of Taber Baits in Bemidji says **Campbell** is probably better known for its good Bluegill population than for anything else, but it does hold "good Northerns and some Walleye." Records show there are plenty of Walleyes, but not too many are caught. This may indicate several things, one of them being that not many Walleye experts fish the lake. The lake is well weeded and has good growths of bulrushes, both at the shoreline and around mid-lake "islands." The weedbeds, in turn, provide excellent spawning and protective areas for panfish and Bass. You can use nightcrawlers on a hook to get panfish after ice-out; add a small jig as the vegetation blooms. While there may not be a lot of Largemouths, there are some healthy-size ones, and these deserve attention. Northerns are pretty well everywhere and can be reached by trolling the outer edges of the weeds. Meanwhile, Chuck Cole, Bemidji angler, says **Deer** "is a nice little lake. Very clean, with big Crappies, Largemouth Bass, and nice Walleye. The Panfishing is excellent." Stocked Walleyes do well enough that the population is above the area average. There are, in fact, lots of fish in the 2- to 3-pound range. The lakeshore is well weeded and has bulrushes and some cabbage weeds where you can get dandy Crappies, as well as plenty of Bluegills.

NOT FOR NAVIGATION

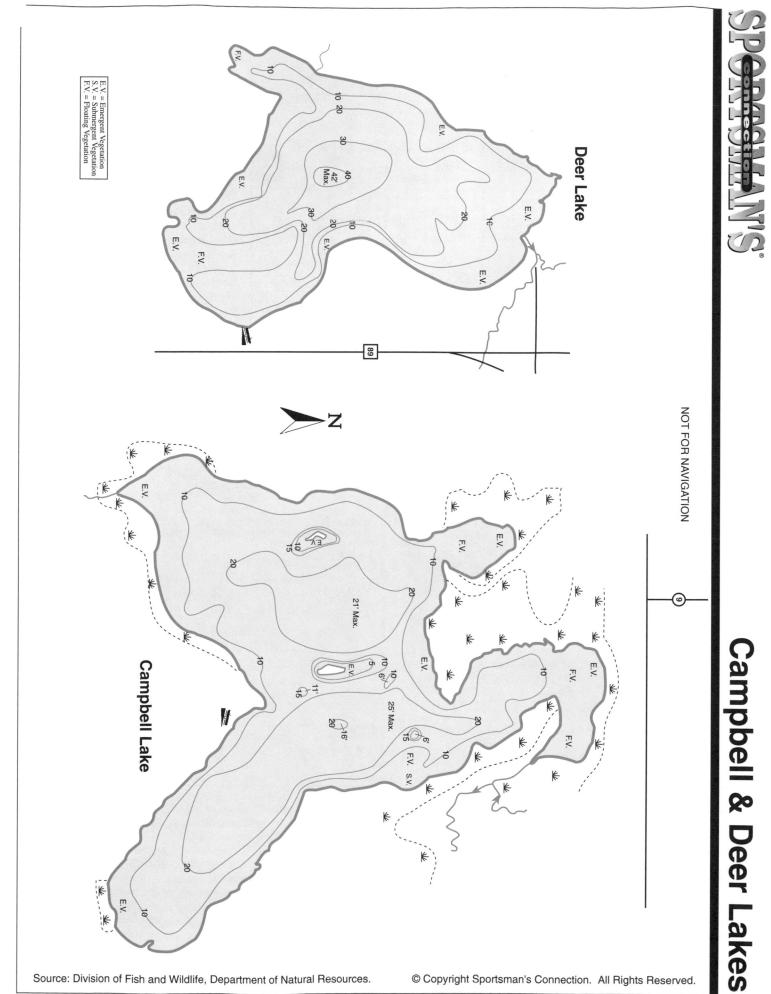

E.V. = Emergent Vegetation
S.V. = Submergent Vegetation
F.V. = Floating Vegetation

Deer Lake

Campbell Lake

N

Source: Division of Fish and Wildlife, Department of Natural Resources.

LITTLE BUZZLE LAKE   WHITEFISH LAKE

Beltrami County

Location: Township 148   Range 35
Watershed: Clearwater
Surface Water Area: 68 acres
Shorelength: NA
Secchi disk (water clarity): 17.0 ft.
Water color: NA
Cause of water color: NA
Maximum depth: 40 ft.
Median depth: NA
Accessibility: Public access on south shore
Boat Ramp: Carry-in
Accommodations: NA
Shoreland zoning classif.: Nat. Envir.
Dominant forest/soil type: NA
Management class: Centrarchid
Ecological type: Centrarchid

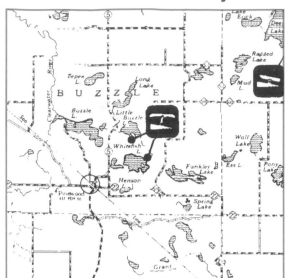

Location: Township 148   Range 35
Watershed: Clearwater
Surface Water Area: 120 acres
Shorelength: NA
Secchi disk (water clarity): 8.0 ft.
Water color: Brownish
Cause of water color: Bog stain
Maximum depth: 30 ft.
Median depth: NA
Accessibility: Public access on northeast corner
Boat Ramp: Carry-in
Accommodations: NA
Shoreland zoning classif.: Nat. Envir.
Dominant forest/soil type: NA
Management class: Centrarchid
Ecological type: Centrarchid

DNR COMMENTS:
Northern Pike numbers remain very high at roughly three times the local median level. Panfish plentiful; a few are large. No Largemouth Bass captured or seen, but this species is known to be present. Yellow Perch numbers very low possibly because of heavy Northern Pike predation.

FISH STOCKING DATA: NO RECORD OF STOCKING

NET CATCH DATA

survey date: 06/20/90

	Gill Nets		Trap Nets	
species	# per net	avg fish wt. (lbs)	# per set	avg fish wt. (lbs)
Rock Bass	1.0	0.10	2.8	0.23
Pumpkin. Sunfish	3.5	0.04	6.0	0.18
Northern Pike	12.5	1.40	1.0	0.60
Bluegill	6.0	0.14	36.5	0.33
Black Crappie	1.0	0.10	0.3	0.60
Black Bullhead	1.5	0.10	-	-
Yellow Perch	-	-	0.3	3.3
White Sucker	-	-	1.8	1.4

LENGTH OF SELECTED SPECIES SAMPLED FROM ALL GEAR
Number of fish caught for the following length categories (inches):

species	0-5	6-8	9-11	12-14	15-19	20-24	25-29	>30	Total
Black Bullhead	-	3	-	-	-	-	-	-	3
Black Crappie	-	2	-	1	-	-	-	-	3
Bluegill	19	113	26	-	-	-	-	-	158
Northern Pike	-	-	-	5	15	8	1	-	29
Pumpkin. Sunfish	9	22	-	-	-	-	-	-	31
Rock Bass	6	3	4	-	-	-	-	-	13
Yellow Perch	-	-	1	-	-	-	-	-	1

FISH STOCKING DATA: NO RECORD OF STOCKING

NET CATCH DATA

survey date: 8/26/97

	Gill Nets		Trap Nets	
species	# per net	avg fish wt. (lbs)	# per set	avg fish wt. (lbs)
Black Bullhead	36.0	0.10	200.1	0.10
Black Crappie	-	-	1.4	0.56
Bluegill	-	-	4.7	0.52
Brown Bullhead	2.5	0.19	13.9	0.21
Northern Pike	2.0	0.89	0.6	0.97
White Sucker	-	-	0.1	1.92
Yellow Perch	6.7	0.17	0.4	0.15

LENGTH OF SELECTED SPECIES SAMPLED FROM ALL GEAR
Number of fish caught for the following length categories (inches):

species	0-5	6-8	9-11	12-14	15-19	20-24	25-29	>30	Total
Black Bullhead	134	51	2	-	-	-	-	-	187
Black Crappie	-	1	11	-	-	-	-	-	12
Bluegill	-	41	1	-	-	-	-	-	42
Brown Bullhead	17	28	12	2	-	-	-	-	59
Northern Pike	-	-	-	4	12	1	-	-	17
Yellow Perch	9	31	4	-	-	-	-	-	44

DNR COMMENTS:
Lake has history of low winter oxygen levels, and fishery shows signs of recovery from a partial winterkill. Northern Pike scarce; average size 16.3 inches and .6 lb.; Neascus common among Pike. Black Crappie numbers near lake class median; average size 9.9 inches and .6 lb. Bluegill abundance down, but 8.6-inch average length is attractive to anglers. Yellow Perch numbers down but within normal range; average length 7.1 inches. Largemouth Bass not found. Black Bullheads extremely abundant but small. Brown Bullhead numbers near average; size small.

FISHING INFORMATION: These two lakes lie on either side of State Highway 5, north of Pinewood. Both have reputations as Northern Pike and panfish producers, and they offer decent numbers of Largemouth Bass as well. **Whitefish Lake** has a large number of Bluegills and Crappies and plenty of good habitat for both. There are weedbeds, cattails, and a shoreline with a fair number of overhanging willows and marsh grass that shade the mucky bottoms. Most of the shoreline is shallow and can be fished with jigs tipped with minnows or nightcrawlers. The water is fairly transparent but somewhat brownish with bog stain, so you may want to use bright jigs to get attention. The south end of the lake may be best for panfish most of the time, but there are so many good areas that you'll want to move around until you hit. Don't overlook the islands at either end, though. Northerns can be anywhere near the lake's weedbeds where they often patrol for Yellow Perch and other forage fish. **Little Buzzle** isn't heavily fished in spite of having a lot of Northerns and excellent Bluegills. The Northerns are on the small side, probably because there are so many of them competing for the forage base. Like neighboring Whitefish, Buzzle is heavily weeded and has a mucky bottom. The weedy areas are prime panfish habitat and hold some good Largemouth Bass. The water is very clear, so you will want to make your presentations carefully to avoid spooking the fish. Earl Taber of Taber's Baits in Bemidji tells us some people like to take Ciscoes from Little Buzzle for smoking. Yum! Both of these lakes have carry-in public access.

NOT FOR NAVIGATION

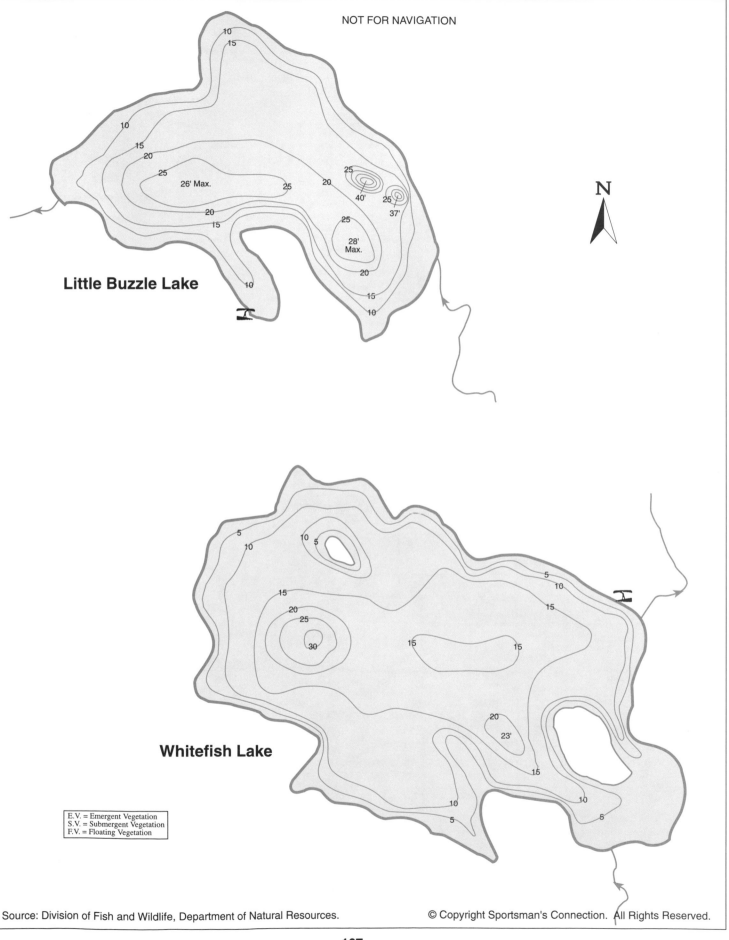

Little Buzzle Lake

Whitefish Lake

E.V. = Emergent Vegetation
S.V. = Submergent Vegetation
F.V. = Floating Vegetation

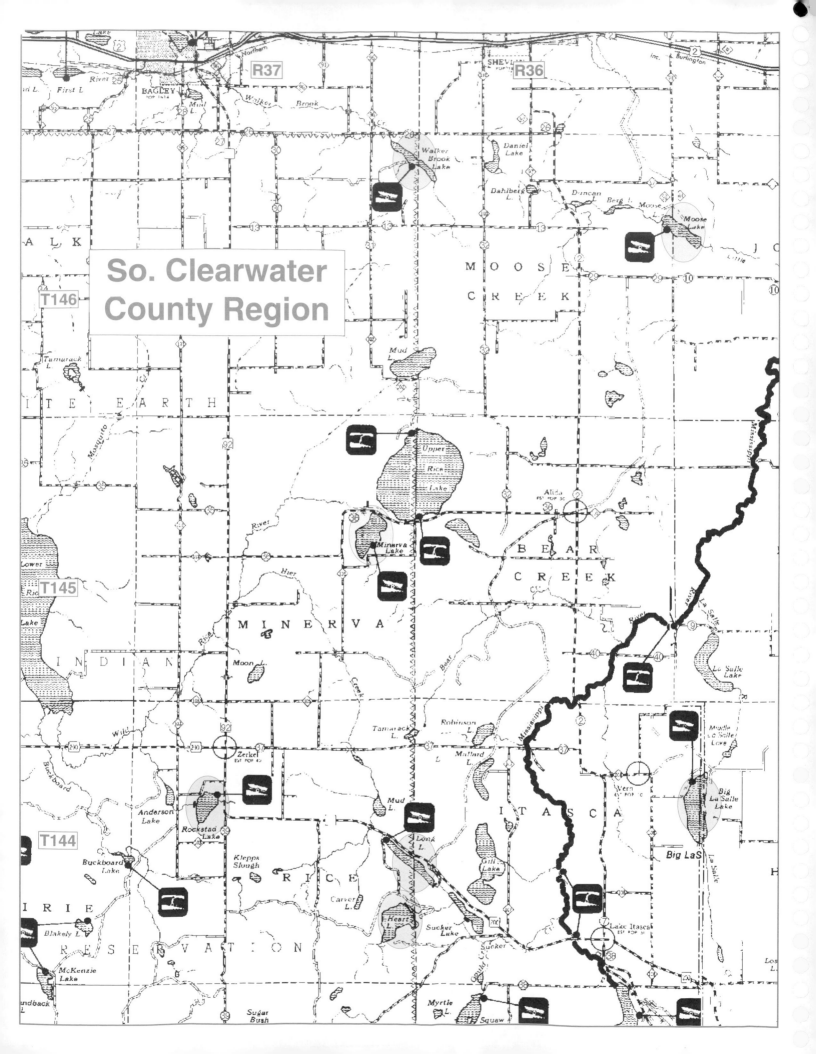

So. Clearwater
County Region

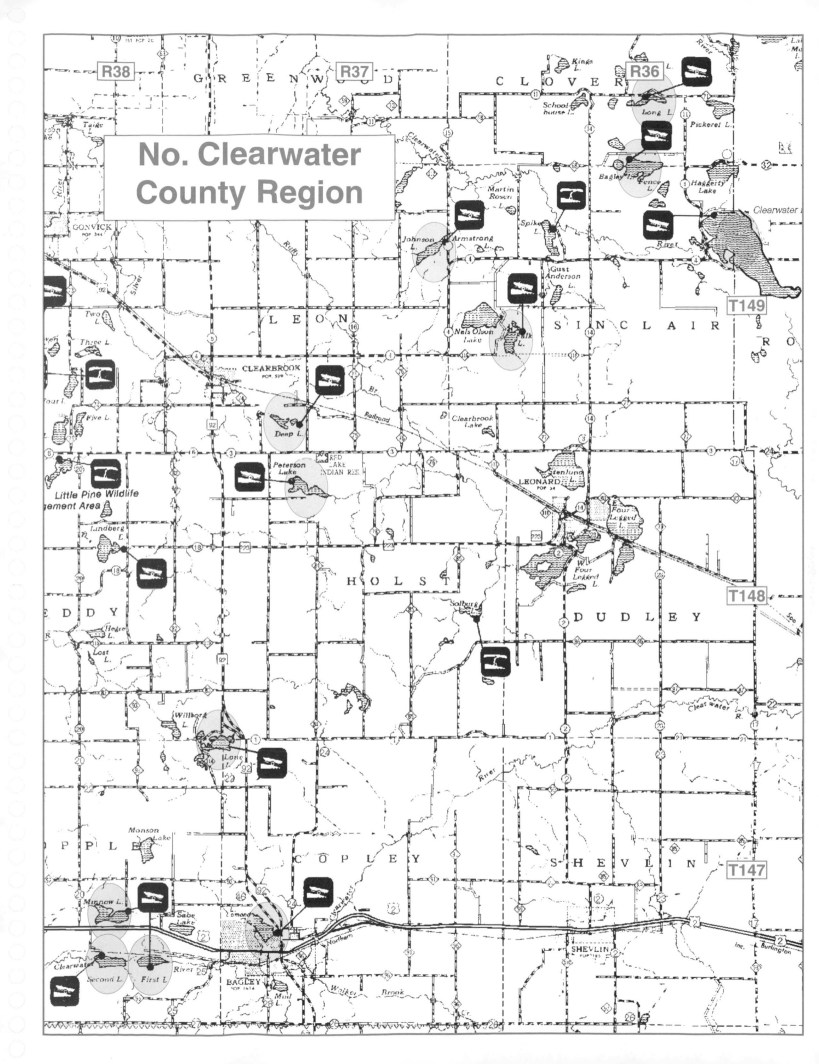

No. Clearwater County Region

BALM LAKE

Beltrami County

SANDY LAKE

Location: Township 150   Range 35
Watershed: Red Lakes
Surface Water Area: 512 acres
Shorelength: 6.6 miles
Secchi disk (water clarity): 11.0 ft.
Water color: Green
Cause of water color: Algae bloom and phytoplankton
Maximum depth: 33 ft.
Median depth: 12 ft.
Accessibility: State-owned access on north shore
Boat Ramp: Earth
Accommodations: Resort
Shoreland zoning classif.: Nat. Envir.
Dominant forest/soil type: Decid/Loam
Management class: Walleye-Centrarchid
Ecological type: Centrarchid-Walleye

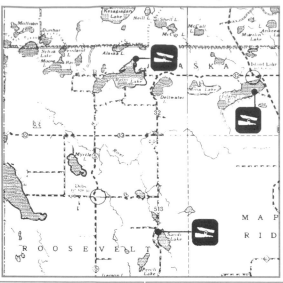

Location: Township 149   Range 35
Watershed: Red Lakes
Surface Water Area: 100 acres
Shorelength: NA
Secchi disk (water clarity): 7.0 ft.
Water color: Green
Cause of water color: Algae
Maximum depth: 72 ft.
Median depth: NA
Accessibility: Public access on north-west corner
Boat Ramp: Gravel
Accommodations: NA
Shoreland zoning classif.: Nat. Envir.
Dominant forest/soil type: NA
Management class: Walleye-Centrarchid
Ecological type: Centrarchid

DNR COMMENTS:
Walleye population in generally good condition; abundance and size above average for lake type; modal length range 16 to 22 inches; population maintained by fingerling stocking. Northern Pike common; most fish between 22 and 30 inches, but larger fish present. Largemouth Bass common. Black Crappie, Bluegill, Pumpkinseed and Yellow Perch populations above average; size generally acceptable to anglers.

FISH STOCKING DATA

year	species	size	# released
92	Walleye	Fingerling	3,300
93	Northern Pike	Adult	292
95	Walleye	Fingerling	6,190

NET CATCH DATA
survey date: 6/23/97

	Gill Nets		Trap Nets	
		avg fish		avg fish
species	# per net	wt. (lbs)	# per set	wt. (lbs)
Black Crappie	3.6	0.30	0.1	0.38
Bluegill	64.9	0.18	76.0	0.23
Golden Shiner	3.6	0.09	0.6	0.08
Hybrid Sunfish	3.3	0.27	0.8	0.27
Largemouth Bass	1.3	1.06	0.9	0.66
Northern Pike	8.0	4.36	0.4	5.07
Pumpkin. Sunfish	20.7	0.16	17.4	0.27
Rock Bass	1.9	0.22	2.4	0.26
Walleye	9.0	2.05	0.3	5.07
White Sucker	0.7	2.11	-	-
Yellow Perch	40.4	0.19	0.9	0.22

LENGTH OF SELECTED SPECIES SAMPLED FROM ALL GEAR
Number of fish caught for the following length categories (inches):

species	0-5	6-8	9-11	12-14	15-19	20-24	25-29	>30	Total
Black Crappie	1	10	15	-	-	-	-	-	26
Bluegill	170	564	-	-	-	-	-	-	734
Hybrid Sunfish	3	27	-	-	-	-	-	-	30
Largemouth Bass	-	2	9	6	-	-	-	-	17
Northern Pike	-	-	-	-	23	28	9	60
Pumpkin. Sunfish	101	201	-	-	-	-	-	-	302
Rock Bass	9	25	1	-	-	-	-	-	35
Walleye	-	-	2	6	37	19	2	-	66
Yellow Perch	39	222	29	1	-	-	-	-	291

FISH STOCKING DATA: NO RECORD OF STOCKING

NET CATCH DATA
survey date: 06/25/90

	Gill Nets		Trap Nets	
		avg fish		avg fish
species	# per net	wt. (lbs)	# per set	wt. (lbs)
Walleye	2.0	0.48	-	-
Rock Bass	5.0	0.19	6.0	0.09
Northern Pike	10.5	1.16	-	-
Largemouth Bass	1.0	0.90	0.5	0.40
Lake Whitefish	1.0	3.00	-	-
Hybrid Sunfish	2.0	0.25	11.3	0.21
Bluegill	1.0	0.35	4.8	0.14

LENGTH OF SELECTED SPECIES SAMPLED FROM ALL GEAR
Number of fish caught for the following length categories (inches):

species	0-5	6-8	9-11	12-14	15-19	20-24	25-29	>30	Total
Walleye	-	-	1	3	-	-	-	-	4
Rock Bass	5	7	1	-	-	-	-	-	13
Northern Pike	-	-	-	2	14	5	-	-	21
Largemouth Bass	-	-	-	1	-	-	-	-	1
Lake Whitefish	-	-	-	-	1	1	-	-	2
Hybrid Sunfish	-	4	-	-	-	-	-	-	4
Bluegill	-	2	1	-	-	-	-	-	3

DNR COMMENTS:
Northern Pike abundant at above-third-quartile values for lake class; mean weight low; length generally 24 inches or less. Walleyes present in average numbers; weight low, but growth rate above average Largemouth Bass present in average numbers; mean weight between first and third quartiles. Lake Whitefish very numerous; growth above statewide average. Rock Bass population down, but still above third-quartile values; mean weight very low. Bluegills scarce; weight low.

FISHING INFORMATION: Located west and southwest of the intersection of County Road 89 and State 32, neither of these lakes gets a lot of fishing pressure. Earl Taber, veteran Bemidji angler and owner of Taber's Bait, calls **Balm** a "good, big lake that's especially good in the summer." It is managed for Walleyes and stocked regularly by the DNR. There are some nice points to fish for Walleyes toward the west side, where the lake narrows. The points lead out to a 27-foot hole. Fish along the points for early-season Walleyes with live bait on a bottom rig. Later on, you will have to fish deeper, but come back to the points at night or early in the morning. There are, meanwhile, several good bays to fish for panfish and Bass. The west bay has good weedbeds with lily pads and bulrushes – just the kind of habitat that yields good fish year round. Two bays at the northeast corner are also excellent. Fish outside the weedbeds for Northerns. Meanwhile, **Sandy Lake** is south of Balm and shouldn't be confused with another lake of the same name northwest of Gull Lake. THIS Sandy is fairly deep, with steep drops off the shorelines. This makes the weedbeds short and not particularly good cover. Sandy has a fair number of Walleyes, thanks to stocking by the DNR, and it holds some Northerns and panfish as well. But it's not one of the more popular lakes among area anglers.

NOT FOR NAVIGATION

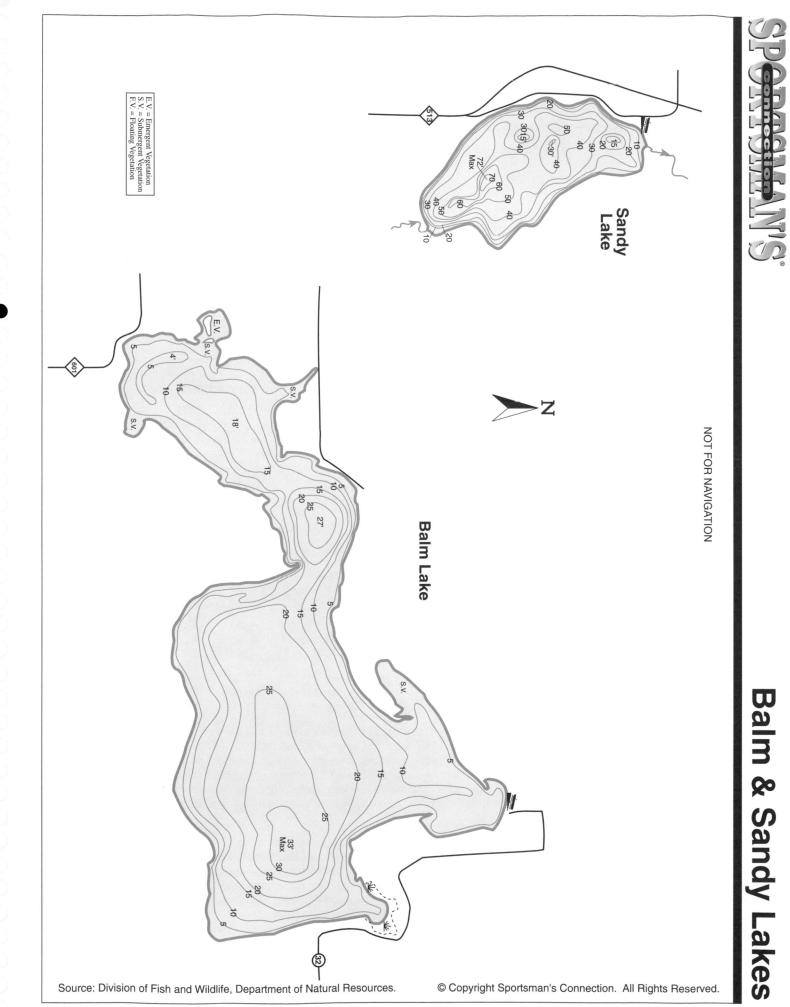

Sandy Lake

513

E.V. = Emergent Vegetation
S.V. = Submergent Vegetation
F.V. = Floating Vegetation

N

Balm Lake

601

E.V.
S.V.

4'

18'

27'

33'
Max

32

Source: Division of Fish and Wildlife, Department of Natural Resources.

CLEARWATER LAKE
Beltrami County

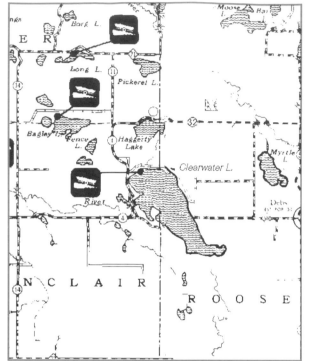

Location: Township 149
Range 35, 36
Watershed: Clearwater
Surface Water Area: 1008 acres
Shorelength: 8.2 miles
Secchi disk (water clarity): 7.0 ft.
Water color: Green
Cause of water color: Algae

Maximum depth: 65 ft.
Median depth: NA
Accessibility: State-owned access on northwest corner
Boat Ramp: Concrete
Accommodations: NA

Shoreland zoning classification: Recreational Development
Dominant forest/soil type: NA
Management class: Walleye-Centrarchid
Ecological type: Centrarchid-Walleye

FISH STOCKING DATA

year	species	size	# released
91	Walleye	Fingerling	14,410
94	Walleye	Fingerling	18,562
97	Walleye	Fingerling	7,410

LENGTH OF SELECTED SPECIES SAMPLED FROM ALL GEAR

Number of fish caught for the following length categories (inches):

species	0-5	6-8	9-11	12-14	15-19	20-24	25-29	>30	Total
Black Bullhead	-	-	1	-	-	-	-	-	1
Black Crappie	-	1	5	1	-	-	-	-	7
Bluegill	12	58	1	-	-	-	-	-	71
Brown Bullhead	-	-	4	2	-	-	-	-	6
Largemouth Bass	-	1	1	-	2	-	-	-	4
Northern Pike	-	-	-	2	35	60	17	5	119
Pumpkin. Sunfish	5	2	-	-	-	-	-	-	7
Rock Bass	27	114	7	-	-	-	-	-	148
Tullibee (Cisco)	-	52	48	27	3	-	-	-	130
Walleye	-	18	3	39	32	18	3	-	113
Yellow Perch	220	285	19	-	-	-	-	-	524

NET CATCH DATA

survey date: 7/24/95

	Gill Nets		Trap Nets	
species	# per net	avg fish wt. (lbs.)	# per set	avg fish wt. (lbs.)
Black Crappie	0.4	0.78	0.2	0.43
Bluegill	2.2	0.41	3.8	0.32
Common Shiner	-	-	1.1	trace
Largemouth Bass	0.2	3.75	0.2	0.36
Northern Pike	9.5	2.49	0.4	2.19
Pumpkin. Sunfish	-	-	0.6	0.12
Rock Bass	3.7	0.42	10.0	0.26
Shorthead Redhorse	1.3	1.91	0.4	1.33
Tullibee (Cisco)	14.4	0.43	-	-
Walleye	8.7	1.54	0.8	0.40
White Sucker	13.3	1.48	0.9	1.36
Yellow Perch	114.5	0.12	47.8	0.13

DNR COMMENTS: Walleye population above lake-class average; most sampled fish were 12 to 17 inches; average weight 1.5 lb., which is slightly below average; fish to 29 inches present. Northern Pike numbers up and near lake-class average; average size 22 inches and 2.5 lb.; fish to 32 inches sampled. Largemouth Bass to 18.7 inches sampled; large numbers of fingerlings sampled during shoreline seining. Black Crappie numbers below average; fish over 12 inches captured. Bluegills relatively scarce; fish to 8.6 inches sampled. Pumpkinseed scarce. Yellow Perch abundance high enough to be a nuisance; average size 6.6 inches; parasite infestation prevalent. Rock Bass abundant; average weight .25 lb. Brown Bullheads scarce, but fish to 13 inches sampled. Only one Black Bullhead found.

FISHING INFORMATION: This lake seems to have just about everything: lots of good-size gamefish and plenty of forage fish to keep them hefty. This makes Clearwater a good producer year round. Tim Falk of Bluewater Bait and Sports in Bemidji says, "There are really big fish in there. Walleyes over 10 pounds are fairly common." Walleyes are stocked as fingerlings by the DNR and survive well. For Walleye, fish the nice points along the south shore, as well as the very steep offshore drops along the north side. The fish like to feed in these spots in spring, and Falk says many anglers simply use nightcrawlers to catch them. Bluegills and Black Crappies are relatively scarce in Clearwater, but the ones you do catch are likely to be memorable. One of the best spots to look for them is the weedy area on the west side next to the public access. This is also a good place to fish for Largemouth Bass which are found in decent numbers. You will want to fish the emergent weeds, too, around the Clearwater River on the lake's south end. Some of the best fishing the lake offers, though, is for Northern Pike, which get fairly nice. The Pike will be around the weeds, searching for food. Here, that means Yellow Perch – in numbers almost beyond count. Earl Taber of Taber's Bait in Bemidji says Northern Pike-fishing is most popular on Clearwater in the fall. He says he's seen 10-, 15-, even 20-pounders taken then by anglers.

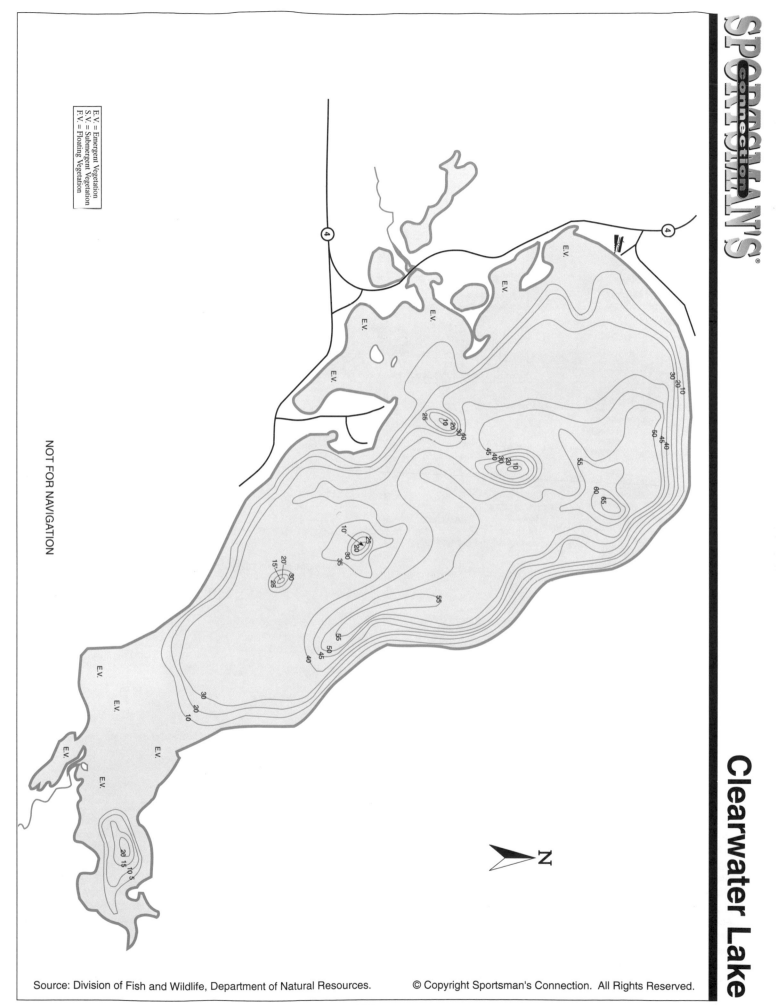

E.V. = Emergent Vegetation
S.V. = Submergent Vegetation
F.V. = Floating Vegetation

NOT FOR NAVIGATION

N

BAGLEY LAKE   LONG LAKE

Clearwater County

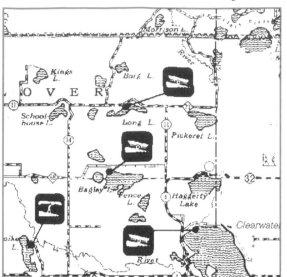

Location: Township 149, 150 Range 36
Watershed: Clearwater
Surface Water Area: 94 acres
Shorelength: NA
Secchi disk (water clarity): 15.0 ft.
Water color: Green
Cause of water color: Suspended solids and phytoplankton
Maximum depth: 39 ft.
Median depth: NA
Accessibility: County-owned access on northwest corner
Boat Ramp: Gravel
Accommodations: NA
Shoreland zoning classif.: Nat. Envir.
Dominant forest/soil type: NA
Management class: Warm-water gamefish
Ecological type: Centrarchid

Location: Township 150 Range 36
Watershed: Clearwater
Surface Water Area: 48 acres
Shorelength: NA
Secchi disk (water clarity): NA
Water color: NA
Cause of water color: NA
Maximum depth: 36 ft.
Median depth: NA
Accessibility: Public access on north shore, off #11
Boat Ramp: NA
Accommodations: NA
Shoreland zoning classif.: Nat. Envir.
Dominant forest/soil type: NA
Management class: NA
Ecological type: NA

DNR COMMENTS:
Walleye, Black Crappie, and Largemouth Bass populations reduced by partial winterkill during 1991-92; numbers well below previous levels. Yellow Perch abundance about double the area average; many fish 10 inches or larger sampled; some Yellow Grub infestation noted. Northern Pike abundant; average size just under 20 inches and about 2 lb. Pumpkinseed numbers good; average size about 6 inches and .2 lb.

FISH STOCKING DATA

year	species	size	# released
91	Walleye	Fry	1,000,000
92	Walleye	Fingerling	950
93	Walleye	Fingerling	1,000

NET CATCH DATA

survey date: 07/06/93

	Gill Nets		Trap Nets	
species	# per net	avg fish wt. (lbs)	# per set	avg fish wt. (lbs)
Black Crappie	1.0	1.08	0.1	1.12
Brown Bullhead	6.3	0.83	6.6	0.79
Largemouth Bass	-	-	0.1	0.46
Northern Pike	10.3	1.76	1.9	1.18
Pumpkin. Sunfish	4.0	0.11	6.2	0.18
Walleye	1.0	1.85	-	-
White Sucker	2.7	2.50	0.1	3.31
Yellow Perch	32.0	0.54	0.9	0.48

LENGTH OF SELECTED SPECIES SAMPLED FROM ALL GEAR

Number of fish caught for the following length categories (inches):

species	0-5	6-8	9-11	12-14	15-19	20-24	25-29	>30	Total
Black Crappie	-	-	-	4	-	-	-	-	4
Brown Bullhead	-	-	18	59	1	-	-	-	78
Largemouth Bass	-	-	1	-	-	-	-	-	1
Pumpkin. Sunfish	14	54	-	-	-	-	-	-	68
Walleye	-	-	-	-	3	-	-	-	3
Yellow Perch	1	10	42	28	-	-	-	-	81

FISH STOCKING DATA: NOT AVAILABLE

NET CATCH DATA: NOT AVAILABLE

LENGTH OF SELECTED SPECIES SAMPLED FROM SURVEY

Not Available.

DNR COMMENTS:

NOT AVAILABLE

FISHING INFORMATION: These two small lakes about 12 miles directly north of Leonard on Highway 14 offer anglers good opportunities for a variety of fish, including Walleyes, panfish, Largemouth Bass, and Northern Pike. **Bagley Lake** is quite clear and has good weedbeds. Its fish population was hard-hit by winterkill in 1991-92, but, with mild winters of late, has largely recovered. There is, accordingly, a decent population of Northerns and lots of Yellow Perch for the Pike to feed on. The Perch and Largemouth Bass, as well as a fair number of Pumpkinseeds, are in the weedbeds and bulrushes around the lake and are caught from ice-out right through the fall. The lake's southwest corner is best for bassing; the broad weedbed there offers plenty of cover and food as well as good spawning habitat. You can do well with spinnerbaits or a pig-and-jig combination. The Northerns are active there, too, as well as around all the other weedbeds, from spring on. They can be trolled for with a long line and live bait or even bobber-fished. Though Walleyes are stocked as fingerlings by the DNR, their population is still fairly small. A few good-size ones, though, are available to the patient angler. **Long Lake** is regarded as a "really good Bass lake," according to Steve Crandall of Crandall's Baits in Bagley. One look at the map and you'll see why: nearly the entire east end of the lake is shallow and loaded with the weeds, rushes, and lilypads favored by Largemouths. The weedbeds are also good Crappie producers, says Crandall. Most of the Walleyes caught in Long are taken by anglers who are after Northerns.

Bagley & Long Lakes

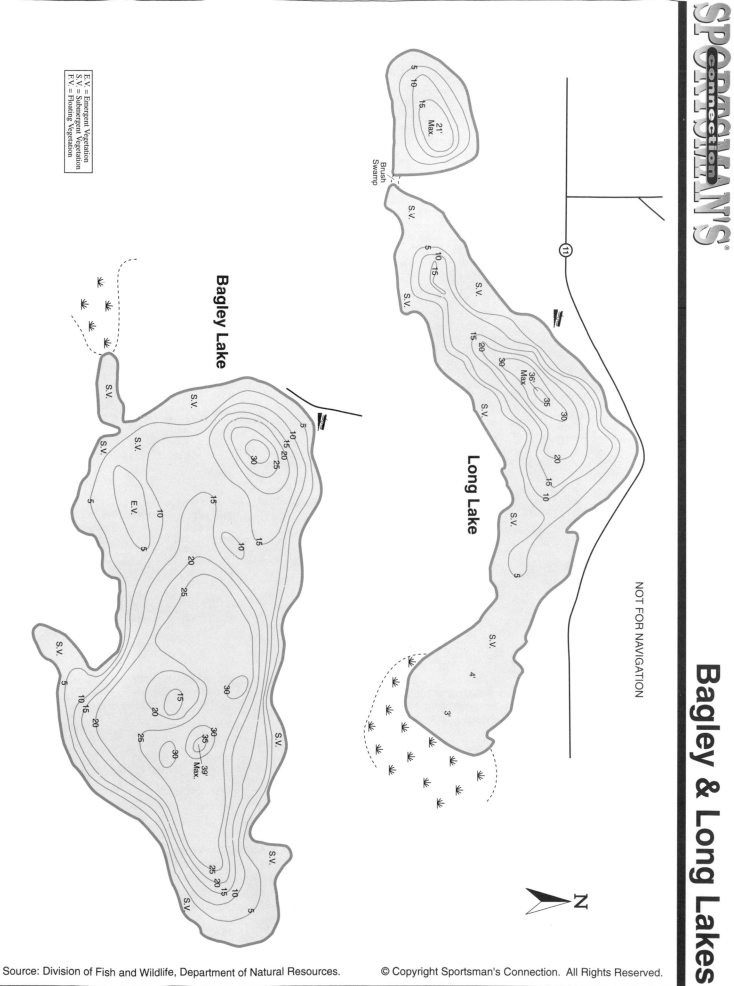

E.V. = Emergent Vegetation
S.V. = Submergent Vegetation
F.V. = Floating Vegetation

Bagley Lake

Long Lake

NOT FOR NAVIGATION

N

Brush Swamp

21' Max.

36' Max.

39' Max.

Source: Division of Fish and Wildlife, Department of Natural Resources.

FALK LAKE

Clearwater County

JOHNSON LAKE

Location: Township 149 Range 36
Watershed: Clearwater
Surface Water Area: 65 acres
Shorelength: NA
Secchi disk (water clarity): 15.0 ft.
Water color: Reddish-brown
Cause of water color: Bog stain
Maximum depth: 33 ft.
Median depth: NA
Accessibility: County-owned access on northeast corner
Boat Ramp: Earth
Accommodations: NA
Shoreland zoning classif.: Nat. Envir.
Dominant forest/soil type: NA
Management class: Walleye-Centrarchid
Ecological type: Centrarchid

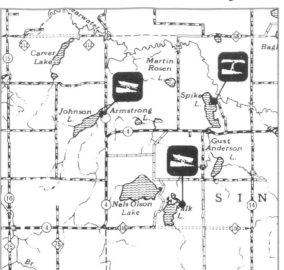

Location: Township 149 Range 37
Watershed: Clearwater
Surface Water Area: 56 acres
Shorelength: NA
Secchi disk (water clarity): 8.0 ft.
Water color: Brown
Cause of water color: Bog stain and suspended solids
Maximum depth: 70 ft.
Median depth: NA
Accessibility: County-owned access on east shore
Boat Ramp: Earth
Accommodations: NA
Shoreland zoning classif.: Nat. Envir.
Dominant forest/soil type: NA
Management class: Centrarchid
Ecological type: Centrarchid

DNR COMMENTS:
Northern Pike numbers high but down from 1986 level; fish generally small. Largemouth Bass quite numerous. Walleye numbers above third-quartile values; most fish from 1989 year class, which either spawned naturally or was illegally stocked; stocking of large fingerlings has generally produced fair Walleye populations. Yellow Perch population down sharply. Bullheads, very abundant in 1980, not sampled.

FISH STOCKING DATA

year	species	size	# released
90	Walleye	Fingerling	2,625
93	Walleye	Fingerling	500

NET CATCH DATA

survey date: 06/20/91

	Gill Nets		Trap Nets	
species	# per net	avg fish wt. (lbs)	# per set	avg fish wt. (lbs)
Yellow Perch	9.5	0.14	4.3	0.14
White Sucker	1.0	2.75	-	-
Walleye	4.0	1.45	-	-
Northern Pike	8.5	2.06	-	-
Largemouth Bass	1.0	1.55	-	-
Hybrid Sunfish	2.5	0.18	8.3	0.21
Pumpkin. Sunfish	-	-	5.0	0.09

LENGTH OF SELECTED SPECIES SAMPLED FROM ALL GEAR
Number of fish caught for the following length categories (inches):

species	0-5	6-8	9-11	12-14	15-19	20-24	25-29	>30	Total
Yellow Perch	-	17	2	-	-	-	-	-	19
Walleye	-	-	-	4	2	2	-	-	8
Northern Pike	-	-	-	-	6	9	4	-	19
Largemouth Bass	-	-	-	2	-	-	-	-	2
Hybrid Sunfish	2	3	-	-	-	-	-	-	5

FISH STOCKING DATA

year	species	size	# released
90	Walleye	Fingerling	660
92	Black Crappie	Adult	15
92	Bluegill	Adult	203
92	Walleye	Fry	40,000
96	Walleye	Fry	50,000
96	Walleye	Fingerling	650

NET CATCH DATA

survey date: 07/30/91

	Gill Nets		Trap Nets	
species	# per net	avg fish wt. (lbs)	# per set	avg fish wt. (lbs)
Yellow Perch	11.5	0.13	20.3	0.10
White Sucker	1.0	0.65	-	-
Walleye	6.5	0.42	-	-
Rock Bass	0.5	0.60	-	-
Pumpkin. Sunfish	1.0	0.05	9.3	0.01
Northern Pike	0.5	2.40	-	-
Black Bullhead	102.0	0.09	1.3	0.08
Golden Shiner	-	-	0.3	0.10
Bluegill	-	-	2.7	0.08

LENGTH OF SELECTED SPECIES SAMPLED FROM ALL GEAR
Number of fish caught for the following length categories (inches):

species	0-5	6-8	9-11	12-14	15-19	20-24	25-29	>30	Total
Yellow Perch	-	21	-	-	-	-	-	-	22
Walleye	-	-	1	12	-	-	-	-	13
Rock Bass	-	-	1	-	-	-	-	-	1
Pumpkin. Sunfish	2	-	-	-	-	-	-	-	2
Northern Pike	-	-	-	-	-	1	-	-	1
Black Bullhead	7	79	-	-	-	-	-	-	86

DNR COMMENTS:
Gillnet catches of Walleye and Black Bullhead considerably above lake-class median. Northern Pike catch well below median; water levels may be affecting Pike recruitment. Size distribution of Yellow Perch suggests only two or three year classes present.

FISHING INFORMATION: Located roughly five miles northeast of Clearwater, these lakes offer a decent fishing experience. They are both small lakes but are fairly deep and stocked with Walleyes. **Falk Lake** holds bunches of Northern Pike averaging 2 to 3 pounds, along with a fair number running much bigger. It also has nice Largemouth Bass, Yellow Perch, and some Walleyes. The water is somewhat stained by bog runoff, but is still quite transparent. Several points on both the east and west sides and some steep breaks at the northeast end offer good fish-holding structure. The Walleye hotspot early in the season is the sunken island near the east shore, where the bottom rises quickly from 20 feet to about 5 feet. That's the sort of habitat Walleyes love in the spring and the kind they return to on summer mornings and nights. Goggle eyes will head for the deep holes during bright days, however, and your best bet then is live bait under a bobber; look for the right depth. **Johnson Lake** holds Northern Pike, Yellow Perch, panfish, and a few Walleyes. The lake is fairly deep and not heavily weeded, but there is some interesting structure, including a sunken island at mid lake. Try there for Walleyes. Good places to look for Northerns are in the weedbeds at the lake's east and west ends, and around the inlet (west) and outlet (east). Both lakes have public access areas with earth ramps. Neither is easy to use.

Falk & Johnson Lakes

NOT FOR NAVIGATION

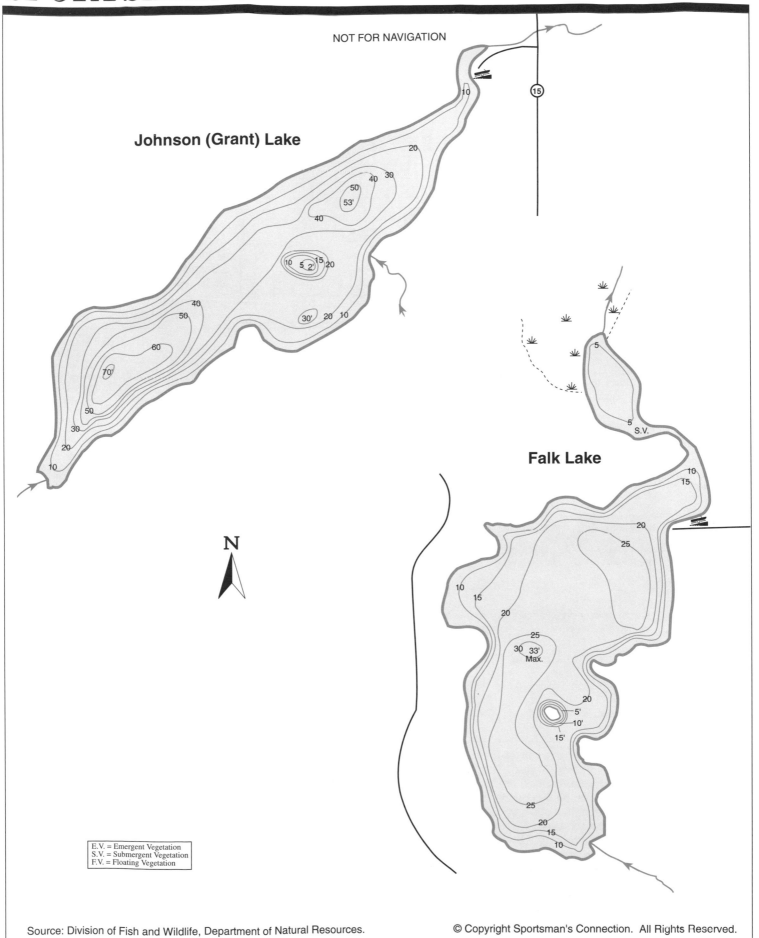

Johnson (Grant) Lake

Falk Lake

15

10
20
40 30
50
53'
40
10 5 2' 15 20
40
50
30' 20 10
60
70'
50
30
20
10

5
5
S.V.

10
15
20
25
10
15
20
25
30 33'
Max.
20
5'
10'
15'
25
20
15
10

N

E.V. = Emergent Vegetation
S.V. = Submergent Vegetation
F.V. = Floating Vegetation

Source: Division of Fish and Wildlife, Department of Natural Resources.

DEEP LAKE

Clearwater County

PETERSON LAKE

Location: Township 149 Range 37
Watershed: Clearwater
Surface Water Area: 47 acres
Shorelength: NA
Secchi disk (water clarity): 14.0 ft.
Water color: Greenish tint
Cause of water color: Algae
Maximum depth: 76 ft.
Median depth: NA
Accessibility: County-owned public access on southeast corner in park
Boat Ramp: Earth
Accommodations: Park
Shoreland zoning classif.: Nat. Envir.
Dominant forest/soil type: NA
Management class: Centrarchid
Ecological type: Centrarchid

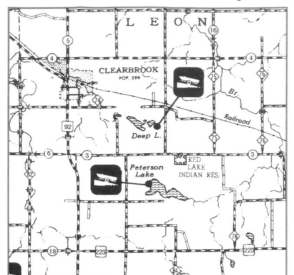

Location: Township 148 Range 37
Watershed: Clearwater
Surface Water Area: 77 acres
Shorelength: NA
Secchi disk (water clarity): 7.8 ft.
Water color: Greenish-brown
Cause of water color: Suspended algae, bog stain
Maximum depth: 74 ft.
Median depth: NA
Accessibility: County-owned access on northwest corner
Boat Ramp: Earth
Accommodations: NA
Shoreland zoning classif.: Nat. Envir.
Dominant forest/soil type: NA
Management class: Centrarchid
Ecological type: Centrarchid

DNR COMMENTS:
Brown and Rainbow Trout stocked in 1978 and 1991, respectively; no Trout found during follow-up sampling. Northern Pike abundance below lake-class average; modal length about 20 inches; fish to 26 inches sampled; Neascus infestation noted. Largemouth Bass common but small; fish to 12 inches sampled. Bluegill numbers near average; average length only 5.2 inches; fish to 7.5 inches sampled. Pumpkinseed and hybrid Sunfish numbers good. Yellow Perch scarce and small. Yellow Bullhead numbers low; average weight under 1/2 lb.

FISH STOCKING DATA

No record of DNR stocking since 1978. Rainbow Trout stocked by private sports group in 1991; numbers and size unknown.

survey date: 8/5/96

NET CATCH DATA

	Gill Nets		Trap Nets	
species	# per net	avg fish wt. (lbs)	# per set	avg fish wt. (lbs)
Bluegill	-	-	18.4	0.10
Hybrid Sunfish	-	-	5.4	0.16
Largemouth Bass	0.5	0.75	2.8	0.21
Northern Pike	1.5	2.08	-	-
Pumpkin. Sunfish	-	-	0.1	0.24
Tullibee (Cisco)	1.0	0.22	-	-
White Sucker	-	-	0.1	0.48
Yellow Bullhead	0.8	0.50	2.8	0.37
Yellow Perch	0.5	0.13	0.3	0.12

LENGTH OF SELECTED SPECIES SAMPLED FROM ALL GEAR
Number of fish caught for the following length categories (inches):

species	0-5	6-8	9-11	12-14	15-19	20-24	25-29	>30	Total
Bluegill	126	40	-	-	-	-	-	-	166
Hybrid Sunfish	24	25	-	-	-	-	-	-	49
Largemouth Bass	6	18	2	1	-	-	-	-	27
Northern Pike	-	-	-	-	3	2	1	-	6
Pumpkin. Sunfish	-	1	-	-	-	-	-	-	1
Tullibee (Cisco)	-	2	2	-	-	-	-	-	4
Yellow Bullhead	-	14	14	-	-	-	-	-	28
Yellow Perch	-	5	-	-	-	-	-	-	5

FISH STOCKING DATA

year	species	size	# released
96	Bluegill	Adult	181

survey date: 07/20/88

NET CATCH DATA

	Gill Nets		Trap Nets	
species	# per net	avg fish wt. (lbs)	# per set	avg fish wt. (lbs)
Yellow Perch	13.0	0.40	0.8	0.13
White Sucker	0.5	2.50	-	-
Pumpkin. Sunfish	0.5	0.50	4.0	0.26
Northern Pike	9.0	1.44	0.8	1.00
Brown Bullhead	0.5	0.40	1.0	0.45
Black Bullhead	44.0	0.15	10.0	0.16
Hybrid Sunfish	-	-	0.3	0.30
Bluegill	-	-	6.0	0.35

LENGTH OF SELECTED SPECIES SAMPLED FROM ALL GEAR
Number of fish caught for the following length categories (inches):

species	0-5	6-8	9-11	12-14	15-19	20-24	25-29	>30	Total
Yellow Perch	-	6	16	4	-	-	-	-	26
Pumpkin. Sunfish	-	1	-	-	-	-	-	-	1
Northern Pike	-	-	-	-	13	4	1	-	18
Brown Bullhead	-	-	1	-	-	-	-	-	1
Black Bullhead	1	83	-	-	-	-	-	-	84

DNR COMMENTS:
Gillnet catches of Northern Pike were triple the state median and local mean values; most fish were in the 16- to 19-inch range. Yellow Perch catches half the local mean; three or four age classes present. Black Bullhead trapnet catches quadruple the state median; most fish were 6-7 inches. Trapnet catches of Bluegill were half local mean and state median; good average size; at least four age classes represented. No YOY Centrarchids and only four YOY Yellow Perch captured in 1/4-inch trapnets; low numbers of YOY Centrarchids observed near shore.

FISHING INFORMATION: These two lakes immediately southeast of Clearbook are known for Northern Pike and panfish. **Deep Lake** is just that, with holes of 40, 50, and 70 feet. The DNR once stocked the lake experimentally with Ciscoes and Brown Trout, but that didn't work well. Neither did a private Rainbow stocking in 1991. Now, according to Steve Crandall of Crandall's Bait in Bagley, Deep has some very big Northerns. "They can be 10 pounds," he notes. There are also a good number of panfish. The lake doesn't have an extensive weedline because of its depth, but you can do fairly well fishing the east and west shores. Northerns will be cruising the weedbeds looking for Yellow Perch and the remaining Ciscoes, and you can troll the outer weed edges effectively. **Peterson** is primarily a Northern Pike lake, and quite a few of the alligators are good-size. The lake has a good forage base of White Suckers and Yellow Perch to keep them that way. You'll also encounter lots of of Black Bullheads and a fair number of Sunfish in this lake. The water is moderately clear, and there is a fairly good weedline, along with several deep holes. The bulrushes in the lake's east end and the small bay in the southwest corner hold good numbers of forage fish. That's where you'll want to look for Northerns most of the year, though the Pike will go deeper on bright summer days. Bigger Northerns like water temperatures of about 50 degrees, so they may be as deep as 30 feet during dog days. Continue, though, to fish the outer edges of the weeds in the mornings and evenings. These areas still draw hungry fish during low-light conditions. Deep Lake has an earth ramp that Crandall tells us is easy to use. Peterson has a dirt ramp in its northwest corner.

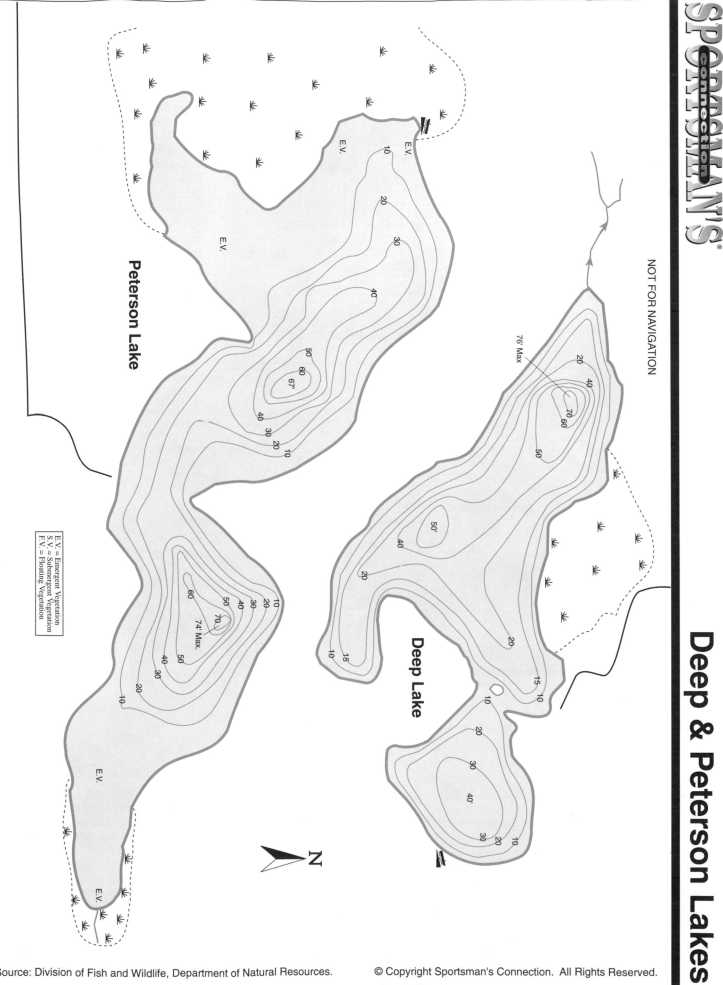

Peterson Lake

Deep Lake

NOT FOR NAVIGATION

E.V. = Emergent Vegetation
S.V. = Submergent Vegetation
F.V. = Floating Vegetation

N

76' Max

74' Max.

67'

Source: Division of Fish and Wildlife, Department of Natural Resources.

LONE LAKE

LOMOND LAKE

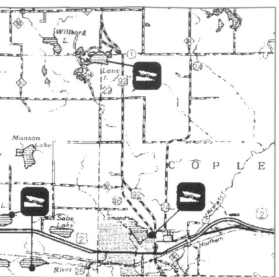

Location: Township 147, 148 Range 37, 38
Watershed: Clearwater
Surface Water Area: 69 acres
Shorelength: NA
Secchi disk (water clarity): 19.0 ft.
Water color: Greenish tint
Cause of water color: Slight algae bloom
Maximum depth: 70 ft.
Median depth: NA
Accessibility: Public access on northwest corner
Boat Ramp: Earth
Accommodations: NA
Shoreland zoning classif.: Nat. Envir.
Dominant forest/soil type: NA
Management class: Walleye-Centrarchid
Ecological type: Centrarchid

Location: Township 147 Range 37
Watershed: Clearwater
Surface Water Area: 91 acres
Shorelength: NA
Secchi disk (water clarity): 6.7 ft.
Water color: Brown
Cause of water color: Bog stain and suspended solids
Maximum depth: 42 ft.
Median depth: NA
Accessibility: Public access in city park on southeast shore
Boat Ramp: Concrete
Accommodations: Park
Shoreland zoning classif.: Gen. Dev.
Dominant forest/soil type: NA
Management class: Centrarchid
Ecological type: Centrarchid

DNR COMMENTS:

Despite regular stocking; Walleye abundance remains low; growth good; size better than average. Northern Pike abundant, but numbers down from previous levels; mean weight low at 1.4 lb.; Neascus infestation noted on about 25 percent of sample. Largemouth Bass trapnet sample nearly twice normal; most fish from 1994 year class; mean length 7.8 inches; fish to 14.1 inches captured. Black Crappies scarce; average length 8.2 inches; fish to 12 inches captured. Bluegill numbers up; mean length 7.4 inches. Yellow Perch abundance slightly above normal.

FISH STOCKING DATA

year	species	size	# released
91	Walleye	Fingerling	1,695
93	Walleye	Fingerling	1,488
95	Walleye	Fingerling	480
97	Walleye	Fingerling	950

survey date: 8/5/96

NET CATCH DATA

	Gill Nets		Trap Nets	
species	# per net	avg fish wt. (lbs)	# per set	avg fish wt. (lbs)
Black Crappie	-	-	0.9	0.40
Bluegill	5.0	0.29	43.5	0.32
Largemouth Bass	0.7	1.09	2.5	0.27
Northern Pike	8.3	1.35	1.4	0.67
Walleye	0.7	2.09	0.1	0.57
Yellow Perch	26.0	0.19	0.8	0.11

LENGTH OF SELECTED SPECIES SAMPLED FROM ALL GEAR
Number of fish caught for the following length categories (inches):

species	0-5	6-8	9-11	12-14	15-19	20-24	25-29	>30	Total
Black Crappie	2	1	3	1	-	-	-	-	7
Bluegill	18	340	5	-	-	-	-	-	363
Largemouth Bass	4	12	5	1	-	-	-	-	22
Northern Pike	-	-	2	10	19	4	1	-	36
Walleye	-	-	-	1	2	-	-	-	3
Yellow Perch	11	60	12	1	-	-	-	-	84

FISH STOCKING DATA

year	species	size	# released
91	Walleye	Fingerling	1,318
93	Walleye	Fingerling	1,312
95	Walleye	Fingerling	612
97	Walleye	Fingerling	950

survey date: 06/21/93

NET CATCH DATA

	Gill Nets		Trap Nets	
species	# per net	avg fish wt. (lbs)	# per set	avg fish wt. (lbs)
Black Crappie	-	-	0.3	0.52
Bluegill	1.5	0.09	257.9	0.25
Green Sunfish	-	-	0.1	0.03
Hybrid Sunfish	-	-	1.0	0.44
Largemouth Bass	0.3	2.17	0.1	3.75
Northern Pike	5.5	3.60	0.4	1.20
Pumpkin. Sunfish	-	-	0.3	0.17
Rock Bass	-	-	0.8	0.23
Walleye	1.0	3.78	0.1	3.09
Yellow Perch	57.0	0.08	-	-

LENGTH OF SELECTED SPECIES SAMPLED FROM ALL GEAR
Number of fish caught for the following length categories (inches):

species	0-5	6-8	9-11	12-14	15-19	20-24	25-29	>30	Total
Black Crappie	-	-	2	-	-	-	-	-	2
Bluegill	22	181	18	-	-	-	-	-	221
Brown Bullhead	-	-	2	-	-	-	-	-	2
Green Sunfish	1	-	-	-	-	-	-	-	1
Hybrid Sunfish	-	6	2	-	-	-	-	-	8
Largemouth Bass	-	-	-	2	-	-	-	-	2
Northern Pike	-	-	-	1	4	15	2	2	24
Pumpkin. Sunfish	-	2	-	-	-	-	-	-	2
Rock Bass	4	-	2	-	-	-	-	-	6
Walleye	-	-	-	-	-	4	1	-	5
Yellow Bullhead	-	1	4	-	-	-	-	-	5
Yellow Perch	-	107	-	-	-	-	-	-	107

DNR COMMENTS:

Walleye fingerling stocking has apparently been ineffective, as no Walleye from 1989 or 1991 stockings captured; those Walleye sampled were from the 1983 and 1987 stocks. Northern Pike numbers near lake-class median; median weight above the third quartile, but two larger fish skewed the median severely from 2.5 to 3.6 lb./net. Largemouth Bass numbers below expected range. Bluegill very abundant at four times third-quartile values; mean length 6.7 inches.

FISHING INFORMATION: If you're on U.S. Highway 2 near Bagley, you have a couple of nice lakes to fish. Lomond is right in town, and Lone Lake just a short distance north. Steve Crandall of Crandall's Bait in Bagley says he's enthusiastic about **Lomond Lake**. "It's good fishing all around," he notes, adding that there's good access and even camping at the city park beside the lake. Lomond has good populations of Northern Pike, Walleyes, panfish, and some nice Largemouth Bass, as well. There are good weedbeds and standing vegetation to provide excellent habitat for Bass and Crappies. The lake is somewhat bog-stained but relatively transparent. The northeast corner is one of the better places to find Bass; the east shore is also good where you see bulrushes. Fish for Northerns along the outer edges of the weedbeds. The northwest side of the lake has good flats to troll with lip-hooked live bait. The steeper breaks along the southeast side can produce some nice Walleyes, also. **Lone Lake** is also a good Largemouth Bass fishery. Although there's a maximum depth of 70 feet, Lone has plenty of weedbeds to hold Bass and Crappies. The water is quite clear, so you'll want to make your presentations carefully to avoid spooking the fish. The lake's west end is shallow and full of weeds, and that should give you a good idea where to start. Walleyes are stocked by the DNR on a regular basis and survive fairly well. Thus there are plenty of 2- to 3-pounders to be had. Lone Lake has an earth ramp on its north side. Lomond has a concrete ramp and plenty of parking in Bagley Park.

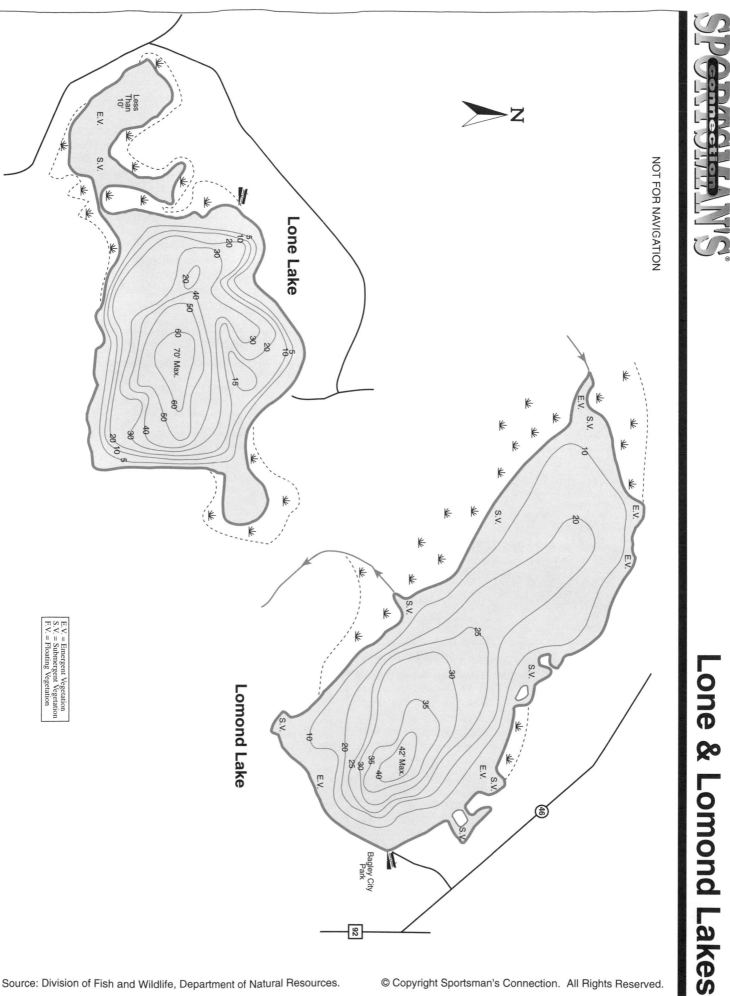

N

Lone Lake

Less Than 10'

E.V.

S.V.

5
10
20
30
20
40
50
60
70' Max.
30
20
10
5
15
60
50
40
30
20 10 5

Lomond Lake

E.V.
S.V.
S.V.
10
20
S.V.
E.V.
E.V.
S.V.
25
30
35
42' Max.
10
20
25
30
35
40
E.V.
S.V.
E.V.
S.V.

46

92

Bagley City Park

E.V. = Emergent Vegetation
S.V. = Submergent Vegetation
F.V. = Floating Vegetation

Lone & Lomond Lakes

Source: Division of Fish and Wildlife, Department of Natural Resources.

Location: Township 147   Range 38
Watershed: Clearwater

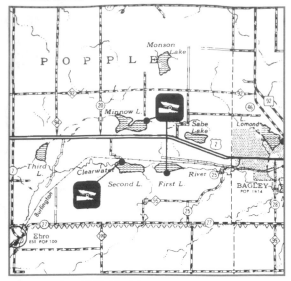

	FIRST LAKE	SECOND LAKE	MINNOW LAKE
		Clearwater County	

	FIRST LAKE	SECOND LAKE	MINNOW LAKE
Surface Water Area:	58 acres	69 acres	102 acres
Shorelength:	NA	NA	NA
Secchi disk (water clarity):	9.0 ft.	14.0 ft.	16.0 ft.
Water color:	Brown-green	Brown	Green
Cause of water color:	Algae, bog stain	Algae, bog stain	Algae
Maximum depth:	36 ft.	47 ft.	24 ft.
Median depth:	NA	NA	NA
Accessibility:	County-owned access on south shore	Public access on northwest shore	State-owned access on northeast corner
Boat Ramp:	Earth	Earth	Earth
Accommodations:	NA	NA	NA
Shoreland zoning classif.:	Natural Environment	Natural Environment	Natural Environment
Dominant forest/soil type:	NA	NA	NA
Management class:	Warm-water Gamefish	Warm-water Gamefish	Walleye-Centrarchid
Ecological type:	Roughfish-Gamefish	Roughfish-Gamefish	Centrarchid

---

DNR COMMENTS:
Fish population dominated by Bullheads and Yellow Perch. Gillnet indices for Northern Pike, White Sucker, and Rock Bass well above state and local medians. Walleye, Bluegill and Black Crappie present in low numbers. Yellow Perch net catch near local mean. Natural reproduction of species other than Bullhead seems poor, though Bullhead dominance may have disturbed tests.

First Lake

FISH STOCKING DATA: NO RECORD OF STOCKING

NET CATCH DATA

survey date: 06/11/87

	Gill Nets		Trap Nets	
species	# per net	avg fish wt. (lbs)	# per set	avg fish wt. (lbs)
Yellow Perch	20.5	0.12	109.5	0.01
White Sucker	14.5	1.16	2.3	1.36
Walleye	0.5	2.75	-	-
Rock Bass	7.0	0.27	0.5	0.25
Northern Pike	9.0	2.42	0.8	1.83
Black Bullhead	196.0	0.08	73.3	0.14
Hybrid Sunfish	-	-	0.3	0.25
Bluegill	-	-	0.5	0.25
Black Crappie	-	-	0.3	0.75

LENGTH OF SELECTED SPECIES SAMPLED FROM ALL GEAR
Number of fish caught for the following length categories (inches):

species	0-5	6-8	9-11	12-14	15-19	20-24	25-29	>30	Total
Yellow Perch	-	38	3	-	-	-	-	-	41
Walleye	-	-	-	-	-	1	-	-	1
Rock Bass	1	13	-	-	-	-	-	-	14
Northern Pike	-	-	-	-	-	16	1	1	18
Black Bullhead	17	59	1	-	-	-	-	-	77

Second Lake

FISH STOCKING DATA: NO RECORD OF STOCKING

NET CATCH DATA

survey date: 07/06/76

	Gill Nets		Trap Nets	
species	# per net	avg fish wt. (lbs)	# per set	avg fish wt. (lbs)
Yellow Perch	33.5	0.15	27.3	0.14
White Sucker	10.3	1.18	1.3	1.24
Walleye	1.3	2.32	-	-
Northern Pike	2.8	2.06	0.3	trace
Brown Bullhead	122.8	0.09	57.3	0.24
Black Crappie	0.5	0.85	0.8	0.76
Rock Bass	-	-	0.7	0.20
Largemouth Bass	-	-	0.2	1.00
Green Sunfish	-	-	0.2	1.00

LENGTH OF SELECTED SPECIES SAMPLED FROM ALL GEAR
Number of fish caught for the following length categories (inches):

species	0-5	6-8	9-11	12-14	15-19	20-24	25-29	>30	Total
Black Crappie	-	-	1	6	-	-	-	-	7
Brown Bullhead	10	208	47	14	-	-	-	-	279
Green Sunfish	1	-	-	-	-	-	-	-	1
Largemouth Bass	-	1	-	-	-	-	-	-	1
Northern Pike	-	-	-	-	2	9	11	-	22
Rock Bass	1	2	1	-	-	-	-	-	4

DNR COMMENTS:
Bullheads, White Suckers, and Yellow Perch dominate the fishery and are below average in size. Northern Pike and Black Crappies present in moderate numbers. Walleye numbers low.

FISHING INFORMATION: Located a few miles west of Bagley on U.S. Highway 2, these three smaller lakes provide good fishing for local anglers most of the year. Steve Crandall of Crandall's Bait Shop in Bagley says **First Lake** is fairly clear, though it has some bog stain. The dominant species is Black Bullhead, but there are decent populations of Northern Pike and Rock Bass, along with some Walleyes. Crandall says the Northerns are big at an average of 3 pounds. Fair numbers are even larger – between 5 and 10 pounds. First is connected to **Second Lake** by the Clearwater River, and the Northerns move easily from one lake to the other. So Second lake has Northerns, as well as decent numbers of Rock Bass and a few Walleyes. Your best bet for taking Pike is to troll the river channel, which runs fairly deep, with spoons and vibrating crankbaits. There are a lot of White Suckers in both lakes. Crandall warns that the earth ramp on Second Lake is crummy, and you'd better have 4-wheel drive if you're going to use it. First Lake has an earth ramp also, but it's easier to use. **Minnow Lake** is heavily weeded and tough to fish. Significant parts of it are also subject to winterkill. The lake has been stocked regularly with Walleye fry, however, and it does provide some fishing for them as well as for Bluegills and Yellow Perch. Minnow sports a sand ramp at the public access on its northeast side.

Minnow Lake

FISH STOCKING DATA

year	species	size	# released
90	Walleye	Fry	80,000
92	Walleye	Adult	371
94	Walleye	Fry	100,000
95	Walleye	Fry	100,000
96	Walleye	Fry	100,000
96	Bluegill	Adult	185
96	Largemouth Bass	Adult	18
97	Walleye	Fry	100,000

NET CATCH DATA

survey date: 06/28/90

	Gill Nets		Trap Nets	
species	# per net	avg fish wt. (lbs)	# per set	avg fish wt. (lbs)
Yellow Perch	33.0	0.15	40.0	0.12
White Sucker	1.0	2.00	-	-
Golden Shiner	9.0	0.07	19.0	0.07
Bluegill	-	-	56.5	0.27

LENGTH OF SELECTED SPECIES SAMPLED FROM ALL GEAR
Number of fish caught for the following length categories (inches):

species	0-5	6-8	9-11	12-14	15-19	20-24	25-29	>30	Total
Black Bullhead	39	71	1	-	-	-	-	-	111
Bluegill	12	67	31	-	-	-	-	-	110
Brown Bullhead	-	17	-	-	-	-	-	-	17
Yellow Bullhead	-	1	13	1	-	-	-	-	15
Yellow Perch	-	83	19	1	-	-	-	-	103

DNR COMMENTS:
Black Bullhead abundant, small, and of little value. Bluegills plentiful; some are of quality size. No Walleye captured but angler catches indicate a modest population of this species.

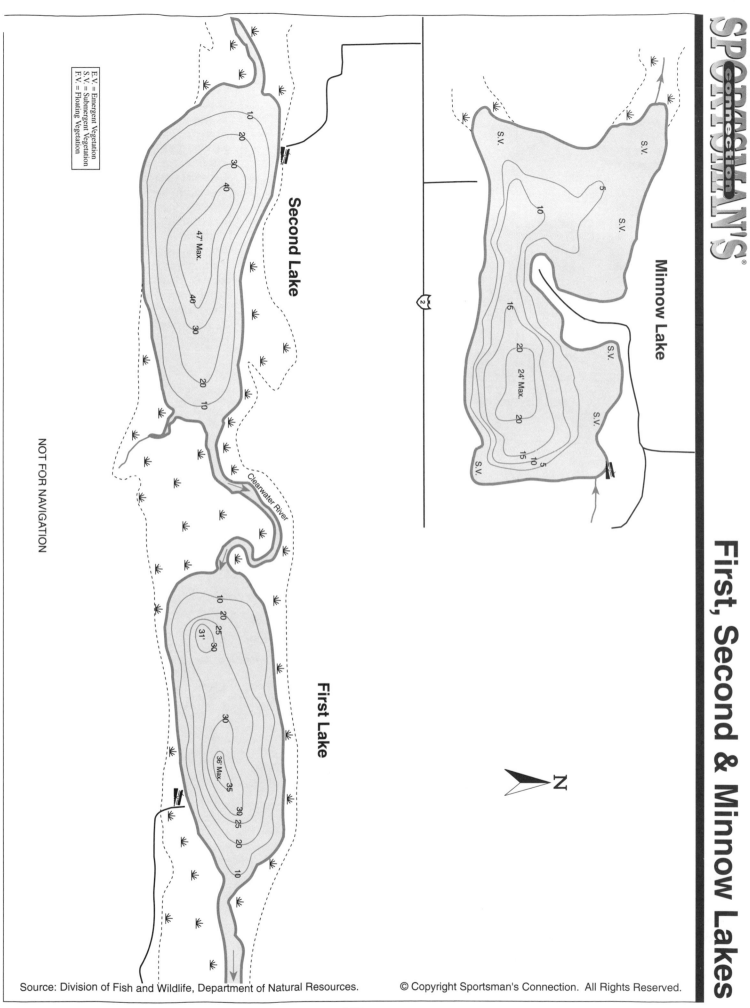

First, Second & Minnow Lakes

Minnow Lake

Second Lake

First Lake

Clearwater River

N

E.V. = Emergent Vegetation
S.V. = Submergent Vegetation
F.V. = Floating Vegetation

S.V.
S.V.
S.V.
S.V.
S.V.
S.V.

5
10
15
20
24' Max.
20
15
10
5

10
20
30
40
47' Max.
40
30
20
10

10
20
25
31'
30
30
36' Max.
35
30
25
20
10

NOT FOR NAVIGATION

Source: Division of Fish and Wildlife, Department of Natural Resources.

MOOSE LAKE   WALKER BROOK LAKE

Beltrami/Clearwater Counties

Location: Township 146 Range 35, 36
Watershed: Mississippi Headwaters
Surface Water Area: 124 acres
Shorelength: NA
Secchi disk (water clarity): 8.0 ft.
Water color: Brownish
Cause of water color: Bog stain
Maximum depth: 13 ft.
Median depth: NA
Accessibility: County-owned access on southwest corner
Boat Ramp: Earth
Accommodations: NA
Shoreland zoning classif.: Nat. Envir.
Dominant forest/soil type: NA
Management class: Walleye-Centrarchid
Ecological type: Centrarchid-Walleye

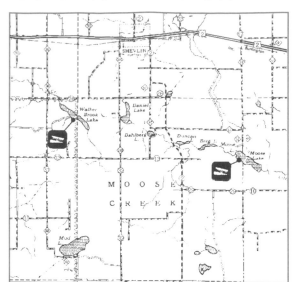

Location: Township 146 Range 36, 37
Watershed: Clearwater
Surface Water Area: 90 acres
Shorelength: NA
Secchi disk (water clarity): 12.0 ft.
Water color: Greenish
Cause of water color: Algae
Maximum depth: 45 ft.
Median depth: NA
Accessibility: State-owned access on west shore
Boat Ramp: Earth
Accommodations: NA
Shoreland zoning classif.: Nat. Envir.
Dominant forest/soil type: NA
Management class: Walleye-Centrarchid
Ecological type: Centrarchid

DNR COMMENTS:
Northern Pike population above local mean. Above-normal Walleye population indicated by trapnet catch; age class distribution shows some natural reproduction occurring. Largemouth Bass near local mean. Black Crappie, Bluegill, Pumpkinseed, Yellow Perch, and Black Bullhead populations all above average Rock Bass numbers below lake-class mean. White Sucker present in above-average numbers.

FISH STOCKING DATA

year	species	size	# released
92	Walleye	Fry	125,000
94	Walleye	Fry	125,000
96	Walleye	Fry	125,000

survey date: 07/13/89

NET CATCH DATA

	Gill Nets		Trap Nets	
species	# per net	avg fish wt. (lbs)	# per set	avg fish wt. (lbs)
Yellow Perch	3.5	0.26	29.5	0.27
White Sucker	10.0	1.58	2.3	2.71
Walleye	2.0	1.60	3.3	1.68
Northern Pike	7.0	1.47	1.3	1.28
Brown Bullhead	2.0	1.00	3.0	0.94
Black Bullhead	67.5	0.30	19.5	0.24
Yellow Bullhead	-	-	12.3	0.35
Rock Bass	-	-	0.3	0.60
Pumpkin. Sunfish	-	-	15.8	0.14
Largemouth Bass	-	-	0.5	1.25
Bluegill	-	-	10.8	0.48
Black Crappie	-	-	1.3	1.20

LENGTH OF SELECTED SPECIES SAMPLED FROM ALL GEAR
Number of fish caught for the following length categories (inches):

species	0-5	6-8	9-11	12-14	15-19	20-24	25-29	>30	Total
Yellow Perch	-	4	2	1	-	-	-	-	7
Walleye	-	-	-	3	1	-	4		
Northern Pike	-	-	-	9	5	-	-	14	
Brown Bullhead	-	-	1	3	-	-	-	-	4
Black Bullhead	-	29	2	1	-	-	-	-	32

FISH STOCKING DATA

year	species	size	# released
91	Walleye	Fingerling	1,665
93	Walleye	Fingerling	1,930
93	Walleye	Adult	8
95	Walleye	Fingerling	732
97	Walleye	Fingerling	950

survey date: 7/1/96

NET CATCH DATA

	Gill Nets		Trap Nets	
species	# per net	avg fish wt. (lbs)	# per set	avg fish wt. (lbs)
Black Crappie	-	-	0.4	0.10
Bluegill	-	-	32.8	0.15
Brown Bullhead	-	-	0.1	1.07
Green Sunfish	-	-	1.1	0.08
Hybrid Sunfish	-	-	7.2	0.14
Largemouth Bass	2.0	1.41	0.4	0.25
Northern Pike	1.3	3.88	-	-
Pumpkin. Sunfish	-	-	2.0	0.16
Walleye	1.0	2.55	0.1	0.18
White Sucker	5.3	0.98	0.6	0.42
Yellow Perch	14.3	0.11	3.3	0.16

LENGTH OF SELECTED SPECIES SAMPLED FROM ALL GEAR
Number of fish caught for the following length categories (inches):

species	0-5	6-8	9-11	12-14	15-19	20-24	25-29	>30	Total
Black Crappie	4	-	-	-	-	-	-	-	4
Bluegill	172	122	1	-	-	-	-	-	295
Brown Bullhead	-	-	-	1	-	-	-	-	1
Green Sunfish	10	-	-	-	-	-	-	-	10
Hybrid Sunfish	47	18	-	-	-	-	-	-	65
Largemouth Bass	-	4	1	5	-	-	-	-	10
Northern Pike	-	-	-	-	-	2	2	-	4
Pumpkin. Sunfish	15	3	-	-	-	-	-	-	18
Walleye	-	2	-	-	1	1	-	-	4
Yellow Perch	21	52	-	-	-	-	-	-	73

DNR COMMENTS:
Walleye gillnet catch near the low end of the normal range for lake class; mean weight 2.5 lb.; mean length 15.1 inches; fish to 24.4 inches present. Northern Pike numbers low; Pike to 25 inches sampled; Neascus infestation noted on most Pike. Largemouth Bass abundance appears good; fish to 13.7 inches sampled. Black Crappie numbers at an all-time low; most fish from the 1993 year class. Bluegill numbers above lake-class average; mean weight only .1 lb., well below average. Yellow Perch numbers down to lake-class average; average length only 6.4 inches.

FISHING INFORMATION: Located some eight miles southeast of Bagley, these two lakes are considered good Largemouth Bass fisheries that also hold fair numbers of Walleyes, panfish, and Northern Pike. **Walkerbrook** is a long, narrow lake, deeper at its southeast end, with long flats in the northwest. Chuck Cole, a veteran Bemidji fisherman, likes it for its Walleyes and the good Crappies it produces. It also holds some nice Northern Pike and Largemouth Bass. The northwest end of the lake has nice weedbeds to fish for Bluegills and Crappies; you can do well right after ice-out with worms or small minnows on a bare hook or a 1/32-ounce jig. After Bass season opens, fish the weedbeds with a pig-and-jig combination or spinnerbaits. Walleyes are stocked as fingerlings, and the southeast end of the lake is the best place to look for their older siblings early in the season. They'll be along the steep drops off both shorelines; jig with live bait. The same spots are also good at night or on dark, cloudy days. Northerns often swim along the outer edges of weedbeds looking for a meal of White Suckers and Perch, and this lake's lengthy weedlines give you a good shot at them. Walkerbrook is a good winter fishery, too, for Yellow Perch and Northerns. **Moose Lake** has a reputation for good Bass and Sunfish. There's lots of good shoreline vegetation to fish in this mostly shallow lake. Veteran anglers use topwater lures as often as possible. The lake's south end is often posted as a Bass spawning area in the spring, and you can't fish there then. Moose Lake's poor ramp doesn't handle larger boats well.

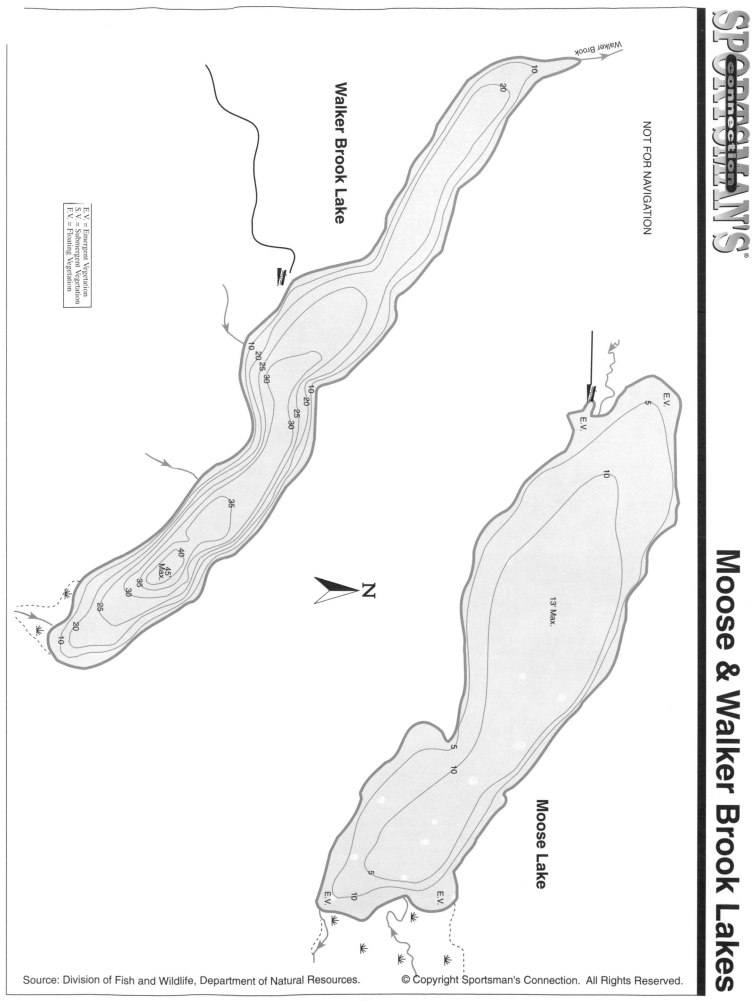

NOT FOR NAVIGATION

Walker Brook

Walker Brook Lake

E.V. = Emergent Vegetation
S.V. = Submergent Vegetation
F.V. = Floating Vegetation

N

10
20

10
20 25 30
10 20
25 30

35
40
45'
Max.
35
30
25
20
10

E.V.
E.V.
5

10

13' Max.

5
10

5
10

E.V.
E.V.

Moose Lake

Moose & Walker Brook Lakes

LAKE MINERVA

ROCKSTAD LAKE

Clearwater County

Location: Township 145 Range 37
Watershed: Eastern Wild Rice
Surface Water Area: 236 acres
Shorelength: 2.8 miles
Secchi disk (water clarity): 4.0 ft.
Water color: Greenish
Cause of water color: Algae, suspended solids
Maximum depth: 16 ft.
Median depth: 7.9 ft.
Accessibility: State-owned public access on southeast shore
Boat Ramp: Earth
Accommodations: NA
Shoreland zoning classif.: Rec. Dev.
Dominant forest/soil type: Decid/Loam
Management class: Warm-water gamefish
Ecological type: Roughfish-Gamefish

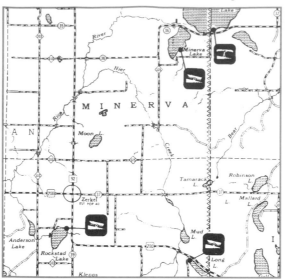

Location: Township 144 Range 37
Watershed: Eastern Wild Rice
Surface Water Area: 128 acres
Shorelength: NA
Secchi disk (water clarity): 3.1 ft.
Water color: Green
Cause of water color: Algae
Maximum depth: 15 ft.
Median depth: NA
Accessibility: Public access on northeast corner, off Hwy. 200
Boat Ramp: Gravel
Accommodations: NA
Shoreland zoning classif.: Nat. Envir.
Dominant forest/soil type: NA
Management class: Walleye-Centrarchid
Ecological type: Centrarchid

DNR COMMENTS:
Walleye numbers very high at triple the lake-class average; average size 15 inches and 1.6 lb.; fish to 29 inches sampled; some natural reproduction occurring. Northern Pike numbers below expected range; average size of 21.3 inches and 2.3 lb. is average for lake class. Largemouth Bass over 17 inches sampled. Black Crappie numbers average, but size excellent at 12 inches and 1.2 lb. Bluegill abundance below lake-class average; average weight over .5 lb. Yellow Perch abundant; average length 7.1 inches; Neascus infestation noted.

FISH STOCKING DATA

year	species	size	# released
91	Walleye	Fry	100,000
94	Walleye	Fry	100,000
96	Walleye	Fry	100,000
96	Bluegill	Adult	140

NET CATCH DATA
survey date: 7/5/95

	Gill Nets		Trap Nets	
species	# per net	avg fish wt. (lbs)	# per set	avg fish wt. (lbs)
Black Bullhead	5.7	0.72	0.7	0.77
Black Crappie	0.5	0.93	4.5	1.25
Bluegill	0.2	0.04	1.7	0.56
Brown Bullhead	23.5	0.78	4.3	0.89
Largemouth Bass	-	-	1.2	0.54
Northern Pike	4.0	2.27	0.3	1.17
Pumpkin. Sunfish	1.8	0.19	4.0	0.18
Walleye	10.7	1.63	1.0	4.07
White Sucker	7.7	1.52	0.8	2.16
Yellow Perch	40.3	0.18	13.3	0.16

LENGTH OF SELECTED SPECIES SAMPLED FROM ALL GEAR
Number of fish caught for the following length categories (inches):

species	0-5	6-8	9-11	12-14	15-19	20-24	25-29	>30	Total
Black Bullhead	-	3	34	1	-	-	-	-	38
Black Crappie	-	-	3	27	-	-	-	-	30
Bluegill	1	9	1	-	-	-	-	-	11
Brown Bullhead	-	7	97	52	-	-	-	-	156
Largemouth Bass	1	5	-	-	1	-	-	-	7
Northern Pike	-	-	-	3	3	17	3	-	26
Pumpkin. Sunfish	14	21	-	-	-	-	-	-	35
Walleye	-	25	2	1	27	10	5	-	70
Yellow Perch	24	220	-	-	-	-	-	-	244

FISH STOCKING DATA

year	species	size	# released
93	Northern Pike	Adult	32
94	Northern Pike	Adult	88
97	Northern Pike	Adult	58

NET CATCH DATA
survey date: 06/15/87

	Gill Nets		Trap Nets	
species	# per net	avg fish wt. (lbs)	# per set	avg fish wt. (lbs)
Yellow Perch	508.0	0.27	63.0	0.26
White Sucker	34.0	0.83	4.7	0.35
Northern Pike	1.0	5.25	-	-
Black Bullhead	37.0	0.22	41.0	0.26
Pumpkin. Sunfish	-	-	0.7	0.18
Creek Chub	-	-	0.7	0.10

LENGTH OF SELECTED SPECIES SAMPLED FROM ALL GEAR
Number of fish caught for the following length categories (inches):

species	0-5	6-8	9-11	12-14	15-19	20-24	25-29	>30	Total
Yellow Perch	-	49	57	-	-	-	-	-	106
Northern Pike	-	-	-	-	-	-	1	-	1
Black Bullhead	-	24	12	1	-	-	-	-	37

DNR COMMENTS:
Fish population dominated by Yellow Perch; gillnet catch well above both state and local median levels; natural reproduction appears limited for this species, but evidence may have been masked by large numbers of Bullheads in the trapnets. Black Bullheads abundant. White Sucker numbers above state and local medians. Northern Pike, Walleye, Creek Chub, and Pumpkinseed numbers very low.

FISHING INFORMATION: These two shallow lakes are south of Bagley and are fairly well-regarded by anglers. **Lake Minerva** is heavily weeded, with an average depth of about 8 feet. It also gets somewhat murky with algae bloom and suspended solids. If that doesn't look too promising, look again: Minerva holds good populations of Walleyes and Northern Pike. That's in addition to slab Crappies and good-size Bluegills. And, of course, gobs of Yellow Perch. Tim Falk of Bluewater Bait and Sports in Bemidji says the lake has a lot of 2-pound Walleyes. The DNR stocks goggle eyes fairly often, and the good forage base of Yellow Perch helps them survive well and grow. The cabbage weeds along the shores offer good protection, and Falk says he's had success backtrolling the edges with live bait and Lindy Rigs. Another angler, Earl Taber of Taber's Bait, says trophy-size Northerns and Walleyes have been taken from Minerva. "In the fall of the year they'll bring in some really big Walleyes," he notes. Although the maximum depth is only about 15 feet, Minerva's Walleyes and Northerns probably get sufficient shade from the cabbage and other emergent vegetation. Still, it wouldn't hurt to still-fish with live bait over the hole in the middle of the lake for Walleyes and Crappies. Fish in the weeds early, of course, for 'gills. They average around 8 inches in Minerva. **Rockstad Lake**, meanwhile, has a local reputation for Northern Pike and Yellow Perch. Chuck Cole of Bluewater Bait tells us that Northerns are plentiful but small. "I must have caught about 35 of them in four hours" on one recent evening, he notes. During recent winters, anglers have done well with Perch. Many of them run to 12 and 13 inches.

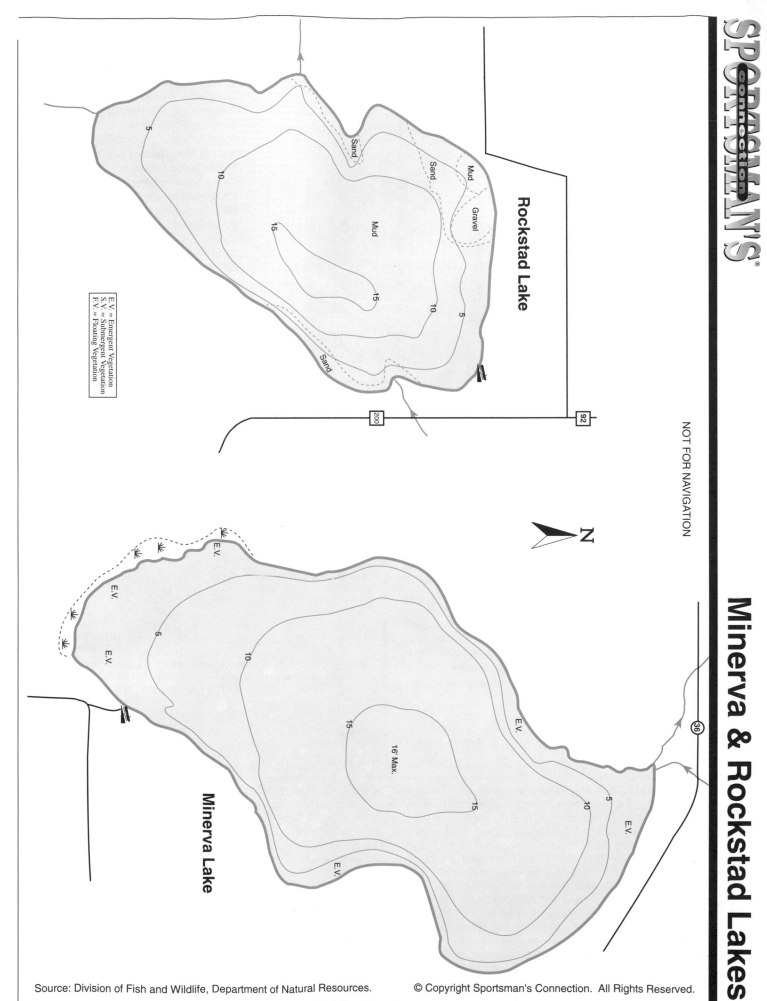

NOT FOR NAVIGATION

N

Rockstad Lake

E.V. = Emergent Vegetation
S.V. = Submergent Vegetation
F.V. = Floating Vegetation

Sand

Mud

Gravel

Sand

5

10

15

15

Mud

10

5

Sand

200

92

Minerva & Rockstad Lakes

Minerva Lake

E.V.

E.V.

E.V.

5

10

15

16 Max.

15

E.V.

5

10

E.V.

E.V.

36

Source: Division of Fish and Wildlife, Department of Natural Resources.

LONG LAKE

Clearwater County

HEART LAKE

Location: Township 144 Range 36,37
Watershed: Mississippi Headwaters
Surface Water Area: 145 acres
Shorelength: 3.0 miles
Secchi disk (water clarity): 18.0 ft.
Water color: Light green/Blue
Cause of water color: Very slight algae bloom
Maximum depth: 80 ft.
Median depth: NA
Accessibility: County park and public access on north shore
Boat Ramp: Concrete
Accommodations: Fishing pier, county park, campground
Shoreland zoning classif.: Rec. Dev.
Dominant forest/soil type: Conifer/Loam
Management class: Trout
Ecological type: Centrarchid

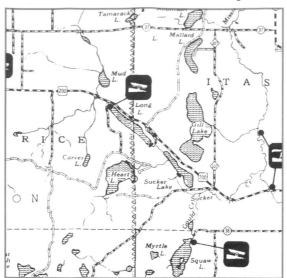

Location: Township 144 Range 36,37
Watershed: Mississippi Headwaters
Surface Water Area: 206 acres
Shorelength: 3.1 miles
Secchi disk (water clarity): 24.0 ft.
Water color: Greenish
Cause of water color: Slight algal bloom
Maximum depth: 55 ft.
Median depth: 29 ft.
Accessibility: County-owned public access on northeast corner
Boat Ramp: Earth
Accommodations: State park
Shoreland zoning classif.: Rec. Dev.
Dominant forest/soil type: Conifer/Sand
Management class: Walleye-Centrarchid
Ecological type: Centrarchid-Walleye

DNR COMMENTS:
Lake managed for stream Trout; Rainbow fingerlings stocked annually. Trout numbers down considerably, likely a result of Northern Pike predation. Northern Pike numbers above the desirable range for Trout lakes; average size 20.8 inches and 2.2 lb.; fish to 31.6 inches captured. Black Crappie numbers lowest since 1951, but average size good at nearly 10 inches. Quality-size Largemouth Bass present. Bluegill numbers at all-time low, but within normal range; maximum length sampled 6.9 inches. Yellow Perch numbers normal; average length 8.2 inches.

FISH STOCKING DATA

year	species	size	# released
92	Rainbow Trout	Fingerling	14,500
93	Rainbow Trout	Fingerling	22,500
94	Rainbow Trout	Fingerling	14,500
95	Rainbow Trout	Fingerling	14,500
96	Rainbow Trout	Fingerling	14,500

NET CATCH DATA
survey date: 6/24/96

	Gill Nets		Trap Nets	
species	# per net	avg fish wt. (lbs)	# per set	avg fish wt. (lbs)
Black Crappie	0.3	0.51	0.4	0.48
Bluegill	0.3	0.14	10.2	0.09
Green Sunfish	-	-	1.1	0.11
Hybrid Sunfish	0.3	0.13	1.4	0.16
Largemouth Bass	0.3	3.47	0.2	1.81
Northern Pike	6.3	2.20	1.0	2.49
Rainbow Trout	0.3	1.82	0.1	1.76
Rock Bass	3.8	0.26	4.3	0.24
Walleye	0.3	5.02	-	-
Yellow Perch	9.5	0.23	4.3	0.21

LENGTH OF SELECTED SPECIES SAMPLED FROM ALL GEAR
Number of fish caught for the following length categories (inches):

species	0-5	6-8	9-11	12-14	15-19	20-24	25-29	>30	Total
Black Crappie	-	-	5	-	-	-	-	-	5
Bluegill	88	5	-	-	-	-	-	-	93
Green Sunfish	7	3	-	-	-	-	-	-	10
Hybrid Sunfish	9	5	-	-	-	-	-	-	14
Largemouth Bass	-	-	-	1	2	-	-	-	3
Northern Pike	-	-	-	-	16	12	5	1	34
Rainbow Trout	-	-	-	-	2	-	-	-	2
Rock Bass	23	29	2	-	-	-	-	-	54
Walleye	-	-	-	-	-	-	1	-	1
Yellow Perch	13	40	24	-	-	-	-	-	77

FISH STOCKING DATA: NO RECORD OF STOCKING

NET CATCH DATA
survey date: 07/20/89

	Gill Nets		Trap Nets	
species	# per net	avg fish wt. (lbs)	# per set	avg fish wt. (lbs)
Yellow Perch	2.5	0.08	0.3	0.20
Rock Bass	2.5	0.76	2.3	0.36
Pumpkin. Sunfish	1.5	0.03	7.3	0.13
Northern Pike	15.5	2.61	1.5	1.80
Largemouth Bass	8.5	1.42	3.5	0.52
Bluegill	20.5	0.09	53.3	0.12
Black Crappie	3.0	0.63	1.0	0.20
Brown Bullhead	-	-	1.5	1.07

LENGTH OF SELECTED SPECIES SAMPLED FROM ALL GEAR
Number of fish caught for the following length categories (inches):

species	0-5	6-8	9-11	12-14	15-19	20-24	25-29	>30	Total
Yellow Perch	-	5	-	-	-	-	-	-	5
Rock Bass	-	1	3	1	-	-	-	-	5
Pumpkin. Sunfish	2	1	-	-	-	-	-	-	3
Northern Pike	-	-	-	1	2	19	9	-	31
Largemouth Bass	-	2	3	8	4	-	-	-	17
Bluegill	25	16	-	-	-	-	-	-	41
Black Crappie	-	2	1	3	-	-	-	-	6

DNR COMMENTS:
Northern Pike gill-net catch above local mean; Yellow Perch catch below. Pumpkin-seed, Largemouth Bass, and Bluegill trapnet numbers all above local means. Black Crappie catch rate near mean values. Brown Bullhead and Rock Bass numbers below mean levels. No Walleye or White Sucker captured in either gill or trapnets, but Walleyes occasionally caught by anglers.

FISHING INFORMATION: Long Lake is one of those fisheries that are too few and far between. Small but deep, this lake is managed as a two-story fishery by the DNR: stream Trout inhabit the "basement," while panfish and Bass enjoy the upper "floor." Rainbow Trout fingerlings have been stocked annually for years. Generally the fish have to be 2-year-olds before they reach keeper-size, and most of them are caught then. But some survive, and there are always some older ones down there, awaiting the patient angler. Long Lake is almost all deep water. The maximum depth is 80 feet, but a lot of the bottom is down there 50 feet or more. Which, of course, means you'll need a lot of lead behind your lure to reach the Rainbows. Live bait is often used, but there are periods when Rapalas or other artificials seem best. As you know, Trout can be picky, and it's a good idea to check with nearest bait dealer to see what's been working *lately*. Long Lake is not a designated Trout lake, so a stamp is not required. Black Crappies, Bluegills, Largemouth Bass and Yellow Perch are in the "upper story" in good numbers. There aren't many Northern Pike, which is a good thing, considering their appetite for Rainbows. Panfishing is good at either end of the narrow lake not far from the public access. Though the lake is too deep for large weedbeds, you'll find enough of them along the shorelines. Fish Bluegills and Crappies there with a jig tipped with a nightcrawler or small minnow. Largemouth Bass can be found in the same weeds. Jigs with plastic worms (purple is a favorite) are often effective. Long Lake is extremely clear, so use a fairly long line when trolling, or present your bait under a slip bobber. Meanwhile, **Heart Lake** in Itasca State Park is chiefly known as a panfish producer. But it also holds fairly good numbers of Northern Pike and Largemouth Bass. A very clear lake that is fairly deep and lacking substantial weeds, Heart is difficult to fish. The northeast corner has the good weedbeds and is the best place to go for Bluegills and Black Crappies. The island in the northeast corner is a good spot both for Largemouths and panfish. You have to cast and troll carefully because it's easy to spook fish here.

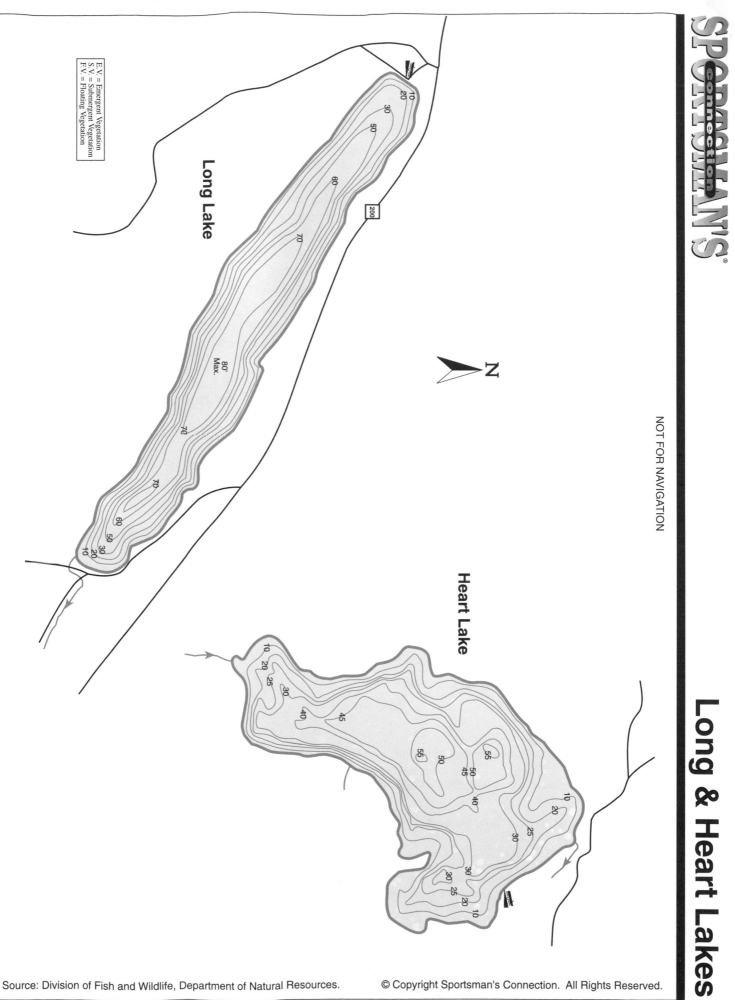

Long Lake

Heart Lake

E.V. = Emergent Vegetation
S.V. = Submergent Vegetation
F.V. = Floating Vegetation

N

NOT FOR NAVIGATION

BIG (Upper) LaSALLE LAKE
Clearwater County

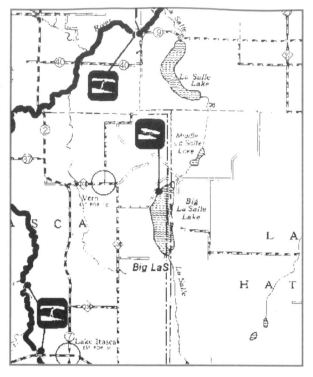

Location: Township 144
Range 35,36
Watershed: Mississippi Headwaters
Surface Water Area: 221 acres
Shorelength: 3.0 miles
Secchi disk (water clarity): 9.0 ft.
Water color: Light green
Cause of water color: Algae

Maximum depth: 48 ft.
Median depth: NA
Accessibility: Public access on northwest corner
Boat Ramp: Earth
Accommodations: NA

Shoreland zoning classification: Recreational Development
Dominant forest/soil type: Conifer/Loam
Management class: Walleye-Centrarchid
Ecological type: Centrarchid-Walleye

FISH STOCKING DATA

year	species	size	# released
91	Walleye	Fingerling	1,644
93	Walleye	Fingerling	800
95	Walleye	Fingerling	624
97	Walleye	Fingerling	3,340

NET CATCH DATA

survey date: 07/10/89

species	Gill Nets # per net	Gill Nets avg fish wt. (lbs.)	Trap Nets # per set	Trap Nets avg fish wt. (lbs.)
Yellow Perch	9.8	0.21	1.1	0.18
Yellow Bullhead	2.5	0.97	3.0	0.63
White Sucker	1.8	1.43	0.1	1.10
Walleye	1.8	2.39	-	-
Rock Bass	3.8	0.78	5.3	0.60
Pumpkin. Sunfish	0.5	0.10	6.6	0.27
Northern Pike	9.5	1.50	1.6	1.00
Bluegill	0.3	0.10	22.3	0.14
Black Bullhead	0.3	0.50	0.1	0.30
Largemouth Bass	-	-	2.4	0.61
Brown Bullhead	-	-	0.4	1.23

LENGTH OF SELECTED SPECIES SAMPLED FROM ALL GEAR

Number of fish caught for the following length categories (inches):

species	0-5	6-8	9-11	12-14	15-19	20-24	25-29	>30	Total
Yellow Perch	-	24	14	1	0	0	0	0	39
Yellow Bullhead	-	2	3	5	-	-	-	-	10
Walleye	-	-	-	-	6	1	-	-	7
Rock Bass	-	5	9	1	-	-	-	-	15
Pumpkin. Sunfish	1	1	-	-	-	-	-	-	2
Northern Pike	-	-	-	8	6	22	2	0	38
Bluegill	1	-	-	-	-	-	-	-	1
Black Bullhead	-	-	1	-	-	-	-	-	1

DNR COMMENTS: Northern Pike gillnet catches above the local mean values. White Sucker catches near the mean, while those of Yellow Perch and Walleye are both below. Trapnet catches show populations of Pumpkinseed, Bluegill, and Largemouth Bass are above local mean values. Rock Bass and Yellow Bullhead catches are near the means, and those of Black Crappie are below.

FISHING INFORMATION: This lake is just northeast of Lake Itasca and is part of the LaSalle River chain which empties into the Mississippi. Upper LaSalle is known especially for producing nice Northern Pike and Bluegills, but it also offers good numbers of Largemouth Bass and some Walleyes. The steep drops off the lake's east and west sides prevent growth of wide weedbeds, but the north and south ends provide good vegetative cover. You can find nice Bluegills and Yellow Perch there, along with Black Crappies. Fish these panfish with nightcrawlers or small minnows on a bare hook or a 1/32-ounce jig. The north and south weedbeds are also the best places to fish for Largemouths in late spring. Bass especially congregate in the south end, where an inlet from LaSalle Creek carries nutrients that attract forage species. Bassing with a jig-and-pig is often effective, as is tossing spinnerbaits. Northerns spend a lot of time at the shallow north and south ends, near both the inlet and outlet. And you can troll either the east or west sides with artificials, strip-ons, or live bait. You can also do well still-fishing the ends with live bait under a bobber. There aren't a lot of Walleyes waiting to be caught, but the ones you do catch will be 2 pounds or better. Early season, they'll be hanging around the steep breaks off the weedlines. Look for bait fish there; the Walleyes will be around. As the season progresses, Wally will be deep during the day. Then, you'll need to get right down there with a minnow under a slip-bobber. Or, troll deep-running crankbaits well down the drops.

NOT FOR NAVIGATION

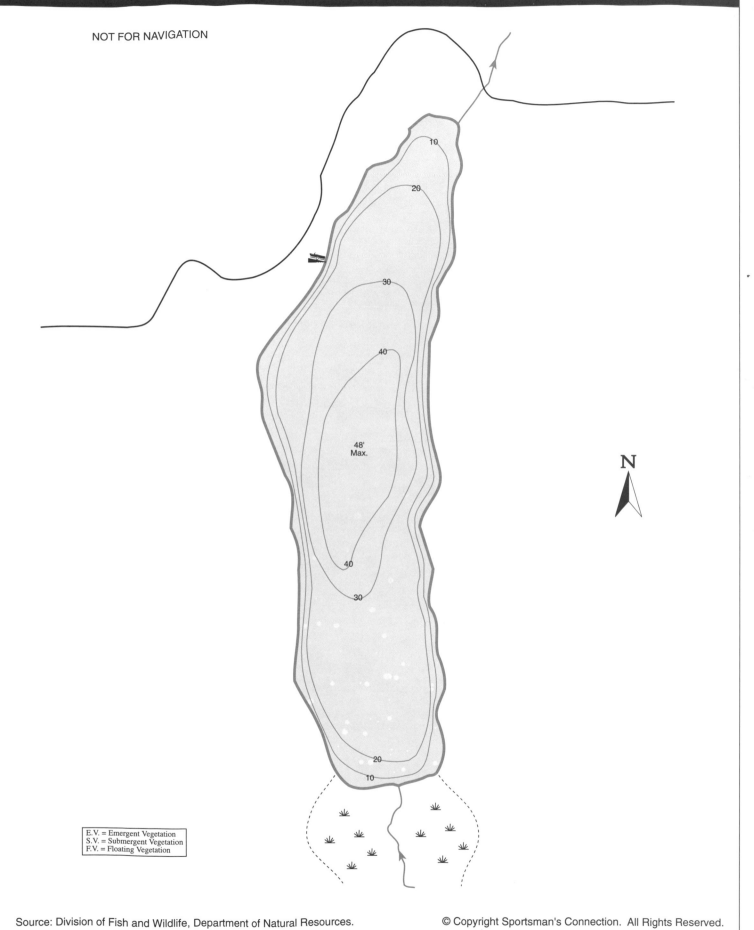

E.V. = Emergent Vegetation
S.V. = Submergent Vegetation
F.V. = Floating Vegetation

Source: Division of Fish and Wildlife, Department of Natural Resources.

Sportsman's Connection publishes a complete line of fishing map guides for the areas that *you* fish

Check with your local retailer for maps of <u>your</u> favorite lakes.

For a complete list, write Sportsman's Connection, 1423 North Eighth Street, Superior, Wisconsin 54880 or phone toll free: 1-800-777-7461
www.sportsmansconnection.com